The Power of IT
Survival Guide for the CIO

Jan De Sutter

Cover Design   Don Weigand
Cartoons   Ted Goff
Web site   http://www.the-power-of-it.com

Copyright © 2003-2004 by Jan De Sutter – All rights reserved

No part of this work shall be reproduced, stored in a retrieval system, or transmitted by any means, electronic, mechanical, photocopying, recording or otherwise, without permission from the author. No patent liability is assumed with respect to the use of the information contained herein. Every reasonable effort has been made to respect the copyrights of other persons or entities. Anybody who believes that his or her copyrights have been infringed is invited to contact the author so that the necessary arrangements can be taken.

All terms mentioned in this work that are known to be trademarks have been appropriately capitalized. The author cannot attest the accuracy of this information. Use of a term in this work should not be regarded as affecting the validity of any trademark.

Although every precaution has been taken in the preparation of this work, the author assumes no responsibility for errors or omissions. Every effort has been made to make this work as complete and as accurate as possible, but no warranty of fitness is implied. The information provided is on an "as is" basis. The author shall have neither liability nor responsibility to any person or entity with respect to any loss or damages arising from the information contained in this work. This work reflects the personal opinions of the author and does in no way engage his current or previous employers.

Library of Congress Control Number: 2004113733
Publisher: BookSurge, LLC
North Charleston, South Carolina

ISBN: 1-59457-867-2

Acknowledgements

First Edition

I would like to thank Professor Carlos De Backer (University of Antwerp) and Professor Eddy Van Dijck (University of Brussels) for their thorough editing, helpful suggestions and thoughtful comments.

Also, a project of this magnitude requires the support of colleagues and friends. I address a special word of gratefulness for Dirk Dons and Niall O'Higgins, who gave useful advice on the purely technical matters.

Finally, this work could not be possible without the love and inspiration of my wife Lut and my children Marieke and Jacob. Thank you for being there!

Second Edition

I received many spontaneous reactions from my online readers and wish to thank them for that. All their remarks have been taken into account.

I also had the occasion to present this book in various international conferences and am very grateful to the organizations that allowed me to do so. During these conferences I had many exchanges with my public who gave some very useful feedback on the book and its content.

To my mother. May she rest in peace.

Table of Contents

INTRODUCTION 1
    Information Technology 2
    The changing role of IT 3
    Evolution of the IT Industry 5
    About this book 6
    Online Resources 9
        IT management magazines and newsletters 9
        IT Business Analysts 9
        IT News sites 9
    Further Reading 10

INFRASTRUCTURE 11
    Introduction 12
    Computing Hardware 14
        Computers 14
        Digital technology 18
        The von Neumann Architecture 19
        Central Processing Unit 20
        Main Memory 21
        Internal buses 22
        Input/Output 23
    Operating Systems 30
    Operating Systems 30
        Purpose of an Operating System 30
        Structure of an Operating System 30
        Characteristics of Operating Systems 31
        Autonomic Computing 32
        Security 32
    Local Services 34
        Storing Data 34
        File Systems 34
        Relational Database Management Systems (RDBMSs) 35
        Object-Oriented Database Management Systems (OODBMS) 40
        Object-Relational Database Management Systems (ORDBMS) 41
        Benchmarking of DBMSs 43
    Networking Services 45
        The OSI Reference Model 45
        The Internet protocols 46
        Physical Layer 47
        Data link layer 48
        Network layer 57
        Transport layer 62
        Application layer 63
        Security 65
    Middleware 69

- *Basic Middleware Services* 69
    - *Advanced Middleware Services* 70
    - *Middleware Technologies* 73
    - *Application Frameworks* 74
    - *Application Servers* 75
- Best Practices 77
    - *Automate your asset management* 77
    - *Automate your systems management* 77
    - *Avoid Single Points of Failure* 78
    - *Centralise your client management* 79
    - *Consolidate and rationalize continuously* 79
    - *Keep control over your architecture* 80
    - *Keep your infrastructure scalable* 80
    - *Printing also deserves a strategy* 82
    - *Reconsider your storage strategy* 83
    - *Rely on open standards, but don't be stubborn* 84
    - *Standardize as much as you can* 85
    - *Use the right tools* 85
- Online Resources 87
- Further Reading 89

INFORMATION SYSTEMS 91

- Information Systems 92
    - *Operational and Informational Systems* 94
- Production 95
    - *Word Processors* 95
    - *Spreadsheets* 97
    - *Drawing tools* 97
    - *Computer Aided Design and Manufacturing (CAD/CAM)* 98
    - *Viewers and Players* 98
    - *Characteristics of Production Information Systems* 99
    - *Potential benefits of Production Information Systems* 99
- Collaboration 100
    - *Collocated – Asynchronous groupware systems* 101
    - *Non-collocated – Asynchronous groupware systems* 102
    - *Collocated – Synchronous groupware systems* 117
    - *Non-collocated – Synchronous Groupware systems* 117
    - *Characteristics of Groupware Systems* 119
    - *Benefits of Groupware Systems* 120
    - *Potential risks of Groupware Systems* 120
- Business Process Support 121
    - *Enterprise Application Integration (EAI)* 123
    - *Exchanging information with other organizations* 127
    - *E-commerce* 130
    - *Characteristics of Business Process Support Systems* 134
    - *Benefits of Business Process Support Systems* 134
    - *Risks Business Process Support Systems* 134
- Tactics 135
    - *Metrics* 135
    - *Benchmarking* 136
    - *Activity Based Costing* 137
    - *Data warehousing* 137
    - *Characteristics of Tactical Information Systems* 142
    - *Benefits of Tactical Information Systems* 143
    - *Risks of Tactical Information Systems* 143
- Strategy 144
    - *Balanced Scorecards* 144
    - *Data mining* 146
    - *Web Farming* 147
    - *Characteristics of Strategic Information Systems* 148
    - *Benefits of Strategic Information Systems* 148
- Best Practices 149

  Also read the small print *149*
  Apply a layered approach where possible *149*
  Beware of biased advice *149*
  Build loosely coupled systems *150*
  Build, buy or borrow? *150*
  Choose for standards *151*
  Do not reinvent the wheel *151*
  Educate the users *151*
  Integrate the Business Processes *152*
  Know the real needs of the users *152*
  Make agility a primary goal *153*
  Rationalize the application portfolio *153*
 Online Resources 154
 Further Reading 156

HUMAN RESOURCES **159**

 Introduction 160
 Getting the Best Employees 162
  Specifying Jobs and Roles *162*
  Recruitment *163*
  The Selection Interview *165*
  Outsourcing *167*
 Getting the Best of Employees 172
  Theories on Human Nature *172*
  Motivating Employees *175*
 Teleworking 185
  A new way of working *185*
  Technological Considerations *186*
 Work Force Planning 188
  Planning techniques *188*
  Human Resources Management Systems (HRMSs) *189*
 Best Practices 192
  Apply an open privacy policy *192*
  Avoid Strategic Outsourcing *193*
  Be fair and treat everyone equally and on merit. *193*
  Behave as a leader, not as a boss *193*
  Build a "win-win" relationship when you outsource *194*
  Concentrate on the Core Employees *194*
  Get legal advice when you outsource *195*
  Hire for Attitude, Train for Skill *195*
  Know the real costs *196*
  Praise loudly, blame softly *196*
  Train your people *196*
  Use Job Enrichment *197*
 Online Resources 198
 Further Reading 199

FINANCIAL RESOURCES **201**

 Introduction 202
 Costing 205
  Cost elements *205*
  Total Cost of Ownership (TCO) *206*
  Activity Based Costing (ABC) *208*
 Charging 211
  Responsibility Centre *212*
 Budgeting 214
  Budgeting Processes *215*
  Budgeting Methods *218*
  The Operations Budget *220*
  The Capital Budget *220*
  Other value factors *227*
 Best Practices 232

      Budget for hardware every year *232*
      Buy your systems "just in time" *233*
      Good enough can be best *234*
      Invest to reduce TCO *234*
      Link the project expenses to the objectives *235*
      Manage your software assets carefully *235*
      Only go for win-win situations *236*
      Push for equal treatment of the IT budget *236*
      Retire your old IT systems in time *236*
      Set up pre- and post-implementation metrics *237*
      Start from the benefits, not the costs *237*
   Online Resources 238
   Further Reading 239

PROCESSES **241**

   Introduction 242
   Business Processes 244
      Typology *244*
      Quality and Quality Management *249*
   Business Process Reengineering 253
      How to succeed a change project *255*
      The relationship between Business Change and IT *255*
   IT Processes 256
      IT Service Management (ITSM) *256*
   Best Practices 263
      Apply the self-service concept where possible *263*
      Build generic solutions *263*
      Create a unified view of the business objects *263*
      Make lightweight Information Systems *264*
   Online Resources 266
   Further Reading 267

PROJECTS **269**

   Introduction 270
   Software Life Cycle 273
   Life Cycle Modelling 274
      Code and Fix *274*
      Waterfall Model *274*
      The Incremental Model *276*
      The Spiral Model *277*
      Time boxing *277*
      Agile Software Development *279*
      Other models *281*
   Concept Exploration 282
   Requirements 283
   Project Initiation 285
      Project Estimation *285*
   Design 294
      Process oriented modelling *294*
      Data oriented modelling *295*
      Object Oriented Modelling *298*
   Implementation 302
      Programming languages *302*
      Software reuse *309*
      Computer Aided Software Engineering (CASE) tools *310*
      Integrated Development Environments (IDEs) *311*
   Project Monitoring and Control 313
      Gantt Charts *313*
      Project Evaluation and Review Technique/Critical Path Method (PERT/CPM) *314*
      Critical Chain Scheduling and Buffer management *316*
   Verification and Validation 319
      White Box testing *319*

Unit Testing 321
Black Box testing 321
Integration Testing 322
System Testing 322
Regression testing 322
Alpha and Beta Testing... 323
Automated testing 323
Test Plan 323
Test Results 324
Software Quality Management 325
Capability Maturity Model (CMM) 325
ISO-9001 326
TickIT 327
Software Process Improvement and Capability dEtermination (SPICE) 327
Software Configuration Management 329
Documentation Development 331
Training 332
Installation 333
Maintenance 335
Typology 335
Problems associated with maintenance 335
Metrics 337
Application Mining 338
Retirement 339
Legal considerations 340
Intellectual Property 340
Best Practices 345
Aim for Conceptual Integrity 345
Design Twice, Code Once 346
Do not be afraid of risks 346
Do not re-invent the wheel 346
Expect the unexpected 347
Fit the methodology to the project, not the other way around 347
Have an Open Source strategy 348
Involve the users 348
Limit the size of the project teams 349
Manage the requirements 350
Not all developers are created equal 350
Organize the refactoring process 351
Rank project elements up front 351
Remember Brook's Law 351
Separate concerns 352
Separate stable and unstable elements 352
Separate Transaction Processing and Analytical Processing 353
Take care of the installation process 353
Think Big, develop small 353
Use the right tool for the job 354
Online Resources 355
Further Reading 356

ORGANIZATION 363

Introduction 364
Organization 364
Objects in the organizational model 365
Management 368
Mapping Managers to Organizational Units 368
Managerial activities and roles 368
Organizational Forms 371
Organizational subunits 371
Coordination mechanisms 372
Organizational forms 374
Organizational Culture 376

- Work Teams...377
- Organizational Structures..379
  - Mechanistic and Organic Structures..379
  - Functional organization...379
  - Process-oriented organization..380
  - Product-oriented organization 380
  - Geographical organization..381
  - Mixed structures...382
  - Organization of projects...383
- Organization of IT...387
  - Types of activities of an IT organization...387
  - Structure of the IT department...387
  - Centralization and decentralization of IT..388
  - IT Staffing 390
  - The CIO/IT manager 392
  - Links between IT and the rest of the organization...393
- Best Practices...395
  - Act normal..395
  - Create high-performance teams 395
  - Eliminate redundant administration..395
  - Every department its own responsibility..395
  - Flat or tall?...396
  - Harmonize, don't centralize...396
  - Integrate in the Organizational Culture..397
  - Know and use the informal organization...399
  - Participate in networks..399
  - Separate development and maintenance 400
- Online Resources 401
- Further Reading..402

STRATEGY AND BUSINESS ALIGNMENT..405

- Introduction 406
- Business Strategy 407
- Integration of business and IT 409
- The Strategic Alignment Model..411
  - Functional Integration 412
  - Strategic Fit 414
- Zachman's Framework...418
- Business Continuity and Disaster Recovery..420
  - Contingency Planning Policy Statement 421
  - Business Impact Analysis (BIA) 422
  - Identify Preventive Controls..423
  - Develop Recovery Strategy...425
  - Develop an IT Contingency Plan 426
  - Plan testing, training, and exercises..427
  - Plan maintenance. 427
- Best Practices...428
  - Apply the right procurement process..428
  - Build a balanced portfolio of IT projects...429
  - Create an "IT-friendly" environment..429
  - Concentrate on the core business 430
  - Do not confuse hypes with trends 430
  - Have a written policy concerning the use of IT in your organization........................432
  - Know your Business..433
  - Protect Your Customers' Privacy...434
  - Reduce complexity..434
  - Select your suppliers carefully 435
  - Set up a knowledge management strategy..437
  - State the alignment with strategies and objectives..438
  - Support the internal communication processes...438
- Online Resources 440
- Further Reading..441

BEYOND THE HYPE 443
- The future and IT 444
- Online Resources 447
- Further Reading 448

GLOSSARY 449
- Online Glossaries 483

INDEX 485

List of Illustrations

Fig. 1.1 – Domains of IT
Fig. 2.1 – Position of Infrastructure in the IT stack
Fig. 2.2 – Layers within the IT infrastructure
Fig. 2.3 – Extract of UNICODE Greek code chart
Fig. 2.4 – Components of a Von Neumann computer
Fig. 2.5 – USB connectors
Fig. 2.6 – NAS vs. SAN
Fig. 2.7 – Storage systems
Fig. 2.8 – XML as a hierarchical structure
Fig. 2.9 – The OSI model
Fig. 2.10 – OSI vs. TCP/IP
Fig. 2.11 - ADSL
Fig. 2.12 – Routing
Fig. 3.1 – Position of Information Systems in the IT stack
Fig. 3.2 – Layers of Information Systems
Fig. 3.3 – Email protocols
Fig. 3.4 – Hierarchical data structure
Fig. 3.5 – XSL transformations
Fig. 3.6 – Workflow vs. paper documents
Fig. 3.7 – Client/Server architectures
Fig. 3.8 – Three-tier model
Fig. 3.9 – Integration scenarios
Fig. 3.10 – Integration at the presentation layer
Fig. 3.11 – Integration at the database layer
Fig. 3.12 – Common database
Fig. 3.13 – Integration at the business logic layer
Fig. 4.1 – Position of Human Resources in the IT stack
Fig. 4.2 – Maslow's Hierarchy of Needs
Fig. 5.1 – Position of Financial Resources in the IT stack
Fig. 5.2 – Financial processes
Fig. 5.3 – Evolution of real costs
Fig. 5.4 – Traditional vs. Activity Based Costing
Fig. 5.5 – Functionality vs. Costs
Fig. 6.1 – Position of Processes in the IT stack
Fig. 6.2 – Process Decomposition
Fig. 6.3 – Business Process Typology
Fig. 6.4 – Process Quality

Fig. 6.5 - ITIL
Fig. 7.1 – Position of Projects in the IT stack
Fig. 7.2 – Waterfall Model
Fig. 7.3 – Incremental Model
Fig. 7.4 – Project estimation
Fig. 7.5 – SA/SD
Fig. 7.6 – Entity Relationship Diagram
Fig. 7.7 – Class diagram
Fig. 7.8 – Sequence diagram
Fig. 7.9 – State diagram
Fig. 7.10 – 4GL+ programming
Fig. 7.11 – Gantt chart
Fig. 7.12 – PERT/CPM
Fig. 7.13 – Integration of tasks
Fig. 7.14 – Cyclomatic complexity
Fig. 7.15 – Bathtub diagram
Fig. 7.16 – Comparison of methodologies
Fig. 7.17 – Communication problems
Fig. 8.1 – Position of organization in the IT stack
Fig. 8.2 – Activities, Processes, Functions and Projects
Fig. 8.3 – Organizational subunits
Fig. 8.4 – Coordination mechanisms
Fig. 8.5 – Organizational forms
Fig. 8.6 – Functional Organization
Fig. 8.7 – Process-Oriented Organization
Fig. 8.8 – Product-oriented Organization
Fig. 8.9 – Geographical Organization
Fig. 8.10 – Mixed Organization
Fig. 8.11 – Coordination of Project by the Functional Managers
Fig. 8.12 – Coordination of Project by a Project Manager
Fig. 8.13 – Weak Matrix Organization
Fig. 8.14 – Balanced Matrix Organization
Fig. 8.15 – Strong Matrix Organization
Fig. 8.16 – Coexistence of centralized and decentralized IT
Fig. 9.1 – Position of Strategy in the IT stack
Fig. 9.2 – Strategic Alignment Model
Fig. 9.3 – Functional Integration
Fig. 9.4 – Balanced Scorecard
Fig. 9.5 – Zachmann's Framework
Fig. 9.6 - Cost Optimization
Fig. 9.7 – Gartner Group Hype Curve
Fig. 9.8 – Boston/IT model
Fig. 9.9 – Complexity
Fig 9.10 - Gartner's Magic Quadrant

List of Tables

Table 2.1 - Storage Architecture strengths and weaknesses
Table 2.2 – IEEE 802.3 standards
Table 3.1 – Categorization of Groupware
Table 3.2 - JSP and ASP
Table 3.3 – HTML and XML
Table 4.1 – Benefits of Teleworking
Table 5.1 – Cost types and cost elements
Table 5.2 – Costing vs. Budgeting
Table 5.3   Depreciation
Table 5.4 – Payback period
Table 5.5 – Net Present Value
Table 5.6 – Decision Criteria
Table 6.1 – Improvement vs. Innovation
Table 7.1 – Life cycle modeling
Table 7.2 – Function points to Lines of code conversion
Table 7.3 – Cost drivers
Table 7.4 – The PERS Cost Driver
Table 7.5 – Comparison of programming languages generations
Table 7.6 – Cyclomatic Complexity and Risk
Table 7.7 – Benefits of CMM
Table 8.1 – Managerial Activities and Roles
Table 8.2 – Knowledge of IT Staff per profile
Table 8.3 – Skills and personality of IT staff per profile
Table 9.1 – Balanced IT scorecard

1

Introduction

"Computer Science is no more about computers than astronomy is about telescopes. "

(E. W. Dijkstra)

Information Technology

"In 1880, about nine out of 10 workers made and moved things; today, that is down to one out of five. The other four are knowledge people or service workers."

(Peter Drucker)

According to Professor Russell Ackoff [1], the content of the human mind can be classified into five categories:

- *Data* – symbols. Data is raw; it simply exists and has no significance beyond its existence. It can exist in any form, usable or not. It does not have meaning of itself. For example, a spreadsheet generally starts out by holding data.
- *Information* - data that is processed to be useful. Answers to "who", "what", "where", and "when" questions. Information is data that has been given meaning by way of relational connection. This "meaning" can be useful, but does not have to be. For example, a relational database makes for information from the data stored within it.
- *Knowledge* - application of data and information. Answers the "how" question; Knowledge is the appropriate collection of information; such that it's intent is to be useful. Most of the Information systems we use exercise some type of stored knowledge (the business rules).
- *Understanding* - appreciation of "why". For example, elementary school children memorize knowledge of the "times table". They can tell you that "2 x 2 = 4" because they have amassed that knowledge (being included in the times table). But when asked what is "123 x 456", they can not respond correctly because that entry is not in their times table. To correctly answer such a question requires understanding.
- *Wisdom* - evaluated understanding. Unlike the previous categories, wisdom deals with the future because it incorporates vision and design.

Technology is the combination of skills, knowledge, materials, machines, and tools used by people to convert or change raw materials into valuable goods and services.

Information Technology (IT) is technology that is used to store, communicate, and manipulate data, information, knowledge, understanding and – ultimately - wisdom.

Organizations use technology in general and IT in particular to become more efficient, more effective, and to innovate.

The changing role of IT

Early computers – mainframes - were too large and expensive to have broad application in business. In the 1960s, they became cost-effective and widely adopted and standards and languages were developed specifically for business use. Initially, though, the mainframe had a purely supporting role, mostly in the accounting department. This was the era of *Electronic Data Processing (EDP)*.

In the beginning of the 1980s IBM introduced the first *Personal Computer* (*PC*) and published the technical details of this machine. This opened the possibility for other companies to make *IBM compatible* computers and cheap clones. Individuals used these machines in their home environment but soon they infiltrated in the offices and on the production floors. At first, the EDP professionals did not know how to cope with this event. Some thought it was just hype that would disappear as fast as it came, others simply ignored it and some began a war against these intruders. After a while, it became clear that the PC was there to stay. It had conquered its place in the organization; first as a stand-alone workstation, but rapidly the need to act as a terminal for the mainframe arose.

A few years later, two other evolutions took place: *departmental computers* and *Local Area Networks (LANs)*. These technologies allowed people to share information and work together in small workgroups or company wide. These evolutions had another effect: where the good old EDP department only had one "client" within the organization, the newly born IT department suddenly had to cope with the whole organization. Almost every white-collar or blue-collar employee had a PC connected to the network. Where the users of traditional EDP were specialists in their branch and were therefore well trained to work with these systems, the newcomers only had a limited knowledge of computers. Specialized services like training classes and help desks had to be organized by the IT department.

Because of the improved productivity of the employees and because of the new ways to communicate and work together, the traditional hierarchies within the organizations began to fall apart. Terms like *flat organizations* and *horizontal departments* became common. Also, and this is an important issue, the dependency of IT increased dramatically. Information Technology supported almost every part of the business. As IT covered more and more facets of the business, it was more and more used to get a better insight in the business. *Management Information Systems, Business Intelligence, Data Warehousing* and *Data Mining* became part of the normal vocabulary of the business managers.

Meanwhile, another technological evolution took place: the digitalization of telecommunications. People and their computers started to join forces over networks and the analog communication technology was digitized. Because of this technological convergence many organizations took the decision to put communications under the same person who was in charge of the data processing business.

"Well, what e-blunder did we make today?"

Today, IT is close to or even part of the *core business* in many organizations. This is the case in service organizations (banking, insurance, publishing, government...) whose nonmaterial products cannot exist without IT. Think of a simple bank account: this is a purely imaginary object without any physical manifestation; it only exists on the disks and in the memories of the bank's computers. The modern stock exchange is another example; all the transactions are merely bits and bytes floating around in the networks of the stockbrokers and again no physical exchanges take place. In many organizations, this is reflected by the presence of a representative in the senior management team: the *Chief Information Officer (CIO)*. The CIO is in charge of both technology managers and business managers and is the link between these two. In other organizations, where IT is merely a support function, the *IT Manager* plays his role as the line manager of a technologically oriented department.

Evolution of the IT Industry

The IT industry is an extremely varied sector of the economy, including thousands of small, medium-sized and big companies serving many different markets. One way of looking at it is to distinguish three segments, centered on *hardware, software,* and *services*. Until the 1980s, these three segments were structured *vertically*. Customers selected an IT solution from a few vendors, such as IBM, DEC, or Wang. These delivered complete solutions, including hardware, software and the adjoining services. Because of the proprietary nature of these solutions, customers were tied to their suppliers and there were few opportunities left for other vendors to offer complementary products or services. Two events led to a fundamental change in this situation: low cost microprocessors and open software standards. These events transformed the IT industry; vendors became specialized in hardware, software or services. In every segment, many competing or complementary products exist, all complying with a limited number of standards.

The IT industry is currently one of the most dynamic in the global economy. As a sector, it not only creates millions of high-level jobs but it also helps other organizations to be more efficient and effective and it stimulates innovation. The importance of IT is not so much the growth of its share of the total economy but in the changes that are introduced in the organizations that use and assimilate it.

Recent events seem to be showing that a new evolution is going on. A tremendous shakeout is now taking place in which smaller vendors are taken over by the big players who are now completing their portfolio with complementary products and services. It looks as if the pendulum is swinging back in the other direction and we can expect new – even more severe – vendor lock-ins. To be watched very carefully by the decision makers!

About this book

IT is not just about computers; it connects at least eight different domains stacked upon each other as building blocks:

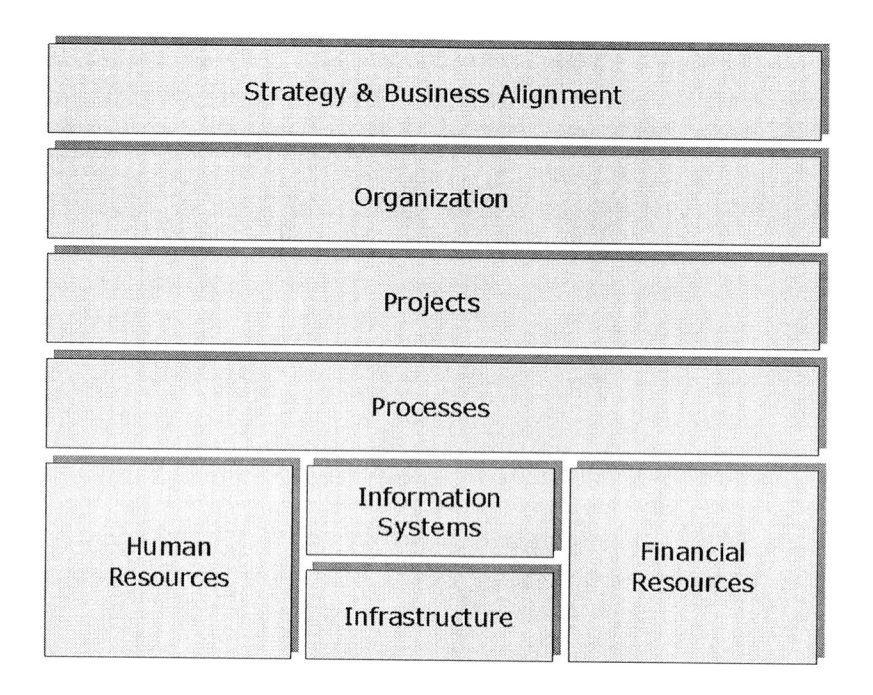

Fig. 1.1 – *Domains of IT*

This framework will serve as the structure of this book. Every chapter will discuss one domain in more detail. Do not expect a comprehensive survey but a management summary. Only the topics contributing to this work will be put in perspective, others will be just mentioned or simply dropped. Several links to Web sites and good books will allow the reader to dig deeper in the discussed items.

As this book has to be a practical help for the IT manager, there will be an important part about the best practices in the different domains of IT. *A best practice* is a policy, procedure, technique, tool, or method that, through experience and research, has proven to lead reliably to a good result. Best practices are a source of competitive advantage as they are often the result of significant experience and costly trial and error. In this work, these best practices will aim at four objectives: information liquidity, availability, agility, and costs.

- *Information Liquidity* - Much like cash liquidity, the liquidity of information is a measure of business success. In a successful organization, data flows smoothly and information changes into economic value. Information liquidity is obtained by integration at all levels. Integration should be the driving force behind design, development, and use of all IT systems.
- *Availability* - As most organizations become more and more dependent on IT, it is important to ensure availability of the services. This does not mean that all the IT systems have to be flawless and failsafe. However, good thought has to be given to what could be the outcomes for the organization if all or part of the IT services are temporarily unavailable, and what can be done to minimize these effects.
- *Agility* - If there is one certainty it is change. The market changes constantly, so do legislation and technology. Product life cycles and their time to market are getting shorter and shorter. As a result, IT has to be agile. We can no longer afford monoliths that cost a fortune to build and are almost impossible to maintain. Cross-compatibility, reuse and lightweight functionality are the ideas to be considered.
- *Costs* - Especially in times of economic slowdown, the costs of IT are under constant scrutiny. Unfortunately, it is difficult to quantify the benefits of IT in Euros or Dollars and it is meaningless to approach the IT investments too much as an accountant. Also the non-quantifiable benefits for the organization must be considered.

It is worth noting that these objectives can be conflicting: for increasing the availability, important investments have to be made, which conflicts with lowering the costs. On the other hand, a close integration will probably get in the way of agility. A good balance will always be required and this balance will depend on the situation your organization is in.

Finally, an extensive glossary ends the content of this book. It can be useful as a quick reference, to "debunk the junk" in the gobbledygook used by IT professionals.

Online Resources

IT management magazines and newsletters

    Byte Magazine - http://www.byte.com
    CIO Magazine - http://www.cio.com
    CIO Worldwide - http://www.cio-worldwide.com
    Computer World - http://www.computerworld.com
    Info World - http://www.infoworld.com
    SearchCIO – http://www.searchcio.com
    ZDNet Magazine - http://www.zdnet.com

IT Business Analysts

    Aberdeen Group – http://www.aberdeen.com
    Bloor Research – http://www.bloor.co.uk
    Boston Consulting Group – http://www.bcg.com
    Business Intelligence – http://www.busintel.com
    Butler Group – http://www.butlergroup.co.uk
    Cambridge Market Intelligence – http://www.cmi.co.uk
    Forrester Research – http://www.forrester.com
    Gartner Group – http://www.gartner.com
    Hurwitz – http://www.hurwitz.com
    IDC Corp – http://www.idcresearch.com
    Headstrong – http://www.headstrong.com
    Jupiter Research – http://www.jup.com
    Killen & Associates – http://www.killen.com
    KnowledgeStorm – http://www.knowledgestorm.com
    Meta Group – http://www.metagroup.com
    OVUM – http://www.ovum.com
    Patricia Seybold Group – http://www.psgroup.com
    Strategic Focus – http://www.strategicfocus.com

IT News sites

    http://dailynews.yahoo.com/headlines/tc
    http://slashdot.org
    http://www.cnn.com/TECH/
    http://www.techweb.com
    http://www.wired.com/news/technology

Further Reading

[1] Ackoff, R. L., *From Data to Wisdom*. Journal of Applies Systems Analysis, Volume 16, 1989 p 3-9.

[2] Applegate, A. et al. *Corporate Information Systems Management*. New York, McGraw Hill. 1999.

[3] Cronin, B. and Davenport, E. *Elements of information management*. London, Scarecrow Press. 1991.

[4] Davenport T.H., *Information Ecology: Mastering the Information and Knowledge Environment*. Oxford University Press, 1997.

[5] Davidow W.H & Malone M.S., *The Virtual Corporation: Structuring and Revitalizing the Corporation for the 21st Century*. Harper Business, 1992.

[6] Dickson, G. and Wetherbe, J., *The management of information systems*, New York, McGraw-Hill, 1985.

[7] Friedman G., Friedman M., Chapman C., Baker J.S., *The Intelligence Edge: How to profit in the Information Age*. Crown Publishers, 1997.

[8] Kahaner L., *Competitive Intelligence: How to Gather, Analyze, and Use Information to Move Your Business to the Top*. Simon & Schuster, 1996.

Infrastructure

"I think there is a world market for maybe five computers."

(Thomas Watson, IBM, 1943)

Introduction

Infrastructure encompasses all permanent facilities that provide services to the higher layers. Infrastructure is *business-unaware*. The ownership of the infrastructure lies with the top of the organization and <u>not</u> with the individual users or organizational entities. This is because the importance of the infrastructure goes far beyond these individual interests and has an influence on the strategic capabilities of the organization.

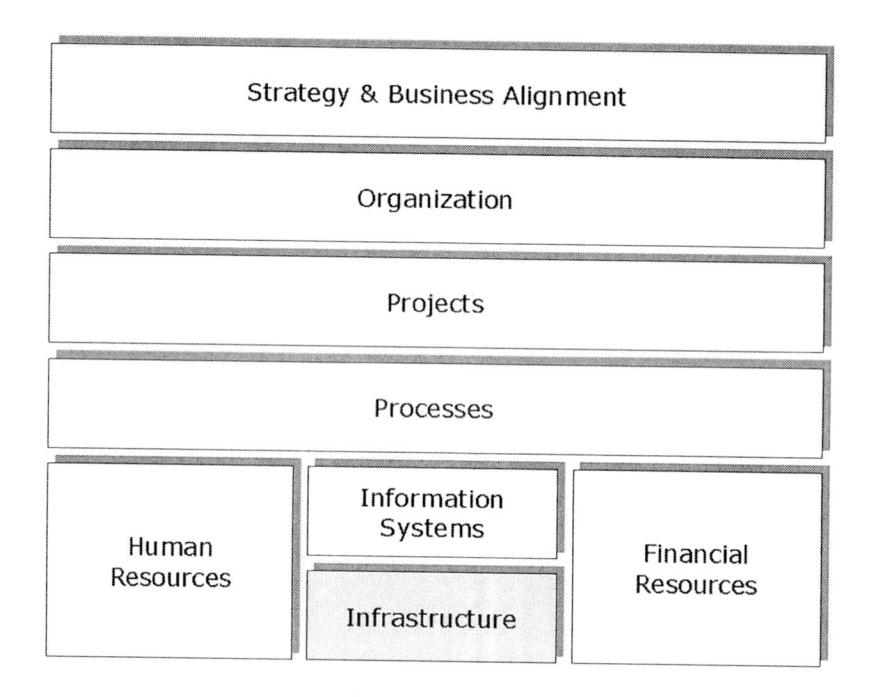

Fig. 2.1 – *Position of Infrastructure in the IT stack*

Fig. 2.2 shows a more detailed breakdown of the infrastructure layer. At the bottom there is the Computing Hardware. Just one layer higher, the Operating System is the first level of System Software that runs and operates this hardware. Local Services and Network Services take care of the connectivity to locally stored data and remote systems. The Middleware layer – finally – hides the implementation details for the Information Systems situated higher up in the stack.

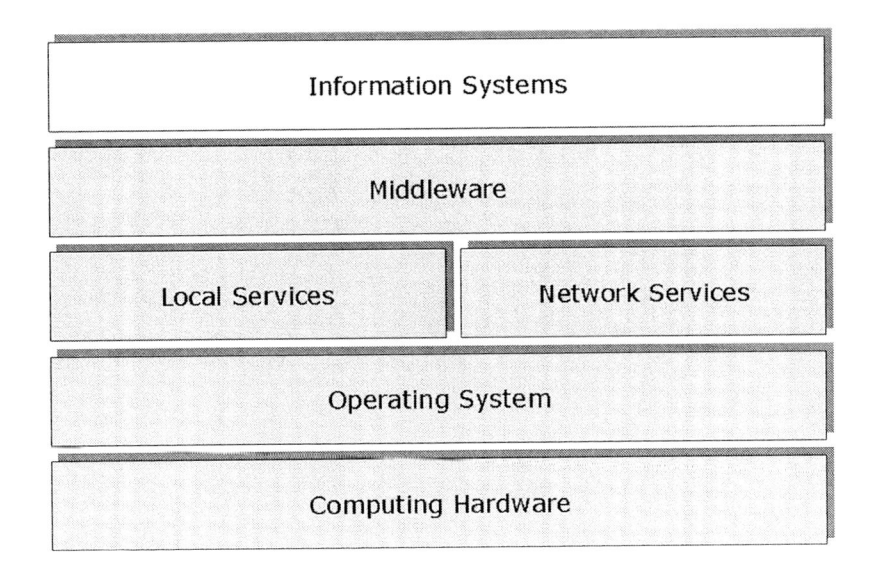

Fig. 2.2 – *Layers within the IT infrastructure*

Computing Hardware

Computers

Various types of computers form the heart of the infrastructure. It is not easy to make a good overview of the different classes of computers. Usually, computers are classified by performance and that is what we will do in this overview.

Personal Computers (PCs)

A *Personal Computer (PC)* is a small, inexpensive computer designed for an individual user. Personal Computers first appeared in the late 1970s. One of the first and most popular Personal Computers was the Apple II, introduced in 1977 by Apple Computer. This changed when IBM entered the market in 1981. The IBM PC quickly became the Personal Computer of choice, and many manufacturers were pushed out of the market. Other companies adjusted to IBM's dominance by building IBM clones, internally almost the same as the IBM PC, but cheaper.

Introduced in 1984, the MacIntosh was the first widely available PC to use a *Graphical User Interface (GUI)* that uses windows, icons, and a mouse. In fact, these concepts were devised much earlier in the research labs of Xerox, but had not been commercialised at that time. A GUI is now common practice on all PCs.

PPCP is Short for *PowerPC Platform,* it was developed jointly by Apple, IBM, and Motorola and was first called the *Common Hardware Reference Platform (CHRP)*. The specification is based on the RISC architecture used for the RS/6000 mini-computer. A computer that meets the PPCP standard allows you to select an application without regard to the underlying Operating System. A PPCP computer can run any Mac, PC, or UNIX-based application program without the usual modifications required to fit an Operating System to a platform.

Notebooks

A *Notebook (computer)* is an extremely lightweight PC, small enough to fit easily in a briefcase. Notebooks are nearly equivalent to Personal Computers; they have similar (but not identical) CPUs, memory, and disk drives. Notebooks use a variety of techniques, to produce a lightweight and non-bulky display screen. Active-matrix screens produce sharp images, but they do not refresh as rapidly as full-size monitors and have a fixed resolution. Notebooks come with battery packs enabling you to run without plugging them in. However, the batteries need to be recharged every few hours.

Battery packs are also the weakest point of these systems. They have a limited lifetime; so make sure to purchase a spare.

Network Computers

Network Computers (NCs) are Personal Computers with minimal memory and processor power and no disk storage designed to connect to a network. The idea behind thin clients is that most users who are connected to a network do not need all the computing power they get from a typical Personal Computer. Instead, they can rely on the power of the network servers. Thin clients are a simpler and easier way to deliver the productivity and application flexibility of a PC without the downsides of high service costs, low reliability and short product life. Thin client computing is not suitable for high performance environments such as graphic design, engineering and software development.

Personal Digital Assistants (PDAs)

PDAs or *Personal Digital Assistants* are handheld devices that combine computing, telephone/fax, and networking. Unlike portable computers, PDAs began as pen-based devices, using a stylus rather than a keyboard for input. Some PDAs can also react to voice input by using voice recognition technologies. PDAs are now available in either a stylus or keyboard version. The field of PDAs was pioneered by Apple Computer, which introduced the Newton Message Pad in 1993. Shortly thereafter, several other manufacturers offered similar products.

"...and if anyone has seen my PDA, which has my speech on it, please pass it forward."

Workstations

A *workstation* is a type of computer used for engineering applications, desktop publishing, software development, and other applications that require a lot of computing power and high quality graphics capabilities. Workstations come with a large, high-resolution graphics screen, a generous amount of main memory and network support. Most workstations also have a mass storage device, but a special type of workstation, called a diskless workstation, comes without a disk drive. In terms of computing power, workstations are situated between Personal Computers and minicomputers, although the line is fuzzy on both ends. High-end Personal Computers are equivalent to low-end workstations as high-end workstations are equivalent to minicomputers.

Servers

Servers are mid-sized computer systems. In size and power, servers lie between workstations and mainframes. In the passed decades, however, the distinction between large servers and small mainframes has blurred in the same way as the distinction between small servers and workstations. But in general, a server is a multiprocessing system capable of supporting from four to about 200 users simultaneously. For example, a *file server* is a computer and storage device dedicated to storing files; any client on the network can store files on the server. A *print server* is a computer that manages one or more printers. Servers are often dedicated, meaning that they perform no other tasks besides their server tasks.

Clusters

The term *cluster* refers to the close connection of several systems to form a group using the appropriate software. Physically, a cluster is a group of two or more servers that serve the same group of clients and can access the same data. From a logical point of view, a cluster represents a unit, in which any server can provide any authorized client with any available service. The servers must have access to the same data and share a common security system. Although clusters can be structured in different ways, they have the same advantages:

- Higher availability of applications and data;
- Scalability of hardware resources;
- Easier administration.

Because of the internal communications needed to distribute the workload among the participating systems of the cluster the scaling of the resulting performance is not linear; that means that increasing the number of systems will not result in a proportional increase of performance of the cluster and the higher the number of nodes, the more this effect will play. On the other hand, the cost of a cluster will probably be lower than the cost of a single system with the same performance.

Blade computers

Blade computers, or blades, are modular computers that look more like circuit boards than traditional computers. Initially, they appealed to customers wanting to reduce the real estate occupied by servers. Conventional server racks can hold 42 two-processor servers, for a total of 84 processors. By contrast, several hundred two-processor blade servers can fit into the same space. Many blades also consume less energy, reducing the need for the big cooling systems now required in some server rooms. Soon after their introduction, designers began advertising another advantage: manageability. Once software is loaded on one blade, it can be replicated on its siblings relatively quickly through software developed specifically for these servers. Other servers require personal attention to do this. Unlike early blades, which were primarily used for relatively simple applications such as Web hosting, the newer blades can be used for running more advanced applications such as databases. The emphasis on versatility has actually reversed some of the gains in density. Future blades will be fatter than their current counterparts, and will likely resemble bricks or blocks. Whatever the eventual buzzword - bricks, blocks or cubes - these systems appear to be the shape of things to come.

Grid Computing

Corporate networks comprise hundreds or thousands of PCs, equipped with some of the fastest microprocessors ever produced. Typically, these processors remain much underused, performing simple tasks like running a word processor, opening e-mail, and printing documents. These tasks rarely consume more than 10% of the PCs' available computing power; the other 90% is going to waste. In *Grid Computing* the idle processing cycles of the PCs on corporate networks are made available for working on computationally intensive problems that would otherwise require a supercomputer or server cluster to solve. Large applications are split into small computing tasks, which are then distributed to PCs to process in parallel. Results are sent back to a server where they are collected and presented. A small program that runs on each PC, allows the server to send and receive jobs to and from that PC. This program runs unobtrusively in the background, never interfering with the routine work being performed by that PC.

Mainframes

A *Mainframe (computer)* is a large and expensive computer capable of supporting hundreds or even thousands of clients simultaneously. In the hierarchy based on performance, mainframes are just below supercomputers. The distinction between small mainframes and big minicomputers is vague, depending really on how the manufacturer wants to market its machines. Historically, mainframes were introduced as computers that run administrative applications such as accounting and stock management for large organizations. They are oriented towards centralized computing, rather than distributed or network computing. Today, many organizations still rely on their mainframes to conduct their business: the important investments of the past make it hard to justify the massive transition to more modern computing concepts, so these legacy systems are there to stay for still some time.

Supercomputers

The main difference between a supercomputer and a mainframe is that a supercomputer uses all its power for the execution of a few programs as fast as possible, whereas a mainframe executes many programs concurrently. *Supercomputers* are employed for specialized applications that require immense amounts of mathematical calculations. For example, weather forecasting requires a supercomputer. Other uses of supercomputers include animated graphics, fluid dynamic calculations, nuclear research, and petroleum exploration.

Digital technology

Human beings are used to calculate with *decimal* (base 10) numbers. This, of course, has to do with the fact that they have ten fingers. Computers, however, only know two states, one and zero, which naturally leads to the use of *binary* (base two) numbers. Consider a decimal number abc:

$$abc_{10} = a*10^2 + b*10^1 + c*10^0$$

Similarly, in the binary system a number with digits a b c can be written as:

$$abc_2 = a*2^2 + b*2^1 + c*2^0$$

Each digit is known as a *bit* and can take on only two values: zero or one. The left-most bit is the highest-order bit and represents the *Most Significant Bit* (*MSB*), while the lowest-order bit is the *Least Significant Bit* (*LSB*).

Besides numerical information, computers also have to be capable to work with other types of data such as text strings. This is done using standardized encoding methods in which a single character is represented by a series of bits.

IBM developed *EBCDIC (Extended Binary-coded Decimal Interchange Code)*; it used an ingenious 5 bit encoding technique.

ASCII (American Standard Code for Information Interchange) was the first non-proprietary method of encoding characters. The standard ASCII character set uses just seven bits for each character and allows encoding standard Latin characters. In 8-bit ASCII the additional 128 codes are used to include characters used by other languages.

The *ISO 8859* series of standards covers almost all extensions of the Latin alphabet as well as the Cyrillic (ISO 8859-5), Arabic (ISO 8859-6), Greek (ISO 8859-7), and Hebrew (ISO 8859-8) alphabets. The first 128 characters in each ISO 8859 code table are identical to 7-bit ASCII, while the national characters are always located in the upper 128 code positions.

Unicode is now becoming widely accepted. ISO 10646 (based on Unicode) is a 16-bit code, meaning that it can represent 65,536 characters instead of the 128 of ASCII or 256 of extended ASCII. The first 256 codes in Unicode are identical to ISO 8859-1. Fig. 2.3 is an extract of the Greek code chart:

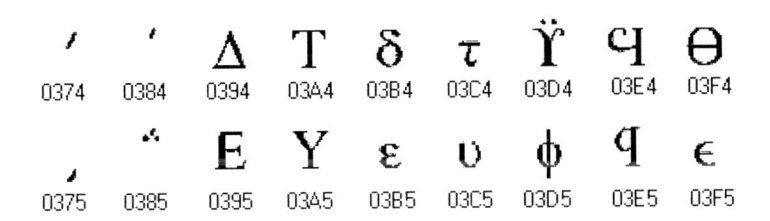

′	′	Δ	Τ	δ	τ	Ϋ	Ϥ	Θ
0374	0384	0394	03A4	03B4	03C4	03D4	03E4	03F4
͵	¨	Ε	Υ	ε	υ	φ	ϥ	ϵ
0375	0385	0395	03A5	03B5	03C5	03D5	03E5	03F5

Fig. 2.3 – *Extract of Greek code chart*

The von Neumann Architecture

Virtually every modern computer is based on the *von Neumann architecture*. The name comes from John von Neumann who was the first to define the requirements for a general-purpose electronic computer. According to von Neumann a general-purpose computer contains three main components. These are identified as relating to *control and arithmetic*, *memory*, and *interaction with the outside world* (Fig. 2.4).

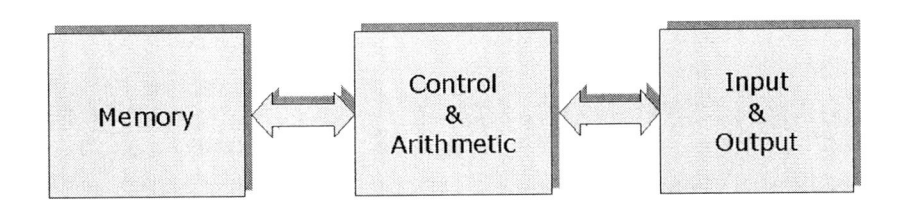

Fig. 2.4 – *Components of a Von Neumann computer*

The von Neumann computer is further able to *store* not only its *data* and the intermediate results of computation, but also to *store the instructions*, that carry out the computation.

Obviously, the computers we use today are the result of numerous improvements of the basic architecture. For example, index registers and general-purpose registers, floating point data representation, indirect addressing, and hardware interrupts, input and output, parallel execution, virtual memory, and the use of multiple processors have been introduced. However, none of these improvements fundamentally changed the original architecture.

Central Processing Unit

The Control and Arithmetic component of a computer is grouped together with the Registers in the *Central Processing Unit or CPU*. The CPU can be seen as the "brain" of the computer. Data and instructions flow between the CPU and main memory in both directions. Instructions arriving at the CPU are decoded and executed, and then the results of the execution go back to the memory.

The CPU has to be able to understand, recognize and execute certain basic programming instructions. This group of basic instructions is known as the *instruction set*. At the lowest level, an instruction is a sequence of 0's and 1's that describes a physical operation the computer is to perform. Different types of CPU's have different instruction sets. In other words, the basic operations one CPU can understand and execute can be different from that which another CPU can understand and execute.

CPUs can be subdivided into two categories: RISC and CISC. *RISC* stands for *Reduced Instruction Set Computer* i.e., the CPU understands only a reduced set of instructions. *CISC* stands for *Complex Instruction Set Computer*, a term that represents the tendency to build ever larger and more complex instruction sets, implying that an ever-increasing amount of complexity is included in the hardware architecture. Since it was assumed that silicon technology would reach its physical limits, researchers began to question whether this was really the best approach to take. The surprising result of their research was that only some 20% of the instructions were frequently used. This led to the idea of a reduced instruction set. Another advantage of the RISC approach was that it became significantly easier for the CPU to process multiple instructions in parallel. Today, nearly all the major computer manufacturers offer computers with the RISC architecture.

Microprocessors

A *microprocessor* is a computer whose entire CPU is contained on one *Integrated Circuit (IC)*. The first commercial microprocessor was the Intel 4004, which appeared in 1971. This chip was called a 4-bit microprocessor since it processed only four bits of data at a time. A single chip microprocessor today includes other components such as memory, memory management, caches, floating-point units, input/output ports, and timers. It has reduced the computer to a small and easily replaceable design component.

In 1965 Gordon Moore, co-founder of Intel, observed that each new memory chip contained roughly twice as much capacity as its predecessor and was released within 18-24 months of the previous chip. So, if this trend continued, computing power would rise exponentially with time. This observation is commonly known as *Moore's Law*. Moore's observation still holds, and probably will for some decades. In particular, microprocessor performance has increased faster than the number of transistors per chip. The performance, measured in *Mega Instructions per Second (MIPS)*, has, on average, doubled every 1.8 years in the last decades. Chip density in transistors per unit area, on the contrary has increased less quickly (doubling every 3.3 years). This is because the automatic layout required to cope with the increased complexity is less efficient than the hand layout used for early processors.

"It's been 18 months and my computer's power hasn't doubled."

Main Memory

"640K should be enough for anybody."

(Bill Gates, 1981)

The early mainframes only had a few kilobytes of memory, made up of small ferrite, core-shaped, elements. Back in the eighties, the first PCs were equipped with 64K of memory and the 640K that was proposed by Bill Gates was considered to be more than enough. Today, however, a "normal" PC has three orders of magnitude more memory than its early predecessors and the internal memory of servers in measured in Gigabytes.

In *Dynamic Random Access Memory (DRAM)* information is stored in capacitors, which can retain energy for a certain time. These capacitors are arranged in a matrix of rows and columns. This technology can be produced at a low cost with high densities. The *Fast Page Mode (FPM)* available with some memory modules is an improvement of the standard DRAM technology. With respect to FPM, *Extended Data Output (EDO)* represents a further development. Like FPM and EDO, *SDRAM (Synchronous DRAM)* is yet another development of the memory technology, in contrast to FPM or EDO however, this technology is not backward compatible i.e., SDRAM memory chips can only be used in computer systems that explicitly support this technology.

Static memory chips operate at a high speed, this is why they are used as *cache* memory between the main memory and the CPU registers ("level 2"). Due to the more complex structure of their memory cells, the density of these chips is much lower than for dynamic memories. They are also considerably more expensive.

These memory components are able to retain their contents, even if the power supply is switched off. *Read-only Memory (ROM)* is an integrated circuit programmed with data when it is manufactured. Creating ROM chips from scratch is time-consuming and expensive. Therefore, a type of ROM known as *Programmable Read-Only Memory (PROM)* was created. ROMs and PROMs can only be programmed once; *Erasable Programmable Read-Only Memory (EPROM)* addresses this issue as these chips can be rewritten many times. All the above types of memory still require dedicated equipment and a labor-intensive process to remove and reinstall them each time a change is necessary. Also, changes cannot be made incrementally. *Electrically Erasable Programmable Read-Only Memory (EEPROM)* chips remove these drawbacks.

Internal buses

The different components of a computer system are all interconnected using an *internal bus*. The *data bus* transports instructions and data between the CPU, main memory, and I/O devices. The CPU uses the *address bus* to select a single address at a time to address either memory or I/O. The *control bus* is used to control the operations: dictate the speed of the operations with the clock signal, show the direction of the data flow, make the distinction between a memory and an I/O operation etc.

The first *Personal Computer Interface (PCI)* bus had 32 bits data bus and a clock rate of 33 MHz. The PCI bus can support a maximum transfer rate of up to 133 Mbps. The 64-bit version supports a maximum transfer rate of up to 267 Mbps. An important advantage of the PCI bus is that it is not dependant on the processor type. Thus, the PCI bus can also be used with non-Intel processors.

The *Accelerated Graphics Port (AGP)* is an individual graphics card slot developed by Intel. The AGP concept allows the graphics card to access directly data stored in the main memory. The main-board chip set and AGP exchange the data at 66 MHz 32 bits at a time, which corresponds with a transfer rate of 266 MB/s. In addition, the AGP card supports the so-called x2 mode or x4 mode, which give a doubled or quadrupled speed. AGP is downward compatible with PCI.

The PC card interface is a standard for credit-card sized expansion cards, which was established by *the Personal Computer Memory Card Interface Association (PCMCIA)* in 1990. The first products that used this standard were memory cards. The standard was gradually expanded so other hardware could be designed and used in accordance with the PC Card standard, such as interface cards, modems, and LAN adapters. It comes in three types (I, II, and III) with different thickness.

The latest development of the PC Card standard is the *CardBus*. This bus has certain improvements such as reduced power consumption, better compatibility, and higher performance. The PC CardBus specification describes a 32-bit bus similar to PCI, with bus master capability and a frequency of 33 MHz with transfer rates up to 132 MB/s. This allows notebooks to use this modern bus with more sophisticated hardware, which requires higher I/O performances (e.g., Fast Ethernet).

Input/Output

The purpose of input/output devices is the transformation of data in a usable form, either by the computer or the outside world. Even though these devices come in a tremendous variety undergoing a constant evolution towards more, faster, and cheaper operations the fact remains that these devices are just commodities. Therefore it has been decided to limit the discussion in this section to the peripheral buses and the important topic of mass storage.

Peripheral buses

The connection of peripheral devices such as disk arrays, tape drives, printers, and scanners to computers is done using standardized interfaces. The simplest ones are the (serial) RS232 interface and the (parallel) Centronics interface, but over the years more elaborate solutions have emerged.

The *Universal Serial Bus (USB)* is a peripheral bus standard developed by industry leaders, eliminating the need to install cards into dedicated computer slots and reconfigure the system (Fig. 2.5). USB allows up to 127 devices to run simultaneously on a computer, with peripherals such as monitors and keyboards acting as additional plug-in sites, or hubs.

USB detects when devices are added and removed. The bus automatically determines what host resources - including driver software and bus bandwidth - each peripheral need and makes those resources available without manual intervention. The current version of USB is 2.0.

Many modern computer systems use the *Small Computer System Interface* (*SCSI*, pronounced "scuzzy") to talk to external devices. Besides faster data rates, SCSI is more flexible than earlier parallel data transfer interfaces. SCSI allows up to 7 or 15 devices (depending on the bus width) to be connected to a single port in a daisy-chain configuration. This allows one card to accommodate all the peripherals, rather than having a separate card for each device.

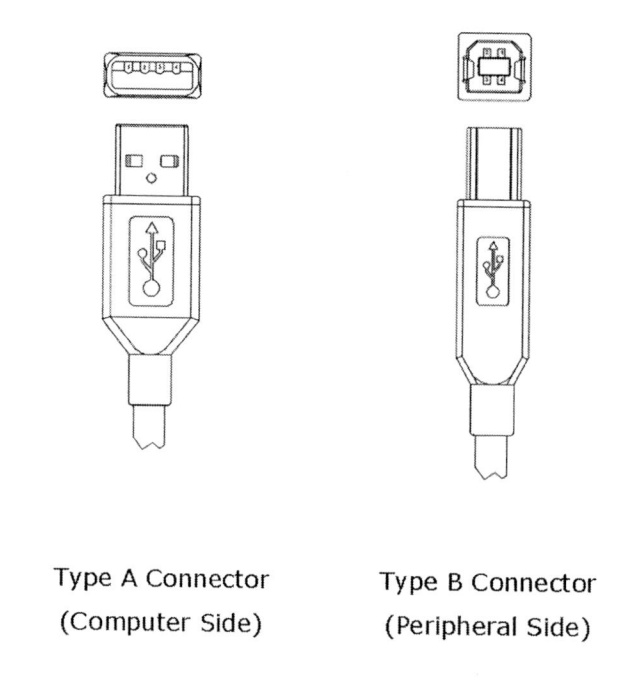

Type A Connector
(Computer Side)

Type B Connector
(Peripheral Side)

Fig. 2.5 – *USB connectors*

There are different successive SCSI standards, which are backwards compatible. This means that, if you attach an older device to a newer computer with support for a later standard, the device will work at the slower data rate. A widely used SCSI standard is Ultra-2 which uses a 40 MHz clock rate to get maximum data transfer rates up to 80 MBps. It provides a greater maximum cabling distance (up to 12 meters). Ultra-2 SCSI sends the signal over two wires with the data represented as the difference in voltage between the two wires. This allows support for longer cables, reduced power requirements, and manufacturing costs. The latest SCSI standards are Ultra-3 (or Ultra-160) and Ultra-320 which increase the maximum burst rate to 160 MBps and 320 MBps. These standards also include *Cyclic Redundancy Checking* (*CRC*) to ensure the integrity of transferred data and domain validation for testing the SCSI network.

Digital video and multimedia applications have brought the need to move large amounts of data quickly between peripherals and PCs together with a simple high-speed connection standard that makes this transmission more efficient. The *IEEE 1394 serial bus* is the industry-standard implementation of Apple Computer, Inc.'s digital I/O system, known as *FireWire*. It's a versatile, high-speed, low-cost method of interconnecting a variety of Personal Computer peripherals and consumer electronics devices. Developed by the industry's leading technology companies, the specification was accepted as a standard by the IEEE Standards Board in 1995, with successive revisions since then. IEEE 1394 has been adopted by the consumer electronics industry and provides a Plug-and Play-compatible expansion interface for the PC. The 100 Mbps, 200 Mbps, and 400 Mbps transfer rates currently specified in IEEE P1394.a and the proposed enhancements in IEEE P1394.b are well suited to multi-streaming I/O requirements. The standard allows the connection of up to 63 devices, without the need for additional hardware; all you need is a flexible six-wire cable.

The *Enhanced Parallel Port (EPP)* and the *Extended Capabilities Port (ECP)* are two modern parallel port standards that support bi-directional communication with external devices. They are about ten times faster than the older Centronics standard.

Data Storage

Data storage can be divided into three categories: primary, secondary, and tertiary data storage.

Primary Data Storage

Apart from the processor speed and the size of the computer's main memory, the performance of the *primary data storage* is the most important factor for a computer's response time. This is data storage that can randomly access the data. Hard disk drives are the devices used for most standard applications.

The *access time* is calculated from the time required for multiple sequential processes. When a program wants to read or write data, the Operating System generates a request that is passed to the hard disk controller. This request causes the drive to position the read/write heads at a point on the disk surface. This time is called the *seek time,* the time required for the head mechanism to travel across the disk. The *settling time* specifies how long the head mechanism requires to rest mechanically after a head movement for oscillations to be extinguished. If the read/write head is positioned on the correct track, it must wait until the desired block is reached. This wait time is called *latency* or *rotational wait time*. This figure is exclusively dependent on the disk's rotational speed. At this point the disk's (internal) *transfer rate* becomes important. It shows the number of bytes transferred per second. The higher a disk's transfer rate, the fewer transfer time is required for the data transfer. Once the data has arrived at the hard disk controller, it is then sent via the peripheral bus to the computer's main memory.

A way to increase performance is *disk caching*. Disk caching works on the same principle as memory caching, but instead of using high-speed SRAM, conventional memory is used. A copy of a part of the disk is held in an intermediate memory block. Smart algorithms are used to determine which parts have to be kept in memory, so that the probability of having the data available in the cache is high (sometimes up to 90%).

Another interesting construction is the *Redundant Array of Inexpensive Disks (RAID)*. As the name implies it is a way of storing the same data in different places (thus, redundantly) on multiple hard disks. By placing data on multiple disks, I/O operations can overlap in a balanced way, improving performance. Since multiple disks increase the *Mean Time between Failure* (*MTBF*), storing data redundantly also increases fault-tolerance. A RAID appears to the Operating System to be a single logical hard disk. RAID employs a technique called *striping*, which involves partitioning each drive's storage space into units. There are several RAID types. The most widely used are RAID-1 (also known as disk mirroring) and RAID-5. RAID-5 stores parity information but not redundant data. It requires at least three and usually five disks for the array. It is commonly used for file and application servers, database servers, and Web, E-mail, News and Intranet servers.

Secondary Data Storage

This is removable data storage, which stores data similar to primary data storage. Data can, however, only be directly reached after the medium has been inserted.

Floppy disk drives - This technology is based on a removable, rotating magnetic disk with an access time of 150-250 ms with the advantage of being widely used. Its limited capacity is a disadvantage. This disadvantage has been largely removed by the ZIP drive from IOMEGA. At 100 MB per storage medium, the capacity of this drive is sufficient even for smaller to medium-size software packages. Since 1999, a HiFD disk drive has been available from SONY, which supports 200 MB of storage capacity and could replace the common drives to date. It is compatible with the drives that are currently used, and can read the 1.44 MB disk.

Removable Disk Drives - Large amounts of data can be managed with removable disks, without losing time in transferring data from one medium to another. In addition, such subsystems are well suited for high-security situations, for example when data needs to be stored in a safe overnight.

CD-ROMs – These are removable optical disks only for reading data that has been recorded as part of the manufacturing process. With a storage capacity of about 650 MB, the CD-ROM is an ideal medium for mass distribution of data, e.g., for software distribution, since the reproduction costs are much lower for greater quantities. The reading speed of the CD-ROM drive is measured in reference to the transfer rate of an audio drive, which is 150 KBps. For example: a 14x drive can read at 2.05 MBps.

CD-R - Using CD recorders, data can be written onto blank CD-ROMs without great expense. CD-Rs are also suitable for long-term archiving. The data media are very stable, but the data cannot be changed once it has been written. With automatic changers that contain a CD recorder there is a cost-effective way to archive and backup in small or medium-sized networks.

CD-RW - This is a technology that allows a medium to be written to repeatedly. These drives can also write a single data session to CD-R media.

Multiread - This specification defines the guidelines necessary for optical devices to be capable of reading discs created in CD formats. Any device adhering to the specification is capable for reading audio CD, CD-ROM, CD-R, and CD-RW.

DVD - With pressure from the video industry, a new optical technology emerged with *Digital Versatile Disk* (*DVD*), which extended the media capacity to 4.7 GB by using a higher density. Using both sides of the medium and employing a second data layer can quadruple this capacity. DVD drives can also read all standard CD formats.

Universal Disk Format (UDF) – This is a CD-ROM and DVD file system standard. UDF is required for DVD-ROMs, and is used by DVD to contain MPEG audio and video streams. UDF was originally developed as a replacement for the file system specifications in the original CD-ROM standard (ISO 9660). This specification is fully compliant with the ISO 13346 standard and allows file interchange between different Operating Systems.

Tertiary data storage

Digital Linear Tape (DLT) – With this technology, data is recorded on tracks that lie parallel to the tape edge. Data is written to magnetic tapes, 1/2-inch wide and enclosed in compact cartridges. DLTs have a capacity of up to 60 GB uncompressed and higher (110 GB for Super DLT and LTO devices). An additional advantage of this technology is that wear and tear on the tapes and read heads is low. This is achieved through stationary magnetic heads and a simple tape threading system. As a result, DLT drives are capable of up to 500,000 tape winding cycles per cartridge. DLT IV tapes are capable of more than 1,000,000 cycles, due to the use of the new technology described above.

Digital Audio Tape (DAT) – This technology also emerged from digital recording methods in the audio field. In comparison to the eight mm Exabyte tapes, however, DAT tapes are only four mm wide. DAT drives can store up to eight GB (120 m tape) at transfer rates of up to one MBps using the DDS-2 standard. The claim of eight GB storage capacities typically represents a figure achievable with data compression. Theoretically, up to 16 GB of data can be stored. Drives with DDS-3 format can record up to 24 GB on a 125 m tape with a data transfer rate of up to 2MBps. At present, the DDS-4 standard ensures capacities of up to 40 GB (with compression) with read and writes compatibility with DDS-2 and DDS-3.

Storage Networking

A study carried out in 2000 by the University of Berkeley showed that 93% of information created today is in digital form. Also, virtually all data has become mission-critical. As a result, the need to add more storage, service more customers and back-up more data has become a difficult task. Today, *Direct Attached Storage (DAS)* is still the most common storage architecture in use, but NAS and SAN are gaining an increased market share A *Storage Area Network* or *SAN* is a high-speed special-purpose network (or sub-network) that interconnects different kinds of data storage devices with associated data servers. This is opposed to the *Network Attached Storage (NAS)* concept, where the normal network infrastructure and protocols are being used (Fig. 2.6).

The SAN was created because early Ethernet/IP networks were not able to handle high volumes of traffic. *Fiber Channel (FC)* was born out of a need for a fast, dedicated, and robust network for storage. With many leading companies supporting FC, it has become the most widely endorsed technology for the storage environment.

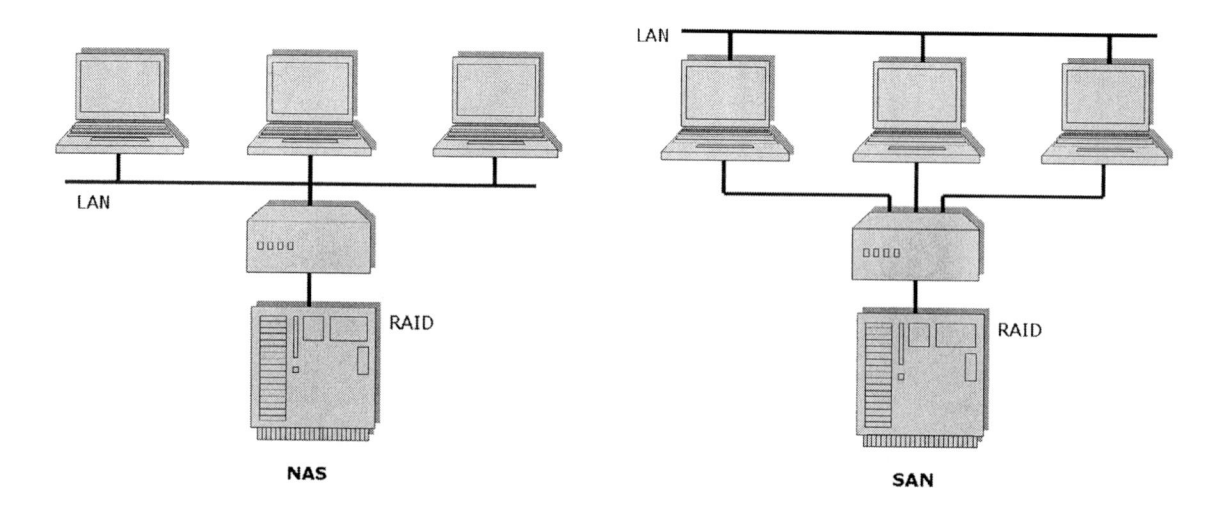

Fig. 2.6 – *NAS vs. SAN*

There are three basic Fiber Channel topologies: point-to-point, arbitrated loop, and fabric.

- *Point-to-point* is a simple setup in which the transmit ports are connected to the receive ports on a pair of devices;
- *Arbitrated loop*, which is by far the most common, is when you have multiple devices connected in a daisy-chain fashion;
- In *fabric mode*, two devices communicate without a direct connection; they are connected to a switch.

Recently, the move has clearly been toward convergence of NAS and SAN technologies. This convergence makes sense because, while both are an improvement over DAS, they tend to have exactly opposite strengths and weaknesses, as is shown in the following table.

	DAS (peripheral device)	NAS (file-oriented)	SAN (block-oriented)
Volume-Sharing	No	Almost never	Yes (same OS)
File-sharing	Does not apply	Yes	Almost never
Robustness	Very Low	Lower	Higher
Manageability	Does not Apply	Higher	Lower
Backup/Recovery	Very poor solution	Poor solution	Good solution
Performance	Good	Lower	Higher
Purchase Cost	Very Low	Low	Higher
Scalability	Very Low	Lower	Higher
Network Topology	Does not Apply	IP (common)	Fiber Channel (uncommon)

Source: The Aberdeen Group

Table 2.1 - *Storage Architecture strengths and weaknesses*

It is clear that NAS provides file intelligence and facilitates file sharing. SAN is actually switched DAS designed to provide volume sharing and efficient backup; without a layer of file intelligence these block-level data cannot be shared.

The advent of *iSCSI* is now changing the terms of the NAS versus SAN debate. Whereas Fiber Channel encapsulates SCSI commands, status, and data in Fiber Channel framing, iSCSI performs the same encapsulation in TCP/IP.

For SAN and NAS to converge, taking the best of both worlds, a Storage Controller is needed, providing multi-OS, high performance file sharing. In addition, Storage Controllers can provide benefits like high-availability, load balancing, LAN-free backup, server-free backup and data replication for disaster recovery.

Operating Systems

Purpose of an Operating System

An *Operating System (OS)* is the software that manages all the other programs in a computer system [23]. Operating Systems perform basic tasks, such as recognizing input from the keyboard, keeping track of files and directories, and controlling peripheral devices like disk drives and printers. For large systems, the Operating System has even greater responsibilities; it makes sure that different programs and clients running at the same time do not interfere with one another. The Operating System is also responsible for *security*, ensuring that unauthorized individuals do not access the system and the data it manages.

Operating Systems provide a software platform on top of which other programs, called *application programs or applications,* can run. The application programs are usually written for a particular Operating System. Your choice of Operating System, therefore, determines to a great extent the applications you can run.

Structure of an Operating System

An operating system can be seen as a layered structure:

- CPU management;
- Memory management;
- Device drivers;
- I/O management;
- User interface.

The first layer of the OS handles the scheduling of the work done by the processor; this is done using *system processes* or *threads*. The Operating System organizes the execution of these processes or threads so that it looks as if several things are happening at the same time.

The *memory management* makes sure that each process gets enough memory without running into the memory space of other processes. It also makes sure that the different types of memory in the system are used properly. A processor can only access memory one location at a time, so the vast majority of memory is unused at any moment. Since disk space is cheap compared to internal memory, moving information from internal memory to hard disk can greatly expand available memory space at low cost. This technique is called *virtual memory management*. Moving data to and from disk is called *swapping*.

Special programs called *drivers* manage the path between the OS and virtually all hardware. Drivers do the translation between the hardware subsystems and the high-level programming languages. One reason that drivers are separate from the OS is that new functions can be added to the driver without requiring the operating system itself to be modified, recompiled, and redistributed. Furthermore, it allows development by the manufacturer of the subsystems rather than the vendor of the operating system. It is important to mention the process of *Simultaneous Peripheral Operations On-Line (spooling),* which consists of putting jobs in a buffer where data can be kept while the slower I/O device catches up.

Just as drivers provide a way for applications to make use of hardware subsystems without having to know every detail of the hardware's operation, *Application Programming Interfaces (APIs)* let application programmers use functions of the computer and OS without having to know all the details of the computer's operation.

Finally, the *user interface* of the OS brings structure to the interaction between a user and the computer. A user normally interacts with the Operating System through a set of commands. For example, the DOS Operating System contains commands such as COPY and RENAME for copying files and changing the names of files, respectively. The commands are accepted and executed by a part of the Operating System called *command processor* or *command line interpreter.* Graphical user interfaces (GUIs) allow you to enter commands by pointing and clicking at objects that appear on the screen.

Characteristics of Operating Systems

Different characteristics of Operating Systems can be distinguished.

Multitasking and multiprocessing - The terms *multitasking* and *multiprocessing* are sometimes confused, even if multiprocessing usually implies that more than one CPU is involved. There are two types of multitasking: *preemptive* and *cooperative.* In preemptive multitasking, the Operating System distributes *time slices* to each program, in cooperative multitasking on the contrary each program can control the CPU for as long as it needs it.

The term *multithreading* refers to the ability of an operating system to execute different parts of a program, called *threads,* simultaneously. The program has to be designed in such a way that all the threads can run at the same time without interfering with one another.

When two or more simultaneous users are allowed, an Operating System is said to be *multi-user.* All mainframes and minicomputers are multi-user systems, but most personal computers and workstations are not.

Autonomic Computing

A new idea in the world of Operating Systems is called *Autonomic Computing*. The central theme is that computers should start to behave as a self-regulating biological system. Why? Because there are always more computers, that are always more complex and we will soon reach the point where we cannot manage it ourselves anymore. So, the computers have to learn to manage themselves (or one another).

Security

According to SEI security is:

"The ability of a system to manage, protect, and distribute sensitive information."

Authentication, authorisation, and accountability

Authentication is the process of determining whether a person or an entity such as another program is who it claims to be. During authentication, credentials presented by an individual or entity are validated and associated with that person or entity's identity.

Authorization is the process of giving a person or entity permission to do or have something. The system administrator defines for the system which users are allowed access to the system and with what privileges (such as access to which file directories, hours of access, amount of allocated storage space, and so forth).

Accountability refers to the ability of a system to keep track of whom or what gained access or made changes to the system.

The Orange Book

The Department of Defense *Trusted Computer System Evaluation Criteria*, (DOD-5200.28-STD) also known as the *Orange Book*, is the de facto standard for computer security today. The evaluation criteria can be used for the evaluation of existing systems and for the specification of security requirements during an acquisition process. In the Orange Book, computer systems are categorized in classes that are part of four divisions, depending on the criteria they satisfy.

Division D is reserved for those systems that have been evaluated but that fail to meet the requirements for a higher evaluation class.

Classes in *division C* provide for discretionary (need-to-know) protection and, through the inclusion of audit capabilities, for accountability of subjects and the actions they start.

The preservation of the integrity of sensitivity labels is a major requirement in *division B*. Systems in this division must carry the sensitivity labels with major data structures in the system. The system developer must also provide the security policy model on which the system is based.

Division A is characterized by the use of formal security verification methods. Extensive documentation is required to demonstrate that the system meets the security requirements in all aspects of design, development, and implementation.

Local Services

Storing Data

The local services are all about *storing data*. In the past, the emphasis was put on high-speed access, the data types were simple and the output devices were standard text devices. This has gradually changed, so that today we are storing complex data (sounds, images) and also the output devices have become more diversified.

The different types of local services can be described in two dimensions. First, there is the complexity of the data they store and second, there is the distinction between those systems that allow for (structured) querying and those who do not. Fig. 2.7 shows the different implementations of these categories:

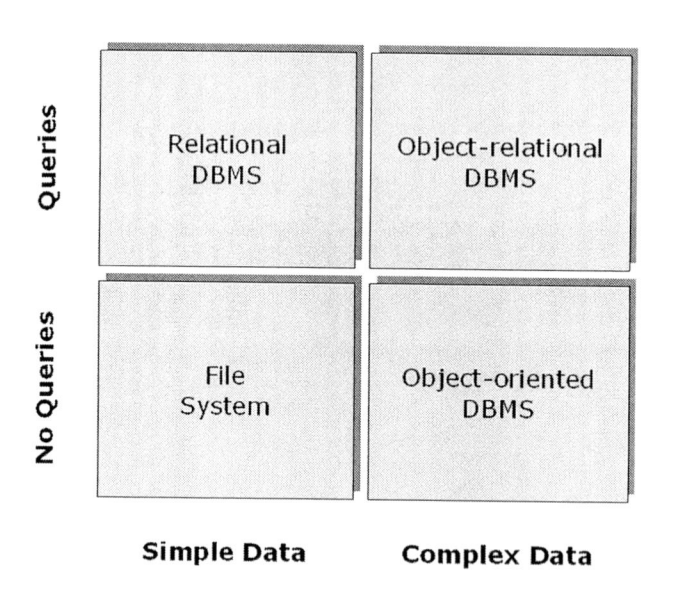

	Simple Data	**Complex Data**
Queries	Relational DBMS	Object-relational DBMS
No Queries	File System	Object-oriented DBMS

Fig. 2.7 – *Storage systems*

File Systems

Market analysts estimate that on average around 85% of all information that is stored in an organization is done by means of files and the volume is growing somewhere between 40 and 120% per year. A *file* is a collection of data that has a name. There are many different types of files: texts (formatted and unformatted), program files, images, movies, etc. Different types of files store different types of data.

A *directory* is a special kind of file used to organize other files into a hierarchical structure. Directories contain bookkeeping information about other files. You can think of a directory as a folder that contains files and perhaps other folders. The topmost directory is called the *root directory*. A directory that is below another directory is called a *subdirectory*.

A *File (Management) System* is the software that an Operating System or other program uses to organize and keep track of files and directories. Although all Operating Systems provide their own file management system, separate file management systems are also available on the market. These systems interact smoothly with the operating system but provide more features, such as improved backup procedures and stricter file protection.

Relational Database Management Systems (RDBMSs)

A *database* is a collection of data that is organized in such a way that its contents can easily be reached, managed, and updated [13].

A *Database Management System (DBMS)*, sometimes just called a *database manager*, is a program that lets one or more users create and access data in a database. The DBMS manages requests from users and programs so that they do not have to understand where the data is physically located. In handling requests, the DBMS ensures the *integrity* of the data (that is, making sure it continues to be accessible and is consistently organized as intended) and *security* (making sure only those with access privileges can access the data). A DBMS can be thought of as a file manager that manages data in databases rather than files in a file system.

Relational databases

The most widely spread DBMSs are *Relational Database Management Systems* or *RDBMSs*. In an RDBMS data are stored as *tables*. Below is a simple example of a table that is part of an order entry application.

Customer

CustID	Name	Address	State	City
100234	AB Corp.	1, Las Vegas Blvd.	Nevada	Las Vegas
222394	Technotools	323, Main Street	Minnesota	Mineapolis
124040	Acme	555, Star Blvd.	Texas	Dallas
449452	Zillion Inc.	123A, Park Ave.	Kentucky	Louisville
553935	Whatsup	8, Silicon Driveway	California	San Diego

Another table holds the orders that were taken down:

Order

OrdID	OrdCustID	Description	Quantity
12345	124040	Baseball Gloves	2
12346	222394	Basketball	3
12347	100234	T-shirt	10
12348	124040	Helmet	6
12349	553935	Bicycle	9

The columns of a database table are known as *fields* or *attributes*, while the rows are called *records*. A *key* is a field that identifies a record. For the Customer table, the company name could be used as a key, but when there are two companies with the same name, there is a problem. The best way is to use an arbitrary whole number or a code (CustID).

There are two types of key fields: primary keys and foreign keys. A *primary key* is a field that uniquely identifies a record in a table (CustID and OrdID). No two records can have the same value for a primary key. A *foreign key* represents the value of primary key for a *related table*. In the Order table, the OrdCustID field holds the value of the CustID field for the customer who placed the order. By doing this, we can link the Customers and Orders tables using the CustID field. By joining the two tables based on this relationship, we can add fields from both tables and see all orders along with any pertinent customer data.

Data not only has to be stored, it also has to be retrieved from an RDBMS. This is done by queries. A *query* is a view of data that represents the data from one or more tables. In Relational Databases, queries are built using *Structured Query Language (SQL)*. SQL includes the capability of manipulating both the structure of a database and its data. In its most common form, SQL is used to create a simple SELECT query.

Let's take the example and build a query to look at customer orders. Here's the SQL for it:

```
SELECT Name, Description, Quantity
FROM Customer
WHERE Customer.CustID = Order.OrdCustID
ORDER BY Name, Description;
```

This query starts with the SELECT keyword. SELECT simply means that we wish to retrieve records from the tables. Following the SELECT keyword is the list of fields. Next comes the FROM keyword. This is used to show where the data is coming from. Here, it is coming from the Customer table and the Order table. The WHERE clause specifies which fields are used to join the tables. Here we are matching the CustID field from Customer to the OrdCustID field (the foreign key) in Order. The ORDER BY clause states the way the results have to be ordered (first by Name, then by Description).

The result that is returned by this query on the given tables looks like this:

Name	Description	Quantity
AB Corp.	T-shirt	10
Acme	Baseball Gloves	2
Acme	Helmet	6
Technotools	Basketball	3
Whatsup	Bicycle	9

One thing that should be noted is that, even though an ANSI standard exists, each RDBMS has its own particular dialect of SQL. Statements that were written for one RDBMS will not necessarily run or be interpreted on another engine.

So far, we have only discussed the SELECT statement, this is known as a *Data Manipulation Language (DML) statement*. Other DML statements allow for the creation or modification of data (INSERT and UPDATE). *Data Definition Language (DDL) statements* such as CREATE TABLE are used to manage the structure of the database and *Data Control Language (DCL) statements* allow the control over the access rights to the data, such as GRANT.

Normalization

Normalization is a theory for designing relational schemas that are efficient and work well. Well-normalized tables avoid unnecessary duplication and reduce inconsistencies. In well-normalized databases semantic dependencies are maintained by primary key uniqueness. Historically, several different types of normalization have been defined (first through fifth normal form); the most important however is the Boyce-Codd Normal Form (BCNF):

"A table is in Boyce-Codd Normal Form if every determinant is a candidate key."

Let A and B be two attributes of a table. A is said to be a *determinant* of B if each value of A has precisely one (possibly null) associated value of B or - said differently - if and only if whenever two tuples agree on their A value they agree on their B value. A *candidate key* is a combination of attributes that can be uniquely used to identify a database record. Each table can have one or more candidate keys. One of these candidate keys is selected as the table's primary key.

Consider the following table:

ID	Product	City	State	Price
9991	T-shirt	San Diego	California	100
9992	Baseball Gloves	San Diego	California	100
9993	T-shirt	Mesa	Arizona	150
9994	Helmet	Los Angeles	California	120
9996	Baseball Gloves	Mesa	Arizona	150
9997	Helmet	Phoenix	Arizona	80
9998	Basketball	Green Valley	Arizona	90
9999	Bicycle	Tombstone	Arizona	110

Transformed to the BCNF this would result in three tables:

ID	Product	City
9991	T-shirt	San Diego
9992	Baseball Gloves	San Diego
9993	T-shirt	Mesa
9994	Helmet	Los Angeles
9996	Baseball Gloves	Mesa
9997	Helmet	Phoenix
9998	Basketball	Green Valley
9999	Bicycle	Tombstone

City	State
San Diego	California
Los Angeles	California
Tombstone	Arizona
Mesa	Arizona
Phoenix	Arizona
Green Valley	Arizona

City	Price
Tombstone	110
Mesa	150
Phoenix	80
Green Valley	90
San Diego	100
Los Angeles	120

Indexing

Conceptually, the relational model is simple: operations on a set of tables yield another table as the result. But simply scanning tables is inefficient, that is why *indexes* exist. Indexes can best be compared with the alphabetical index of a book; they are easy to scan and point to occurrences of the searched word in the actual text.

There are different types of indexes but the common point is that they can speed up the search for a particular row or the sorting of a set of rows. Most databases have some kind of *query optimizer* that chooses the best path to get the data that satisfy a given query. An index can speed up considerably joins, ORDER BY and GROUP BY clauses from a SELECT statement. It can also speed up queries for which the conditions match the columns and sort order of the index. When you have a primary key, you already have an implicitly defined unique index on the primary key columns. It is a good idea to define non-unique indexes on the foreign keys.

Parallel databases

Today, database research is focusing on technology that allows multiple, smaller machines to achieve the same throughput as single, larger machine, with greater scalability and reliability. A so-called *parallel DBMS* runs across multiple processors and disks and executes operations in parallel, whenever possible, to improve performance. Parallel database architectures can be broadly classified into three categories: shared memory, shared disk, and shared nothing. The first two architectures require a special hardware arrangement; the last one uses a standard communication network.

The advantages of a parallel DBMS are obvious:

- Improved Performance;
- Improved Availability;
- Improved Reliability;
- Lower Total Cost of Ownership (TCO);
- Scalability.

The price, however, is paid in terms of:

- Increased complexity;
- More difficult security;
- More difficult integrity control.

The *Open Group* has formed a Working Group to provide specifications for a common SQL *Application Programming Interface (API)* and a common database protocol that enables DBMS from one vendor to communicate directly with DBMS from another vendor without the need for a gateway.

Object-Oriented Database Management Systems (OODBMS)

Relational database technology fails to handle the needs of complex Information Systems; they require the application developer to force an information model into tables with relationships between them.

The study of databases is centered on the problem of *data modeling*. A data model is a collection of well-defined concepts that help people to consider and express the properties of data intensive information systems.

A data model consists of:

- *Static properties* such as objects, attributes and relationships;
- *Integrity rules* over objects and operations;
- *Dynamic properties* such as operations or rules defining new database states based on applied state changes.

Relational databases are capable of supporting the first two points and rely on separate software programs for defining the dynamic properties of the model. The disadvantage of delegating the dynamic properties to separate programs is that they cannot be applied uniformly in all scenarios since they are defined outside the database.

Object-oriented databases can model all three of these points directly within the database thus supporting a complete problem/solution modelling capability. Object-oriented databases provide a unifying paradigm that allows one to integrate all three aspects of data modelling and to apply them uniformly to all customers of the database. OODBMSs have, however, some drawbacks as well. First, there is no common query language such as SQL for the relational databases. The performance of Object-oriented databases is much lower than that of RDBMSs. Moreover, there is a lack of standardized industry support, and finally, high-tech features such as multi-threading and parallel processing are not available.

Today, there are many companies marketing commercial object-oriented databases that are second-generation products. OODBMSs have established themselves in niches such as e-commerce, engineering, and special purpose databases in areas such as securities and medicine.

Object-Relational Database Management Systems (ORDBMS)

The relational database vendors considered the arrival of OODBMSs as a threat. As a result they started to add features and functionality to their products to stay competitive. Real-life implementations of the *Object Relational Databases (ORDBMSs)* as well as theoretical extensions of the relational model such as the "Third Manifesto" [14] started to appear mid 1990s.

Stored procedures are collections of SQL statements and flow-control language that are stored in a precompiled way into the database. Stored procedures are supported by most RDBMSs, but there is a fair amount of variation in their syntax and capabilities. *Triggers* are Stored Procedures that are launched on a given event, such as inserting or updating a row in a table.

The addition of complex data types such as *BLOBs (Binary Large Objects)* is another example of how the relational database vendors have reacted to OODBMSs. A BLOB is a large block of data stored in a database, such as an image or sound file. A special subtype of BLOB is CLOB; characters are used instead of pure binary information. A BLOB cannot be interpreted by the database management system but is known only by its size and location. Modern RDBMSs allow for some relatively simple operations on BLOBs such as storing, retrieving, and even some sort of indexing. There remains, however, a fundamental mismatch between BLOBS and RDBMSs.

The net result of these enhancements was that the purely relational databases evolved into Object-Relational Databases (ORDBMSs), also described as *hybrid databases*. These systems are much more like RDBMSs than OODBMSs. They make use of a proprietary object model and are designed for large-grained objects.

More recently, another challenge for the database vendors was set by the appearance of the *eXtensible Markup Language (XML)* [43]. XML is a powerful communication mechanism; it contains both the data and its description in a well-structured way. In fact, it is a text format with a particular way of representing information in a hierarchical structure (Fig. 2.8).

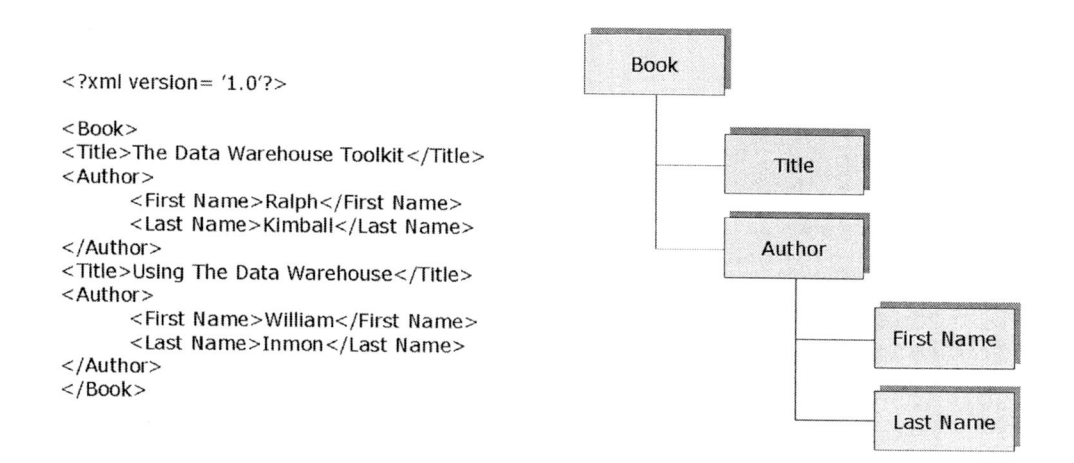

```xml
<?xml version='1.0'?>

<Book>
<Title>The Data Warehouse Toolkit</Title>
<Author>
    <First Name>Ralph</First Name>
    <Last Name>Kimball</Last Name>
</Author>
<Title>Using The Data Warehouse</Title>
<Author>
    <First Name>William</First Name>
    <Last Name>Inmon</Last Name>
</Author>
</Book>
```

Fig. 2.8 – *XML as a hierarchical structure*

We observe that:

- The document starts with the XML declaration `<?xml version="1.0">`;
- All elements have start and end tags: `<element name></element name>`;
- All elements are contained within one root element: `<Book></Book>`.

In XML, a clear distinction is made between data and metadata, syntax and semantics. Much like in a relational database the same structure stores different types of information but in XML the structure is not fixed; it can be altered on-the-fly, as long as the syntax is respected. XML is the basis for new architectures in various domains of IT: storage, exchange, and representation of information. The database vendors could of course not neglect the importance of XML, so different ways to store and retrieve XML documents were developed. Traditional database vendors have all extended their products and propose two possible strategies:

- In the *mapping approach* all elements of the XML file are stored as separate rows. The advantage of this approach is that, once stored, the data are accessible with traditional tools (SQL). This is why it is recommended for data-centric applications;
- In a RDBMS XML can also be stored in one piece: as a *CLOB* or a derived data type (e.g., `XMLType` in Oracle). This approach is best suited for text-centric applications.

Some OODBMS vendors have used their know-how and technology to build *native XML databases*. The idea is to store the elements of the XML document as objects using a special query language data can then be retrieved and updated.

Working with XML documents in databases sparked the need for a standard query language. Several attempts have been undertaken by W3C, one of them being *Xquery*. XQuery has an SQL-like syntax combined with Xpath, a query language designed to address parts of XML documents:

```
FOR $b IN //Book
WHERE $b/Author/First Name = "Ralph"
AND $b/Author/Last Name = "Kimball"
RETURN $b/title
```

Xquery statements are known as *FLWR expressions*. FLWR (pronounced *flower*) is an acronym that stands for the four possible sub expressions; this expression type can contain: FOR, LET, WHERE, and RETURN. The FOR statement creates a collection of variable bindings, one for each node in the "ordered forest" returned by the path expression. For each of these bindings, the subsequent statements are executed. The nodes in the collection are filtered by the WHERE clause. RETURN constructs the result. The LET subexpression (not shown) binds a variable to a value.

Benchmarking of DBMSs

The performance of DBMSs is compared using *benchmarks*. The *Transaction Processing Performance Council* or *TPC* is a non-profit corporation founded by database manufacturers to define transaction processing and database benchmarks and to disseminate objective and verifiable performance data. The term *transaction* is often applied to a wide variety of business and computer functions. Looked at as a computer function, a transaction could refer to a set of operations including disk read/writes, operating system calls, or some form of data transfer from one subsystem to another. The TPC defines a transaction, as it is commonly understood in the business world: a commercial exchange of goods, services, or money. A typical transaction would include the updating to a database system for such things as inventory control, airline reservations, or banking. In these environments, several customers or service representatives input and manage their transactions via a terminal or desktop computer connected to a database.

The benchmarks that are currently in use are TPC-C, TPC-H, TPC-R, and TPC-W.

- *TPC-C* – This benchmark simulates a complete computing environment where a population of customers executes transactions against a database;
- *TPC-H* – This is a decision support benchmark. It consists of a suite of business oriented ad-hoc queries and concurrent data modifications;
- *TPC-R* – This is a decision support benchmark similar to TPC-H, but which allows additional optimizations based on advance knowledge of the queries;
- *TPC-W* – This is a transactional web benchmark. The workload is performed in a controlled Internet environment that simulates the activities of a business oriented transactional web server.

Networking Services

The OSI Reference Model

The *Open Systems Interconnection* (*OSI*) networking model is a layered representation of network services made available in a computing environment [22]. The *International Standards Organization* (*ISO*) developed this networking suite. Each entity interacts only with the layer immediately beneath it, and provides facilities for use by the layer above it. Protocols enable an entity in one host to interact with a corresponding entity at the same layer in a remote host.

The *OSI Reference Model* arranges a common ground for communications development. The OSI Reference Model provides a seven-layer definition of functions of protocols (Fig. 2.9). Each layer is assigned a different task whose final goal is to prepare data to transmit or receive it; adding extra information to the packets of the lower layer does this. A layer does not define a single protocol. Instead, it represents a single function carried out by one or more protocols.

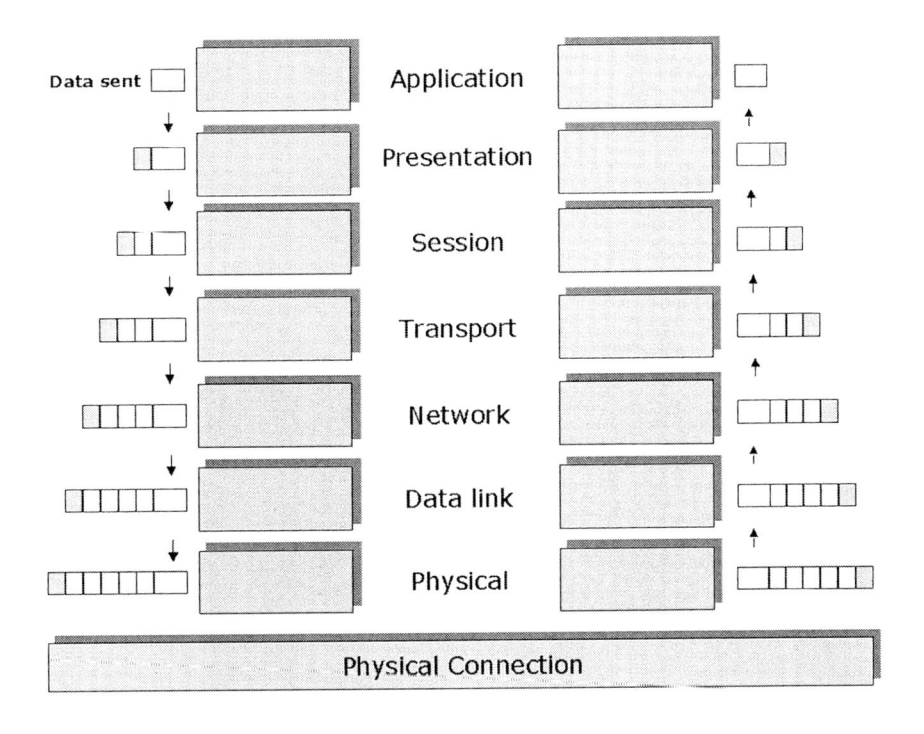

Fig. 2.9 – *The OSI model*

Somebody makes a request to the Application Layer. Here it is encoded in such a way that its peer layer protocol on the other side understands it. Then it is passed down to the Presentation Layer. This layer packages it in such a way that the peer layer protocol on the other side will understand it and also knows what to do with it. This process of re-encapsulation of higher-level data continues all the way down until it gets to the physical layer.

The Internet protocols

The OSI Model is a theoretical model that emerged in parallel with another model: TCP/IP. Much like in OSI, TCP/IP is divided into layers. Regardless of the difference in the number of layers, the principle is the same. Each layer controls a part of the communication process and the ultimate goal is to represent data in a way that a different host can read it. This is why the so-called *IP stack* does not exactly match the OSI model. Figure 2.10 shows an attempt to position the two models versus one another.

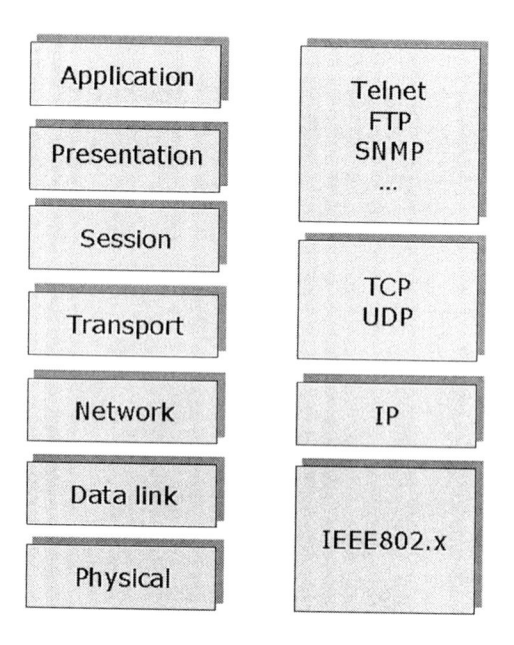

Fig. 2.10 – *OSI vs. TCP/IP*

In the rest of this section we will describe, from bottom to top, the practical implementations of the OSI and TCP/IP layers.

Physical Layer

Cabling

There are three major types of cable in use in networks today:

- Coaxial (coax);
- Unshielded twisted pair (UTP);
- Fiber optic.

Coax can be a good solution for small networks; it does not require hubs and is easy to install. Coax also offers relatively high immunity to interference from noise sources, so it is often used in manufacturing environments. There are some disadvantages to coax, though: it is difficult to isolate problems and the new high-speed standards are not supporting coax, so coax can be a dead end street.

Unshielded Twisted Pair (UTP) cable is rated by the EIA/TIA standards into categories. Categories 3, 4, and 5 are rated to 10, 20, and 100 MHz. Category 6 is recommended for new installations expected to support 1000Base-T. The specification of Category 7 is in preparation. Most of the network types require only two pairs (four wires). However, if you install four pairs cabling, it will support any possible combination without requiring you to put new connectors if you change network types.

Fiber optic - In recent years fiber optics are steadily replacing copper wire as an appropriate means of communication signal transmission. A fiber-optic system is similar to a copper wire system; the difference is that fiber-optics use light pulses instead of electronic pulses to transmit information. At one end of the system is a *transmitter*. The transmitter accepts coded electronic information coming from copper wire. It then processes and translates that information into equivalently coded light pulses. A *Light-Emitting Diode (LED)* or an *Injection-Laser Diode (ILD)* can be used for generating the light pulses. Using a lens, the light pulses are funnelled into the fiber-optic medium. Once the light pulses reach their destination they are channelled into the *optical receiver*. The basic purpose of an optical receiver is to detect the received light and to convert it to an electrical signal.

There are several advantages associated with fiber-optic cable systems. Compared to copper, optical fiber is relatively *small* and *lightweight*. Optical fiber is also desirable because of its *electromagnetic immunity*. Since fiber-optics use light to transmit a signal, it is not subject to electromagnetic interference, radio frequency interference, or voltage surges. This can be an important consideration when laying cables near electronic hardware such as computers or industrial equipment. As well, since it does not use electrical impulses, it does not produce electric sparks which can be a fire hazard.

Wireless technologies

Manufacturers have a range of technologies to choose from when designing a wireless communication solution. Each technology comes with its own set of advantages and limitations.

Narrowband – A narrowband radio system transmits and receives information on a specific radio frequency. Narrowband radio keeps the radio signal frequency as narrow as possible just to pass the information. Undesirable cross talk between communications channels is avoided by carefully coordinating different customers on different channel frequencies. A drawback of narrowband technology is that the end-user must obtain a license for each site where it is employed.

Spread Spectrum - This is a wideband radio frequency technique developed by the military for use in reliable, secure, mission-critical communications systems. Spread-spectrum is designed to trade off bandwidth efficiency for reliability, integrity, and security. In other words, more bandwidth is consumed than for narrowband transmission, but the signal is easier to detect, provided that the receiver knows the parameters of the spread-spectrum signal being broadcast. There are two types of spread spectrum radio: frequency hopping and direct sequence:

- *Frequency-Hopping Spread Spectrum Technology (FHSS)* uses a narrowband carrier that changes frequency in a pattern known to transmitter and receiver;
- *Direct-Sequence Spread Spectrum Technology (DSSS)* generates a redundant bit pattern for each bit to be transmitted.

Infrared (IR) - Infrared systems use high frequencies, just below visible light in the electromagnetic spectrum, to carry data. Like light, IR cannot penetrate opaque objects; it is either directed (line-of-sight) or diffuse technology. Inexpensive directed systems provide limited range (1 m) and typically are used for personal area networks but are also used occasionally wireless LAN applications. High performance directed IR is impractical for mobile users and is therefore used only to implement fixed sub-networks. Diffuse (or reflective) IR wireless LAN systems do not require line-of-sight, but cells are limited to individual rooms.

Data link layer

Local Area Networks (LANs)

A *Local Area Network* (*LAN*) is a high-speed data network that covers a relatively small geographic area. It typically connects workstations, Personal Computers and printers. LANs offer many advantages, including shared access to devices and applications, file exchange among connected users, and communication among users. LAN standards are to be situated at the lowest levels of the OSI model: they describe the implementation of the physical and data link layers. LAN protocols typically use one of two methods to reach the physical network medium: *Carrier-Sense Multiple Access Collision-Detect (CSMA/CD)* and token passing.

In *CSMA/CD*, network devices contend for use of the physical network medium. The CSMA/CD scheme is a set of rules determining how network devices respond when two devices attempt to use a data channel simultaneously (called a *collision*). After detecting a collision, a device waits a random delay time and then attempts to re-transmit the message. If the device detects a collision again, it waits twice as long to try to re-transmit the message. This is known as exponential back off.

With *token passing*, network devices access the physical medium based on possession of a token. A token, which is a special bit pattern, travels around the network. To send a message, a device catches the token, attaches a message to it, and then lets it continue to travel around the network.

Ethernet/IEEE 802.3

Xerox created Ethernet [19][20] in the 1970s, but the term is now often used to refer to all CSMA/CD LANs. Ethernet was designed to serve in networks with occasional heavy traffic requirements and the IEEE 802.3 specification was developed in 1980 based on the original Ethernet technology. Today, many different versions exist.

	Ethernet	IEEE 802.3 10base5	IEEE 802.3 10base2	IEEE 802.3 10baseT	IEEE 802.3 10baseFL	IEEE 802.3 100baseT	IEEE 802.3ab 1000baseT	IEEE 802.3z 1000baseX
Data rate (Mbps)	10	10	10	10	10	100	1000	1000
Media	50 Ohm coax (thick)	50 Ohm coax (thick)	50 Ohm coax (thin)	UTP	Fiber	UTP	UTP	Fiber
Topolog	Bus	Bus	Bus	Star	Point-to-point	Star	Star	Point-to-point

Table 2.2 – *IEEE 802.3 standards*

Token Ring/IEEE 802.5

IBM originally developed the Token Ring network in the 1970s. The related IEEE 802.5 specification is almost identical to and completely compatible with IBM's Token Ring network. In fact, IBM Token Ring inspired the IEEE 802.5 specification. The term Token Ring is used to refer to both IBM's Token Ring network and IEEE 802.5 networks. Token Ring and IEEE 802.5 networks are compatible, although the specifications differ slightly. IBM's Token Ring network specifies a star, with all end stations attached to a device called a multi station access unit (MSAU). In contrast, IEEE 802.5 does not specify a topology, although virtually all IEEE 802.5 implementations are based on a star. Other differences exist, including medium type and routing information field size.

Wireless LAN

Wireless LANs (WLANs) offer the following advantages over traditional wired networks:

- *Mobility* - Wireless LAN systems provide access to information anywhere in the organization;
- *Installation Speed and Simplicity* - Installing a wireless LAN system is fast and easy and eliminates the need to pull cable through walls and ceilings;
- *Reduced Cost-of-Ownership* - While the initial investment required for wireless LAN hardware is probably higher, overall installation expenses and life-cycle costs can be significantly lower;
- *Scalability* - Wireless LAN systems can be configured in a variety of topologies to meet the needs of specific applications and installations.

IEE802.11

The IEEE 802.11 committee, a subgroup with the IEEE, has been working on industry-wide, vendor-independent standards for wireless LANs. In July 1997, IEEE 802.11 was adopted as a worldwide ISO standard. Since then, different flavours covering various implementations of the physical layer have been approved For example, two radio transmission methods and one infrared have been defined: Frequency Hopping Spread Spectrum (FHSS) and Direct Sequence Spread Spectrum (DSSS). The radiated power is limited to 1W for the United States, and 10mW in Europe and Japan. There are different frequencies approved for use in Japan, United States and Europe and any WLAN product must meet the requirements for the country where it is sold.

Bluetooth

Another wireless technology is known as *Bluetooth*. This technology provides for a 10-meter personal "bubble" that supports simultaneous transmission of both voice and data for multiple devices. Up to eight data devices can be connected in a *piconet* and up to ten piconets can coexist within the 10-meter bubble. Each piconet supports up to three simultaneous full duplex voice devices. The gross data rate is 1 Mbps, but the actual data rate is 432 Kbps for full duplex transmission and 721/56 Kbps for asymmetric transmission. Bluetooth operates in the 2.4 GHz band. This is the same band as 802.11b thus creating an interference problem when these devices are used in the same environment. Moreover, 2.4GHz is also the resonant frequency of water molecules and therefore the operating frequency of microwave ovens. So, a leaky oven can obliterate communications with Bluetooth devices. This industry standard is mainly intended as a cable replacement technology to connect peripheral devices to mobile phones and PCs in a *Personal Area Network (PAN),* whereas IEEE 802.11 and HiperLAN2 is a more cable replacement technologies for Local Area Networks supporting speeds up to about 54 Mbit/s. The IEEE has formed a working group called 802.15 that is looking to adopt Bluetooth.

Infrared Data Access (IrDA)

Since 1994, IrDA defines a standard for an interoperable universal two way cordless infrared light transmission data port. IrDA technology is being used in devices such as desktops, notebooks, printers, digital cameras, public phones/kiosks, cellular phones, pagers, PDAs, electronic books, electronic wallets, and other mobile devices. IrDA has a speed advantage over Bluetooth products (4 Mbps versus 1 Mbps). As it is based on infrared technology, it will not interfere with other, radio frequency based technologies like IEEE 802.11b and Bluetooth. On the other hand, IrDA requires line of sight, which limits the agility and makes the technology more difficult to use.

IEEE 802.11/HiperLAN2 on the one hand and Bluetooth/DECT/IrDA on the other hand, operate in different application areas and thus complement each other.

Wide Area Networks (WANs)

Wide Area Network (WAN) is the term used to describe a network that connects various Local Area Networks (LANs) or stand-alone systems together, via remote links.

Analog Dial-Up Connections

Probably, the most extensive and familiar WAN is the *Public Switched Telephone Network* (*PSTN*), in which dial-up connections are established to set up communication links. The use of this network as a platform for data transmissions will continue to be significant in the foreseeable future. The main attraction of this method is that it is ubiquitously available. This is a major advantage compared to other options and makes it a particularly attractive option for mobile users, who cannot assume that other services will be available wherever they go. For these users, connectivity is as close as the nearest phone jack or cellular phone. The usage-based charges with the relatively inexpensive modems make this a cost-effective but performance-constrained option for users with limited bandwidth requirements. As this method relies on analog transmission in the local loop, line quality is often a problem that prevents users realizing the speed capabilities of their modems. The network management and security features of analog dial-up lines are also inferior to those of other options. For data transmission in the analog public telephone network use is made of modems. The term *modem* is derived from the original functions of Modulation and Demodulation. The modem receives data from the computer in digital format and converts them into analog signals suitable for transmission through the telephone lines. The receiving modem demodulates these analog signals, reconverting them back into digital format. The two major factors that distinguish the variety of modems are their transmission mode and transmission rate.

Asynchronous transmission uses characters as the basic data unit. Each transmitted character is assigned a supplementary start bit and one or two stop bits. In *synchronous transmissions* all the data bits are sent in a continuous sequential stream.

With respect to *transmission rate*, there is often confusion between baud rate and bits-per-second (bps). The *baud rate* is the modulation rate while bps expresses the quantity of data that is transferred. Some modems send multiple bits per modulation cycle, meaning that the bps will be higher than the baud rate. So you should be interested in the bps, as this is the modem's actual speed.

Error Correction is an important feature in the fastest modems. It allows fast and reliable connections over standard phone lines. All modems in a network must be using the same error-correction protocols. Fortunately, most modems use the same protocol: V.42.

Data compression allows modems to use higher transmission rates. A 14.4 modem with data compression can boost transmission rates of 57,600 bps. A 28.8 modem will boost transmissions of 115,200 bps.

The *Hayes-compatible command set* has become the standard tool for configuring and controlling modems. It is also called the AT command set, as the commands are prefixed with the letters AT (for "ATtention").

The *installation arrangements* vary according to the type of modem; modems can be installed on cards that can be inserted in a PC, or they can be external devices, which are connected via a RS232 serial interface. Yet another, more recent alternative is a modem with a PC-card interface (PCMCIA). These are popular, as virtually all the modern portable Personal Computers are equipped with the corresponding connection.

Digital Subscriber Lines (DSL)

DSL technology (*Digital Subscriber Lines*) is a new method of data transfer via an analog two-wire line. It supports a data transmission rate of up to two Mbps, which is scalable in steps of 64 kbps. A DSL modem is required at each end. A distinction is made among the following standards: ADSL (Asymmetric DSL), HDSL (High Bit Rate DSL), RADSL (Rate Adaptive DSL), SDSL (Symmetric High Bit Rate DSL), and VDSL (Very High Bit Rate DSL).

A popular implementation is *ADSL*; this technology is intended for the last leg into a customer's premises. As its name suggests, ADSL transmits an asymmetric data stream, with more going downstream to the subscriber and less coming back upstream (Fig. 2.11). Fortunately, the prevalence of target applications for digital subscriber services is asymmetric. Video on demand, home shopping, Internet access, remote LAN access, multimedia access, specialized PC services all feature high data rate demands downstream, but relatively low data rate demands upstream.

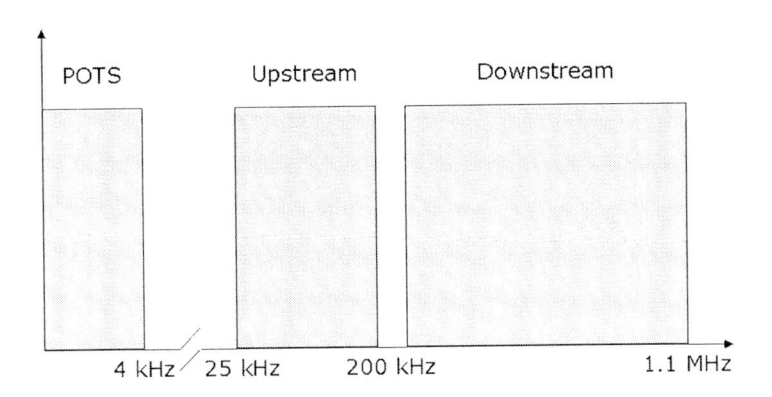

Fig. 2.11 - *ADSL*

Upstream speeds range from 16 kbps to 640 kbps. Individual products incorporate a variety of speed arrangements, from a minimum set of 1.544/2.048 Mbps down and 16 kbps up to a maximum set of nine Mbps downstream and 640 kbps upstream. All these arrangements operate in a frequency band above the one required for voice telephony (0-4 kHz), leaving the *Plain Old Telephony Service* (*POTS*) independent and undisturbed. ADSL includes error correction capabilities. Error correction introduces about 20 msec of delay, which is too much for certain applications. Consequently ADSL must know what kind of signals it is passing, to know whether to apply error control or not.

Cable modems

In countries with a high density of TV cabling use can be made of *cable modems* to bring a data connection such as Internet access to the homes. Access to the network is established using a special high-speed cable modem, which is connected to the computer via a network. In the download direction, these modems are capable of transferring data to cable customers at up to ten Mbps.

Leased lines

Leased lines are private reserved pathways (or pipelines) through a service provider's network. For networks with moderate traffic requirements, use is made of 56 or 64 Kbps leased lines, for higher speeds there are so-called T1 (US) or E1 (Europe) and Fractional solutions. T1 lines provide 1.544 Mbps (2 Mbps for E1) of bandwidth. Fractional lines can be used where bandwidth requirements do not justify a full T1/E1 connection. The advantage of leased lines is that the circuit is available on a permanent basis and does not require a connection to be set up before traffic is passed. The disadvantage is that the bandwidth is being paid for, even if is not being used, which is typically about 70 percent of the time. Leased lines are an expensive alternative for networks spanning long distances or requiring extensive connectivity between sites. They also lack agility. For example, adding a new site to the network requires a new circuit to be provisioned end-to-end for every site with which the new location must communicate.

Integrated Services Digital Network (ISDN)

ISDN (*Integrated Services Digital Network*) combines the use of voice and data in a single network. This means that only a single ISDN connection is needed for access to a variety of telecommunications services such as telephone, fax, file transfer utilities, etc. The high speed, error-free data transmission, and quick connect times make ISDN not only attractive for newcomers to data communications, but also for users who up to now have been dependent on analogue modems.

"Your room has six data ports and an ISDN line, but no heat. Will that be okay?"

X.25

X.25 is a packet switching technology that is typically used in a public network environment, in contrast to the private nature of leased lines. This allows it to exploit the statistical nature of data traffic to share the resources of the carrier's network among several different users, which, in turn, results in lower costs to each customer than dedicated lines. X.25 has extensive error detection and recovery capabilities to provide a high quality of service. Unfortunately, this results in performance sacrifices in terms of speed and latency due to the increased processing that is required, which limits actual throughput to about 70 percent of the circuit speed. X.25 is obsolete.

Frame Relay

Frame Relay exploits high-quality digital infrastructure by eliminating the extensive error detection and recovery performed in X.25 networks, which results in both speed and performance improvement.

Since most Frame Relay service providers price it on a distance-independent basis, the economic benefits of Frame Relay increase as the distance between sites increases. Frame Relay's benefits also increase as the number of connected sites increases, since it allows a single access line to be used to communicate with multiple remote sites via its multiplexing capabilities. Available at speeds up to the T1 (E1) rate of 1.544 (2) Mbps, Frame Relay imposes fewer overheads than X.25 so the customer has more usable bandwidth. Frame Relay is likely to be cost-effective compared to private line networks for meshed networks connecting four or more sites.

Asynchronous Transfert Mode (ATM)

ATM is a cell-based technology that is expected to unify the currently separate networks used for voice, video, and data applications. Consolidation of these networks has the potential to provide significant economic benefits. The service is available in speeds ranging from 1.544 Mbps (T1 or DS-1) to 155 Mbps (Optical Carrier Level 3 or OC-3), with rates expected to be available down to 64 Kbps and up to 622 Mbps (OC-12). Ultimately, ATM is expected to scale up to the gigabit range.

ATM is being used by large organizations with substantial bandwidth requirements for applications such as LAN interconnection, multimedia, video conferencing, and imaging. ATM has the potential to provide a seamless connection between the local and wide area networks, thereby eliminating the distinction between the two. Deployment of ATM is more complicated than other alternatives, since a variety of parameters must be defined to optimize the performance of the network.

Infrastructure

Wireless WANs

Global System for Mobile Communications (GSM)

Global System for Mobile Communications (GSM) Networks operating in the 900 & 1800 MHz bands is standard in Europe, most of Asia, and Australia (Japan has its own proprietary network type). GSM is also available in some North American cities (1900 MHz), but the USA mostly uses analog systems.

The *Wireless Application Protocol (WAP)* is an open specification that offers a standard method to gain access to the Internet from wireless devices. The mobile device has embedded browser software that understands the content written in *Wireless Markup Language (WML)*.

"Could you hold, please? The phone in my other pocket is ringing."

NTT DoCoMo introduced i-mode in Japan in February 1999. It is one of the world's most successful wireless services offering web browsing and e-mail from mobile phones. I-Mode supports speeds of 384 Kbps or faster, making mobile multimedia possible. I-mode uses a simplified version of HTML, *Compact HTML (cHTML)* instead of WAP's WML. The most basic difference with WML is the graphics-capability; while it is true that I-mode only supports simple graphics, which is far more than WAP allows.

General Packet Radio Services (GPRS)

General Packet Radio Services or *GPRS* is a packet based data service that uses the existing GSM network. The current *Circuit Switched Data (CSD)* method of connecting to the WAP Gateway creates a dedicated circuit or channel for the entire length of the session. This efficient use of the network resources allows a theoretical bandwidth of 171.2 Kb/s. GPRS can be used as a bearer for WAP.

Universal Mobile Telecommunications System (UMTS)

UMTS is a part of the International Telecommunications Union's vision of a global family of *third-generation (3G)* mobile communications systems. UMTS will deliver low-cost, high-capacity mobile communications offering data rates up to 2Mbps with global roaming and other advanced capabilities.

Network layer

The Internet Protocol

The *Internet Protocol (IP)* is a network protocol. This means that an IP-packet can be transported over different types of subordinate services (Ethernet, Token Ring, FDDI, etc.) The IP-packet is "encapsulated" in the packets of the subordinate levels.

Concepts

Every station that is connected to the network is recognized by its IP-address. Every address is unique, much like a telephone number. The IP address of the Source and that of the Destination is part of every packet that circulates on the network. Every packet has the following structure:

Type	Length	Time to Live	Protocol	Address Source	Address Destination	Data	

An IP address has 32 bits:

Binary	10010000	01111000	11111101	00111010
Hexadecimal	90	78	FD	3A
Decimal	144	120	253	58

This IP-address will be called 144.120.253.58

IP addresses are organized in a hierarchical order, much like in the telephone numbering system. The *Internet Service Provider (ISP)* can be compared with a telephone company. These ISPs manage different classes of IP-addresses that are distributed over their clients.

Every client gets a pool of IP-addresses that can be used for the internal addressing of his network. An IP-address is composed of two parts: a *network part* (like the prefix in a telephone number) and a *station part* (like the internal extension). The number of bits used for these parts can vary, depending of the "address class".

Infrastructure

The most commonly used address classes are A, B, and C.

Class A - If the first bit of an IP-address is 0, it is said to be a "Class A" address. There are seven bits left to define the network and 24 for the station. So there are only 128 class A networks (2^7), which can contain millions of stations (2^{24}).

	Network ID (7 bits)	Station ID (24 bits)

Class B - The first two bits are 1 and 0. There are 2^{14} different network IDs and 2^{16} stations.

	Network ID (14 bits)	Station ID (16 bits)

Class C - The first three bits are 1.1.0. There are 2^{21} networks and 2^8 (256) stations per network.

	Network ID (21 bits)	Station ID (8 bits)

It is thanks to the splitting of the IP-address that the routing of packets is possible. A packet that has its destination inside the same network does not have to be routed. On the other hand, a packet for a station in another network is passed to the communication port of the network: the default gateway. This means that the address of the default gateway has to be known by every station.

In *Classless IP* these networks are divided into smaller networks by breaking them on bit boundaries. Classless IP also allows multiple classical networks to be aggregated to form a *supernet*. Classless IP uses a 32-bit number called a *mask* to define the network. This value is sometimes called a *netmask*. The netmask is a 32-bit value that starts with a contiguous group of ones followed by a contiguous group of zeroes. For example, the following values are valid netmasks:

```
11111111 11111111 11111111 11111000    255.255.255.252
11111111 11111111 11111111 11100000    255.255.255.224
11111111 11111111 11111111 00000000    255.255.255.0
11111111 11111111 11111000 00000000    255.255.252.0
11111111 11111111 00000000 00000000    255.255.0.0
11111111 11100000 00000000 00000000    255.32.0.0
11111111 00000000 00000000 00000000    255.0.0.0
```

Classless IP subnetting allows the assignment of a block of addresses that fits better with the actual number of addresses needed on a network. For example, if an organization only has 24 hosts, they can be assigned a subnet using a mask of 255.255.255.224 that will give them a block of 30 host addresses. If an organization has 900 hosts, rather than assign a class B network and waste over 64 thousand addresses, a network with a mask of 255.255.252.0 can be used. This will total four consecutive class C networks, or subnet parts of a class A, or class B network, to yield a block of about 1000 host addresses. Under classless IP, rather than having networks assigned to individual organizations by a central authority, large blocks of IP addresses are assigned to the major ISPs. Using netmasks, a block of 1024 class C addresses uses a single routing table entry rather than 1024 individual entries. The ISP then breaks up the block inside his network, assigning aggregated or sub netted blocks of addresses as needed.

Distribution of IP-addresses within an organization

The pool of official addresses given to an organization can be managed in two different ways: direct access or indirect access.

Direct access - every station is configured with an official address given by the ISP. This is a simple structure, but there are some inconveniences:

- A station that shares no data monopolizes an official address.
- All stations are potential targets of hackers.
- The number of stations is limited.

Indirect Access - the connection to the Internet is done through a Proxy or a Firewall that implements the *Network Address Translation (NAT)*. The *Demilitarized Zone (DMZ)* is an optional part of the organization's network that contains stations configured with an official IP-address. In general, these stations are running shared services that are directly accessible via the Internet (Web server, Mail gateway, DNS). The other stations of the network are configured with a private IP-address, chosen by the network administrator. A special case is formed by *DHCP (Dynamic Host Configuration Protocol)*. Here the ISP disposes of a pool of official addresses, which he dynamically allocates to his customers. This technique is used when there is no permanent connection to the Internet, like in a Dial Up configuration using the Public Switched Telephone Network (PSTN).

IPv6

"32 bit ought to be enough address space"
(Vinton G. Cerf, co-designer of the Internet Protocol, 1977)

The designers of the IP-protocol had never expected its tremendous success. However, the explosive growth of the Internet made it obvious that something had to be done. The answer is *IP version 6 (IPv6)* also called *IP Next Generation (IPng)*. Ipv6 offers:

- Extended address space (128 bits);
- A standardized header format and size;

- Header and payload compression;
- *Quality of Service (QoS)* and differential service features;
- Security: authentication, integrity, confidentiality and key management;
- Auto configuration in both stateful and stateless modes;
- Updated routing protocols (RIPv6, OSPFv6, BGP4+, IDRPv6);
- Multi-homing possibilities;
- Interoperability with the installed base of older IP devices;
- Support for mobile and nomadic scenarios.

The Ipv6 protocol and some related topics are described in the following documents:

- RFC1883 – The Ipv6 base protocol;
- RFC1884 – The address specification;
- RFC1885 – The control protocol;
- RFC1886 – Enhanced domain name service;
- RFC1933 – The transition mechanism.

Clearly Ipv6 will be the next thing in internetworking and because of the offered advantages many organizations are already planning the migration towards this new technology.

Routing and switching

Routing is the act of moving information across a network from a source to a destination. Along the way, at least one intermediate node typically is encountered. Routing is often contrasted with *bridging;* the main difference between the two is that bridging occurs at Layer 2 of the OSI reference model, whereas routing occurs at Layer 3. Routing involves two basic activities: determining best routing paths and transporting *packets* through a network. In the context of the routing process, the latter is called *switching*. For the process of *path determination*, routing algorithms start and maintain *routing tables*, which contain route information.

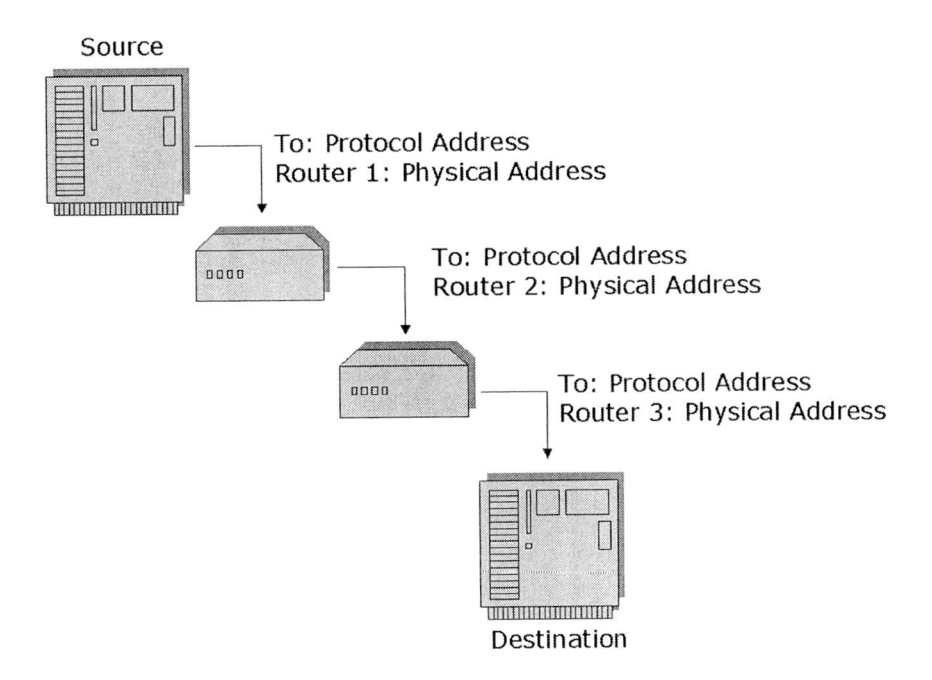

Fig. 2.12 - *Routing*

Switching [18] is a relatively simple task and is the same for most routing protocols. Usually, a host determines that it must send a packet to another host. Having acquired a router's address, the source host sends a packet addressed specifically to a router's physical address (the so-called *Media Access Control* or *MAC* address), with the IP address of the destination host. As it examines the packet's destination protocol address, the router determines that it either knows or does not know how to forward the packet to the next hop. If the router does not know how to forward the packet, it typically drops the packet. If the router knows how to forward the packet, it changes the destination physical address to that of the next hop and transmits the packet, as the packet moves through the network, its physical address changes, but its protocol address remains constant (Fig. 2.12).

Internets, intranets, and extranets

An *internet* (not capitalized) is a set of interconnected networks. Of course, the *Internet* (capitalized) is the best-known example of an internet. The Internet is a global network connecting millions of computers. The Internet is decentralized by design: each Internet computer is independent. Its operators can choose which Internet services to use and which local services to make available to the global Internet community. Technically, the Internet is based on the IP-protocol as discussed above.

An *intranet* is a network which provides similar services within an organization to those provided by the Internet, but which is not necessarily connected to the Internet. Like the Internet, intranets are based on IP protocols. Intranets look and act just like the Internets, but a *firewall* fends off unauthorized access. Firewalls are widely used to give users of an intranet secure access to the Internet, as well as to separate the organization's public Web server from its internal network. Intranets are cheaper to build and manage than private networks based on proprietary protocols.

An *extranet* is a network that crosses organizational boundaries, giving outsiders access to information and resources from within the organization's internal network. An extranet links the intranet to business partners using the Internet Protocol suite. An extranet is also called *Virtual Private Network (VPN)* as it uses a public network to create a closed (private) community. Security is a critical component of extranets, especially those built over the Internet.

Transport layer

So far we have seen how systems communicate at a low level, using IP addresses to identify each other. The IP layer does not provide many capabilities other than sending data packets back and forth. Much more is needed than that, which is where TCP and UDP come in the picture.

Transmission Control Protocol (TCP)

The *Transmission Control Protocol (TCP)* provides a virtual connection between two systems. So, strictly speaking TCP goes beyond the transport layer into the session layer of the OSI model. TCP also provides certain guarantees on the data packets that are passed between the systems; retransmission of packets that are dropped, ensuring that the packets are received in the same order that they are sent. Another guarantee is that each packet received has exactly the same content as when it was sent. If a bit has changed or been dropped for some reason, TCP will detect it and cause the packet to be re-transmitted. TCP is common on the Internet, and is almost always mentioned together with IP, making the acronym TCP/IP (TCP running on top of IP).

User Datagram Protocol (UDP)

Some applications use a different protocol running on top of IP called *User Datagram Protocol (UDP)*. UDP sends data one chunk (called a datagram) at a time to the other system and does not provide a virtual connection like TCP does. UDP also does not provide the same guarantees that TCP does, which means that datagrams can be lost or arrive out of sequence. Each received datagram is checked for internal integrity (like TCP), but if it has been corrupted it is dropped, rather than re-transmitted (as TCP does). To provide the extra guarantees, TCP has a lot of overhead compared to UDP, which makes TCP slower than UDP. For applications where performance is more important than reliability, UDP makes more sense. Some examples include audio and video streaming over the Internet and Internet telephony applications.

Application layer

Simple Network Management Protocol (SNMP)

The *Simple Network Management Protocol (SNMP)* has become the de facto standard for network management. To achieve its goal of simplicity, SNMP includes a limited set of management commands and responses. The management system issues Get, GetNext, and Set messages to retrieve single or multiple object variables or to establish the value of a single variable. The managed agent sends a Response message to complete the Get, GetNext or Set. The managed agent sends an event notification, called a *trap* to the management system to identify the occurrence of conditions such as threshold that exceeds a predetermined value.

Telnet

Telnet is a way to remotely login to another system on the Internet. A telnet server must be running on the remote system, and a telnet client application is run on the local system. When you are logged in to a system using telnet, it is as if you were logged in locally and using the operating system command line interface on the telnet server system.

File Transfer Protocol (FTP)

The *File Transfer Protocol or FTP* is a way to upload and download files on the Internet. Typically a site on the Internet stores several files (they could be application executables, graphics, or audio clips, for example), and runs an FTP server application that waits for transfer requests. To download a file to your own system, you run an FTP client application that connects to the FTP server, and request a file from a particular directory or folder. Files can be uploaded to the FTP server, if appropriate access is granted. FTP differentiates between text files (usually ASCII), and binary files (such as images and application executables), so care must be taken in specifying the appropriate type of transfer.

Domain Name System (DNS)

IP-addresses are useful for computers to communicate with each other. For human beings, however, they are hard to use. This is why the addresses were given a human-readable name, the mapping between these names and the IP-addresses in a file known as the *host table*. This mechanism is known as the *Domain Name System (DNS)*.

A *DNS host* is a computer that is running DNS software. DNS software is made up of two elements: the actual *name server* and something called a *resolver*. The name server responds to requests by supplying name-to-address conversions. When it does not know the answer, the resolver will ask another name server higher up the tree for the information. If that does not work, the second server will ask yet another - until it finds one that knows.

Directories – Lightweight Directory Access Protocol (LDAP)

A *Directory* is much like a database: you can put information in, and later retrieve it, but a directory is optimized for reading not for writing; it offers a static view of the data.

A *Directory Service* supports all the above, and in addition it provides for:

- A network protocol used to gain access to the directory;
- A replication scheme;
- A data distribution scheme.

The growing popularity of Internet email created the need for a good address book. Indeed, every email program has a personal address book, but how do you look up an address for someone who has never sent you an email? And how can an organization keep one centralized up-to-date phone book that everybody has access to? This is the reason why the *Lightweight Directory Access Protocol (LDAP)* was designed. "LDAP-aware" client programs can ask LDAP servers to look up entries in a wide variety of ways. LDAP servers index all the data in their entries. Permissions are set by the administrator to allow only certain people to gain access to the LDAP database, and optionally keep certain data private. LDAP servers also provide an authentication service, so that other servers can use a single list of authorized users and passwords. LDAP is a vendor- and platform-independent standard. It was designed at the University of Michigan to simplify a complex enterprise directory system (called X.500). An LDAP server runs on a host computer on the Internet, and various client programs that understand the protocol can log into the server and look up entries.

Other Protocols

There are many other Internet application protocols in use, with the same underlying client/server model of communication: HTTP, SMTP, POP, and IMAP ... These protocols will be discussed later.

Security

Secure communications have for a long time been the monopoly of the defense-world. Now that corporate networks are systematically being connected to the Internet, these too have become a possible target for malicious attacks.

When talking about secure communications, most people have the following goals in mind:

- *Secrecy or confidentiality* – only the intended receiver can read information;
- *Authentication* – receiver and sender want to be sure of each other's identity;
- *Integrity* – we want to be sure the message has not been altered;
- *Non-repudiation* – senders cannot deny that they sent a message.

Cryptography

All the above goals can be realized with *cryptography*. Cryptography is the conversion of data into a secret code before transmission over a (public) network. The original data is converted into a coded equivalent using a key and an encryption algorithm. The encrypted data is decoded (decrypted or deciphered) at the receiving end, and turned back into the original data. This is done using a decryption algorithm, again using a key.

One basic principle of cryptography is that the security should be based on the secrecy of the keys, NOT on the secrecy of the algorithms. Another element is that every encryption can be "broken;" it is sufficient to find the key(s). A good algorithm, however, forces the intruder to try all the possible key values, the higher this number, the more computing time it will take him to do so. The idea is to make this effort big enough to discourage possible intruders.

There are three types of encryption algorithms:

- Symmetric key cryptography;
- Asymmetric key (or public key) cryptography;
- One-way encryption (or hashing).

In *symmetric key* cryptography both sender and receiver have the same key, which of course has to be kept secret from the rest of the world. The encryption and decryption algorithms are fast; the disadvantages are related to the difficulty to distribute the key (you cannot communicate with someone for whom you have no prior arrangements). Furthermore, a lot of keys are needed. Examples of these algorithms are DES, 3DES, IDEA, RC4, and AES (Rijndael).

In *asymmetric or public key* cryptography use is made of a key pair. One key is announced to the public, the other is kept secret (e.g., on a smartcard). A message that has been encrypted with one key can be decrypted with the other (of the same pair). The advantage of this method is of course the ease of the key distribution (it can be published on a directory service, yellow guide, etc.). The disadvantage is that both encryption and decryption are much slower. This technology guarantees the confidentiality towards the receiver (the sender uses the public key of the receiver to encrypt the message) or to authenticate the sender (the sender uses his private key to encrypt the message, which can be decoded with his public key). An example of a public key algorithm is RSA. A *Certification Authority (CA)* is an authority that issues and manages security credentials and public keys. As part of a *Public Key Infrastructure (PKI)*, a CA checks with a *Registration Authority (RA)* to verify information provided by the requestor of a digital certificate. Depending on the implementation, the certificate includes the owner's public key, the expiration date of the certificate, the owner's name, and other information about the public key owner.

In practice, the best of both worlds is used, and a communication session is set up in two phases:

- First, a session key is exchanged by using an asymmetric algorithm;
- Then, a symmetric encryption algorithm with this key is used.

The third type of encryption is by use of a *one-way* (or hashing) algorithm. As the name suggests it is not possible do decrypt a message that has been encrypted in this way. This type of algorithm generates a so-called signature of a file. This signature is a small string (e.g., 128 bits) that is joined to the original file. So, when you want to verify the integrity of the file it is sufficient to perform the hashing algorithm again and to verify if the result is the same as the signature.

IPsec

IPsec stands for IP security, security built into the IP-layer. This standard provides for a host-to-host encryption and authentication. In the "normal" IP-protocol it is optional, for Ipv6 it is mandatory. IPsec was developed by the IETF to support secure exchange of packets at the IP layer. IPsec has been deployed widely to implement *Virtual Private Networks (VPNs)*.

IPsec supports two encryption modes: Transport and Tunnel. In the *Transport mode* only the data portion (*payload*) of each packet is encrypted, and the header is left untouched. In the *Tunnel mode* both header and payload are encrypted, which is more secure. Officially spelled IPsec by the IETF, the term often appears as IPSec or IPSEC.

Firewalls

A *Firewall* is a system designed to prevent unauthorized access to or from a private network. Firewalls can be built in software or hardware, or a combination of both. There are several firewall techniques:

- *Proxy server* – a proxy server effectively hides the true network addresses;
- *Packet filtering* - each packet entering or leaving the network is inspected and accepted or rejected based on user-defined rules. Packet filtering is effective and transparent to users, but it is difficult to configure;
- *Application gateway* - security mechanisms are applied to applications such as FTP and Telnet servers. This is an effective technique, but can cause performance degradation;
- *Circuit-level gateway* - applies security mechanisms when a TCP or UDP connection is established. Once the connection has been made, packets can flow between the hosts without further verification.

In practice, many firewalls use two or more of these techniques in concert.

Other security issues

Viruses

A *virus* is a piece of software that causes some undesirable effect and which is often designed so that it is automatically spread to other computer users. Sending them as attachments to an email, by downloading infected programming from other sites, or on a diskette or CD can transmit viruses. Most viruses can also replicate themselves. Sometimes, a distinction is made between viruses and *worms*. A worm is a special type of virus that cannot attach itself to other programs.

© 2000 Ted Goff

"Excuse me, could you see if this virus ruins your computer, too?"

There are three main classes of viruses:

- *File infectors* - these viruses attach themselves to program files. When the program is loaded, the virus is loaded as well;
- *System or boot-record infectors* - these viruses infect executable code found in certain system areas on a disk. They attach to the boot sector on diskettes or on hard disks;
- *Macro viruses* - these are among the most common viruses, and can do a lot of damage. Macro viruses infect your data files (texts or spreadsheets) and typically insert unwanted words or phrases.

Denial-of-service

A *denial-of-service attack* is characterized by an explicit attempt by attackers to prevent legitimate clients of a service from using that service. Examples include:

- Flooding a network, thereby preventing legitimate network traffic;
- Disrupting connections, thereby preventing access to a service;
- Preventing a particular individual from gaining access to a service;
- Disrupting service to a specific system or person.

Illegitimate use of resources can also result in denial of service. For example, an intruder can use your anonymous ftp area as a place to store illegal copies of commercial software, consuming disk space and generating network traffic.

Electronic Mail abuse

Repeatedly sending of an email message to a particular address is known as *Email bombing*. *Email spamming* is a variant of bombing; it refers to sending email to hundreds or thousands of destinies. These practices can be combined with spoofing, which alters the identity of the account sending the email, making it more difficult to determine who actually sent the email. Recently, spam has become a real nuisance, forcing network administrators into a lot of work.

Middleware

Middleware is the term used for common, business-unaware services that enable applications to interact, usually across a network; the term is used to designate separate products that serve as the glue between two applications. Middleware is sometimes called *plumbing* as it connects two sides of an application and passes data between them.

Basic Middleware Services

The basic middleware services can be listed as follow:

- Client/Server Connectivity;
- Platform Transparency;
- Network Transparency;
- Application and Tool Support;
- Language Support;
- Database Support.

Client/Server Connectivity - Middleware provides the mechanisms by which network applications communicate across a network. For database networking for example, this includes the service of putting packages of query results data in network transport packets. This session layer interaction can also have its own timers and even error control to handle automatic retransmission of lost packets. One common feature is the ability for the client to interrupt the current operation on the server to cancel a large query response download.

Platform Transparency - Client and server do not need an intimate knowledge of each other in order for work to be done. Differences between platform encoding like EBCDIC, ASCII and UNICODE are typically hidden by middleware. Middleware often runs on a variety of platforms, letting the organization use all its hardware platforms as required.

Network Transparency - Middleware often makes networking choices transparent to application programmers. In reality, every middleware product runs on TCP/IP.

Application and Tool Support - Before middleware can be used, it must present its own *Application Programming Interface* (*API*) to client applications that could use it. For shrink-wrapped tools like a database query tool, the API support can be critical.

Language Support - Middleware should provide transparency across different SQL database dialects. Outside the database specific middleware products, generic middleware products often allow different programming languages to be used to create the distinct pieces of an application (pieces that reside on different machines).

Database Support - In the area of database networking, middleware also provides a level of transparency across different data storage formats. It will make different RDBMSs look like the same RDBMS. A common way of solving this transparency is *Open Data Base Connectivity (ODBC)*, a standard database access method developed by Microsoft. The goal of ODBC is to make it possible to gain access to any data from any application, regardless of which database management system (DBMS) is managing the data. ODBC manages this by inserting a *driver*, between the application and the DBMS. The purpose of this layer is to translate the application's queries into commands that the DBMS understands.

Another solution is *Java Database Connectivity (JDBC)*, a Java API that enables Java programs to execute SQL statements. This allows Java programs to interact with any SQL-compliant database. Since nearly all RDBMSs support SQL, and as Java itself runs on most platforms, JDBC makes it possible to write a single database application that can run on different platforms and interact with different DBMSs. JDBC is similar to ODBC, but is designed specifically for Java programs, whereas ODBC is language-independent.

There are four different types of JDBC drivers:

- The *type 1* driver is the JDBC-ODBC Bridge, which provides JDBC access to most ODBC drivers. One drawback in this approach is that the performance overhead of ODBC can affect overall speed;
- The *type 2* driver is considered partly native and partly Java. The driver can convert JDBC calls into calls for the RDBMS;
- The *type 3* driver is an all Java driver which translates JDBC calls into a database management system independent network protocol;
- The last driver, *type 4*, is a native protocol, 100% Java driver. This allows direct calls from a java client to a DBMS server.

Advanced Middleware Services

Besides the basic services, middleware products can also offer more advanced services:

- Single System Login;
- Enhanced Security;
- Location Transparency;
- Database Oriented Services;
- Transaction Monitoring;
- Application-to-Application Integration.

Single System Login - Many database connectivity solutions lack a separate authentication service. Without any security service tied into an organization-wide directory service, users have to log into each server separately. This means they will either forget usernames and passwords or they will breach security by keeping a list of everything on paper taped on their monitor. This situation also forces the database administrators to add a username and password to each server independently. More advanced middleware solutions let the user log in once to the middleware's security, which in turn handles authentication from there on. That security can or cannot be the same system used in a file and print environment.

Enhanced Security - Some middleware vendors have security options much better than just usernames and passwords; support of smart card or biometric solutions and encryption are some examples.

Location Transparency - Simple middleware solutions do not offer a name service. If the user wants to connect to a server and cannot remember the name of it, they will have to call the helpdesk. Advanced middleware solutions offer centralized naming services with some level of distribution. The issues are the same as those associated with DNS on the Internet.

Database Services - In the database connectivity world, other services can be offered by middleware. An example is heterogeneous join support; if the middleware does a multi-RDBMS join transparently, then the client itself does not have to worry about the problems of handling differences and enhancing performance.

Transaction Monitoring - In computing jargon, a *transaction* means a sequence of information exchange and related work (such as database updating) that is treated as a unit for satisfying a request and for ensuring database integrity. For a transaction to be completed and database changes to be made permanent, a transaction has to be completed in its entirety. A typical transaction is an order placed by a customer and entered into a computer by a customer representative. The order transaction involves checking an inventory database, confirming that the item is available, placing the order, and confirming that the order has been placed and the expected time of shipment. If we view this as a single transaction, then all the steps must be completed before the transaction is successful and the database is changed to reflect the new order. If something happens before the transaction is successfully completed, any changes to the database must be tracked, so that they can be undone. When a transaction completes successfully, database changes are said to be *committed*; when a transaction does not complete, changes are *rolled back*.

Transactions must have the so-called ACID properties (ISO/IEC 10026-1:1992):

- *Atomicity* – Actions of a transaction are indivisible; all succeed or all fail;
- *Consistency* – Actions must keep the database in a consistent state;

- *Isolation* – Actions of one transaction must not affect other transactions;
- *Durability* – All actions of a transaction, once committed, must persist in the database regardless of failures that occur after the commit operation.

A program that manages the sequence of events that are part of a transaction is called a *Transaction Monitor or TP monitor*. A TP monitor must coordinate transaction control over a network and maintain the data consistency, even if a network or system failure occurs. Imagine there are five participating nodes at different places and a network failure occurs, the TP monitor will send a signal to all the nodes to be ready to commit or rollback (known as Prepare Phase), if all the five nodes in return send a yes to commit (known as Commit Phase) to the server then the distributed transaction is committed. If one node in return sends a rollback signal then the whole transaction is rolled back. This mechanism is known as *two-phase commit*.

Application-to-Application Integration – Three different mechanisms can be used for application-to-application integration: message queuing, component buses and peer-to-peer communication.

Message queuing is an asynchronous method to integrate different systems. There are two forms: Point-to-Point and Publish-and-Subscribe.

- In *Point-to-Point* message queuing, both correspondents have an input and output message queue. This can be compared somewhat to a post office box or an e-mailbox. When needed, the client puts a message in its output queue. A queue manager takes care of the transfer to the input queue of the server, which retrieves and processes the message. The response message is placed in the output queue from where it is transferred to the input queue of the client,
- *Publish-and-Subscribe* messaging is a one-to-many publishing paradigm, in which client applications publish messages to topics, to which other interested clients in turn subscribe. All subscribed clients will receive each message (subject to quality of service, connectivity, and selection factors).

Message queuing provides a loose coupling of systems with a high level of scalability and availability. It allows load balancing and prioritization of messages. It affects the application design and is not suited for all types of applications.

Components are pieces of software that are modular, have a well-defined and documented interface, are callable from any language, are disconnectable and replaceable and are distributable. A complete system can be assembled making use of components: user-interface components, business components, database components etc. Assembling is done using a *Component Bus*, which can reside physically on one machine, or be distributed over several machines.

An alternative solution to message queuing and component buses is *Peer-to-Peer (P2P)*. If message queuing is like the e-mail system, then Peer-to-Peer can be compared to the telephone system. P2P is a synchronous mechanism.

Middleware Technologies

Middleware is realized on the *Distributed Object Computing* paradigm. In object-oriented computing every system component is seen as an *object*. An object not only has a data structure but also includes the methods that allow it to change its state. Objects can only communicate with the external world and with one another using messages. Distributed object computing extends an object-oriented programming system by allowing objects to be distributed across a heterogeneous network. The most popular distributed object paradigms are Microsoft's *Distributed Component Object Model (DCOM/COM+)*, OMG's *Common Object Request Broker Architecture (CORBA)* and JavaSoft's *Java/Remote Method Invocation (Java/RMI)*.

DCOM/COM+ is the distributed extension to *COM (Component Object Model)* that is why it is sometimes called "COM on the wire." A COM server can create object instances of multiple object classes. A COM object can support multiple interfaces, each representing a different view or behaviour of the object. An interface consists of a set of functionally related methods. A COM client interacts with a COM object by acquiring a pointer to one of the object's interfaces and invoking methods through that pointer, as if the object resides in the client's address space. COM specifies that any interface must follow a standard memory layout. Since the specification is at the binary level, it allows integration of binary components possibly written in different programming languages such as C++, Java and Visual Basic. COM+ became available with Windows 2000 and is a complete standard. The fact that it is a Microsoft only standard can be seen as a disadvantage.

CORBA [16] is a distributed object model proposed by a consortium of more than 700 companies called the *Object Management Group (OMG)*. The core of the CORBA architecture is the Object Request Broker (ORB) that acts as the object bus over which objects transparently interact with other objects located locally or remotely. CORBA relies on a protocol called the Internet Inter-ORB Protocol (IIOP). A CORBA object is represented to the outside world by an interface with a set of methods. A particular instance of an object is identified by an object reference. The client of a CORBA object acquires its object reference and uses it as a handle to make method calls, as if the object is located in the client's address space. The ORB is responsible for all the mechanisms required to find the object's implementation, prepare it to receive the request, communicate the request to it, and carry the reply back to the client. Although technically superior, this standard is not popular.

Java/RMI relies on a protocol called *Java Remote Method Protocol (JRMP)*. Java relies heavily on *Object Serialization*, which allows objects to be transmitted as a stream. Since serialization is a mechanism that is specific to Java, both server and client objects have to be written in Java. A server object defines an interface, which accesses the object outside the current *Java Virtual Machine (JVM)*. The interface exposes a set of methods, which indicate the services offered by the server object. For clients to locate server objects for the first time, RMI depends on a naming mechanism called RMI Registry that runs on the server machine. Since Java/RMI is based on Java it can be used on many platforms, however, it cannot be used with other languages, which is a disadvantage.

Application Frameworks

Having a distributed object model is one thing, developing and deploying real world applications, however, requires more than that:

- *Developer productivity* – By providing pre-existing components to the developers along with a programming model that makes it easy to reuse code components created by others, the productivity of development teams can be enhanced;
- *Reliability* – Older programming languages such as C allowed for error-prone constructs like indirect pointers. The new programming models force all interactions between components to be clearly defined, thus isolating the impact of mistakes and making errors easier to track;
- *Security* – There is a need to control what applications can and cannot do. There also have to exist mechanisms that allow the verification that code was written by a trusted entity and has not been altered;
- *Simplifying installation and deployment* – Embedding component description within the code itself makes it possible for application software to install automatically, with little or no user or administrator intervention.

Two competing application platforms that achieve these goals have emerged: Sun's *Java 2 Enterprise Edition (J2EE)* and the newer Microsoft's *.NET* framework. Both frameworks are similar in their intentions and architecture, but completely different in their underlying implementations. Corresponding architectural features include:

- A *virtual machine* that inspects loads and executes programs in a secure way: *Java Virtual Machine (JVM)* or *Common Language Runtime (CLR)*. The virtual machine executes programs that are compiled from their original code to a processor-independent, intermediate language (Java byte code or Microsoft's Intermediate Language). These intermediate code modules are then translated into native code by *a just-in-time (JIT)* compiler;

- *Class libraries* provide developers with prewritten functionality such as networking services, transaction processing, etc.
- The *programming languages* include improvements such as strong typing and garbage collection that reduce the likelihood of bugs. Microsoft's CLR supports many languages such as C# and Visual Basic while there is a support for Java, COBOL, ADA and other languages given by the JVM;
- A *development environment for dynamic Web pages* is also available in both architectures: ASP.NET and Java Server Pages.

Since the .NET framework and J2EE offer similar architectures and capabilities, the decision to adopt either one of them will be based on non-technical issues such as maturity (J2EE is older than .NET), availability of developers, portability and interoperability. It is even likely that, in bigger organizations, both frameworks will coexist and bear collaborating applications using Web services or some other XML-based data exchange mechanism.

Application Servers

The explosive growth of the Web, the increasing popularity of PCs and the advances in high-speed network access has brought distributed computing into the main stream. One result has been the rise of a new class of products, called *Application Servers*. An Application Server is a piece of middleware, created specifically for the deployment of Web based applications. Application Servers handle all the application logic and connectivity that old-style client-server applications contained. A lot has been written about these products, but what are they? Well, it is not obvious to give a clear definition as this definition depends largely on the origin of the companies that market the products.

At the low end of the price scale the *application development toolmakers*, see application servers as an extension of their existing tool sets. The toolmakers offer combined tool-and-application server packages that offer an integrated development environment and runtime server that lets organizations assemble and deploy Web systems quickly and for a modest price.

At the opposite end of the price and complexity scales are the *transaction processing monitor makers*. These high-end systems are the luxury class of application servers, typically used by banks. Many have been around since the dinosaur age of the computer business. The application server wave gives TP monitor makers a new way to market their products to Web developers.

In the middle are the *database vendors*. These companies are now putting Application Servers in a starring role in their product suites. Application Servers and databases go hand-in-hand, and these vendors are emphasizing the back-end connectivity of their products, along with the application development potential. Most large companies already use software from the database and Web server companies, so moving into the application server space should be an easy transition for them.

The *Open Source* application servers such as JBoss and Jonas form another, special group. These systems can be used as an inexpensive alternative for organizations that first want to acquire some hands-on experience with this technology before spending a lot of money on a full-blown commercial solution or as a license-free implementation in the development or test environment.

All these groups agree on some common features that an Application Server product has to have. First, application servers need to support the creation of server components *conforming to one of the popular application frameworks*. Also required is *clustering support, load balancing, and fail over features*. Connectivity to *legacy systems* like mainframes and older transaction and database systems is a must, as is support for some sort of *business and application logic*.

Best Practices

Automate your asset management

Automated asset management consists of electronically supported procurement, automated inventory, and centralized data repository that are available to financial, administrative and technical planners, system administrators, and the service desk. Data managed within the asset management system consists of contract terms, hardware inventory, software inventory, accounting, maintenance records, change history, support history, and other technical and financial information.

A *hardware inventory* consists of a listing of all IT hardware in an organization. It includes all network components such as clients, servers, peripherals, and network devices. The data includes relevant identifications (serial numbers, asset tags, bar codes, etc.) of each discrete component (system units, add in cards, peripherals, and monitors) of the client computers, servers, peripherals and network hardware. The financial, physical, and technical history of the asset should also be maintained.

A *software inventory* is an up-to-date listing that contains detailed information about the client, network and server software installed within an organization. Inventory information should be stored in a central repository.

These inventories should include acquisition records, moves, adds, changes, service records, contract information, depreciation history, lease terms and usage for hardware and license terms and conditions, date of acquisition, user name and location, system installation details, maintenance agreements and usage monitoring for software. Inventories should be automatically updated and maintained, and include history, and other relevant data. This information is used for technical planning, support and financial management.

Automate your systems management

Automated systems management proactively and reactively notifies system operators of failures, capacity issues, traffic issues, virus attacks and other transient events. The tools allow monitoring of system status, performance indicators, thresholds, notification of users, and dispatch of trouble tickets. It provides optimal system performance, quicker resolution of problems, and minimizes failures. The automated system should be fully integrated with processes and policies that provide manual intervention when needed, support for remote/mobile users, and include policies for file/disk sharing and download.

Avoid Single Points of Failure

Redundancy is the provision of multiple interchangeable components to perform a single function to cope with failures and errors. The idea is to avoid what is called *Single Points of Failure (SPOFs)*. The proverbial chain is as strong as its weakest link, and this is true for IT as well. Often, the failure of one single element can cause the non-availability of a complete system. If that element cannot be replaced, very rapidly it is a SPOF.

Redundancy can be achieved by installing two or even three computers to do the same job. There are several ways this could be done. They could all be active all the time thus giving extra performance as well as extra availability (*clustering*); one could be active and the other simply monitoring its activity so as to be ready to take over if it fails (*hot standby*); the spare can also be kept turned off and only switched on when needed (*cold standby*). Redundancy also often allows for repair actions with no loss of operational continuity (*hot swappable devices*).
Another common form of hardware redundancy is *disk mirroring*; writing duplicate data to more than one hard disk, to protect against loss of data in the event of device failure. This technique can be realized in either hardware (sharing a disk controller) or in software. It is a common feature of RAID systems. When this technique is used with magnetic tape storage systems, it is called *twinning*.

The Internet has made that more and more businesses are online 24 hours per day and seven days a week. This means that they can no longer afford to have their IT systems down for reason of failure or scheduled maintenance. The market has discovered this need and almost any vendor now has *High Availability (HA)* products in his offerings. These systems make use of redundancy at component level, usually combined with a software solution to guarantee 99.999% ("five nines") availability; in practical terms this means a downtime of five minutes or less per year!

Many people stop thinking about redundancy at this point. However, if the main system and it backup are placed side-by-side, a power outage or a fire can affect both. Consequently, an entire building, a site or even a town (earthquakes or other disasters) can be a SPOF! Such major disasters can be handled by locating the backup node(s) in different building and at a certain distance from the main site.

Remember that disaster recovery depends on people as well. September 11 taught us that having good and geographically separated backup facilities is not sufficient. Qualified people must be able to get to the backup facility to manage fail-over operations. Disaster scenarios must be tested periodically, and backup data must be verified as correct and complete.

Centralise your client management

Client image control is the ability to create a client specific configuration of applications, settings, and privileges on a server. These can then be automatically downloaded to a specific address or set of addresses on the network; therefore, configuring the clients initially, and ultimately standardizing the maintenance of configurations. A client agent is used to synchronize the server and client images for change management.

Automated software distribution is the ability to install software on a client device without having to physically visit it. When this is integrated into a comprehensive change management process, it can significantly reduce the time and cost of software changes, enable a more frequent change cycle, be used to upgrade applications, operating systems, utility software, as well as "patches" to troubleshoot software problems and update data files.

Unattended Power Up is the ability for a client computer to power up (from a sleep mode) remotely on the network. This feature allows network and systems management tasks to be executed regardless of whether a system is powered on or off.

Client hardware event management is the ability for networked components to identify and communicate abnormal operating and performance conditions to a systems manager or operator that can respond with corrective measures. This feature, when integrated into management systems and support practices, can enable the support team to be proactive in service calls, minimizing unplanned downtime, and preventing cascade effects of hardware failures as well as providing valuable trend information for service providers.

Consolidate and rationalize continuously

The idea is – of course – to benefit from economy of scale and reduced complexity through standardization. Some points to consider are:

- Consolidation of computing power (bigger servers, clusters);
- Consolidation of storage capacity (SAN and NAS);
- Consolidation of networks (LAN and WAN);
- Consolidation of geographically distributed data centers;
- Standardization of desktops and other end-user equipment.

In this context it could be a good idea to think of the deployment of a thin client infrastructure. For many organizations this could be the solution with the lowest Total

Cost of Ownership (TCO), not only because the hardware is cheaper but also because of:

- *Extended Lifetime* - The currently accepted lifetime of a PC is two years, although often depreciated over three years. Thin clients can be used until they die, which can be longer than a PC because of the lack of moving parts;
- *Lower Bandwidth requirements* - The highest bandwidth user is a worker that performs the same tasks repetitively. In a thin client configuration, these users typically need only 20 kbit/s, thus reducing the need for high-speed LAN and enabling teleworking over dial-up connections. With thin clients, bandwidth requirements for backup are also reduced, as data is stored centrally;
- *Lower Power consumption* - Power consumption of a thin client is typically 14% of a PC. This leads to an important saving in the exploitation costs;
- *Simpler Licensing* - By centrally installing applications, licensing is simpler to manage, making it possible to grant access from the server on a "need to have" basis without creating packages and visiting local workstations or installing licenses for "in case of;"
- *Better Backup* - Having all data centrally creates an economy of scale advantage by using more efficient backup mediums;
- *Physical security* - PCs are prime targets for theft; thin clients are not. Of course the servers have to be protected adequately;
- *Better Support* – Higher quality and consistency of deployment, repair and replacement.

Keep control over your architecture

Because the infrastructure has an influence on the strategic capabilities of the organization outsourcing the control over its architecture is comparable with outsourcing a core business activity, we will see further in this book why this is a bad idea.

Keep your infrastructure scalable

Scalability is the aptitude to logically and physically increase performance and capacity to meet reasonable growth and change over time. A scalable infrastructure enables the rollout of homogeneous platforms across users and departments with different processing requirements, while providing technical staff with a common platform to support.

To reduce costs many infrastructure planners design infrastructure to satisfy minimum short-term business requirements. However, this strategy can negatively impact the organization's long-term ability to respond to change. Therefore, infrastructure design should take into account the future, encompassing not only the initial costs of a solution, but also the cost of change.

Computing Hardware – Truth is that there are no clear-cut engineering rules to determine the needs and consequently the level of investment required in computing hardware. One can only observe *a posteriori* whether the processor power of a server is sufficient to support several users with a given application. Indeed, the numbers of *MIPS* (*Mega Instructions per Second*) or *MegaFLOPS* (*Mega Floating Point Operations per Second*) of a processor are theoretical measures and it is difficult to project these figures to your daily working environment. Because of this, scalability, which is factoring out these uncertainties, is particularly important when choosing new computing hardware.

Storage - The required amount of storage of course depends on the applications you run. Audio and Video- applications and graphics programs produce particularly high volumes of data. In addition, the Operating System and application programs require a lot of disk space. As a result, a hard disk that originally seemed large can quickly fill up. The conclusion is that storage should be planned generously, since more space is usually required than originally calculated. One should also consider that the performance suffers when the capacity limits are reached. The constant decrease in hard disk prices, however, is a reason for not purchasing much more than is initially needed. Purchasing a smaller disk with little reserve capacity and later upgrading to a larger disk could prove to be more economical than initially investing in a larger disk, but only if the time between the initial purchase and the upgrade is long enough.

If your storage needs are important enough, a Storage Area Network could be a good option.

Network - A good networking design must answer both the LAN and WAN needs of its users. I challenge anybody who can make an accurate calculation of the required number of Megabits per second for a given operational environment. The powerful network analysis tools that are available on the market today can only give you an image of the past, and it are rules of thumb that are applied to state whether a network has enough bandwidth or not.

Many LAN applications depend on lots of surplus bandwidth. This is especially true for Ethernet, which begins to show performance degradation once about 20% of the theoretical capacity is exceeded.

WANs tend to operate with tight bandwidth margins. Probably the best advice here is the same - plan for expansion, but in a different way. Plan so that you can upgrade your WAN service without changing your LAN configuration. Dialup SLIP or PPP is fine for one or two computers. Once you have half a dozen computers in use, shift to a router configuration, even if it is still using PPP. Static IP address assignment is probably the best option, as are intelligent inverse name server entries.

Cabling - The biggest start up cost for a network is the labour needed to install it. So do not just install two-pair cable, install eight-pair and leave six unused. Do not just install one Ethernet cable; install two or three, and maybe run some fibre alongside it. Seriously consider a *Structured Cabling System (SCS)*. The initial investment will rapidly pay off. The term Structured Cabling System refers to all the cabling and components installed in a logical, hierarchical way. It is designed to be as independent as possible of the network which uses it, so that can this can be modified with a minimum of rework to the cabling.

The advantages SCSs are:

- *Consistency* - An SCS means the same cabling system for everything: telephony, LAN, etc...
- *Support for multi-vendor equipment* - A standards-based cable plant will support your applications and hardware even after you change or mix & match vendors;
- *Simplify moves/adds/changes* - Need to move a connection from one room to another? Add a modem connection to the office? Add a two-line phone, modem, and fax to the office? Share a file server or colour printer? A SCS should be devised to be able to cope with all this, without any problem;
- *Simplify troubleshooting* - Even cables that were installed correctly can fail. With a structured wiring system, problems are less likely to down the entire network, they are easier to isolate and easier to fix;
- *Support for future applications* - If you install Category 6 your cable plant will support future applications like multimedia, video conferencing, and who knows what else, with little or no upgrade effort.

Printing also deserves a strategy

Few terms are so frequently used in the IT domain as Total Cost of Ownership (TCO) and Return on Investment (ROI); many IT strategies are actually based on the reduction of TCO or the improvement of ROI and this by all possible means. However, few IT strategies take into account the possibilities of optimising TCO and ROI in the area of physical production of documents.

According to IDC, up to ten percent of the turnover of an organization can go to the production, the management and the distribution of documents. In some organizations, printing alone is good for three percent of the revenues, says Gartner, and the total cost of printing is between ten and twenty percent of the IT budget. On top of that, about half the calls to helpdesk have to do with printing. In the same time, other studies indicate that 70 percent of the organizations have no idea of what is spent on document management and the output on paper is still growing by about twenty percent every year. Even if these figures are exaggerated they are important enough to have a closer look.

It may be an overstatement to say that there is no attention at all for the cost of printers and consumables, but often the TCO analysis stops with the number printers and toner cartridges. This is not surprising when considering the price of these consumables; the Financial Times calculated that toner costs about seven times more per litre as the finest champagne and it is by far not that good to drink!

Many suppliers are convinced that the best way to save money on printing is to invest in the newest technologies, allowing for a centralized management. Having the printers send their usage and maintenance information directly to the supporting organization can dramatically reduce downtime and the number of helpdesk calls and give a detailed insight in the usage of a printer and hence in the possibilities to improve.
It must be clear by now; a good printing strategy is based on more than the Cost per Page (CPP), which only takes into account the purchase and maintenance costs of printers and accessories. A simple example is the extreme centralization of printing devices. Of course, it is possible to save money by centralizing all print jobs, but when you centralize too much this will reduce the efficiency of the employees, so you have to take into account the distance between the users and their printers.

On the other hand, one has to decide on what types of documents really have to be produced on paper. Maybe it is more efficient to scan incoming documents, such as invoices, and to treat them electronically further down the chain. Also, a good archiving infrastructure will help the users to get rid of their habit to print every document for filing purposes only.

Reconsider your storage strategy

While backup is designed for recovery of active data and systems, the process of *archiving* is meant to preserve semi-active or inactive information in order to mitigate the risk of litigation or to ensure regulatory compliance. The access requirements for archived information can span years or even decades.

An interesting fact is that most of the data on your systems is probably "inactive", meaning that it is not updated anymore and that the access frequency is very low. Keeping these data on fast, high-end disks can be very expensive in many respects.

Imagine you have 1 TB on high-end storage. At a price of $0.20 per MB this costs you some $200,000. Migrating the 80% of "inactive" data to low-end disk (@ $0.02 per MB) will make you save $124,000. Moving these data to tape (@ $0.005 per MB) can even make you save $136,000.

Making backups also costs in terms of media. A 1 TB full backup to tape @ $0.05 per MB costs $ 5000 in tapes. Suppose you make a full backup every two weeks and keep the tapes for one year you will have an annual tape cost of $130,000. This can be reduced to $26,000 when migrating the 80% of "inactive" data in our example.

Migrating "inactive" data to off-line or near-line storage can also be a solution for your backup window. If a full backup would take you 10 hours you can reduce this to 2 hours by migrating 80% of your unused data. By the same occasion, the time it takes to restore in case of a catastrophe will be reduced proportionally.

It is clear that these considerations can give you a strong business case when planning to invest in storage infrastructure and tools.

Rely on open standards, but don't be stubborn

Many organizations, especially the larger ones, have a big variety of IT systems, both on the hardware side as in the software field. There are many, perfectly good reasons for this:

- There have been mergers with other organizations in the past;
- There have been internal reorganizations;
- Technology has evolved;
- Different managers had different ideas;
- There have been commercial opportunities.

The result of this can be that several segments of the infrastructure are incompatible or cannot interoperate. These problems can be avoided by using an open architecture.

Open architectures use off-the-shelf components and conform to established standards [49]. An open architecture allows the systems to be connected easily to devices and software made by other manufacturers. The main advantage of open architectures is that anyone can design add-on products for it, which in turn generates the availability of a wide variety of products on the market. A system with a closed architecture, on the other hand, is one whose design is *proprietary* (owned by a company). It also implies that this company has not divulged specifications that would allow other companies to duplicate the product, making it difficult to connect the system to other systems. Manufacturers often use this approach to bind their customers to their products thus ensuring a continuous revenue flow.

Sometimes, it is not possible to use an open architecture, because there is a monopoly of a certain manufacturer or the technology is new and there are no established standards yet. In the first case it is best not to be stubborn and conform to the *de facto* standard (*if you can't beat them, join 'em*). In the second case it is better to wait until it becomes clear which choices will be made (and they will be made, if the technology is there to stay).

Standardize as much as you can

Platform standardization is the standardization of specific system models and operating system platforms for servers, client computers, and peripherals. Platform standardization is the limiting of available operating systems, client computer models, mobile computer models, server models, printer models, and network communication device models that may be purchased. The standards are set for specific user types and designate specific model number and operating system platforms that can be purchased.

Vendor standardization limits the number of vendors that an organization purchases from. By standardizing on fewer vendors, an organization can gain purchasing leverage and reduce incompatibility issues, support issues, vendor liaison requirements, testing of new technology, and administrative costs of vendor management. While it may limit the available selection of technology and features, it enables larger discounts with volume purchasing.

Use the right tools

"When the only tool you have is a hammer, every problem looks like a nail."

(Unknown)

It is a normal human reaction to defend what is best known; this is not different with IT people. Somebody who has worked for the last ten years in a mainframe environment will try to solve everything with a mainframe. The person who has been educated at the university in a UNIX world will look for UNIX solutions and the programmer who only has experience in a PC environment will always first try to write a PC program. Be aware of the fact that this can end in wars of religion between the adepts of different schools. They will always come back on their own arguments and refuse to listen to those of the other party. These discussions are of course completely pointless so the IT Manager should not allow them to take place. He has to select the best-suited technology and force his collaborators to use it, even if it is initially against their opinion.

In a somewhat different context, but equally applicable here, this idea can best be described by Steven Covey's word-picture [12]:

Infrastructure

Suppose you were to come upon someone in the woods working feverishly to saw down a tree.

"What are you doing?" you ask.

"Can't you see?" comes the impatient reply. "I'm sawing down this tree."

"You look exhausted!" you exclaim. "How long have you been at it?"

"Over five hours," he returns, "and I'm beat! This is hard work."

"Well why don't you take a break for a few minutes and sharpen that saw?" you inquire. "I'm sure it would go a lot faster."

"I don't have time to sharpen the saw," the man says emphatically. "I'm too busy sawing!"

Sharpening the saw is about learning new things and using the right tools.

Online Resources

.NET – http://msdn.microsoft.com/net/
AES - http://csrc.nist.gov/encryption/aes/
ANSI - http://www.ansi.org
ATM - http://www.atmforum.com
Autonomic Computing – http://www.research.ibm.com/autonomic/
Biometry - http://www.biometrics.org
Bluetooth – http://www.bluetooth.com
Cable Modems – http://www.cable-modems.org
Computer Benchmarking - http://www.specbench.org
COM/DCOM - http://www.microsoft.com/com/default.asp
CORBA - http://www.omg.org
Database Benchmarking – http://www.tpc.org
DBMS - http://www.dbmsmag.com
DSL forum - http://www.dslforum.com
DVD, Mulitread – http://www.osta.org
EIA - http://www.eia.org
Grid Computing - http://www.gridcomputing.com
Hardware - http://www.computerworld.com/hardwaretopics/hardware
HiperLAN 2 – http://www.etsi.org
IEC – http://www.iec.ch
IEEE standards - http://standards.ieee.org
IETF - http://www.ietf.org
Ipv6 - http://www.ipv6.org
IrDA – http://www.irda.org
ISO - http://www.iso.org
ITU – http://www.itu.org
JDBC – http://java.sun.com/products/jdbc/
MacOS - http://www.apple.com/macosx/
Microprocessors – http://www.amd.com
Microprocessors - http://www.intel.com
Network wiring - http://www.network.wiring.com
Networking - http://www.computerworld.com/networkingtopics/networking
ODBC - http://www.microsoft.com/data/odbc/default.htm
Open source implementation of UDDI in java – http://www.juddi.org
Operating Systems - http://www.computerworld.com/softwaretopics/
PDA – http://www.palm.com
SCSI – http://www.scsita.org
Security - http://www.w3.org/Security/
Security - http://www.cert.org/tech_tips/security_tools.html
Smartcards - http://www.scia.org

Storage - http://www.nsic.org
Storage - http://searchstorage.techtarget.com
Storage networking, SNIA – http://www.snia.org
Supercomputing - http://www.top500.org
UMTS – http://www.umtsworld.org
UMTS forum - http://www.umts-forum.org
UNICODE – http://www.unicode.org
UNIX - http://www.eco.utexas.edu/Help/UNIXhelp/
USB – http://www.usb.org
VDSL Alliance – http://www.vdslalliance.com
VDSL Coalition – http://www.vdslcoalition.net
WiFi – http://www.weca.net
WiFi – http://www.wi-fi.org
Wireless LAN Association – http://www.wlana.com

Further Reading

[9] Bourne, S.R., *The UNIX System*. Addison-Wesley, 1983.

[10] Brockschmidt, K., *Inside OLE*, Redmond, Washington: Microsoft Press, 1993.

[11] Chappell, D., *Understanding ActiveX and OLE*, Redmond, Washington: Microsoft Press, 1996.

[12] Covey, S. The Seven habits of highly effective people, Simon & Schuster; 1st edition, 1990.

[13] Date, C.J., *An Introduction to Database Systems*, Addison-Wesley Publishing Company, 1999.

[14] Date, C.J. and Darwen, H., *Foundation for Object/Relational Databases: The Third Manifesto*, Addison-Wesley Publishing Company, 1998.

[15] Krause, M., Harold F. Tipton, H.F., *Information Security Management Handbook, Fourth Edition, Volume I,* CRC Press - Auerbach Publications; 4th edition, 1999.

[16] Orfali, R., Harkey, D., Edwards, J., *Instant CORBA*, Wiley Computer Publishing, John Wiley & Sons, Inc., 1997.

[17] Rosen, K.H., Rosinski, R.R., Faber, J.M., Osborne, *UNIX System V, An Introduction*. McGraw Hill.

[18] Seifert, R., *The Switch Book*, John Wiley & Sons, 2000.

[19] Seifert, R., *Gigabit Ethernet*, Addison Wesley, 1998.

[20] Spurgeon, C.E., *Ethernet: The Definitive Guide*. O'Reilly and Associates.

[21] Tanenbaum, A.S., *Structured Computer Organization*. Prentice Hall, 1990.

[22] Tanenbaum, A.S., *Computer Networks*. Prentice Hall, 1996.

[23] Tanenbaum, A.S., *Operating Systems: Design and Implementation*. Prentice Hall, 1996.

[24] Umar, A., *Object-Oriented Client/Server Internet Environments*, Piscataway, New Jersey, 1997.

3

Information Systems

"Information systems will maintain the corporate history, experience and expertise that long-term employees now hold. The information systems themselves - not the people - can become the stable structure of the organization. People will be free to come and go, but the value of their experience will be incorporated in the systems that help them and their successors run the business."

(Applegate et al.)

Information Systems

An *Information System* is a system of functions concerning the acquisition and transfer of data, information, knowledge, understanding, and wisdom. Information Systems are also called *applications*. According to the Meta Group a typical large corporation depends on 49 different applications to run its business and spends up to a third of its IT budget getting those applications to communicate with each other.

Within the framework of this book, Information Systems are situated on top of the infrastructure, in support of processes.

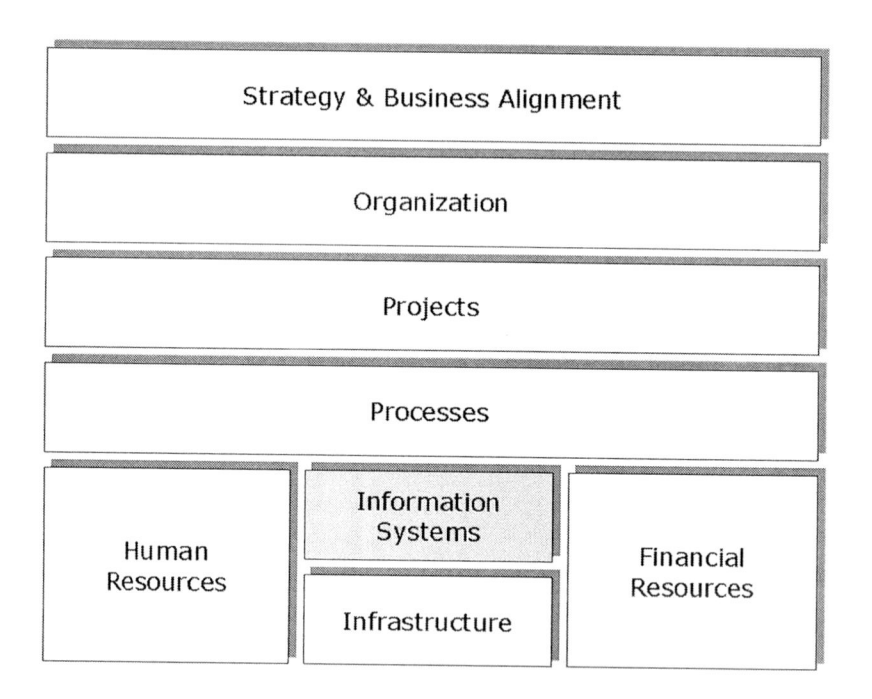

Fig. 3.1 – *Position of Information Systems in the IT stack*

Information Systems can further be split down into sub layers as is shown in Fig. 3.2.

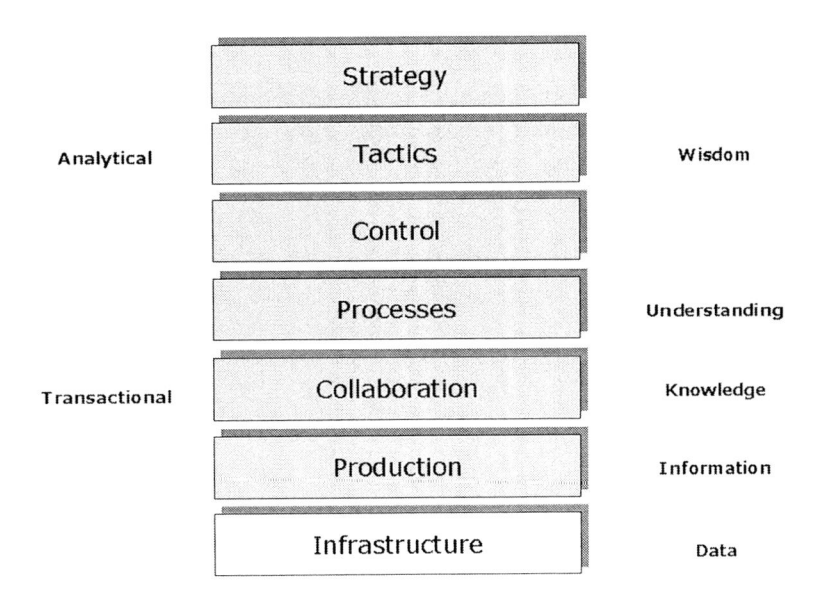

```
                    Strategy
Analytical          Tactics              Wisdom
                    Control
                    Processes            Understanding
Transactional       Collaboration        Knowledge
                    Production           Information
                    Infrastructure       Data
```

Fig. 3.2 – *Layers of Information Systems*

Production

In the lowest layer we find the *personal productivity tools*. These Information Systems are nothing more than a way to gain access to data so, in a way, they can be considered as just specialized user interfaces. They can be specialized (e.g., word processor) or generic (e.g., browser).

Collaboration

The tools in this layer are designed to improve group productivity; this is why they are also called *groupware*. These Information Systems are used to communicate, cooperate, solve problems, and negotiate. They systematically rely on a network. Typical Information Systems are email, group calendars, newsgroups, chatting and videoconferencing.

Processes

The purpose of these layers is to generate added value for the organization through the *combination of information*. In these layers we find the direct support to the Business Processes. The Information Systems in the lower layer consist of input, verification and calculation programs (creation, modification and deletion of information on a unitary basis) while the upper layer will aggregate these data (sorted lists, totals, averages...).

Tactics

The purpose of the systems in this layer is to provide the Management with *quantitative information* about the Business Processes. This information can be used to compare the organization with others; it can be of an analytical nature or be used to apply corrections to internal Business Processes. This layer supports the short-term change processes.

Strategy

The Information Systems in this layer aim to provide *strategic information* to the Management. They support the long-term change processes.

Operational and Informational Systems

The lower three layers are managing operations on individual entities (creation, modification and deletion of objects, files, records, entities...); they are oriented towards transaction processing. The upper three layers are managing groups of entities; they are oriented towards analytical processing. The layers in the lower part of the model are directed towards the daily operations of the organization, they are called *Operational Systems*. The upper layers are supporting the change processes and are called *Informational Systems, Decision Support Systems (DSSs)* or *Business Intelligence (BI) systems*.

Production

The tools situated in this layer are intended to enhance the capabilities of the individual worker. They can work on a standalone machine; there is no need for network support.

There is a large variety of *Personal Productivity Tools*. The most commonly known are:

- Word processors;
- Spreadsheets;
- Drawing tools;
- Viewers and Players.

Word Processors

Compared to old typewriter and carbon copy technology, the way of producing documents has become much more efficient with the introduction of word processing software. There are many flavors of word processing programs. Different programs are better for different types of jobs.

Text Editors

The simplest programs that do word processing are known as *text editors*. These programs are designed to be small, simple, and cheap. Most text editors save files in ASCII. The biggest advantage of this scheme is that almost any program can read and write ASCII text. The ability to write ASCII is the biggest benefit of text editors, but it is also their biggest disadvantage. ASCII is a good way of storing text information, but it has no way of handling more advanced formatting. Text editors do not allow you to do things like change font sizes or styles, spell checking, or columns.

Integrated Packages

Often, when you buy a new Personal Computer an *integrated* package is preinstalled. This is a program that usually contains a word processor, a spreadsheet and some other software tools. An integrated application package is somewhat a "Swiss army knife." The advantages derive from the fact that all the modules are part of the same program. Therefore, it should be relatively easy to use the parts of such an integrated package together. Integrated packages are often designed with casual users in mind. This could make them easier to use than more elaborate programs. The word processor built into an integrated package is normally more powerful than a typical text editor.

Modern Word Processors

Word processing programs have evolved a lot from the early days of computing. In the beginning these word processors were running on dedicated hardware. This has changed with the Personal Computer. A *modern word processing program* can do many things besides simply handling text. Since the early 1990s, most word processors feature a WYSIWYG interface. WYSIWYG (pronounced 'whizeewig') stands for *What You See Is What You Get*. This means that the screen looks much like the finished document. This feature is important as the real strength of word processors is in the formatting they allow. Formatting is the manipulation of characters, paragraphs, pages, and complete documents. Modern word processors also are designed to have numerous features for advanced users. Some of the additional features one can expect to find on a modern word processor are spelling and grammar checkers, the ability to handle graphics, tables, and formulas and outline editors. Word Processors usually save the result of your work in a special, proprietary format. Most of them also allow for saving in a simple text format (with loss of mark up and formatting) or in a special format called *Rich Text Format (RTF)*. The Open Source product OpenOffice (previously StarOffice) and the latest versions of Microsoft Word use XML as native saving format.

Desktop Publishing (DTP)

Desktop Publishing (DTP) software is taking text that has already been created with some other tool, and applies powerful formatting features to that text. Such a program makes it easy to create other kinds of documents than plain pages. Desktop Publishing Software is used to prepare materials such as brochures, flyers, full-page advertisements, newsletters, books, proposals, forms and much more. The quality of graphic material that can be produced in this way is so high that only a professional can detect the difference between material designed by desktop publishing and material that has been typeset. The latter has a somewhat higher resolution but this is not noticeable to the naked eye. In fact, much of the material you see in newspapers and magazines was prepared through Desktop Publishing. The high-end word processing programs give you most of the features you could expect in a desktop publishing program. Yet DTP tools are still popular in certain specialty fields (graphic arts, printing, and publishing…).

Web Authoring Tools

A special class of word-processing programs is the *HTML editors* also called *Web Authoring Tools*. They allow the user to create Web pages with a WYSIWYG user interface, much like a normal word processor, but the document is saved in HTML, a special format suitable for publishing on the Internet.

Spreadsheets

In 1978, a Harvard Business School student, Daniel Bricklin, came up with the idea of an interactive visual calculator. Together with Bob Frankston he co-invented or co-created the software program VisiCalc, the first *spreadsheet* program. A spreadsheet is in essence a table, but instead of having fixed values in the cells these contains formulas that refer to values (or the results of formulas) in other cells. This is useful for computational work and simulations.

The introduction of spreadsheet software made individual *knowledge workers* a lot more productive: where they had to do their analyses and simulations on paper in the past, the spreadsheet concept now offers a tremendous flexibility. Modern spreadsheet software allow for graphical representation of the data (bar graphs, line graphs, pie charts) and for database access. Other possibilities include sorting and filtering.

As with the Word Processors there has been a market shakeout so that only a few packages remain. These are usually interoperable; that is: they can read one another's output file formats.

Drawing tools

Drawing tools allow their users to create graphics or drawings. There are two big groups of graphic file formats: bitmap and vector.

A *bitmap graphic* (also called *raster*) is created from rows of different colored pixels. In their simplest form, bitmaps have only two colors, with each pixel being either black or white. With increasing complexity, an image can include more colors; photograph-quality images can have millions. Some examples of bitmap graphic formats are BMP, PCX, GIF, JPEG and TIFF.

Vector graphics (also known as *object-oriented*) are constructed using shapes, curves, lines, and text, which together make a picture. While a bitmap image contains information about the color of each pixel, a vector graphic contains instructions about where to place each of the components. Examples of vector graphic formats are PICT, EPS, and WMF as well as PostScript.

Bitmap and vector graphics both have their strengths and weaknesses:

- In general, a bitmap graphic file is much larger than a vector graphic file;
- Bitmap graphics are resolution dependent;
- Vector graphics are not appropriate for complex images.

Computer Aided Design and Manufacturing (CAD/CAM)

Computer Aided Design/Computer Aided Manufacturing (CAD/CAM) tools are a special class of drawing tools. These tools can generate files that can be used as an input for manufacturing machines. For example, a photo-plotting machine generates photo masks that can be used in the manufacturing of Printed Circuit Boards (PCBs). The industry standard photo plotting language is the *Gerber Format* (also known a RS-274-D). This format also contains *aperture codes*, i.e., the coordinates and the diameter of the holes that have to be drilled in the PCB; this information is fed directly to a drilling machine in a further step of the manufacturing process. Many specialized tools and formats exist for almost every industry.

Presentation software

Another specialized class of drawing software is *presentation software*. These programs are specialized in the preparation and rendering of good looking business presentations. These tools come with an important gallery of backgrounds, graphics etc. Furthermore, users can select between a set of animations to make their presentations even more attractive.

Instead of being a personal productivity tool, presentation software sometimes becomes a "productivity killer": the user spends more time in making fancy presentations than in concentrating on the essence: the content.

Viewers and Players

Viewers allow their users to visualize the content of a document, without having the possibility to alter it. A well-known example of a viewer is the Acrobat Reader. This freeware allows the visualization of PDF files (Portable Document Format).

A special class of viewers is formed by Web-browsers. These will be handled further on this chapter.

Players allow for the (read-only) exploitation of multimedia files (sound, video, animations).

Characteristics of Production Information Systems

A first characteristic of the Information Systems in this layer is that they have only affect the activities and *productivity of individual staff members*. If there is any resistance against the introduction of these tools it will be on an individual basis, not structural. This resistance will be inspired by the natural reluctance of people to change. It will have to be overcome using training and coaching in which the potential benefits for the individual worker are made clear. The introduction of these tools does not imply any changes in the existing procedures and working methods. The only difference is that information is handled electronically and no longer on paper.

Personal productivity tools are *generic* (not specialized) and *low cost*. There is also a high change rate: every one or two years there is a new "generation" of products on the market. Often, however, the changes are not fundamental; they are just small improvements or new functionalities that are added.

Potential benefits of Production Information Systems

The most obvious benefit is of course the *improved personal productivity*.

A second benefit is the possibility for *efficient storage, retrieval, and reuse* of information.

Another more qualitative advantage will be that you will have *satisfied customers*. This will be good for the working atmosphere and thus for the productivity of the entire organization.

Collaboration

Whereas personal productivity tools most certainly have improved the individual information processing capabilities, they did not affect the global office worker's productivity. Staff spends more and more time in looking for relevant information and less and less time in using it in a significant and productive manner. The Information Systems of level 2 are designed to improve the productivity of groups; this is why they are also called *groupware*.

Groupware systems typically reside on a network (an LAN, a WAN or the Internet). Today, the most commonly used computing model remains the Client Server model. The Server is running on a central platform (or *host*) while the Clients are executing on the individual workstations of the users. In almost all cases, the Server is general-purpose and business-unaware. Likewise, the Clients are general-purpose and only used by a single user, so they could be classified as personal productivity tools. The combination of these two lower-level components however, can be seen as a higher-level entity in the value-chain of the organization.

The introduction of groupware in an organization is an important step. Not only are the infrastructure requirements a lot higher than for level 1 Information Systems (there is a need for a network) but also, more importantly, the way the organization works will change completely.

Groupware systems can be categorized along two dimensions: time and space. Table 3.1 gives an overview of the possible combinations and some typical examples.

	Asynchronous	**Synchronous**
Collocated	Resource sharing Document Management	Voting systems Decision support
Non-collocated	Email News groups Mailing lists Hypertext Enterprise portal Web content management Group calendar Workflow	Chat systems Voice telephony Videoconferencing Shared whiteboards

Table 3.1 – *Categorization of Groupware*

Collocated – Asynchronous groupware systems

Resource sharing

The simplest form of groupware is the *sharing of resources* (files, printers, public folders…). This kind of elementary groupware is normally included in the Network Services part of the IT infrastructure.

Document Management Systems

Document Management Systems (DMSs) are software applications that are related to Database Management Systems (DBMSs). Whereas DBMSs handle *structured data* – short records such as a name, address, and social security number – DMSs store, retrieve, and manage *unstructured data* such as files, text, spreadsheets, images, sound clips, multimedia, and compound documents. The benefits of using DMSs are well established, including improved productivity, shorter process times, and better access to information. They are increasingly being used for business-critical Information Systems in financial services, insurance, energy, manufacturing, government, and many other industries.

Some years ago, document management standards efforts were started at two levels. One was focused on a simple *Application Programming Interface (API)* to let any kind of client interact with a DMS that also realized the API, for storing and retrieving files. Desktop applications like word processing and spreadsheet packages are on those clients and must interact with the DMS to store and retrieve the files. In that sense, the DMS replaces the Operating System's file system. With this standard, the client must know the specific design, construction, capabilities, etc. of the DMS to use it, including its proprietary document structuring, indexing, and query facilities. As all this knowledge is inside the client, the API itself is simple and inexpensive, yet very valuable as it makes the power of a proprietary DMS available to a wide range of desktop applications. This API standard, called *ODMA* (for *Open Document Management API*) has been built into many different kinds of clients, and is used widely today.

In parallel, a second, more ambitious, standardization effort was launched to create interoperability across the different proprietary DMSs. This effort was carried out by an ad hoc alliance: the *Document Management Alliance* or *DMA*. The DMA specification can be combined with the ODMA standard for universal client access, and adds what is needed for completely vendor-independent cross-repository interoperability. In addition, as it accommodates international multi-language conventions, it is even language-independent.

Non-collocated – Asynchronous groupware systems

Email

Email is a groupware application that has seen a tremendous growth in popularity with the introduction of the Internet. The basic functionality is to pass text messages between two persons but almost all email packages include features like forwarding, organizing of the messages in folders, and attaching files.

An email system consists of two components: a server and a client (one for every user).

The *server component* resides on a central host and has two distinct roles: it relays the messages between the other participants of the network (other hosts or clients) and it stores the messages that are intended for the clients it serves.

The *client component* usually resides on the workstation of the users allowing them to send mail to other users and to retrieve messages that are stored on the server.

The interaction between the different players in an email system can be handled using several protocols:

- Simple Mail Transfer Protocol (SMTP);
- Post Office Protocol (POP);
- Internet Message Access Protocol (IMAP).

The purpose of the *Simple Mail Transfer Protocol (SMTP)* is to transfer email around the Internet. SMTP forms the backbone for email transmission from one host to another. A receiving SMTP host continuously listens for incoming SMTP conversations, and when it detects one, will exchange information about the sender and intended recipients of the message and the email message itself. When the conversation is completed, the two hosts will disconnect from each other, and the receiving host will carry on listening for new conversations. In reality, a listening host will listen while talking to one host, and can cope with several concurrent conversations. Most users on the Internet today use SMTP to send out messages, but few receive SMTP mail directly. As SMTP requires machines to continuously listen for incoming conversations which can occur at any time, SMTP is mainly used by Internet Service Providers (ISPs) who have email relay hosts that run 24 hours a day.

POP is an abbreviation for *Post Office Protocol*, and came about as Personal Computers became popular. A prime requirement of an SMTP host is that it continuously listens for incoming email conversations, which is impractical for a PC to do. POP works by querying what is known as a *mailbox* for new mail. The mailbox will usually reside on a host that has a permanent connection to the Internet. When a user wishes to check if there is any email waiting, he will connect to one of these email hosts using POP. The user will then authenticate himself to the remote host, normally using a username and password combination. Once properly logged on, the user can request a list of the email messages in his mailbox, and choose to retrieve them, look at their headers, delete them or do nothing. It is usual that once an email message has been retrieved it will be deleted from the server, thus preventing it is retrieved several times. When the user's host has retrieved the email messages it wants, it will simply log off and drop the connection to the remote host. The whole process of sending and receiving email is analogous to the postman delivering letters between houses (SMTP), and you picking the letters up from your mailbox when it is convenient for you to do so (POP).

IMAP stands for *Internet Message Access Protocol*. With IMAP, you can define a hierarchy of folders (i.e., mailboxes on the mail server), which lets you organize and store mail messages where users can access them from multiple locations. IMAP supports shared folders, so a workgroup can share one copy of a message. IMAP supports both clear text and more secure authentication methods.

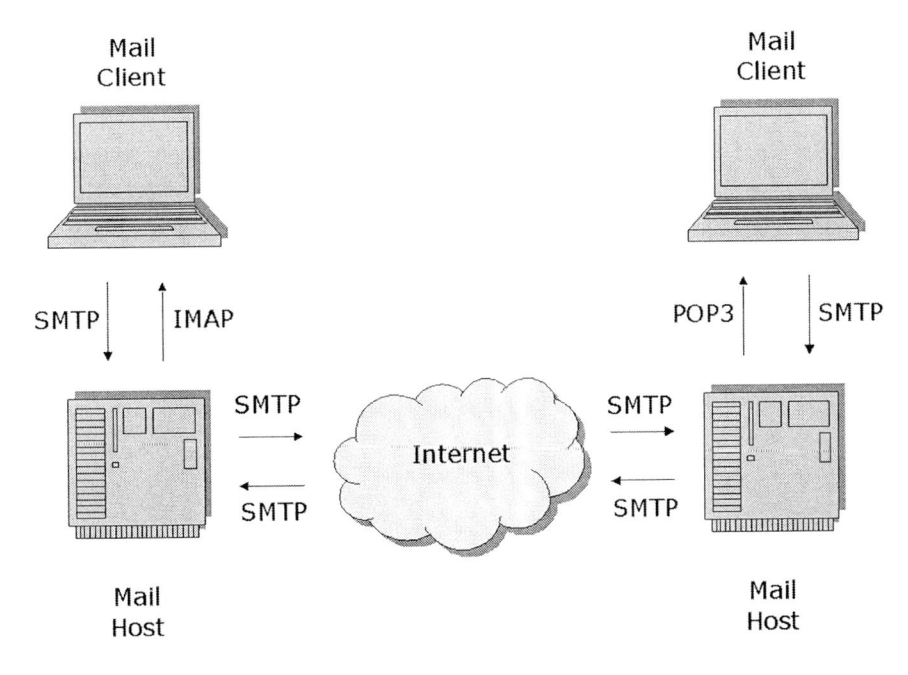

Fig. 3.3 – *Email protocols*

In the early days of the Internet, the only use of mail was the exchange of simple textual messages made of ASCII characters. ASCII needs only seven bit words to map its set of characters, so SMTP was defined to handle words this long. This makes SMTP unable to transmit files made up of eight bits, known as *binary* files. To overcome this limitation, algorithms for transforming 8-bit files into 7-bit files (encoding) and vice-versa (decoding) have been defined. So for sending binaries you need to encode the file before sending it out with your mail tool and the recipient must know which encoding scheme you used and have the right decoder to go back to the original file. An encoding scheme used in the DOS and UNIX world is *uuencode*. The Mac community has chosen for *BinHex*. The *MIME* (*Multipurpose Internet Mail Extensions*) standard foresees as encoding scheme known as *base64* that is more robust than the others and is therefore recommended.

Newsgroups and mailing lists

These Information Systems have the same fundamentals as email but they are intended for messaging among groups of people, instead of one-to-one communication. The main difference between newsgroups and mailing lists is that newsgroups are *pull services* (the user explicitly requests to see the content) while mailing lists are *push systems* (the user receives a message when it becomes available). Both systems can be found as public services on the Internet (often at no cost) or as a private service set up on the Intranet of an organization.

Hypertext Markup Language (HTML)

The *Hypertext Markup Language (HTML)* is a special text format, which is based on *tags*. These are in-line commands to show the formatting the information. Usually tags come in pairs; the first one shows the beginning of an entity and the second one the end. The end tag is identical to the begin tag, except that it is preceded by "/." For instance, the title of a document is indicated by the <TITLE></TITLE> tag pair. There are two groups of tags:

- Tags that structure the document by itself;
- Tags that structure the contents of the document.

Tags like <HEAD>, <BODY> and <FRAMESET> are used to *structure the document*. They allow the segmentation of the document in a part that contains *meta-information* (information about the document) and a part containing the useful information.

The second group of tags is used to *structure the content of the document*. With these tags you can for instance declare that a piece of text is the title of a paragraph or subparagraph (<H1>...<H6>), a table (<TABLE>) or a list (<OL> or <UL>). An important element in this group is the *anchor* tag (<A>). This allows delimiting an active part of the text, a *hyperlink*; clicking on a hyperlink instructs the browser to load the referred document. This is a powerful feature that made HTML so popular. Below is a simple example of a HTML file:

```
<HTML>
<HEAD>
    <TITLE>Hello World!</TITLE>
</HEAD>
<BODY>
    <P>Hello World!</P>
</BODY>
</HTML>
```

Hypertext can be used to create group work, for example to build an Intranet site containing documentation about the internals of the organization (telephone directories, internal procedures, vacancies...). During the past decade, however, these Intranet sites have evolved to true groupware tools that do not simply display information but also allow for interaction with underlying databases.

In the beginning mainly intended for the rendering of HTML files available on the World Wide Web, browsers have gradually evolved into powerful pieces of software that have a multitude of possibilities like the execution of scripts (JavaScript, VBscript), Java applets, and cascading style sheets. The program below is the source code of a complete *Java applet*. The compiled version is stored on the server and loaded on request by the browser which will also execute it:

```
import java.applet.*;
import java.awt.Graphics;

public class HelloWorld extends Applet
{
    public void init()
    {
    resize(150, 50);
    }
    public void paint(Graphics g)
    {
    g.drawString("Hello world!," 20, 20);
    }
}
```

The way to embed this in the HTML page goes like this:

```
<HTML>
<HEAD>
    <TITLE>Hello World! with applet</TITLE>
</HEAD>
<BODY>
    <P><APPLET CODE="HelloWorld" HEIGHT=50 WIDTH=200></APPLET></P>
</BODY>
</HTML>
```

It is also possible to pass parameters to an applet (not shown here) and to make the applet communicate with the server it originated from.

The protocol used to exchange hypertext files is the *Hypertext Transfer Protocol (HTTP)*. This protocol is optimized for one task: allow a browser on a client machine to gain access to hypertext documents on a server. The software that is run on the server is called a *HTTP server* or a *Web server*. The way HTTP works is simple:

- The client opens a connection to the server and sends its request;
- The server responds by sending the requested document;
- The connection is closed.

So, every request requires a new connection to be opened and the server "forgetting" all about the previous request. That is why HTTP is called a *stateless* protocol. HTTP has three basic commands:

- GET, which allows the client to request for a document;
- POST, which allows the client to send data to the server;
- PUT, which allows sending a document.

The hyperlink mechanism uses an addressing method known as *Uniform Resource Locator* (*URL*). An URL is a human-readable string that identifies the location of a resource on the Internet (for example, a page of HTML data or a .GIF file) and the protocol used to retrieve it. An URL is formed of three parts:

- The *identifier of the used protocol*. For HTTP this is `http://`, but a browser can also use other protocols such as FTP (the prefix then being `ftp://`).
- The *name of the server*. This can be formed of different elements ordered in a hierarchical way: the name of the machine (e.g., `www`), the domain name (e.g., `somedomain`) and the top-level domain (e.g., `com`). These elements are separated by dots. Optionally, the port number can be added (the default value is `80`). This number is separated from the rest of the name with ":"
- The *identifier of the document*. If this is a file, the identifier is the complete filename, path included, preceded with "/" However, the path is only given starting at a root directory.

An URL is not necessarily referring to a document; it can also invoke the *execution of a program*. The output of the program is then sent as the answer to the request. In this way it is possible to dynamically create Web pages. There are several techniques to do this. The most frequently used are CGI-scripts, servlets, and server pages.

CGI stands for *Common Gateway Interface*. CGI is not a language; it is a simple protocol that can be used to communicate between Web forms and a program. A CGI script can be written in any language that can read STDIN, write to STDOUT, and read environment variables, including C, Perl, or even shell scripting. Below is a little example written in C:

```c
#include <stdio.h>
void main() {
    printf("<HTML>\n");
    printf("<HEAD>\n");
    printf("<TITLE>Hello World! CGI </TITLE>\n");
    printf("</HEAD>\n");
    printf("<BODY>\n");
    printf("<P>Hello World!</P>\n");
    printf("</BODY>\n");
    printf("</HTML>\n");
exit(0); }
```

This program runs on the server and generates *on-the-fly* the required HTML code to be sent to the client.

Another possibility is the use of *servlets*. A servlet is a Java program that provides a special server side service. They can also be used to generate HTML:

```java
import java.io.* ;
import javax.servlet.* ;
public class helloworld extends GenericServlet
{
public void service(ServletRequest req, ServletResponse res)
throws ServletException, IOException
    {
    ServletOutputStream out = res.getOutputStream();
    out.println("<HTML>");
    out.println("<HEAD>");
    out.println("<TITLE>Hello World! Servlet </TITLE>");
    out.println("</HEAD>");
    out.println("<BODY>");
    out.println("<P>Hello World!</P>");
    out.println("</BODY>");
    out.println("</HTML>") ;
    }
}
```

Servlets share an inconvenience with CGI: every line of HTML code has to be generated separately, and this can be a tedious operation for complex web pages.

Java Server Pages (JSP) and the Microsoft alternative *Active Server Pages (ASP)* are two other techniques for generating dynamic Web content. The idea is to embed program code in HTML-templates. The server executes (expands) this code before it is sent to the client, the result being a perfectly normal HTML file.

JSP	ASP
| ```
<HTML>
<HEAD>
<TITLE>Hello World! with JSP</TITLE>
</HEAD>
<BODY>
<P>
<%@ page language="java" %>
<%System.out.println("Hello World!"); %>
</P>
</BODY>
</HTML>
``` | ```
<%@ Language=VBScript %>
<HTML>
<HEAD>
<TITLE>Hello World! With ASP</TITLE>
</HEAD>
<BODY>
<P>
<% Response.Write("Hello, world!") %>
</P>
</BODY>
</HTML>
``` |

Table 3.2 - *JSP and ASP*

Both JSP and ASP allow session management and database access. As can be seen JSP and ASP are similar, but JSP has a slightly steeper learning curve. The main difference between JSP and ASP is that ASP is interpreted while JSPs are compiled to servlets, which makes them faster, whereas ASP is only found on Microsoft platforms (as part of the .NET framework), JSP can operate on any platform that conforms to the J2EE specification. JSP allow component reuse by using Java beans and EJBs, ASP provides the use of COM/ActiveX controls. With JSP 1.1 the notion of *custom tags* was introduced. The advantage here is that most of the complex Java code is moved out of the JSP document to a reusable component accessible by using a simple tag.

Extensible Markup Language (XML)

HTML is simple but has some major drawbacks as well. First, as the needs have evolved much more rapidly than the standards, the different browsers have started to add non-standard tags. This means that HTML is not really platform independent. Second, many HTML authors are abusing HTML, as they use it mainly as a tool to take care of the presentation and not to show the logical structure. This makes it impossible to use HTML as a structured way to exchange information. As from 1996 the W3C has been looking for a solution to solve these problems. The first version of the new standard was published in 1998; it was called *XML (eXtensible Markup Language)*. This standard for documents and data provides the protocol, required to aggregate disparate data types, including text, graphics, relational data, and software components. The authors can define their own tags and XML also supports hyperlinks. The language applies a formal structure to documents and data and is far more flexible and intelligent than HTML. XML makes it possible to programmatically access, assemble, search and interchange data and documents. Once information is encoded in XML, any program supporting the standard can understand it. Below is an example of a HTML document and its equivalent in XML.

HTML	XML
| ```
<HTML>
<BODY>
<CENTRE>
<TABLE BORDER="1">
<TR>
<TD>Title</TD>
<TD>Author, First Name</TD>
<TD>Author, Last Name</TD>
</TR>
<TR>
<TD>The Data Warehouse Toolkit</TD>
<TD>Ralph</TD>
<TD>Kimball</TD>
</TR>
<TR>
<TD>Using the Data Warehouse</TD>
<TD>William</TD>
<TD>Inmon</TD>
</TR>
</TABLE>
</CENTRE>
</BODY>
``` | ```
<?xml version="1.0"?>
<Book>
<Title>The Data Warehouse Toolkit</Title>
<Author>
    <First Name>Ralph</First Name>
    <Last Name>Kimball</Last Name>
</Author>
</Book>
<Book>
<Title>Using the Data Warehouse</Title>
<Author>
    <First Name>William</First Name>
    <Last Name>Inmon</Last Name>
</Author>
</Book>
``` |

Table 3.3 – *HTML and XML*

We can observe some interesting differences:

- XML is *case sensitive* `<First Name>` and `<first name>` are not the same;
- Data is enclosed by *metadata*: `<First Name> Ralph </First Name>`;
- Users can define their *own tags*: `<Book>, <Author>`;
- In XML there is *no layout specification* such as `<CENTRE> </CENTRE>`.

In fact, the XML document is a hierarchy of *elements*:

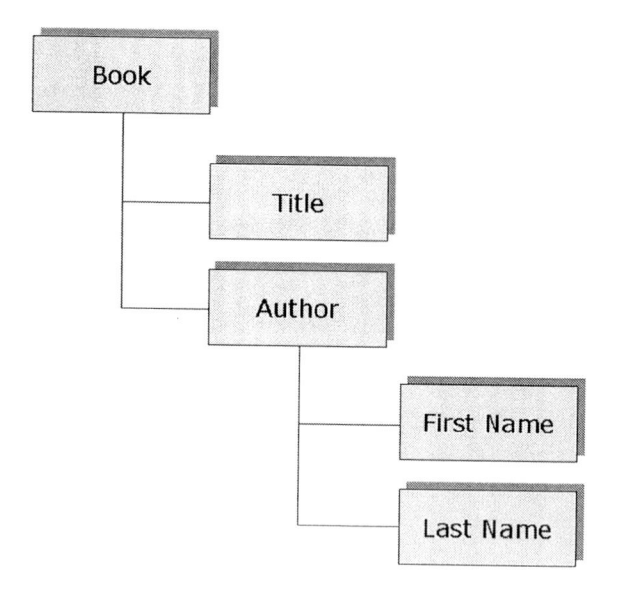

Fig. 3.4 – *Hierarchical data structure*

These elements can also have *attributes*. Adding the attributes "Language," "Publisher" and "Year" to the Book element would go like this:

```
<Book Language="English" Publisher="John Wiley & Sons" Year="1996">
<Title>The Data Warehouse Toolkit</Title>
<Author>
        <First Name>Ralph</First Name>
        <Last Name>Kimball</Last Name>
</Author>
</Book>
```

With a *Schema Language* it is possible to specify the rules (the *semantics*) that apply to the elements and attributes. These rules say what elements must be present and which ones are optional, what their attributes are and how they can be structured with relation to one another. Consider the following piece of code:

```
<!DOCTYPE page [
   <!ELEMENT page (head, body)>
   <!ELEMENT head (title)>
   <!ELEMENT body (title, para)> ]
```

This is part of the specification of how a HTML page should be composed; it says that:

- A page element consists of a head followed by a body;
- A head element contains a title element;
- A body element contains a title element followed by a "para" element.

An XML document that conforms to the structural and notational rules of XML is *well formed*. A well-formed XML document does not have to contain or reference a DTD, but can implicitly define its data elements and their relationships. Well-formed XML documents must follow these rules:

- The document must start with the XML declaration <?xml version="1.0">;
- All elements must be contained within one root element;
- Elements must be nested in a tree structure without overlapping;
- All non-empty elements must have start and end tags.

Well-formed XML documents that also conform to a DTD are *valid*. When an XML document containing or referencing a DTD is parsed, the parsing application verifies that the XML conforms to the DTD and is therefore valid, which allows the parsing application to process it with the assurance that all the data follows the rules defined in the DTD.

We already observed that there are no layout specifications in a XML document. The way in which the information has to be rendered by the output device is specified separately with the *Extensible Style Language (XSL)*. The idea is that the same XML document can be reproduced in different formats, by applying different XSL.

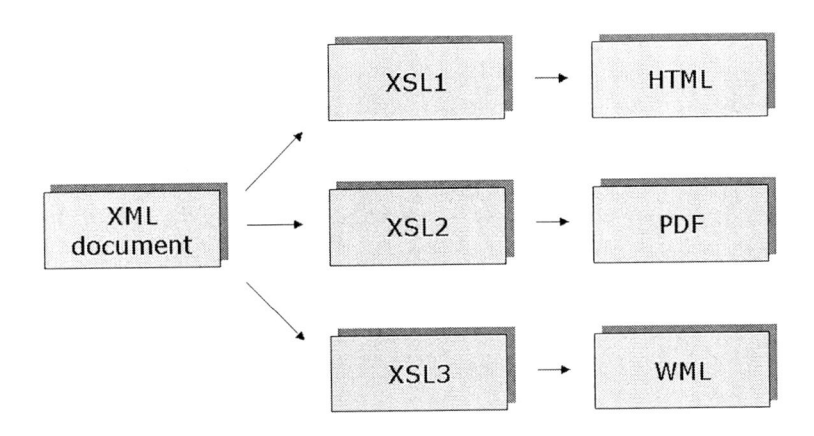

Fig. 3.5 – *XSL transformations*

Web Content Management

Putting a simple homepage on the Web is easy. Getting a group of people to do so properly is a lot more difficult, and getting a whole organization to manage a combination of static and dynamic pages with different views for different target groups, tracking revisions and making it all scalable and secure is a real challenge. The creation of content and its management and maintenance is a human activity, labor-intensive and thus expensive. *Web Content Management* systems help to reuse the effort put into it, and make it show a higher return.

"Please remove the body and find us another webmaster."

The term *Web Content Management* has been adopted by almost every vendor of a software product that has something to do with HTML. Vendors are taking their older technologies, adding support for XML and then repositioning them as content management systems. However, none of these products really are, because they fail to accomplish a major task of a true content management system: distributing the management of Web development. Control over content is a routine when one person or a small group creates content for an entire site. But as more people are involved, the difficulties of managing the flow of data are growing exponentially. Managing these difficulties is the true challenge for the Web Content Management Systems.

Data has to be *input at source*, by the back office employees, not by the Webmaster. The authors should continue to work with their usual word processor, thus taking off much of the load of the technical staff, which means everyone can concentrate on his own tasks. These tools should also allow for the automatic importing and organization of existing web sites, ensuring uninterrupted operation with minimum effort.

More elaborate products integrate a *workflow system*, enabling the organization to create a model of the publishing process and then to create an instance of that process, assigning users to tasks, setting deadlines, and associating items such as documents and files to each task. When the process is activated, the tool pushes the first task (and its associated data) to the correct user and, on completion, immediately notifies those assigned to the next task in the process. The project manager can review the status of each task in a workflow, collect statistics, and configure the tool to send a notification whenever a task deadline expires.

An *electronic review tool* captures the electronic comments of local and remote reviewers, which are immediately available to authors and editors. As documents are routed from person to person, the reviewer uses query and viewing facilities to insert corrections, suggested replacement text, supporting documentation, and so on. The author can then list all comments based on parameters such as priority, reviewer and date. Accepting a comment will automatically update the document with the suggested change. All changes are versioned and stored in a database.

A standard related to this matter is called *Web Distributed Authoring and Versioning (WebDAV)*. WebDAV defines extensions to the HTTP protocol, which would allow Web pages to be created with one Web authoring tool, to be revised using a different Web authoring tool. As the WebDAV group has proposed including features such as "checking out" a Web page, or tracking versions of Web pages (which are features commonly found in Document Management Systems), there has been some confusion about WebDAV possibly competing or conflicting with ODMA. In reality, WebDAV and ODMA are complementary. ODMA creates interoperability of Web servers with a variety of document repositories. WebDAV creates interoperability of the tools used to write and revise Web pages. Both have the effect of increasing openness and interoperability for Web-based applications.

Enterprise Information Portals (EIPs)

A *Portal* is an application that allows users to view and manipulate data from different sources, anywhere through a single gateway in a personalized form.

An *Enterprise Information Portal* (*EIP*) is the application of the portal concept to an organization's information and knowledge base for employees and possibly for customers, business partners, and the public as well.

The definition given by Merril Lynch (1998) is:

"Enterprise Information Portals (EIPs) are applications that enable companies to unlock internally and externally stored information and provide users a single gateway to personalized information needed to make informed business decisions."

An EIP is composed of the following elements:

- *Security* – users have access only to authorized information;
- *Personalization* - roles, preferences and habits of the individual user;
- *Access/search* - access to all the necessary information in the desired context;
- *Collaboration* - people can collaborate regardless of where they are;
- *Expertise and profiling* - individuals within an organization are profiled according to their experience and competencies;
- *Application integration* - individuals can deliver, access, and share information regardless of applications used.

An EIP can give its customers access to many sources of information:

- *Personal data on a network* – reached by starting local applications;
- *Company databases* – with SQL or an OLAP tool;
- *Internal applications* – access via middleware or XML;
- *External applications* – access with EDI, XML, Web Services, etc.
- Web sites – access via XML or SOAP.

The suppliers of software systems have discovered the EIP-market and are currently doing a lot of marketing to sell their solution that is often integrated with their main product, an ERP package or a DBMS. Fortunately for the customers, however, there are also good Open Source implementations (such as JetSpeed, part of the Jakarta project). These products can be helpful in acquiring experience with this technology.

Portal Mark-up Language (*PML*) is the application of XML for the configuration of Portals.

Group calendars

In today's environment, organizations are continuously challenged to find new and more efficient ways to manage their people's time. Scheduling meetings between individuals and groups via telephone or email is replaced by solutions known as *Group Calendars*. These tools allow scheduling, management and coordination of resources (people, equipment, meeting rooms...). Every individual disposes of a personal calendar, which he can make accessible (read-only or read and write) to other members of the organization. In this way it becomes easy to verify the availability of persons or resources, for example to schedule a meeting. These programs also allow for detection and resolution of planning conflicts.

Modern group calendar products allow for the synchronization with off-line devices such as *Personal Digital Assistants* (*PDAs*). The exchange of information is done using a transport and platform-independent format known as iCalendar. The IESG has approved the specification for iCalendar as proposed standards. The three *Requests For Change (RFCs)* are RFC 2445, Internet Calendaring and Scheduling Core Object Specification (iCalendar), RFC 2446, iCalendar Transport-Independent Interoperability Protocol (iTIP): Scheduling Events, BusyTime, To-dos and Journal Entries and RFC 2447, iCalendar Message-based Interoperability Protocol (iMIP).

Workflow systems

Workflow systems allow information to be routed through organizations following a predefined procedure. These systems are well suited for the materialization and follow-up of administrative processes, especially when many different parties are involved. They have the tremendous advantage over tailor-made systems that the process flow can always be modified thereby providing a high agility.

"At this point, you'll step in and do all the work over."

The main features of a workflow system are:

- Process modeling;
- Workflow enactment;
- Work case coordination and tracking;
- Integration with the rest of the IT environment;
- Providing metrics and statistics.

Workflow systems can yield an important productivity gain by a dramatic acceleration of the information flow within the organization. The diagram below gives the typical difference between a process that is run by a paper flow and the same process that is handled with a workflow system (Fig. 3.6).

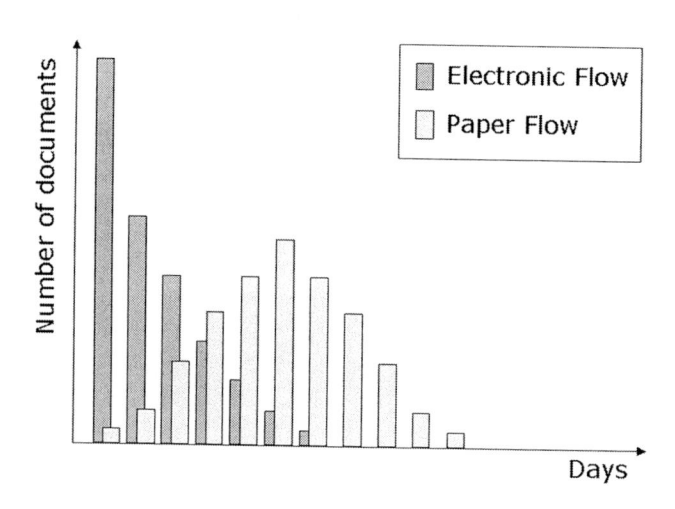

Fig. 3.6 - *Workflow vs. paper documents*

The *workflow definition tools* allow the mapping of Business Processes in the computer system. These tools are often graphical. These tools are message driven, decision driven, or event driven.

The *workflow servers or engines* are the programs that execute and track the workflow processes. The *workflow client systems* are the programs that participants use to interact with the workflow. This software is not necessarily a part of the workflow software; in fact it is better if it is not. Some workflow systems can simply use a normal email client or a Web browser instead of proprietary software. The advantage of this is of course, that the users do not need to learn how to use this client software. Moreover, it makes installation and administration a lot easier.

Workflow systems should also include some way to *administer and track* the status of the different processes.

There are three types of workflow systems:

- Messaging based workflow;
- Web based workflow;
- Production based workflow.

The *messaging based workflow* systems make use of the organization's email system to route tasks. Some of these systems do not require proprietary client software; the participants can simply use their normal email client. The *Web based workflow* products use an Intranet or Internet Web server to which the participants connect. Using their preferred Web browser they can then interact with the workflow system. Some systems provide a proprietary client with a normal Web browser included. The *production based workflow* systems are solutions that implement all the components (definition, server, client, and monitoring) as an independent Application package.

Collocated – Synchronous groupware systems

Voting systems

These systems allow to a large group of people to make a selection within a limited number of possibilities and render an immediate score for every possibility. These systems are typically used in democratic decision organs like national parliaments, trade unions, and boards of directors.

Decision Support Systems

These tools help groups in decision-making. They provide functionalities for brainstorming, debating ideas, applying weightings and probabilities, and voting.

Non-collocated – Synchronous Groupware systems

Voice telephony

The oldest form of groupware is of course *voice telephony*. The telephone set of today acts more and more like a computer: you can check your bank accounts with it, it is an answering machine, it stores a list of names and numbers in its memory, you can use it as a fax or an email client. If it is really necessary, you can also make a phone call with it. On the other hand, the personal computer is also being used as a communication device (via a modem, the sound card and a microphone, or via the Internet). You can listen to music with HiFi quality, listen to the radio or even watch TV with your PC. The integration of different functionalities into one device is a strong trend that will probably continue for some time, especially in the context of the ever-expanding Internet.

A typical example of this trend is *Voice over IP (VoIP)*. The possibility of voice communication over the Internet, rather than the PSTN, first became a reality in 1995. The software that was used was designed to run on a personal computer equipped with a sound card, speakers, microphone, and modem. It compressed the voice signal and translated it into IP packets for transmission over the Internet. This PC-to-PC Internet telephony works only if both parties are using the same software. The next step was the development of gateway servers that act as an interface between the Internet and the

PSTN. Equipped with voice-processing cards, these gateway servers enable users to communicate via standard telephones. Although progressing rapidly, Internet telephony still has some problems with reliability and sound quality, due primarily to limitations both in bandwidth and compression technology. As a result, most organizations looking to reduce their phone bills today confine their Internet-telephony applications to their intranet. With more predictable bandwidth available than the public Internet, intranets can support full-duplex, real-time voice communications. Organizations generally limit their Internet voice traffic to half-duplex asynchronous applications (e.g., voice messaging). Internet telephony within an intranet enables users to save on long-distance bills between sites; they can make point-to-point calls via gateway servers attached to the network. No PC–based telephony software or Internet account is required.

In May 1996, the *International Telecommunications Union* (*ITU*) ratified the H.323 specification, which defines how voice, data, and video traffic will be transported over IP–based local area networks. The recommendation is based on the *Real-Time Protocol (RTP)* for managing audio and video signals. The transport protocol RTP is a new protocol layer for real-time applications; RTP–compliant equipment will include control mechanisms for synchronizing different traffic streams. However, RTP does not have any mechanisms for ensuring the on-time delivery of traffic signals or for recovering lost packets. RTP also does not address the *Quality of Service (QoS)* issue, related to guarantee bandwidth availability for applications. This is realized with the *Resource Reservation Protocol (RSVP)* that will be built in routers to establish and maintain requested transmission paths and quality-of-service levels.

Chat systems

The Internet gave birth to a new way to share thoughts and information: *chat systems*. Each participant can submit messages, which then appear at the bottom of a scrolling screen. These groups are usually formed by topic of discussion. They can be moderated or non-moderated. An interesting feature is of course the fact that a direct transcript of the conversation is generated. This allows for backward reference and people to drop into a conversation and still pick up on the ongoing discussion. These systems are already useful in a research environment but are enjoying a growing popularity in business environments.

Video conferencing

Video conferencing systems allow two-way or multi-way calling with live video and sound. Simple systems make use of the desktop computer of the users, more sophisticated systems provide in specially equipped meeting rooms with large screens and translation services.

With the growing availability of bandwidth both on intranets and on the Internet, this type of Information System most probably has a bright future ahead.

"I'd like to thank those of you in the nighttime parts of the world for joining us at such short notice."

Characteristics of Groupware Systems

Unlike the production tools, these tools are integrated into the daily job of the users: they will influence how the users interact with one another and participate in the Business Processes. Because this there could be a resistance against these tools at a higher level, typically the Middle Management.

The introduction of these tools will have as a consequence that the traditional hierarchy will become "flatter" because of the improved and specialized mechanisms for direct communications between people.

Finally, these tools make IT visible in the organization and hence considered as an added value rather than a cost factor.

Benefits of Groupware Systems

Groupware offers significant advantages over single-user Information Systems:

- They help communication (faster, clearer, more reliable);
- They reduce paper instructions, forms, and procedures;
- They enable teleworking, thus cutting down travel expenses;
- They bring together multiple viewpoints and expertise;
- They enable the creation of groups with common interest;
- They allow time and cost savings through better coordination;
- They can help group solving of problems;
- They enable logging, tracking, and reporting on processes.

Potential risks of Groupware Systems

If not properly handled, the introduction of groupware tools can be dangerous because the blurring of responsibilities. Make sure there is a clear and documented policy or even better; embed the responsibilities in the tools (e.g., workflow).

Be aware that, if the usage of these tools is not generalized, you could end up with *information haves and have-nots*. Avoid this by aiming for a full penetration.

A frequently heard complaint is a problem of *information overflow*. A clear communication strategy has to be set.

The management of this layer has to be active and conscious. This is more than a technical matter; this is why it should NOT be given entirely in the hands of the IT department.

Business Process Support

These systems are all about supporting the Business Processes. Now, why are we handling two layers at a time? Well, this is just a little conceptual trick to make clear that there are two types of operations in these systems: the *Operations* create and maintain information (lower layer) and the *Control* gives a view of the information (upper layer). These operations are indeed different. If we consider for example a payroll application, the operations part will consist of input programs (files, screens) and computational programs (compute the salary, taxes, bonuses). The control part will be the production of individual pay states, lists, output files for the accounting system or the bank. The "lower layer" operations will typically be a-periodic: whenever a new element comes up, it is introduced into the system. The "upper layer" operations are likely to be periodic: once a month, a quarter or a year. The role of the applications in these layers is to integrate individual activities into complete business processes. These systems typically make use of the services of the underlying systems, which, in turn are built on top the IT infrastructure.

Today, most applications are based on the *Client/Server architecture*. The Gartner Group distinguishes five possible configurations:

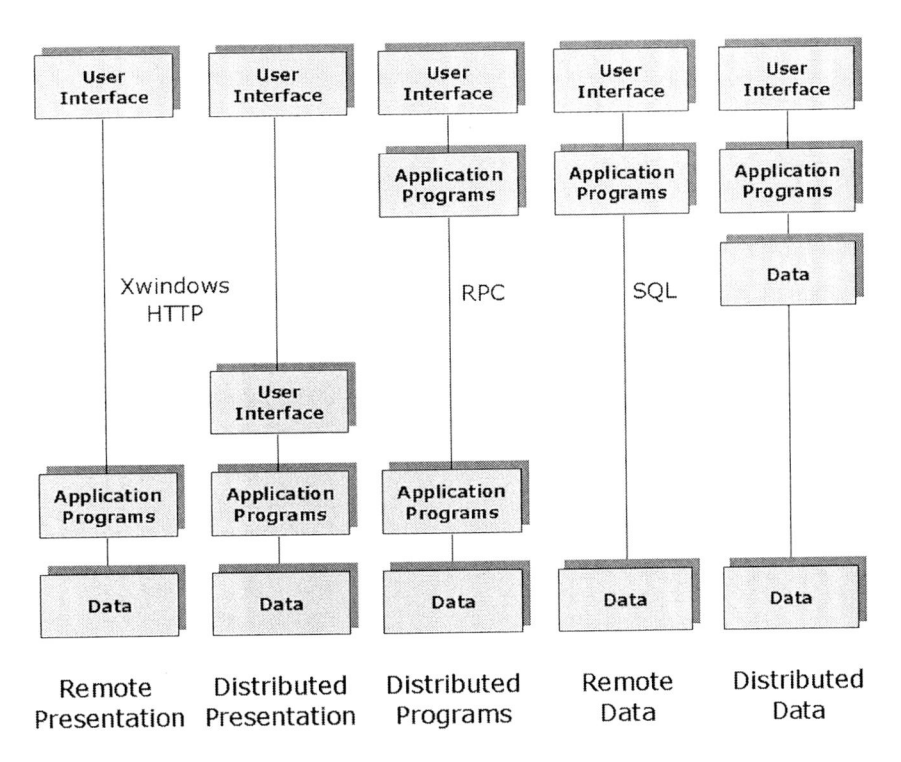

Fig. 3.7 – *Client/Server architectures*

The first configuration is used in presentation intensive applications (multimedia) and Web-based applications. This configuration is also known as *thin client*. The second configuration is used to provide a "face lift" to legacy applications by building a graphical interface that invokes the older text-based user interface. In the third model the application programs are distributed between the client and the server machines, they communicate with each other through *Remote Procedure Calls (RPCs)* or a messaging middleware. In the fourth configuration (*fat client*) both user interface and business logic are performed at the client side, the data are typically retrieved with SQL calls. Finally, in the last architecture data exist on both client and server machines.

For these architectures three parts can be distinguished: the software associated with the user-interface, the actual business logic, and the storage of the information.

Fig. 3.8 – *Three-tier model*

Any application indeed integrates the activities from different parties into one coherent system. The efficiency of the supported processes is improved because duplication of activities is avoided, errors are reduced and repetitive operations can be automated. Furthermore, an accurate follow-up of the processes is made available using built-in reporting tools.

Enterprise Application Integration (EAI)

Usually, applications are built to support a group of business processes; they are specialized and do not cover all the processes of an organization; it is easier to build or buy specialized systems. However, the different processes within an organization are interrelated, sometimes directly (e.g., order processing and invoicing) sometimes indirectly (e.g., the price of a product will be influenced by the production process). This is why, often, two or more applications have to be connected: *Application-to-Application integration (A2A)*. The problems of course occur because these applications were not initially designed to interoperate or share data. Application integration is NOT a new problem; the need was there already in the mainframe era, in the client server era and now, in the Internet era. The needs and principles have remained the same; the only things that have changed are the technological solutions. Application integration is also an expensive activity: according to Forrester Research some 35% of all development time is devoted to creating interfaces and point of integration for applications and data sources.

Application Integration can take place between different layers:

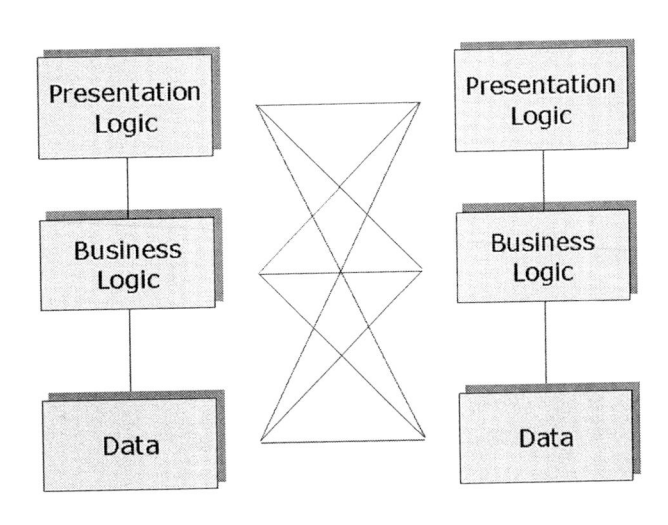

Fig. 3.9 – *Integration scenarios*

One system can act as the master and the other as the slave, or they can interoperate on a peer-to-peer basis. Also, both systems do not necessarily have to be owned by the same organization, this is the case of *Business-to-Business (B2B)* integration.

The issues involved in application integration are both technical and organizational:

- Departments/Organizations use different technologies or products;
- Speed, availability, and security of communication link;
- Need for inter-departmental or inter-organizational procedures;
- The speed of change is dependent on the speed of change of the partner;
- Who is responsible for what?
- Who pays for what?

And things can even get worse when more than two parties are involved...

Integration at the presentation layer

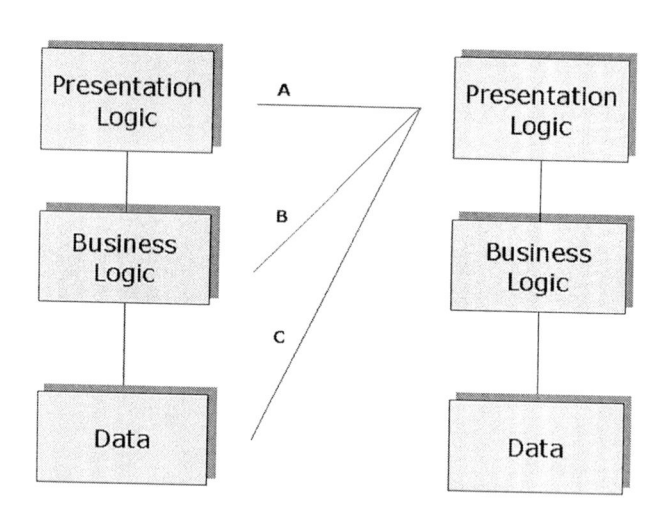

Fig. 3.10 – *Integration at the presentation layer*

Situation A is only a superficial form of integration; two applications are accessible in two different windows on the user's desktop and the only thing they can do is copy-paste information from one window to another.

In *situation B* the user interface of one application is modified to be able to show/manipulate data from the other application. Typically, a technique known as *screen scraping* is used: the dialog to the other application is simulated and the response e.g., an HTML file is then analyzed to filter out the desired data.

There are situations in which this approach could be used:

- Legacy mainframe applications (e.g., IBM 3270 terminal) could be made available as web pages;
- Portal sites accessing different other sites or applications;
- Delivery of virtual services as an integration of other, individual services (e.g., job offers, find cheapest offer…)

The inconveniences of such a solution are obvious:

- Every change in the sending system has a consequence in the receiving system;
- Peer-to-peer integration is impossible;
- There can be a performance penalty.

As this is not a nice solution it is sometimes called "putting lipstick on a pig."

Situation C would represent a situation in which there is no business logic, which is therefore purely academic.

Integration at the database layer

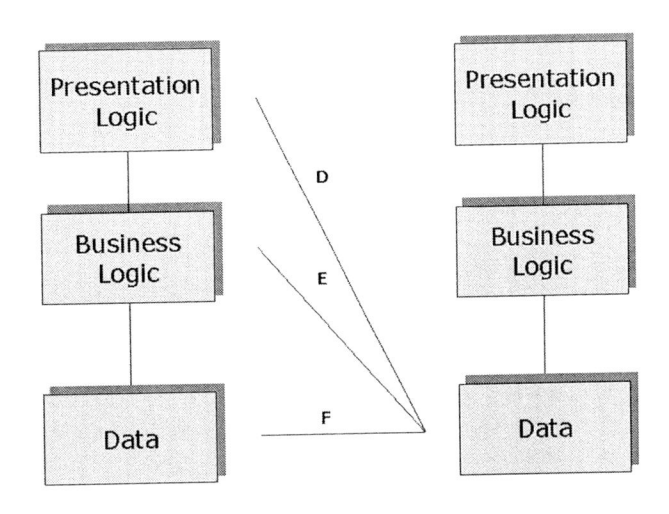

Fig. 3.11 – *Integration at the database layer*

Situation D is the same as C above and is purely academic.

Situation E is technically the easiest form of application integration, given of course that the source database contains all the necessary data. This is, in fact the approach that is used by the commercially available business integration packages (ERP, CRM, and SCM). The problem of course is that the database schema can become complex (a typical ERP implementation needs thousands of tables).

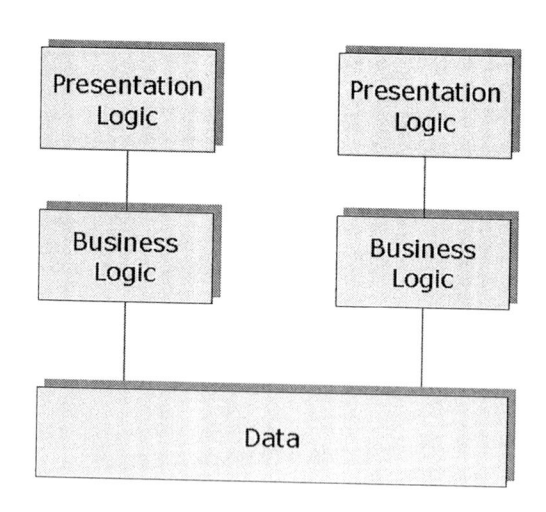

Fig. 3.12 – *Common database*

Finally, *situation F* can also be a good solution but only if the number of links remains limited and manageable. Batch processes or a combination of triggers and stored procedures can be used to synchronize the data.

Integration at the business logic layer

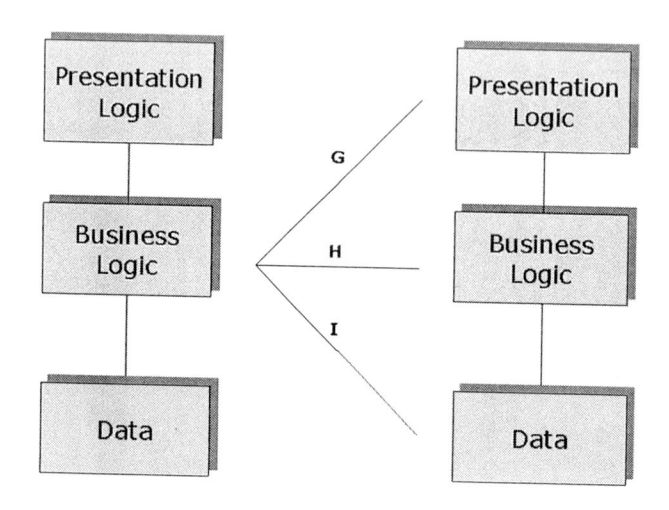

Fig. 3.13 – *Integration at the business logic layer*

Situations G and I have already been discussed.

Situation H is interesting. It is the best choice for cross-organization integration. There are, however some prerequisites:

- The new application has to "understand" the logic of the existing one;
- The existing application has to be modular or at least provide some way to hook up an adapter.

This type of integration is usually done with some kind of (asynchronous) messaging mechanism. This will be discussed in the next paragraphs.

Exchanging information with other organizations

Electronic Data Interchange (EDI)

Traditionally, organizations have used paper as the medium for exchanging information. Business records are filed on paper, and paper forms are mailed between organizations to exchange the information. The arrival of office computers has enabled companies to process data electronically. However, in many organizations the exchange of data still relies heavily on the postal system. Often, an organization will enter data into an Information System, print a form containing the data, and mail this form to a partner. The partner, after receiving the form, re-keys the data into another Information System. Inherent to this process are poor response times - use of the postal system can add days to the exchange process, excessive paperwork for both parties, and the potential for errors as information is transcribed. These problems can be solved with *Electronic Data Interchange (EDI)*. EDI is the computer-to-computer exchange of business data in standard formats. In EDI, information is organized according to a specified format set by parties, allowing a "hands off" computer transaction that requires no human intervention or re-keying on either end.

EDI was first developed by the shipping and transportation industries to reduce the burden of paperwork, a significant factor in the cost of doing business. Traditional applications of EDI are purchase orders, bills of lading, invoices, shipping orders and payments. However, the development of standards and the widespread use of computers has encouraged the use of EDI in many new domains including health care insurance and management, record-keeping, financial services, government procurement, and transactions over the Internet. The benefits of EDI are a reduction of the administrative costs, more rapid and accurate information processing and an improved inventory control.

```
ISA*00*          *00*    *08*61112500TST     *01*DEMO WU000003
*970911*1039*U00302000009561*0*P?
GS*PO*6111250011*WU000003 *970911*1039*9784*X*003020
ST*850*397822
BEG*00*RE*1234**980208
REF*AH*M109
REF*DP*641
REF*IA*000100685
DTM*010*970918
N1*BY*92*1287
N1*ST*92*87447
N1*ZZ*992*1287
PO1*1*1*EA*13.33**CB*80211*IZ*364*UP*718379271641
PO1*1*1*EA*13.33**CB*80211*IZ*382*UP*718379271573
PO1*1*1*EA*13.33**CB*80213*IZ*320*UP*718379271497
PO1*1*1*EA*13.33**CB*80215*IZ*360*UP*718379271848
PO1*1*1*EA*13.33**CB*80215*IZ*364*UP*718379271005
CTT*25
SE*36*397822
GE*1*9784
IEA*1*000009561
```

(Example by xedi.org)

Although today there is more than one syntax for EDI, only two are widely recognized: *X12* in the US and the *Electronic Data Interchange For Administration, Commerce, and Transport (EDIFACT)* in Europe. Both these standards can be viewed as hierarchical in structure; simple data structures at the bottom of the hierarchy are combined to form more complex data structures. At the top of the hierarchy are the information units exchanged between the partners. The X12 and EDIFACT standards provide a lot of agility regarding how business data is represented. To remove some of the ambiguities of the standards and to ensure the successful exchange of information, trading partners adhere to *EDI Implementation Conventions*. Implementation conventions reflect interpretations and common practices regarding the usage of EDI standards. They are developed and published by specific industries to help the implementation of selected standards within that industry.

XML

Another, more recent, approach for exchanging business information is *XML*. Once information is encoded in XML, any program supporting the standard can understand it.

There are numerous ways to transmit XML documents between applications: File Transfer with FTP or NFS, HTTP with servlets, Web Forms built with applets or Javascript, using the Java Messaging Service or the Peer-to-Peer standard JXTA. Many e-business standards have been defined by either individual organizations such as Microsoft's BizzTalk or by industry consortia like xedi.org and ebXML.org.

```xml
<?xml version="1.0" ?>
<?xml:stylesheet?>
<purchase-order>
	<header>
		<po-number>1234</po-number>
		<date>2000-08-08</date><time>12:05</time>
	</header>
	<billing>
	<company>XYZ Supply Store</company>
	<address>
		<street>601 Pensylvania Ave. NW</street>
		<street>Suite 900</street>
	<city>Washington</city><st>DC</st>
	<postcode>20004</postcode>
	</address>
	</billing>
	<order items="1">
	<item>
		<reference>097251</reference>
		<description>Widgets</description>
		<quantity>4</quantity>
		<unit-price>11.99</unit-price>
		<price>47.96</price>
	</item>
	<tax type="sales">
		<tax-unit>VA</tax-unit>
		<calculation>0.045</calculation>
		<amount>2.16</amount>
	</tax>
```

(Example by xedi.org)

Web Services

A whole new mechanism for the exchange of data across the organizational borders is known under the common name of *Web Services*. Web services are applications that are self-contained, self-describing and modular, and that can be published, located, and invoked across the Web. Once a Web service is deployed, other applications (and other Web services) can discover and invoke the deployed service.

Web services are based on three standards: WSDL (Web Services Description Language), UDDI (Universal Description Discovery and Integration), and SOAP (the Simple Object Access Protocol).

The *Web Services Description Language (WSDL, pronounce as "whistle")* is an XML-based language used to describe the services an organization offers and to provide a way to gain access to those services via the Web.

Universal Description, Discovery, and Integration (UDDI) is an XML-based registry, a kind of yellow pages for Web services. UDDI lets two organizations share a way to query one another's capabilities and describe their own capabilities.

SOAP stands for *Simple Object Access Protocol*. It is a lightweight and simple XML/HTTP-based protocol that is designed to exchange structured and typed information on the Web. SOAP uses XML messages to invoke remote methods in a platform- and language-independent manner; a request for the famous "Hello World!" Web Service could look like this:

```
<?xml version="1.0" encoding="UTF-8"?>
<SOAP-ENV:Envelope
xmlns:SOAP-ENV="http://schemas.xmlsoap.org/soap/envelope/">
        <SOAP-ENV:Body
        SOAP-
ENV:encodingStyle="http://schemas.xmlsoap.org/soap/encoding/"
            xmlns:SOAP-ENC="http://schemas.xmlsoap.org/soap/encoding/"
            xmlns:xsd="http://www.w3.org/1999/XMLSchema"
            xmlns:xsi="http://www.w3.org/1999/XMLSchema-instance">
                <namesp1:HelloWorld xmlns:namesp1="World"/>
        </SOAP-ENV:Body>
</SOAP-ENV:Envelope>
```

You can see where the envelope and its body begin in the XML. The `HelloWorld` method is called inside the body.

Although a Web service could interact with remote machines through HTTP's POST and GET methods, SOAP is better, as it is much more robust and flexible. There are, however, some drawbacks as well: SOAP does not provide for transaction monitoring (for this the *Business Transaction Protocol (BTP)* has been proposed by the *Organization for the Advancement of Structured Information Standards (OASIS)*). There is also no location transparency (i.e., the URLs are hard coded).

E-commerce

The Internet has changed the way in which the world conducts business; *e-commerce* is rapidly taking a share of global trade [180]. Goods are purchased and sold, services are rendered, stocks are traded, newspaper and magazine subscriptions are sold, and up-to-the-minute news and financial information is readily available, all from the convenience of the consumer's home or office. Organizations around the world are increasingly turning to the Internet to improve their efficiency and profitability. Lower purchasing costs, reduced inventory, lower cycle times, more efficient and effective customer service, lower overhead, lower sales and marketing costs, new sales opportunities and a global customer base are only some of the benefits enjoyed by businesses conducting electronic commerce.

There is a general consensus that international cooperation is needed to help e-commerce worldwide. The goal of is to create a legal framework that will help global electronic commerce without unnecessarily hampering the freedom of governments to pursue their own objectives. The US and major international organizations such as the European Commission [184][185], the *United Nations Commission on International Trade Law (UNCITRAL)*, and the *World Trade Organization (WTO)*, are engaged in discussions regarding the development of domestic and global legal frameworks that will help electronic commerce worldwide.

E-commerce web sites

Many organizations only have a straightforward publicity site; the objective of this site is to promote the organization and to supplement traditional marketing activities. E-commerce sites are different; the objective is to close sales electronically with payment (and sometimes delivery) made over the Internet. E-commerce sites generally have three sections: marketing and added value information, an on-line catalog, and order processing.

Marketing and added value information - This is aimed at attracting customers and building a one-to-one relationship with them. Ideally, this section is linked with the organization's CRM system but usually the visitors' preferences are recorded, so they can be presented the right special offers when they return. This has to be done carefully: you have to tell your customers that their information is recorded and explain your organization's privacy policy.

The On-line Catalog contains detailed information on products, specifications, and pricing. The customer must be able to find the product they need with few clicks. It has been estimated that you lose 20% of visitors every time you ask them to link to a new page so good navigation is essential. Also, the information must be comprehensive once the customer has located the product of interest. Provide pictures and diagrams to help the customer understand what is being offered.

The *Order Processing* section includes methods for specifying and paying and sometimes a method to verify progress and delivery of the order. In the catalogue part, the customer can flag products; these are then added to an electronic *Shopping Cart*. At any point the customer can review the contents of this cart, the cost and so on. When the shopping session is complete, the customer clicks on a hyperlink that takes him or her to the checkout page. At this stage the customer is presented with a list of the goods marked for purchase, the total cost, shipping, handling, tax, etc. The customer can then add shipping instructions, name, and address. The next operation is payment. There is normally a range of payment options. The most common is to use a credit card; other options are "electronic wallets," "electronic checks." Proprietary systems such as First Virtual, contact the purchaser later by phone or post/print a form that has to be faxed.

Online contracts

Most real world contracts are formed on a person-to-person basis. By contrast most Internet contracts are made remotely, impersonal and automated. This can be problematic if there is ambiguity or uncertainty over the transaction but a more likely issue is whether there was a contract at all. In a poorly designed ordering system it could be possible to argue that the contract occurred by accident because the buttons marked "buy" and "cancel" are next to each other. Likewise if the contractual terms are contradictory or ambiguous the validity or enforceability of any contract can be in question.

Income Tax

The Internet makes it difficult to link an item of income with a geographical location to transactions conducted through electronic commerce. As a result, the focus on and importance of concepts of source-based taxation decreases and the significance of residence-based taxation increases. The selection of a corporate domicile will become increasingly important as corporations seek to benefit from the most advantageous local tax laws and international treaties.

Sales Tax

A consensus exists among international organizations that efforts should be made to avoid inconsistent and redundant taxes on electronic commerce. In the United States, legislation was introduced in the House of Representatives and the Senate, creating the *Internet Tax Freedom Act*. The Act allows state and local governments to impose sales tax on electronic sales in a similar fashion as imposed on sales made via the telephone or mail order.

Jurisdiction

The rules are not always easy to guess and as a result lawyers almost always advise that a clause determining which country has the jurisdiction and which laws should apply. Often this will be determined to be in a country, which is most convenient for the more powerful party and where the contract is most likely to be interpreted in favor of the party most likely to sue.

Privacy and data protection

Privacy is one of the more contentious issues in e-commerce. At its simplest level this means ensuring that communications with the customer are protected. It is a reasonable expectation of the customers that encryption is used to protect their information from hackers while in transit. Failure to this could render a merchant liable for negligence or breach of contract.

The other expectations of privacy relate to the use that is made of client data. Most companies regard this as a valuable marketing asset since it represents a base from which further sales can be made. Consumers on the other hand, often feel threatened by the pervasive data gathering undertaken by merchants and the data mining used to build up uncomfortably precise pictures of their inner life. It is therefore of the greatest importance that a privacy statement is published and respected on your e-commerce site.

Characteristics of Business Process Support Systems

One of the most important characteristics of these Information Systems is that they affect the operations of the organization. This is why you will have to persuade the top of the organization of the introduction or evolution of these tools.

Business Processes tend to change frequently and there is an ever-increasing demand for shorter deployment times. This is reflected in the shortening development time that is allotted to the project teams.

Projects related to the automation of Business Processes tend to be *complex and expensive*. There is also an important impact of non-technical issues (optimization of existing processes, Change Management).

Benefits of Business Process Support Systems

The benefits that can be obtained with the introduction of these systems are overall improvement of the effectiveness and the efficiency of the organization.

Risks Business Process Support Systems

- Badly matched to the needs of the organization;
- Inability to keep up with technological or organizational evolutions. Project deliverables can be late and thereby be more a hindrance than help for the organization;
- Dependency on external suppliers (products, services, know-how);
- Loss of internal knowledge on one's own Business Processes. This knowledge has to be managed in a conscious way. It should NOT be situated in the IT department but with the business users;
- Disproportional investments: spend more money and energy on a project than it will ever generate or save. Also take the (hidden) running costs into account when you make a cost-benefit evaluation.

Tactics

The purpose of this layer is to provide the Management with *quantitative information* about the business processes. This information can be used to compare the organization with others. It can be of an analytical nature or be used to apply corrections in the internal processes of the organization. This layer supports the short-term change processes.

The software tools that are used in this layer are also called *Business Intelligence (BI)* tools, but do not be mislead: they are just tools. The important thing is that they are used properly, after all "*A fool with a tool stays a fool.*"

The potential in added value of this layer is much higher than for the lower layers, but so is the potential risk. When not used properly, these techniques can also do much harm to an organization.

Metrics

"Without data you are just another person with another opinion."

(Unknown)

In every organization or process, there are elements that can be used to monitor the performance; they are called *metrics* or *Key Performance Indicators* (*KPIs*). These measures can be simple ones such as number of units sold or turnover, they can also be complex and hard to define such as market share or customer satisfaction. The purpose is always clear: use this information to improve the performance of the organization.

Often, it is possible to extract the metrics from the operational data. Where operational systems typically create, modify, and delete elementary units of information (products, customers, orders...) the analytical approach will handle totals, averages, and ratios. Also, the users of this information are different: the people that are involved in the execution of the operational processes use the operational data. The Middle Management typically uses metrics. For these two reasons it makes sense to implement them as separated systems.

Benchmarking

The *American Productivity & Quality Centre* (*APQC*) defines a *Benchmark* as:

"A measured, "best-in-class" achievement; a reference or measurement standard for comparison, this performance level is recognized as the standard of excellence for a specific business process."

APQC further describes *Benchmarking* as the process of identifying, learning, and adapting outstanding practices and processes from any organization, anywhere in the world, to help an organization improve its performance. Benchmarking gathers the tacit knowledge, the know-how, judgments, and enablers that explicit knowledge often misses.

Organizations can benefit from benchmarking because it:

- Prevents reinventing the wheel (Why invest the time and costs when someone else can have done it already and often better, cheaper, and faster?).
- Accelerates change and restructuring by:
    - Using tested and proven practices.
    - Convincing sceptics who can see that it works.
    - Overcoming inertia and complacency and creating a sense of urgency when gaps are revealed.
- Leads to out-of-the-box ideas by looking for ways to improve outside your industry.
- Forces organizations to examine present processes, which often leads to improvement in and of itself.

There are different types of benchmarking:

- *Internal* – a comparison of internal operations, e.g., to similar processes in different units or divisions of the same organization;
- *Competitive* – a comparison of products or processes of the competition;
- *Functional* – a comparison of similar processes from the same industry or industry leaders from dissimilar industries, they should be driven by the same customer requirements however;
- *Generic* – a comparison of processes that are the same, regardless of industry (e.g., order intake).

The problem of course is where to get the information you can compare with; it is highly improbable that your competitors will give you access to their internal metrics or that you get that kind of information from a whole industry. This is why organizations like APQC, Benchmarking Exchange and industry organizations like the *International*

Government Benchmarking Association (IGBA) have been created; your organization can become a member and exchange benchmarking information with your peers and competitors.

Activity Based Costing

All organizations are subject to strict financial accounting procedures. However, these processes are based on historical information and provide little scope for looking forward. Information is rarely presented in a format that helps the day-to-day business, where operational management and staff can fully understand and exploit it.

Organizations have to know if they are operating in the most efficient and effective way. The ability to calculate and control activity costs, to communicate key elements of cost information to relevant parts of the organization, enabling informed management decisions to be made, can provide a competitive advantage.

A popular costing system is known as *Activity Based Costing (ABC)*, Cooper and Kaplan devised it in 1988 [46][47]. They developed a methodology that recognizes the need to understand how costs relate to individual products and services.

The benefits, which can be derived from introducing an Activity Based Costing system, depend on the diversity of the services or products of an organization, the level and degree of competition, and the number of products or services produced. The more competitive the operating environment is, the greater the need for accurate costing. ABC costing provides information in a format that focuses management attention on the underlying causes of cost. ABC systems can, therefore be a trigger to improving processes.

ABC tools enable you to import information from other systems, such as ERP packages, to perform the necessary analysis.

Introducing ABC is a non-trivial operation that involves every segment of the organization. It will be discussed in one of the next chapters.

Data warehousing

In the last decades, a set of significant new concepts and tools have evolved into a new technology that makes it possible to attack the problem of providing all the key people in the organization with access to whatever level of information needed to survive and prosper in an increasingly demanding world.

Bill Inmon [35][36][37][38][39] first introduced the term that has come to describe this technology; it is *Data Warehousing (DW)*. The definition he gave is:

"A data warehouse organizes and stores the data needed for informational, analytical processing over a long time perspective. A data warehouse is a subject-oriented, integrated, time-variant, non-volatile collection of data in support of management's decision-making process."

A related item is the *data mart*: unlike the data warehouse, this database does not contain enterprise-wide information, but is limited to a part of the organization (e.g., marketing, finance, and manufacturing).

Data Warehousing is a field that has grown out of the integration of several different technologies and experiences over the last decades. These experiences have allowed the IT industry to identify the key problems that have to be solved.

A DW is made up of three different functional areas, each of which must be customized to meet the needs of a business:

- Data Acquisition;
- Storage Management;
- User Access.

Data Acquisition

The process of *data acquisition* is complex, tedious, and costly. Warehouse developers usually wind up spending an inordinate amount of time doing three things. First, they catalogue all the data, developing an inventory of where it is and what it means. Second, they clean and prepare the data. This includes extracting it from legacy files and reformatting it to make it usable. And third, they devote a lot of energy transporting data from one location to another. These steps are commonly called *Extraction, Transformation and Loading (ETL)*.

Although it is certainly possible for organizations to accomplish these operations without the assistance of any software (and many do just that), there are a host of products designed to help manage and automate the acquisition process. The vendors of metadata management products take on data inventory and catalogue management. Most of these products are updated versions of the *data dictionaries* of the 1970s and 1980s. New, specialized products, however, also do data cleaning and preparation. Some of these products include *Artificial Intelligence (AI)* that can look at data and decide how it should be repaired to make it usable. Data transportation can be handled by simple system utilities or automated by products, which automatically extracts, cleans, and delivers data nightly without human intervention. Some data acquisition product vendors integrate several of these products into complete offerings. Their product families include separate modules that perform the three acquisition functions.

Most warehouse *storage* today is being managed by relational databases running on UNIX platforms. These RDBMSs often use special indexing techniques such as inverted lists, bitmap indexes, and aggregates.

Inverted List Indexes provide much greater functionality and agility than B-tree indexes. They store the data from the database as keys so the data content can be quickly searched on, with pointers back to the database as data in the index so the data records can be quickly retrieved.

Customer

CustID	Name	Address	State	Region	City
100234	AB Corp.	1, Las Vegas Blvd.	Nevada	W	Las Vegas
222394	Technotools	323, Main Street	Minnesota	N	Mineapolis
124040	Acme	555, Star Blvd.	Texas	S	Dallas
449452	Zillion Inc.	123A, Park Ave.	Kentucky	E	Louisville
553935	Whatsup	8, Silicon Driveway	California	W	San Diego

In this example, a Region index would contain the key values "N," "E," "S," and "W" with the customer record numbers as pointers back to the records in the Customer table. The Region index looks like this:

N	E	S	W
222394	449452	124040	100234 553935

When a user queries on a region, he will get an immediate answer by reading the inverted list. Inverted list indexes can also perform keyword lookups, provide an instant, up-front qualifying count, and support unlimited multi-column and multidimensional queries.

Another type of advanced indexing technology is a *bitmap* or *bitmapped index*. Bitmapped indexes provide high-speed index-only query processing for instant counts, keyword searches, and multi-column combinations using multiple criteria.

The structure of a bitmapped index looks like a spreadsheet. The possible values go across the top, the record numbers down one side, and a flag or "bit" is set to ON or OFF in each cell, depending on whether the data record contains a particular value.

Order

OrdID	OrdCustID	Description	Quantity	Class	Category
12345	124040	Baseball Gloves	2	2	A
12346	222394	Basketball	3	2	B
12347	100234	T-shirt	10	1	A
12348	124040	Helmet	6	2	A
12349	553935	Bicycle	9	1	B

For example, the index for the combination of the fields "Class" and "Category" in the Order table looks like this:

OrdID	Index
12345	01
12346	00
12347	11
12348	01
12349	10

The first bit represents the value of the "Class" field the second bit the "Category" field. Bitmap indexes reduce the quantity of data to be loaded in memory by a factor of ten or more, thereby reducing disk access and allowing the computer to do what it is good at: comparing binary data.

Bitmaps are limited to low cardinality columns (columns which can hold only a few possible values) such as "Y/N," "M/F," or "0 to 10" as they grow unmanageably large for high-cardinality. Moreover, they cannot be updated online, so bitmaps are limited to fields that do not change over time (such as the gender of a person).

Another technique that is used in data warehouses is the storage of *aggregated information* (sums, totals, averages). This can be seen as a form of denormalization with some extra disk space usage as result, but in this way, that information will not have to be recalculated at run time yielding a better performance. The purpose of aggregates is to speed up the "group by" clauses of your queries.

Storage Management

Storage Management of a DW sometimes calls for more exotic hardware solutions. When a typical UNIX server or mainframe computer seems incapable of handling the envisioned workload, help is sought from *Symmetric Multiprocessor (SMP)* or *Massive Parallel Processor (MPP)* architectures.

The same companies who make the typical UNIX-based server machines usually manufacture *SMP hardware*. These machines run a slightly modified version of the UNIX operating system but take advantage of extra processors. SMP hardware lets warehouse managers greatly increase the capacity of their systems without sacrificing the current UNIX and database administration skills required to run it.

But for the really big jobs, SMP is not enough. In those cases, some organizations are turning to *MPP machines*. MPP systems incorporate the use of dozens or even hundreds of processors. The power of these machines cannot be approached by any other hardware. Unfortunately, this hardware requires a large investment in specialized software and support expertise.

User Access

By far the widest range of products in the DW marketplace can be found in the area of *User Access*. These products can be broken down into several different categories:

- *Executive Information Systems (EISs)*: a fixed set of queries, pre-developed by IT experts, is presented in a user-friendly way to the executive;
- *Dashboards (or cockpits)* contain a fixed set of queries, pre-developed by IT experts, but the queries are run periodically (usually in batch, during the "calm" hours);
- *Managed Query tools*: the user has the freedom to create his own queries, but he has to know the structure of the database and is very SQL oriented;
- *Online Analytical Processing (OLAP)* [28][50] also allow the user the freedom to create his own queries, but the database structure is hidden behind an intermediate layer. These tools typically allow for a type of analysis known as *drill-down*: launching more and more detailed queries, based on a more general (aggregated) result.

Warehouse development

Of course, each of these products contributes only a part of the overall warehouse development picture. To build a warehouse for your own organization, you must assemble a unique collection of these tools and perhaps combine them with your own customized software to tie the different pieces into a coherent system.

In many respects developing a good data warehouse is not different with any other IT project; it requires careful planning, requirements definition, design and implementation. There are, however, some major differences as well [26][31][34][40][41].

The best data warehousing strategy is to select a user population based on value to the organization and make an analysis of their needs. Based on these needs, a prototype data warehouse is built and populated so the end-users can experiment and modify their requirements. Once there is general agreement on the needs, the data can be acquired from existing operational systems across the organization or from external data sources and loaded into the data warehouse. If it is required, information access tools can also be enabled to allow end-users to have access to required data using their own favorite tools or to allow for the creation of high-performance multi-dimensional information access systems using the core data warehouse as the basis.

One key to data warehousing is *agility*. It is critical to keep in mind that the more successful a data warehouse is, the more end-users are going to want to add to it. This is why designing data warehouses is different from designing traditional operational systems. For one thing, data warehouse users typically do not know nearly as much about their requirements as operational users; as a result, designing a data warehouse is like aiming at a moving target. Second, designing a data warehouse often involves thinking in terms of much broader, and more difficult to define, business concepts than does designing an operational system.

It looks like the definition that was given by Bill Inmon will have to be revised in some not so distant future. Indeed, the new e-commerce systems (which are transactional by nature) are more and more connected to a data warehouse to create a personalized environment for the person that is managing the system. A well-known example is the on-line bookstore that suggests related book titles when buying a book. In the background there is a data warehouse that contains information about books that are likely to be bought together. This warehouse is consulted *on the fly* by the transactional system to support the commercial process. Right now, the transactional and analytical systems are often two different databases, each specialized in their domain, but in the future, technology will certainly allow for a re-integration into a single database, thus allowing a more efficient support of the business process. The database vendors have already detected this trend and adapted their products by including ETL tools, special indexing techniques, and OLAP functionalities in their offerings.

Another remark regarding Inmon's definition concerns the *customers* of the data warehouse. Inmon limits the use of data warehouses to the manager's decision-making process, the on-line bookstore example clearly illustrates that this is likely to change: a regular customer purchasing a book can certainly not be confused with a business manager.

Characteristics of Tactical Information Systems

The most significant characteristic of these Information Systems is that the business aspects are more important than the technological issues.

The whole organization is involved in the deployment of these systems: everybody has to be activated to provide the information that is needed to feed these systems and the Management has to be trained to interpret the information and to react properly.

Benefits of Tactical Information Systems

It is obvious that the benefit of these Information Systems has to be sought in an overall improvement of the efficiency, effectiveness, and quality of the organization. In that way they have a large contribution in the competitiveness and long-term survivability.

Risks of Tactical Information Systems

An obvious risk is situated in the quality of the underlying data. An old axiom of IT is often called *Garbage In, Garbage Out (GIGO)*: you cannot expect the output to be of good quality if the input is incorrect or incomplete, which is unfortunately often the case in the real world. This problem is particularly true for decision support systems that rely on the data manipulated and stored by the underlying operational systems.

The biggest risk of these systems, however, is that they are considered as control mechanisms ("big brother") rather than instruments to improve the overall performance of the organization. If such is the case, the project will fail, as the information necessary to make it all work will not be provided or will be inaccurate, and therefore become useless.

Strategy

"If you know the enemy and you know yourself, you need not fear the result of a hundred battles."

(Sun Tzu, 500 BC)

If there is a single key to survival, it is being able to analyze, plan, and react to changing business conditions rapidly. To do this, top managers, analysts, and knowledge workers need more and better information [8].

IT itself has revolutionized the way organizations operate today throughout the world. But the truth is that in many organizations, despite the availability of more and more powerful computers on everyone's desks and communication networks that span the globe, many decision makers cannot get their hands on critical information. Every day organizations large and small create billions of bytes of data about all aspects of their business, millions of individual facts about their customers, products, operations, and people. But for the most part, this data is locked up in a myriad of computer systems and is exceedingly difficult to get at.

This phenomenon is known as the *Data Access Crisis*.

Balanced Scorecards

Professor Robert Kaplan and Dr. David Norton introduced the concept of *Balanced Scorecard* (*BSC*) in 1992. The BSC is a framework for describing, carrying out and managing the operations of an organization by linking objectives, measures, and initiatives. The BSC provides an overall view by integrating *financial measures* with other Key Performance Indicators (KPIs) concerning *customers, internal processes, learning, and innovation*. The BSC is not just a static list of measures, but a framework for realizing and aligning complex programs of change.

The basic idea of the methodology is that focusing solely on the (short term) financial performance of a business is not a good thing for the long-term survivability of the organization. Indeed, a business with unsatisfied customers is unlikely to survive, so is an organization with badly organized internal processes or an organization that is not able to cope with both technological and environmental changes in its operating environment. The BSC concept aims at finding a set of performance indicators in these four domains (Finance, Customer, Processes, and Innovation). As optimization in every separate domain inevitably conflicts with one or more of the others a good balance has to be found. The BSC methodology has a tremendous potential for business benefit. Therefore, organizations should not consider a balanced scorecard as just a performance measurement tool. They should consider it as a method to align the organization and its processes with the strategic objectives.

According to Gartner, the Balanced Scorecard tools available on the market today can be subdivided into four categories:

- Stand-alone tools;
- OLAP-based tools;
- Templates;
- Enterprise Management Suites.

The *Stand-alone tools* have been developed with the purpose to support the scorecard functionalities. Data are usually stored in a file structure or in a simple relational database. This is not a problem, because the number of performance indicators is small. The advantage of these tools is that they are easy to implement, but they are difficult to integrate with other data sources.

The *OLAP-based tools* are built on top of an existing OLAP tool. A strong point is of course the underlying multidimensional database with drill-down capability. A weakness can be that the focus is often put on the visualization of the performance indicators, without support for the analysis of the processes.

Template tools are not complete applications but off-the-shelf modules that allow the IT department to build a BSC application more rapidly. These modules typically provide functionality for the visualization of the performance indicators such as executive dashboards, traffic lights, and cause-effect diagrams. Using these tools to build an application requires an important effort of the IT department.

An *Enterprise Management Suite (EMS)* is composed of a set of tools that together support the management of the enterprise. Apart from the BSC component they contain tools for planning, budgeting, forecasting, and ABC. These tools offer an integrated image of the organization but not every organization has the need for the implementation of all components. If not all modules are built; the advantage of integration is lost by the same occasion.

As a conclusion it can be said that every category has its advantages and inconveniences, so for the selection of a tool it is important to know the real needs of the organization.

Data mining

"We are drowning in information, but are starved of knowledge."

(John Naisbett, Megatrends)

"Ten crates of data and one little envelope of information. Sign here."

Databases today can range in size into the terabytes - more than 1,000,000,000,000 bytes of data. Within these masses of data lies hidden information of strategic importance. But when there are so many trees, how to see the wood? A possible answer is *Data Mining*; this technology finds patterns and relationships in data by using sophisticated techniques to build models - abstract representations of reality. A good model is a useful guide to understanding your business and making decisions [27][28][29][33].

The definition of the Gartner Group (1995) is:

"Data Mining is the process of discovering meaningful new correlations, patterns, and trends by sifting through large amounts of data stored in repository, using pattern recognition technologies, and statistical and mathematical techniques."

The most common types of problems to which data mining is applied today are classification and regression.

Classification, as the name implies, predicts class membership. For example, a model predicts that a potential customer will respond to an offer. With classification the predicted output (the class) is categorical. A categorical variable has only a few possible values, such as "Yes" or "No," or "Low," "Middle," or "High."

Regression predicts a value. For example, a model predicts that a customer's profitability will be $500. Regression is used in cases where the predicted output can take on an unlimited number of (or many) possible values.

Data miners use classification and regression to predict customer behavior, to signal potentially fraudulent transactions, to predict store profitability, and to identify candidates for medical procedures, to name just a few of many applications. A common characteristic of these applications is that they have a high payoff. Data mining can increase revenue, prevent theft, save lives, and help make better decisions.

Various data mining techniques are available and these techniques use several algorithms. While these techniques will produce different models, each generates a model based on historical data. All these techniques can generate *predictive models*. Some also provide *descriptive models*, information that provides insight or further understanding of relationships in the data, independent of the predictive nature of the model. This information could be of the form "income is the most important factor in determining whether someone is a good credit risk." Such descriptive information can be presented in text form or through a visualization tool such as a decision tree graphic or sensitivity analysis.

The world of data mining is polarized between those who believe data mining tools should be sophisticated weapons for statisticians, and those who believe general business managers have to be able to use them. While it's not difficult to find data mining tools that business users of some intelligence can use, the most powerful data mining tools remain beyond the understanding of typical query tool users, since they require significant mathematical background and statistical training. Consequently, an organization that is big enough to afford a data mining facility should provide itself with a team of qualified experts with a good scientific background and a thorough understanding of the business. This team of experts should report directly to the Business Managers who can use their input to make better decisions.

Web Farming

All the techniques that have been described so far are *introspective*: they are mainly based on information that finds its origin somewhere inside the own organization. But there is a whole new source of information out there: the Web. As a consequence, a new technique of discovering information that is useful for the organization has been developed; it is called *Web Farming*.

Web Farming is the systematic discovery and acquisition of business-relevant Web content as input to your data warehouse.

The objectives of Web farming are:

- *Discover* Web content that is highly relevant to the business;
- *Acquire and validate* the content within a historical context;

- Structure the content into a form compatible with the organization's data warehouse;
- *Disseminate* the content to the proper people within the organization;
- *Manage* all the above as part of the production operations of an IT department.

Characteristics of Strategic Information Systems

Strategic Information Systems are the preferred toys of the Top Managers. They provide the information to think ahead and make strategic decisions about the organization.

This type of Information System will typically be found in big or rich organizations.

Benefits of Strategic Information Systems

The introduction of these Information Systems is a time consuming and costly process. However, the return on investment can be tremendous.

Best Practices

Also read the small print

Are there besides lawyers, other people that read the legal conditions regarding the standard software products? Nevertheless, these legal conditions can have serious consequences; take for instance the following statement from IBM found in the license agreement for one of their products:

"NOTE: The developer license agreement in the DB2 Universal Developer Edition gives you the right to develop, but not to deploy applications in a production environment using the products in the box. Please read the developer license for exact terms. When you are ready to deploy your application, you must purchase a full-use license for the products that you used to build your application. To purchase full-use license, go online at ShopIBM or please contact your local sales office."

In clear, this means that you are not allowed to deploy or sell the results of your work, without first paying a fee to the owner of the tools you used to develop them. How many managers, project leaders or developers are aware of this? The message is: be aware of the terms and conditions before you plan to use a tool, or it can cost you much more than expected.

Apply a layered approach where possible

The layered approach that has been used throughout this chapter is a good way of looking at Information Systems. The layers should be as independent as possible, so do not embed Word processors or email functionalities in your Information Systems but make them call for the services of the lower layers. Make sure that the way these services are called is done in a known and standard way so that, whenever some part is replaced by a newer version there will be minimal compatibility problems.

Beware of biased advice

There are many sources of advice available; they all have their own bias:

- Hardware vendors can promote products that only run on their platforms;
- Software vendors will try to lock you in with proprietary products;
- Service companies favor products for which they provide implementation services;
- The press only writes about well-marketed products;
- Industry analysts tend to have likes and dislikes;
- End-users and IT professionals try to stick to what they know.

The important thing is to be aware of these biases and to take them into account when you form your own opinion.

Build loosely coupled systems

The layered approach handles hierarchical relations between Information Systems, but there are also relations between Information Systems of the same level. These Information Systems should be highly independent of each other, rather than parts of a big super system. In such an environment Information Systems can be quickly adapted to fit the changing business, without bringing the entire organization to a halt. In the same context it is highly recommended that the logical design of applications and databases be partitioned, so that changes in one application or database will not affect the other applications or databases.

If application integration is done badly it can waste time and money. If it is performed via "hard coded" connectors, those connectors will have to be modified or rebuilt each time one application is enhanced or modified. Today's technology offers better application integration solutions (e.g., XML and web services) which can be programmed once and do not require rebuilding when applications change; moreover, these new application integration techniques can be created more quickly and at lower cost than custom connectors because they do not require specialized expertise in each application.

Build, buy or borrow?

An element to be considered when deciding to automate a Business Process is how it will be done: doing everything with your own staff (Build), try to find an off-the-shelf product (Buy) or outsource the Process (Borrow).

Building your own IT systems can look attractive, because you have perfect control over the end product but this option should only be considered if the process that has to be automated is specific for your organization and if it is part of the core business. In other cases it will usually turn out that others have already solved your problem and even if they did not there can be an opportunity to set up collaboration to come to a shared development effort.

Buying is usually a good option when the Business Process (or group of) is common to many organizations. The danger of buying a software solution is the dependency on the supplier. You, as a client, are dependent and vulnerable, so you cannot afford to select products without any kind of guarantee that they will be supported in the future.

Borrowing can be another interesting option. This can be the (tactical) outsourcing of a Business Process and everything that goes with it (infrastructure, staffing…) or just outsourcing of an application (Web hosting, Mail service, Application Service Provider…).

Choose for standards

Standards can be "de jure" or "de facto."

Do not try to find a "better" product based on technical arguments. Compatibility and interoperability are more important than technical features.

Do not reinvent the wheel

Others have already solved many automation problems; there are excellent commercial products on the market, the Internet is stuffed with freeware, shareware, and Open Source Software or maybe another department of your own organization has already done a development.

Therefore you should always look around you before developing a new Information System of your own; even if the available products are not exactly what you're looking for they could be adapted to fit your needs and you will find interesting ideas that could be applied in your own system should you decide to go for a development after all.

Using or applying existing solutions will improve the availability by providing a quicker answer to the business question and by reducing down time for maintenance, as the products are more mature.

Educate the users

IT can be a blessing for an organization, provided it is used properly. This has to be explained to the end-users either through formal training, information sessions, pamphlets, intranet information pages or a combination of all these. Typically, general guidelines will be established for ubiquitous systems such as personal productivity tools and groupware while more targeted and formal sessions will be organized for the higher-layer systems. The helpdesk can have an important role to play in the education of the users. Also the advanced users can play the role of ambassador of IT towards the rest of the organization.

Integrate the Business Processes

A lack of integration between processes means replication of functionality, double work, unnecessary expenses, and loss of business time and, finally, loss of revenue. Integration means that the Information Systems – which support these processes – are not considered as independent blocks but as a part of a whole, interacting in an organized way. At a technical level, there are mainly three reasons for integrating applications:

- *Data Consistency integration* - Several applications use the same information and have to be synchronized;
- *Multistep Process integration* - A Business Process is partly realized in different Information Systems, so these must communicate their input/output to avoid multiple data entry. Workflow is an example of the multistep process way of integration;
- *Composite applications* - New applications (e.g., Web applications) need to use data and logic owned by other applications.

Know the real needs of the users

For Information Systems *availability* means that they can be used maximally, so minimal downtime due to bad design, bugs or maintenance, and a short development cycle. Some examples of poor availability due to bad design are:

- A travel agent wants to find an arrangement that matches the requirements of his customer but cannot do so as the reservation system does not allow him to do a search based on criteria such as period, region and hotel type. He has to go over all the possible combinations of dates, places, and hotels;
- A customer wants to have a book sent to his home address and the invoice to his professional address, but the order intake system does not make a distinction between these two addresses;
- On a Friday evening, the financial manager of a subsidiary of a multinational organization has to send a report to the head office that is located in a different time zone where the operations have not started yet;
- In a hotel, a customer wants his consumptions from the mini bar to appear on a different invoice than the one he has to hand in to his employer to get his expenses reimbursed; the billing system does not allow for two invoices for the same room number on the same date;
- In a Human Resources Management system a new employee has to be created to give him access to the network, however, certain fields are mandatory and the necessary proofs have not yet been produced. Provisional information has to be entered and a track record has to be kept manually.

The consequences of these types of unavailability are:

- *Work overload* – to obtain the desired result the work has to redone in another way or later, tracking and rescheduling are necessary;
- *Parallel procedures* – a manual tracking system has to be put in place, the work is done twice: once on paper and once in the IT system;
- *Workarounds* – certain operations are avoided or executed differently, leading to other results;
- *Unhappy customers* – they have it difficult to accept the delays, the double work and the errors and run away to another supplier;
- *Impossible to satisfy the customers* – the IT system does not allow the same possibilities as the manual procedures, customers are lost.

Clearly, all this has to be avoided by a good requirements analysis - to know the needs of the users - is of the highest importance.

Make agility a primary goal

As a general rule, the systems should fit to the processes, not the other way around. This is particularly true for higher-layer systems, as their impact on the business is important.

Ask the manager of a failed IT project what his primary design goals were and he will give you a list that always contains the same elements. The system had to be client-server, it had to fit on the existing hardware and network infrastructure, and it had to deliver data to everybody, everywhere at any time. The user interface of course had to be graphic and intuitive and the response times better than before. Furthermore, the system had to be there by the next day and the project had a limited budget. All these requirements are of course difficult to combine.

During the 1970s and 1980s organizations did not change that fast. Today, Business Processes are constantly being re-invented. As a consequence, *agility* has to be the primary goal, the other requirements such as these listed before, have to come second.

Rationalize the application portfolio

A permanent worry of the IT manager should be the rationalization (read simplification) of his application portfolio. This can be done by the creation of common application platforms, killing discretionary projects and outsourcing legacy systems.

Online Resources

ABC - www.betterManagement.com/abcmauthority
Balanced Scorecards - http://www.balancedscorecard.com
Balanced Scorecards – http://www.balancedscorecard.org
BPML - http://www.bpmi.org
Cascading Stylesheets - http://www.w3.org/Style
Content Management – http://www.webdav.org
Content Management (open source) - http://www.zope.org
Desktop Publishing - http://desktoppublishing.com
Datawarehousing - http://datawarehouse.ittoolbox.com
Datawarehousing - http://www.compinfo-centre.com
Datawarehousing - http://www.data-warehouse.com
Datawarehousing - http://www.dmreview.com
Datawarehousing - http://www.dwinfocentre.org
Datawarehousing - http://dssresources.com
Datawarehousing - http://www.intelligententerprise.com
Document Management - http://www.aiim.org
DOI – http://www.crossref.org
DOI – http://www.doi.org
DOI – http://www.handle.net
DOI – http://www.indecs.org
EDI - http://www.x12.org/x12org/index.cfm
EDI - http://www.unece.org/trade/untdid/
Graphics - www.elementkjournals.com/tma/9508/tma89501.htm
ICalendar - http://www.imc.org/pdi/
Metrics – http://www.cio.com/metrics
Personal productivity tools (open source) – http://www.openoffice.org
Protocols - http://www.ietf.org/rfc.html
RTF - http://msdn.microsoft.com/library/specs/rtfspec.htm
Semantic Web – http://www.semanticweb.org
Site hosting service - http://www.virtualdomains.net
SOAP - http://www.w3.org/TR/SOAP/
Spreadsheets - http://dssresources.com/history/sshistory.html
Spreadsheets - http://www.bricklin.com/visicalc.htm
URL - http://www.w3.org/pub/WWW/Addressing/Addressing.html
UDDI – http://www.uddi.org
Videoconferencing - http://netconference.about.com
Voice-data integration - http://www.w3c.org/voice
Web services – http://www.ws-i.org
Web standards - http://www.w3c.org
Workflow systems - http://www.wfmc.org
Workflow systems- http://www.waria.com

Webfarming - http://www.Webfarming.com
Web Services - http://www-106.ibm.com/developerworks/webservices/
Web Services - http://www.cbdiforum.com
XML - http://www.xml.com
XML - http://www.w3.org/pub/WWW/XML
XML/EDI – http://www.xedi.org

Further Reading

[25] Ackoff, R. L., *From Data to Wisdom*, Journal of Applies Systems Analysis, Volume 16, 1989.

[26] Anahory S. and Murray D., *Data Warehousing in the Real World.* Addison-Wesley Publishing Company, 1997.

[27] Berry M. and Linoff G., *Data Mining Techniques*, John Wiley & Sons, 1997.

[28] Berson A. and Smith S.J., *Data Warehousing, Data Mining, and OLAP*, McGraw-Hill, 1997.

[29] Cabena P., *Discovering. Data Mining; from Concept to Implementation*, Prentice-Hall, 1998.

[30] Davis G., *Management Information Systems: Conceptual Foundations, Structure, and Development.* McGraw-Hill, 1974.

[31] Devlin B.A., *Data warehouse; from Architecture to Implementation*, Addison-Wesley Publishing Company, 1997.

[32] Gill H.J. and Rao P., *The Official Guide to Data Warehousing*, CQue, 1996.

[33] Groth R., *Data Mining; a Hands-on Approach for Business Professionals*, Prentice-Hall, 1998.

[34] Hammergren T., *Data Warehousing; Building the Corporate Knowledgebase*, International Thomson Computer Press, 1996.

[35] Inmon W.H., *Using the Data Warehouse*, John Wiley & Sons, 1994.

[36] Inmon W.H., *Building the Data Warehouse*, John Wiley & Sons, 1996.

[37] Inmon W.H., Welch J.D., and Glassey K.L., *Managing the Data Warehouse*, John Wiley & Sons, 1997.

[38] Inmon W.H., Terdeman R.H., and Imhoff C., *Exploration Warehousing*, John Wiley & Sons, 2000.

[39] Inmon W.H. et al., *Data Warehouse Performance*, John Wiley & Sons, 1999.

[40] Kimball, R. *The Data Warehouse Toolkit*, John Wiley & Sons, 1996.

[41] Kimball R. *The Data Warehouse Lifecycle Toolkit*, John Wiley & Sons, 1998.

[42] Leventhal M., Lewis D. and Fuchs M., *Designing XML Internet Applications.* Prentice Hall, 1998.

[43] Light R., *Presenting XML*. Sams.Net, 1997.

[44] Mattison R., *Data Warehousing. Strategies, Technologies and Techniques*, McGraw-Hill, 1996.

[45] Morse S. and Isaac D., *Parallel Systems in the Data Warehouse*, Prentice Hall, 1998.

[46] Ness, Joseph A., Cucuzza, Thomas G., *Tapping the Full Potential of ABC*, Harvard Business Review, July-August 1995.

[47] O'Guin, Michael C., *The Complete Guide to Activity Based Costing*, Englewood Cliffs, NJ, Prentice Hall, 1991.

[48] Poe V., *Building a Data warehouse for Decision Support*, Prentice Hall, 1996.

[49] Shaffer, S.L. & Simon, *Transitioning to Open Systems: Concepts, Methods & Architecture*. A.R. Morgan Kaufmann, 1996.

[50] Thomsen E., *OLAP Solutions*, John Wiley & Sons, 1997.

[51] Yeager, N.J & McGrath R.E., *Web Server Technology: The Advanced Guide for World Wide Web Information Provider.* Morgan Kaufmann, 1996.

Human Resources

"The soft stuff is always harder than the hard stuff."

(Roger Enrico, Vice Chairman Pepsico)

Introduction

It can sound as a commonplace, but the *Human Resources (HR)* are the second most important assets of an organization (after its customers). Without the knowledge, the skills, and the right attitude of its employees no organization can survive in the long run. Consequently, in any organization, small or big, commercial or non-profit, private or public, an explicit and prevailing Human Resources Policy must exist. In larger organizations this policy will be defined and enforced by a Human Resources Department, a component with a growing importance in modern organizations, therefore to be regarded as a key partner of the IT department.

From a management perspective, the Human Resources are one of four types of assets that are available to obtain the corporate goals (the others being Infrastructure, Information Systems, and Finance). Human Resources, however, are more difficult to manage than the others as all individuals are unique and have their own free will. Furthermore, these resources are not available in unlimited quantities and there are a lot of legal aspects to be considered.

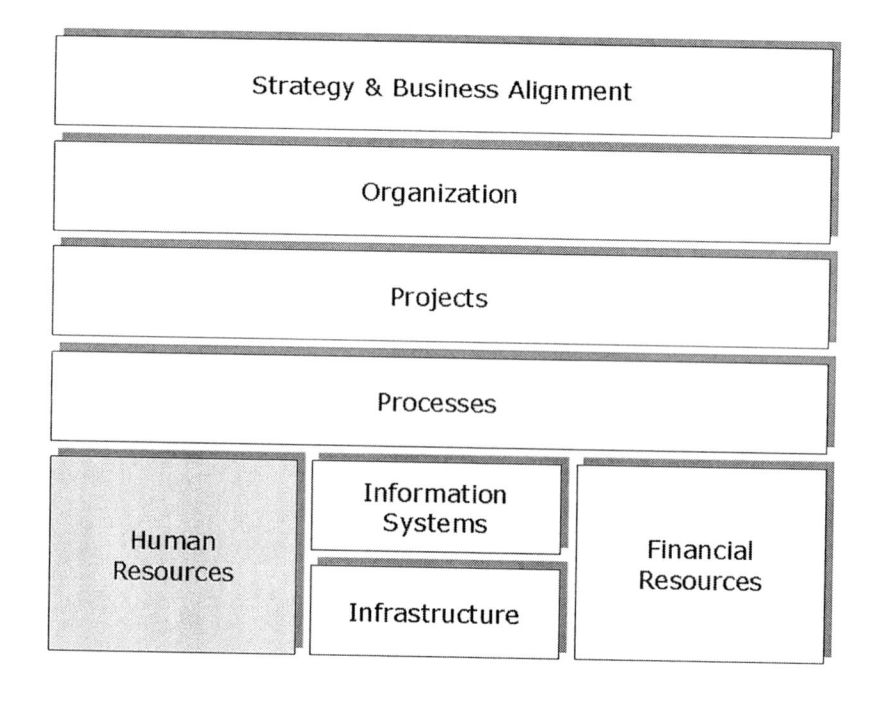

Fig. 4.1 – *Position of Human Resources in the IT stack*

Although this work is intended for IT managers, and therefore not a reference on Human Resources Management, the soft resources or an organization are so important that the manager of the IT department must at least have some basic knowledge on these matters.

Getting the Best Employees

Specifying Jobs and Roles

A *task* is a unit of work, that is, a set of activities needed to produce some result.

A *job* is a collection of tasks and responsibilities that an employee is responsible to conduct. Jobs have titles.

A *role* is the set of responsibilities or expected results associated with a job; a job usually includes several roles.

A *career* is something that someone wants to pursue for the rest of his or her life.

Complex positions in the organization can include many tasks, which are sometimes called *functions*.

Job analysis is the most basic activity in HRM. Accurate information on all jobs is necessary to direct and control the operations of an organization. *Job descriptions* are the most visible output from *job analysis*; they are used in selection, training, performance appraisal, and compensation.

Job descriptions are lists of the general tasks, or functions, and responsibilities of a position. Typically, they also include to whom the position reports, specifications such as the qualifications needed by the person in the job, salary range for the position, etc. It is important to make a job description practical by keeping it dynamic, functional and current. A well-written, practical job description will help you avoid hearing a refusal to carry out a relevant assignment because "it isn't in my job description." The Internet is full of sites that can provide you with job descriptions. Don't make the mistake of simply copying these and using them for your applicants but customize them for your specific position. The result will be better because the focus will be greater. Many jobs are subject to change, due either to personal growth, organizational development, and the evolution of technology. A poor job description will keep your employees from trying anything new and learning how to perform their job more productively. *Flexible job descriptions,* on the contrary, will help them to grow within their positions and learn how to make larger contributions to your organization.

Other commonly used job analysis terms include:

- *Knowledge* - information applied directly to the performance of a duty;
- *Skill* - a present, observable competence to perform a learned activity;
- *Ability* - a competence to perform an observable behavior or a behavior that results in an observable product.

Recruitment

The need to hire an employee arises from various events such as voluntary or involuntary terminations, increased workload or restructuring of a department.

Recruitment is the first step in the hiring process. A successful recruitment program will ensure a good pool of qualified candidates to choose from. This will increase the chances of selecting an individual with the skills, knowledge, and abilities to become a successful employee. The quality, not quantity, of applicants should be the focus of the recruiting program.

"Well, you certainly have a lot of experience in tech support."

It is important to maintain accurate records of the requirements for the open position (i.e., a current job description), recruitment methods used, applications received, candidates interviewed, candidate selected and reason for selection. Another important element of the recruitment process is *uniformity*, to minimize the risk for claims of discrimination or other legal problems. Therefore, a clearly written and widely communicated recruitment policy should be developed.

Following are some of the most commonly used recruitment methods and some of the advantages and disadvantages of each.

Internal Job Posting

Internal job-posting programs can serve a variety of HRM objectives. It can help to minimize employee complaints of unfair treatment, unlawful discrimination, and favoritism. It also allows for the identification of potential problems: if employees from a particular department are constantly applying for the posted positions, it can be a sign that the department's working conditions, job requirements or supervisory staff can be a problem.

Employee Referral Program

Employee referral programs are another effective and cost efficient way to attract qualified candidates. Typically, this type of program gives employees who refer candidates for employment a financial reward if the candidate is hired and remains employed for a certain period of time (e.g., six months).

Advertising

Classified advertisings in the newspaper or professional magazines are yet another means of filling open positions. An effective ad outlines the qualifications for the position and job duties, which will attract qualified candidates.

Online Recruitment

In recent years, there has been an explosive growth in the number of *online recruiting venues* for employers. These include corporate web sites, industry-related web sites, newsgroups, and job and resume sites.

Job Search Agents are automated programs or services that can be set up to search databases and notify the user when listings matching his requirements are found.

Meta-Search Tools are software programs that give the capability to search more than one online site at a time, pulling the results together into a single list for the user to review.

Employment Agencies

Employment agencies are typically used by employers to help in the recruitment of qualified candidates and are paid a fee for their services if they refer the candidate who is ultimately hired. The government employment services and unemployment offices form a special category; these can be a good source of recruitment for employers and can be a cost effective method of attracting candidates. These agencies provide screening and testing of prospective job candidates at no fee to the employer.

Executive Search (headhunting)

Executive Search is a specialized branch of management consulting in which outside professionals are authorized by organizations to identify, attract, and refer qualified candidates for important executive, managerial and technical positions. This usually confidential process involves research, search, and evaluation based on clear understanding of position and person specifications.

Educational Institutions

High schools or – in Europe, secondary schools - are excellent sources of clerical employees. Vocational schools train students on a variety of skills, such as secretarial, electronics, mechanics, data entry, computers, and others which can be applied in the workplace. Universities are excellent sources for entry-level professional, administrative, and sales employees.

The Selection Interview

Whatever the recruitment mechanism that has been used to identify a possible new employee, there will be a first contact between the employer and the candidate under the form of a selection interview.

The interviewer's first concern should be to make the interviewee feel at ease. It should be explained clearly what the purpose of the meeting is and that it would be possible to ask questions about the job and the organization. Make sure there is a relaxed and friendly atmosphere.

The interview room should be protected from any interruptions. Phone calls should be diverted and the possibility of visitors interrupting the interview should be eliminated. The physical conditions should be as unobtrusive as possible. Reduce the visible symbols of status difference, for example by letting the applicant have the same chair like yours.

All good interviews are prepared by setting out the *objectives*. For a selection interview these are to verify that the candidate is suitable, create goodwill for the organization, and explain the job. In particular, it must be checked to which extent the applicant has the qualities and skills needed for the job. A study of the application form will help you draw up the main questions you must ask. Writing down these questions will increase your confidence and ensures that you cover all the areas you intend to cover.

During the interview itself, the following points have to be watched for:

Manner and Appearance – Be aware of your personal bias. It is quite common to find prejudices, which vary from people's names to unfounded notions about a firm handshake, a high forehead or direct eye contact. It is impossible to get rid of your prejudices completely, but at least be aware of them.

Intelligence – Intelligence may be indicated by achievements at work or at school. Private interest can also be helpful, particularly for young candidates who have no previous work experience. Breath of interest is not closely associated with intelligence, but depth of interest is.

Sociability – It is important to get an idea of the applicant's ability to get on with others. Is he ma member of any clubs or social groups? During the interview traits of stubbornness or arrogance may be spotted. If a person heavily criticizes the last company he worked for, it is not unreasonable to assume that he may continue to behave this way when he comes to work for you.

Skills and Traits – When you are looking for a special skill, experience or personal qualities you must seek evidence that the applicant has shown that he used this faculty in the past. However, if you are looking for a standard skill you will look at the candidate's education and training, the examinations he has passed and the levels of skill his previous jobs required. Past performance may provide the only reliable evidence on which to predict the future. For example, if most of his previous employments have been short-lived and the stated reason is an inability to get on with his superiors then it would be reasonable to assume that all his superiors could not have been at fault.

The relative importance of the above points will depend on what exactly you are looking for. When selecting a project manager you will attach more importance to the person's sociability than you would for a programmer, whose technical skills will be more relevant.

It is important to make frequent use of *open questions*, starting with "what", "where", "why", "when", and "how". Closed questions that can be answered with "yes" or "no" will bring you little information, as will suggestive questions because they tell the interviewee the type of answer you want.

When you have finished asking questions, ask the applicant if there are any questions he would like to ask. When you have answered his questions you should close the interview by telling the person when he can expect to hear from you.

Once you have finished the interview and got a feeling about the person it usually helps to get a second opinion; this can be done by checking out the person's references and having a talk with one or some of his previous employers. You must of course make sure that, by doing so you will not embarrass the person and ask for his permission to do so during the interview. It is my experience that you get a lot of information out of this, information that would be impossible to collect otherwise.

Outsourcing

Another way to complete the work force of an organization is to make temporarily use of the resources of other organizations. This is known as *Outsourcing*.

In the domain of IT, outsourcing is used for conducting projects, to fill skill gaps, for work force reinforcement and for services.

There are three types of outsourcing: global (or strategic), partial (or tactical), and contracted (or targeted). Each of these has different strategic, management, and economic issues.

"We've outsourced all our repair work to Taiwan. You'll have to take your car there now."

Global or Strategic Outsourcing - This type of outsourcing involves the complete transfer of an entire function. For IT this could involve the development team, the support people, system administrators, network people, and the complete IT infrastructure. These arrangements typically involve previously internal or permanent organization staff being transferred to the outsourcing organization.

Partial or Tactical Outsourcing - Tactical Outsourcing involves major sub-functions or projects being outsourced. The Tactical outsourcing of the operation and maintenance of computer equipment and infrastructure is an example; the outsourcing of major projects is another. Typically, Tactical Outsourcing does not involve staff transferring to an outsourcing organization.

Contracting or Targeted Outsourcing - This is the most common form of outsourcing. It involves the contracting out of parts of projects or sub-functions. This form of outsourcing does not raise the major issues associated with Strategic or Tactical outsourcing. The word *body shopping* emerged in the early 1980s as a pejorative term to describe the activity of providing inexpensive labour on an hourly basis for low value-added programming services at customer sites. This type of contracting has now evolved into a more mature activity where specialized companies send out staff for project work or to fill temporary shortages in their client's own staff. Another form of Targeted Outsourcing is known as *Offshore Development*. These services include the development of software in a distributed model, with some phases of the project being conducted offshore. For instance, the requirements analysis is conducted at the client's location. Successive phases of the project, like design, development, and unit and system testing are performed at an offshore location. Finally the tested product is brought back on site to the client for Acceptance testing.

Pros and cons of Outsourcing

Many observers see *Outsourcing* as a pillar of modern management. It is, however, one of the most delicate management topics to discuss. Often, outsourcing has become a major strategic concern but unfortunately, many organizations have found that outsourcing, like so many other management trends, can be a strategic and financial disaster.

In many organizations, the word "Outsourcing" is not an economic or management concept but an emotional and political issue. One should, however, try to weigh pros and cons in this discussion.

Following are typical arguments used to support the case of outsourcing:

- *Lower costs* – An outsourcing organization can spread both the costs of support and the spare capacity resulting in lower costs for all clients;
- *Risk sharing or reduction* - Exporting high-risk projects or processes can reduce risks, however, there will normally be additional charges or a cost-premium for assuming the risk;
- *Economy of scale* - The outsourcing company has existing infrastructure, expertise and capacity that can be offered to the client. This is a compelling argument for smaller organizations that cannot afford to maintain services, equipment and expertise in-house;
- *Access to greater skill pool and intellectual capital* - Large multi-national outsourcing organizations can have access to international experts, knowledge repositories and infrastructures that are typically not available to most organizations. This is a compelling justification provided that the outsource contract stipulates which experts are required;
- *Greater focus* - By eliminating non-essential activities, the organization can use outsourcing to either release key people to concentrate on core functions. Strangely enough, the size, cost and contractual issues of the outsourcing effort often results in Senior Management giving more focus to the areas being outsourced than they were when the function was undertaken in-house;
- *More Control* - This is an often-used justification for outsourcing. IT people sometimes abuse their expert power to dominate their business and external clients. Consequently, many business people think that they have lost control of the IT strategy and technology. By outsourcing their IT, they expect to regain control;

- *More Professionalism* - Similar to the control justification, there is an expectation that the outsourcing organization will have more professional development and management standards and procedures than internal IT groups.
- *Ideological Purity* - In an era of economic rationalism there are elements of ideological purity in the concept of outsourcing, especially in the public sector. The belief in reducing the size, cost and impact of government has supported the move to major outsourcing of many government functions.

Those who are opposed to outsourcing also have several equally valid arguments:

- *Higher costs* - Especially in the outsourcing of projects the actual costs can be higher than when the work is done by the internal staff. This can be caused by several factors. A significant reason is that internal IT project groups often generate 30 - 50% additional effort without additional costs, on the contrary, there are few outsourcing companies that would tolerate those levels of unpaid and uncharged work. In addition, there is a clear profit motive from the outsourcing company's perspective: the need for profit margins of, at least 20 - 30%, must lead to increased costs;
- *Higher Risks* - The key risk areas associated with IT outsourcing are loss of control of major projects, potential financial litigation and loss of intellectual capital. Clearly, it is in the interest of both parties in a failed outsourcing arrangement for the failure not to become public, this is why so few cases are documented as opposed to the success stories that will be used extensively by the outsourcing organizations to make their own publicity;
- *Poor Service* - The smaller and less high profile the outsourcing client, the larger the incentive for the outsourcing organization to downscale the attention that client receives. Given the size of most outsourcing organizations, the client can in fact receive a more bureaucratic and unresponsive service than he receives from his internal IT department;
- *Limited access to knowledge base* - The access to worldwide experts is often inhibited by the fact that outsourcing organizations are working more on strategic clients and projects. This leads them to use the contract as a vehicle of placing "B-team" and trainees. This is of course encouraged by poorly developed contracts, which do not stipulate the skill and experience levels required from the outsourcing organization;
- *Loss of intellectual capital* - There are two primary types of knowledge: explicit and tacit. Explicit knowledge is published and public while, tacit knowledge is in the heads of the experts. In the IT area, little knowledge has been made explicit. As a result, the loss of IT personnel associated with outsourcing leads to a loss of tacit intellectual capital and capability;
- *Loss of control over core activities* - By outsourcing the people and intellectual capital required for developing new products, services and systems, many organizations risk losing control of their future; they are outsourcing the future core of their business.

From this discussion it will be clear that outsourcing is a topic that has to be considered carefully. It is, in fact, a major topic in the strategy of an IT department and even of the organization as a whole.

Outsourcing contracts

The key to a successful IT outsourcing relationship is a *good contract*. This contract defines the expectations, rights and liability of both the outsourcer and the customer. Outsourcing contracts are often long lasting and of high value. Furthermore, outsourcing vendors and customers are not partners because their profit motives are not the same. It is therefore of high importance to get the contract right the first time. The following issues are typically part of such a contract.

Scope – The contract should describe in precise, verifiable, terms the scope, nature and types of all the services required along with the times when these services should be available and the level of performance.

Transfer of Assets – Typically, computer hardware, software licenses and leases for equipment or telecommunication circuits can need to be transferred to the outsourcing vendor. The way this is handled has to be described in the contract.

Transfer of Staff – A common feature of many outsourcing arrangements is the transfer of staff from the customer to the outsourcer. This can be a delicate operation for which the legal implications have to be examined carefully. On the other hand, new staff can be hired by the outsourcer to work on the contract and it seems natural that the customer wants to have a say in the selection process to ensure quality and suitability.

Pricing and Payment Terms – When, how and to whom payments should be made can be complicated issues. It is important to ensure that the price agreed covers all the services required. Since the cost of technology is decreasing constantly it is interesting to include a mechanism for periodic re-negotiation or price review.

Dispute Resolution – Proper mechanisms should be built in for dispute resolution through an independent third party.

Warranty and liability – To avoid costly lawsuits it is convenient to stipulate the compensation for any losses, costs and liabilities arising from the outsourcer's breach of the contract.

Termination – There should be an explicit agreement relative to the termination of the contract in cases where service levels are not met or when the vendor goes out of business.

Intellectual Property – There should be an agreement on the ownership of intellectual property rights such as copyright and patents arising from the outsourcing contract.

Security and Confidentiality – It is important to reach an agreement concerning what type and what level of information security will be provided. Since the outsourcer can have access to the customer's data, which can be commercially sensitive, it is important that confidentiality is respected

Getting the Best of Employees

Theories on Human Nature

It is impossible to have a discussion on Human Resources Management without having a look at the raw material: the people. People behave according to certain principles of *Human Nature*, the common qualities of all human beings. Therefore, to understand and motivate people it is important to know Human Nature. Many theories have been developed over the years; we will elaborate on a few in the following paragraphs.

Maslow's Hierarchy of Needs

Human Needs are an important part of Human Nature. Ethics, ideas, and behavior differ from country to country and group to group, but all people have similar needs. According to Abraham Maslow [60] the human needs are arranged in a hierarchical order. There are two major groups of human needs: Basic Needs and Meta Needs.

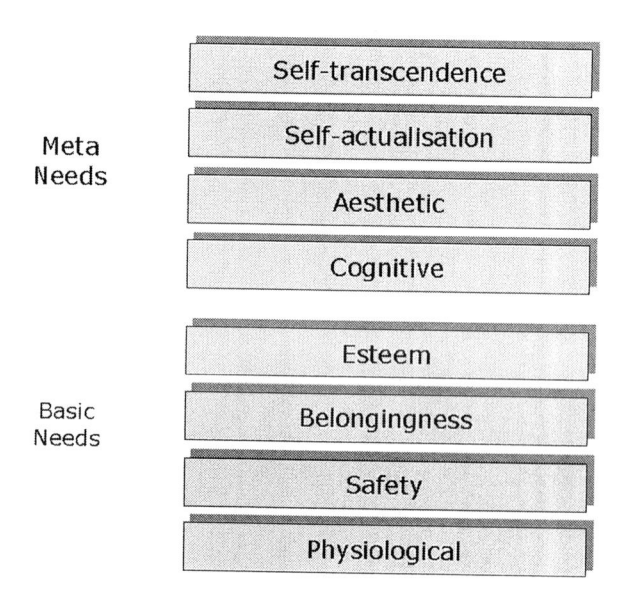

Meta Needs:
- Self-transcendence
- Self-actualisation
- Aesthetic
- Cognitive

Basic Needs:
- Esteem
- Belongingness
- Safety
- Physiological

Fig. 4.2 – *Maslow's Hierarchy of Needs*

A need higher in the hierarchy can only become a motivator as long as the needs below it have been satisfied. Unsatisfied lower needs come before unsatisfied higher needs and must be satisfied first.

Herzberg's Hygiene and Motivational Factors

Herzberg [57] developed a list of factors, which are based on Maslow's Hierarchy of Needs, but more closely related to work:

- Hygiene Factors or Dissatisifiers:
    - Working Conditions;
    - Corporate Policies;
    - Salary and Benefits;
    - Supervision;
    - Status;
    - Security;
    - Fellow workers;
    - Work-life Balance.
- Motivators or Satisfiers:
    - Recognition;
    - Achievement;
    - Advancement;
    - Growth;
    - Responsibility;
    - Job Challenge.

Hygiene factors must be present (without them there is dissatisfaction) before motivators stimulate an employee. Herzberg used the term *job enrichment* to describe the process of redesigning work to build in Motivators.

Theory X and Theory Y

Douglas McGregor [61] developed another view of humanity with his *Theory X and Theory Y*. These are two opposing perceptions about human behavior at work and in organizational life.

Theory X

- People have an inherent dislike for work and will avoid it whenever possible;
- People must be coerced, controlled, directed, or threatened with punishment to get them to achieve the organizational objectives;
- People prefer to be directed, do not want responsibility, and have little or no ambition;
- People seek security above all else.

Theory X is the view that traditional management has taken towards the work force.

Theory Y

- Work is as natural as play and rest;
- People will exercise self-direction if they are committed to the objectives;
- Commitment to objectives is a function of the rewards associated with their achievement;
- Creativity, ingenuity, and imagination are widely distributed among the population. People are capable of using these abilities to solve an organizational problem;
- People have potential.

Observe that Maslow, Herzberg and McGregor's theories all tie together. Indeed, Herzberg's theory is the application of Maslow on the work place and McGregor's theory X is based on workers caught in the lower levels, while theory Y is applicable to workers who are in the higher levels.

Expectancy Theory

In recent years, probably the most popular motivational theory has been the *Expectancy Theory*. Although there are several theories found with this general title, they all have their roots in Victor Vroom's work on motivation [64]. Vroom defines motivation as:

"A process governing choices ... among alternative forms of voluntary behavior."

Imagine an individual, occupying a role in an organization, faced with a set of alternative voluntary behaviors, all which have outcomes attached. The traditional view is that the choice reflects the strength of the individual's desire or avoidance of a specific outcome at a certain time. Vroom's theory suggests that behavior results from conscious choices among alternatives whose purpose it is to maximize pleasure and minimize pain. The key elements to this theory are called *Expectancy (E)*, *Instrumentality (I)*, and *Valence (V)*:

- *Expectancy (E)* refers to the strength of a person's belief about whether a particular job performance is attainable;
- *Instrumentality (I)* is a probability belief linking one outcome (a high level of performance, for example) to another outcome (a reward);
- The term *Valence (V)* refers to the level of satisfaction people expect to get from the outcome.

The resulting *Motivation (M)* is given by:

$$M = E * I * V$$

Motivating Employees

The aforementioned theories are of course useless if they cannot be put in practice in the day-to-day working environment. Following is a discussion based on Herzberg's Hygiene and Motivational Factors, whenever applicable reference will be made to the other theories.

For this work *motivation* is the inner force that drives individuals to accomplish personal and organizational goals. Motivated employees are more productive; they also have lower absenteeism and lower turnover, which leads to higher productivity of the organization as a whole.

Working conditions

The science that seeks to adapt work or working conditions to suit the worker is known as *Ergonomics*. Working Conditions are not something that only need to be considered when a workplace is built, or when a new process or piece of equipment is introduced. Workplace design and layout need ongoing attention for problems that become evident during work, and to handle changes in the type of work being done or the way in which it is done. The factors that need to be considered when assessing workplace design and layout include not only the physical layout of the workplace, but also lighting, temperature, and ventilation:

- Desks, benches, and chairs have to be suitable and adjustable for the people using them and for the tasks they are performing;
- Passages and exits should be kept clear at all times;
- Equipment with dangerous moving parts has to be properly guarded;
- Electric cords have to be kept clear of areas where people could trip over them and from areas where they could get wet;
- Suitable lifting and carrying devices have to be supplied;
- Well-designed storage areas and work areas can reduce the amount of bending, twisting and lifting needed by the workers to carry out their tasks;
- Lighting levels should be suitable for the tasks being performed. Lighting problems - such as flickering lights, glare, and a lack of natural light - can cause eyestrain and vision problems;

- Noisy equipment should be enclosed or located away from where people are working. Noisy equipment not only affects concentration, it can also cause permanent hearing loss;
- The workplace should be kept at a comfortable temperature. Badly designed air-conditioning can create draughts, cause discomfort and contribute to health problems;
- Chemical agents have to be stored and manipulated in well-ventilated rooms.

Some considerations concern the use of computers:

- Computer equipment should comply with the industry guidelines concerning ergonomics (TCO95 and TCO99);
- People should learn how to type and be familiar with keyboard layouts;
- Poorly placed computer screens - for example in a position that causes screen glare from reflected lights - can cause eyestrain;
- Keyboards that are not adjustable for height or placement and badly designed mice can add to the strain associated with keyboard use;
- Keyboard work should be alternated with other non-repetitive tasks. Regular breaks should be taken;
- Devices to help keyboard work, such as document holders, wrist rests, foot rests, and angle boards should be supplied if required.

The workplace is located in a broader environment: a building, a plant, an industrial area, and a city. The quality of this environment is also important for the quality of the working conditions. The following elements can play a role:

- Availability of facilities like coffee-corner, smokers corner, cafeteria and restaurant;
- Accessibility by car or public transportation, parking space;
- Neighborhood (city centre, industrial area...)

The employer can also provide facilities such as babysitting, fitness room, shopping service etc., which can be attractive for new employees and which contribute to the motivation of existing employees.

Policies and Administrative Practices

An organization's Policies and Administrative Practices can be a great source of frustration for employees if they are unclear or unnecessary or if not everyone is required to follow them. In order not to become a dissatisfier, Corporate Policies and Administrative Practices should comply with the following criteria:

- They should be clear, simple, and easy to understand for everyone;
- They should be well-known by and communicated to everyone;
- They should be fair and non-discriminating.

Salary and Benefits

The package of *Salary and Benefits* is an important motivation factor for an employee but it also represents a major cost factor for the employer. An organization has to balance this cost against what the employees perceive as its value, and that varies by employee. Of course, the most important aspect of a compensation plan for the employees is to keep them motivated to do the job the best they can.

Salary levels have to be measured against other employees in the organization, against other employees in other organizations in similar positions, and against performance. Salary ranges have to be determined for existing positions and adjusted periodically to compensate for economic factors (cost of living changes, inflation) and competitive pressures (industry demand for that type of employee, profit margins). Often, a salary for a new position has to be determined, or for someone promoted to new responsibilities. All this has to comply with government regulations regarding discrimination, contractor versus employee determinations, and other contractual obligations.

In a *Variable Pay Program* persons are paid fully or partly on individual or organizational performance. In this way, a part of the labor costs is turned into variable costs. Variable Pay programs are consistent with the Expectancy Theory: employees should perceive a strong relationship between performance and rewards [58]:

"Pay serves to motivate employees when it is closely tied to performance...people are most satisfied with their pay when they feel that it is based on performance."

(E.E. Lawler)

There are four widely used types:

- *Price-rate pay plans* – Workers are paid a fixed sum for each unit of production completed;
- *Bonuses* – Given to employees if a preset objective is met;
- *Profit sharing plans* - Compensation based on an established formula designed around the company's profitability;
- *Gain sharing* – Formula based group incentive plan.

Skill-based Pay sets pay levels on how many skills employees have or on how many jobs they can perform. The attractiveness of skill-based pay is the agility: staffing becomes easier and generalists help communication and downsizing. Skill-based pay is consistent with Maslow and Herzberg's theories (learning and growth as motivators) as well as with the Expectancy theory.

Employee Benefits typically refer to retirement plans, health insurance, life insurance, disability insurance, vacation, employee stock ownership plans, etc. Benefits play an increasingly important role for the employees and their families and affect an organization significantly. Designing a good benefit plan is a complex task; there are many issues to consider, including tax and legal aspects, funding, and finding the right partners. Employers must be aware of these issues and be able to make informed decisions when they select employee benefits. The following are some of the reasons why employers offer benefits to their employees:

- To attract and hold capable people;
- To keep up with the competition;
- To foster good morale;
- To provide opportunities for promotion as older workers retire.

A *Benefit Plan* usually includes the following elements:

- Health insurance;
- Disability insurance;
- Life insurance;
- A retirement plan;
- Leave;
- Bonuses, service awards, etc.

To accommodate today's many variations in family relationships, life-styles, and values, *Flexible Compensation* or *Cafeteria Plans* have emerged. Besides helping meet employee needs, cafeteria plans also help employers control overall benefit costs. Cafeteria plans offer employees a minimum level of basic benefits, and employees are able to choose from several levels of supplemental coverage or different benefit packages. All packages are of relatively equal value, but can be selected to help employees achieve personal goals or meet differing needs.

Supervision

Organizations are different from other forms of social arrangement because of the preoccupation with controlled performance; the scarcity of (human) resources leads to the need to control performance to ensure that it is good enough and to take corrective action if necessary. In this perspective the term *control* has a positive meaning, as it is necessary for predictability, order, reliability, and stability.

Objectives provide guidelines for performance. If they are set too high they are ignored, if they are too low they impede performance. Overly complex objectives can lead to an ineffective organization.

Management control or *supervision* is the process through which plans are created and objectives are achieved by setting objectives, measuring performance, comparing performance with objectives and selecting corrective actions and feedback. Establishing effective control processes is one main function of management. The role of supervisor is extremely difficult. It requires leadership skills and the ability to treat all employees in a fair way. Supervisors should use positive feedback whenever possible and punish only if there is no alternative.

Social control is a process by which compliance and conformity to predetermined standards are achieved through interpersonal and group interactions. People also have a psychological need for control as feedback on performance enables learning and motivates through recognition and most people want to know what is required and how they are evaluated.

However, if not applied properly, control can also be dysfunctional:

- If it is too rigid and bureaucratic; attention is too much focused on whatever criteria are chosen; the rules and procedures are strictly followed, regardless of whether these rules apply to or are effective in the particular circumstances;
- When inaccurate information is fed in the control process; employees want to look good, hide mistakes or perceive imposed standards as unfair;
- Controls can be resisted when they threaten need satisfaction.

Status

Material symbols such as ranks, titles, size of offices, type of furnishing, reserved parking spaces, and the like show to the employee who is important. In some organizations, like the military, this is pushed to the extreme; indeed from a military uniform it is immediately obvious what the rank and the achievements of the individual are. These powerful symbols are also necessary as military leaders can be required to ask for the ultimate form of motivation from their subordinates: give their life for a cause.

Security

Another Hygiene Factor or potential dissatisifier is *job security*. In different part of the world there are different perceptions about this topic: in the United States the labor market tends to be flexible and massive layoffs are common because of fluctuations in economy. In Europe, under pressure of trade unions and social security legislation, these movements are much more restricted and people have a bigger tendency to stick to their jobs. Traditionally, big corporations in Japan promised a life-long job and even a complete social environment to their employees. It is a fact that, under pressure of globalization and increased competition, the labor market is becoming more volatile. Over their lifetime, people change job and employer several times. The question is if this has to be encouraged: a high turnover inevitably leads to a lower productivity as people have to be retrained on every job switch and show less loyalty, thus lower motivation and lower performance.

Fellow Workers

Part of the satisfaction of being employed is the social contact it brings, so employees should be allowed a reasonable amount of time for socialization (e.g., over lunch, during breaks...). At the same time rudeness, inappropriate behavior, and offensive comments should be discouraged.

Work-Life Balance

It will undoubtedly remain an eternal question: do we work to live or live to work? Some people consider a job as a means to make money and a living; others think that their life would be pointless without their job and strongly identify with their position and employer. The fact is that this balance is different from individual to individual and varies with time and circumstances. It is accepted that people who are stuck in Theory X will consider work as a necessary evil while Theory Y employees find more pleasure and satisfaction in their professional life. On the other hand, young people with small children will probably make the balance swing more towards the personal life than older people without children.

Flextime is a scheme that lets the employee choose when he starts and finishes work, within certain limits agreed with his employer. For example, employer and employee could agree to:

- Start work between 7:30 am and 10:00 am (flextime)
- Guarantee to be there from 10:00 am until noon (core time);
- Take lunch break between noon and 2:00 pm (flexible lunch hour);
- Guarantee to be there from 2:00 pm to 4:00 pm (core time);
- Leave between 4:00 pm and 7:30 pm (flextime).

Most schemes allow a credit or debit margin. If an employee goes beyond his/her credit margin, into surplus, he can lose those extra hours; if he/she goes beyond the debit margin, into debt, he or she could be disciplined or lose pay. Credit hours can be turned into time off; depending on the scheme, this could be two half days a month or one full day, or days can be added to the holiday entitlement. Besides flextime a Human

Resources Policy can provide for a whole array of other work/life balance options like part-time work, job sharing and sabbaticals.

Recognition

Individuals at all levels of the organization want to be recognized for their achievements on the job. Their successes do not have to be monumental before they deserve recognition, but praise should be sincere. If employees do something well, their good work should be acknowledged immediately; publicly thank them, write them a note of praise or give them a bonus, if appropriate. *Employee recognition* can be a powerful motivator and can take numerous forms; they are often formalized in an *Employee Recognition Program* (e.g., "employee of the month"). The best programs use multiple sources and recognize both individual and group accomplishments. These programs are popular because of the low cost.

Achievement

One premise inherent in Herzberg's theory is that most individuals sincerely want to do a good job. Therefore people should be placed in positions that use their talents and are not set up for failure. Clear, achievable goals and standards for each position have to be set. Individuals should also receive regular, timely feedback on how they are doing and should feel they are being adequately challenged in their jobs. Do not overload individuals with challenges that are too difficult or impossible, as that can be paralyzing.

Management By Objectives (MBO) is a popular technique in which individual goals are set to motivate people; the emphasis is on converting overall organizational objectives into objectives for organizational units and individual employees. Objectives should be *Specific, Measurable, Acceptable, Realistic*, and *Timely* (*SMART*).

Advancement

Loyalty and performance should be rewarded with *advancement*. If there is not an open position to which to promote a valuable employee, consider giving him or her a new title that reflects the level of work he or she has achieved.

Growth

"An organization's ability to learn, and translate that learning into action rapidly, is the ultimate competitive advantage"

(Jack Welch, former chairman GE)

"Are you finished with the training policy yet? I need something to wedge under the corner of my desk to keep it level."

To be able to grow in their job, employees have to be trained and developed. There are a variety of reasons why training and development can be started. Training and development can be part of an overall professional development program or a part of succession planning in the context of a change in the organization. They can test the operation of a new performance management system or when a performance appraisal shows that improvement is needed. Training can also be needed simply to train employees about a specific topic.

The following are some typical topics that are covered by an employee training:

- *Computer skills* – Being able to work with computer has become necessary for conducting administrative and office tasks;
- *Safety* - Safety training is critical where working with heavy equipment, hazardous chemicals, repetitive activities, etc.
- *Quality initiatives* – Total Quality Management, Quality Circles, Benchmarking, etc., require training about concepts, guidelines, and standards;
- *Human relations* - The stress of today's workplace can introduce tension and conflicts. Training can help people to get along in the workplace;
- *Customer service* - Increased competition makes it critical that employees understand and meet the needs of customers.

Besides an increased motivation several other benefits can be expected from employee training and development:

- Increased efficiency in processes, resulting in financial gain;
- Innovation of strategies, methods, and products;
- Reduced employee turnover.

In the recent past there has been a lot to do about *E-learning* or *Internet-enabled learning*. The advantages of this method are multiple.

- *It overcomes distance and time barriers* - People can learn anywhere and on their own schedule;
- *It promotes collaboration* - Students can interact with each other or with experts conveniently over extended periods of time;
- *It leverages experts and instructors* - E-learning approaches allow instructors to teach more classes at a distance, and allow subject matter experts to respond to questions conveniently;
- *It reduces travel, facility, and distribution costs.*

Note that E-learning is not applicable for all subjects (interpersonal skills and high-level strategic skills are difficult to teach via this method) and that the initial cost of developing e-learning courses is higher than for classroom learning.

There are at least three good reasons why particular attention has to be paid to the *training and development of IT staff*:

- IT is a fast moving domain so knowledge is rapidly outdated;
- IT is a wide and complex domain, so you can never know enough;
- IT people want to maintain their value on the employment market.

These elements distinguish IT from most other disciplines and require a special training program, different from and complementary with the training program of the other staff. Normally, IT professionals have a good background, which they received during their formal studies at school or university. However, this is only a basis for the construction of their knowledge and skills they will need during their further career. The concept of *life-long learning* is, more than in other disciplines a fact of life for the IT professional. Every person who is serious about his job in IT will spend an important part of his time (at work or after hours) in learning new concepts or technology. It is important that the employer recognizes this and some special arrangements should be made to acknowledge this reality. Some examples are:

- Financial support for formal training outside the organization;
- Training leave;
- Allow for non-productive experimentation time in project plans;
- Reimbursement of books and other didactical materials;
- Elaboration of a library with technical books;
- Circulation of technical magazines (paid by the employer);
- Membership of interest groups, discussion forums, etc.

Besides these measures, of course, formal trainings can be organized around a number of topics.

- Tools and technology;
- Knowledge of the business and its processes;
- Team Building;
- Management techniques.

Usually, training of IT staff is project related. However, a more general employee development program has to be considered in an IT department worthy of this name. A special and permanent budget should be set aside for the training and the development of IT staff, if not the costs for the organization will be manifold because of loss of efficiency during project development, poorly motivated IT staff, and personnel turnover.

Responsibility

Employees will be more motivated to do their jobs well if they have the *ownership* of their work. This requires giving employees enough freedom and power to carry out their tasks so that they feel they "own" the result. As individuals mature in their jobs, provide opportunities for added responsibility. *Employee Involvement* is a participative process that is designed to encourage an increased commitment to the organization's success. It is more than just participation but also an increasing of the employee's autonomy and control to make them committed to be more productive and satisfied.

There are different ways to implement this:

- *Participative Management* – This is joint decision making between management and employees;
- *Representative Participation* – Workers are represented by a small group of employees who participate in work councils or as board representatives;
- *Quality circles* – Groups of eight to ten employees and supervisors who meet regularly for solving quality problems.

Teleworking

"Work is not necessarily going to take place in offices or factories. It's going to take place everywhere, anytime."

(Alvin Toffler)

A new way of working

New communications technologies are radically transforming the way we work and provide services together. Armed with cell phones, PDAs, notebook computers, and other technologies, today's work force is equipped to work anywhere.

Jack Nilles is commonly considered to be the father of *teleworking*. During the 1960's he began teleworking from Los Angeles to Washington DC while working as a consulting rocket scientist to the US Air Force Space program. Today, over 10% of the US work force does teleworking. While the private sector is leading the way in the number of people teleworking, public sector teleworking increases as well.

Teleworking can be defined as:

"A work arrangement in which employees work at any time or place that allows them to accomplish their work in an effective and efficient manner."

In other words, teleworking - also called *telecommuting* - is an arrangement that enables employees to work away from the traditional office. Teleworking has the potential for several benefits for Employer, Employee, and Society:

Employer	Employee	Society
Attract and retain skilled workers	Reduce commuting time	Reduce traffic congestion
Increase employee satisfaction	Reduce stress	Reduce air pollution
Increase employee productivity	Reduce job-related costs	Improve accommodation for disabled
Reduce absenteeism	Provide better work environment	
Reduce office space	Provide better Work-Life Balance	
Reduce overhead costs		

Table 4.1 – *Benefits of Teleworking*

Teleworking can be done in a variety of places: some work at *home-based offices* on the days that they are not reporting to their main office site, others prefer to work in *telecenters*, which can provide facilities such as videoconferencing, faxing, and helpdesk and a growing number of individuals have a virtual *office*.

Telecommuting should be *voluntary*. No employee should be forced to teleworking. If you have employees that you think would be good candidates for teleworking, discuss it with them. Determining which of your employees will make good telecommuters requires consideration of the individual's work responsibilities and habits and whether their home situation is favorable to teleworking.

Not everyone is suitable for telecommuting. If an employee is unsuitable, discuss any characteristics the employee could change, such as organization skills or the need for supervision and feedback.

Managing telecommuters is not much different from managing people on-site. It involves basic management skills that include setting goals, assessing progress, giving regular feedback, and managing by results. Close supervision is not necessarily good supervision. To manage from a distance, there must be objective standards of measurement to assess progress, give performance feedback, and set timetables.

Technological Considerations

To successfully telecommute, an employee must have access to the computing resources he needs to do his job. Today's technology provides a wide range of solutions; the key is to choose the right one.

Personal Workstations

If an employee already makes extensive use of a Personal Computer at the office, he/she has most of the equipment he/she needs to telecommute. Today's trend toward an open computing environment means that more and more vendors have designed their products for a heterogeneous environment. Most Personal Computers can run software that emulates a wide variety of other devices, even workstations. Software can turn a Macintosh into a PC, a PC or Macintosh into a variety of terminals, or a UNIX workstation into a PC or a MacIntosh. If information has to be stored on the home workstation, remember that it has to be backed up. For administrative work, thin client computing could be the answer.

Printers

Whether a printer is needed or not depends on how much has to be printed, what kind of information is printed, and what percentage of time the employee telecommutes. If somebody telecommutes one or two days a week, then he can probably manage without a printer. If he/she needs to print only occasional information, he/she can probably defer printing until the next time he/she is at the office. Printing at the office not only reduces the cost of the equipment needed to telecommute but also reduces the space needed for equipment.

Data Communications Link

The choice of communications link depends on what kind of information is accessed and how frequently it accessed. Technology has evolved to the point where one has a tremendous variety of choices in terms of link speed and cost. Start by thinking about the type of access (file transfer, terminal emulation, etc.), the volume of data transferred, how far home is from the office and how long the link will be needed each day. The access and the volume of data will determine how fast the link should be, while the distance from the office and hours will determine the most cost-effective technology.

Application Software

Once a decision has been made on the workstation, it has to be determined which application software will be used. If the workstation at home is the same as the one at the office then obviously the same application packages will be used. Many license agreements today recognize that people use the packages both at the office and at home and permit to treat the software as a book. In other words, it is permitted to install the software on both office and home workstations as long as there is no possibility that two people will use the software at the same time. Large companies often have *site licenses* for packages adopted as company standards. If the home workstation is different from the office workstation, the choice of software depends on whether you emulate some form of terminal or run application packages that support different platforms.

Work Force Planning

Planning techniques

As an organization grows or changes, its needs for Human Resources evolve. Therefore, an important aspect of Human Resources Management is to know at every moment what the needs of the organization are. The toolbox of the Human Resources Managers contains a variety of techniques to do so.

Administrative Databases – These databases contains all necessary data for the administration of the employees: identification, addresses, contracts, position, title, salary information, holidays, etc. It is important that these data are correct and up-to-date as they are the legal link between the employee and the organization.

Organization Charts and Head Count – This is a detailed and up-to-date situation of the different positions and the associated job description and the names of the persons occupying them.

Inventories of Skills, Competencies, and Interests - To reassign resources and fill unexpected vacancies HR Departments develop computerized inventories of skills, competencies, and interests of the employees. Such inventories allow assigning talented people to a problem, as we are aware of which individuals have the needed skill or experience to solve that problem.

Training Management – Organizations are becoming increasingly aware that a major competitive advantage occurs when they can rapidly acquire information and solutions and share them throughout the company. HR can help managers in developing individual and corporate wide learning plans and strategies to increase the speed of learning and the application of that knowledge within the organization. Training management typically contains records on training sessions and providers, and training budget.

Succession Plans - These are strategies for ensuring that individuals are available to fill vacant key positions. Many succession plans fail because they are too broad. Targeted plans allow the focus and forecasting to be more narrowly applied with the goal of increasing the accuracy of the planning. Targeted areas often include major software projects and product development.

Retention Plan - A retention plan is a corporate strategy to lower turnover. The first step is to identify key performers and hard to fill positions. Individuals that can be at risk are identified. Strategies are then developed to increase their retention rates.

Additional efforts are made to identify why people stay in their jobs and why people leave.

Employee Challenge Plans - One primary reason why employees leave their job is due to a lack of challenge. HR can increase retention rates if it gets managers to develop individual *Challenge Plans*. The plan is reviewed regularly to ensure that the individual is constantly growing and feels challenged.

Bad Management Identification Program - Another important reason why employees quit their jobs are the bad management practices of their direct supervisor. Through metrics such as absenteeism, surveys, 360° assessments and interviews organizations can identify bad managers. The organization can then develop strategies for fixing these managers, transferring them back to more technical jobs or for releasing them.

Job Rotation Plans - Because many organizations now have a flat hierarchy there are fewer opportunities for promotion to stimulate workers. As a result, there is a need to develop horizontal transfer and job rotation plans to ensure the continued development of both technical and managerial skills of the employees.

Career Plans – A career plan identifies the most appropriate career direction or job options for an employee or group of employees and highlights the required skills and training.

Metrics - If HRM is to be proactive it has to expect problems. Developing performance indicators that show potential problems give sufficient time to develop plans and strategies to either avoid the problem or minimize its impact.

Work-Life Balance – HR needs to develop strategies to assess accurately what the Work-Life demands will be. It must also be able to forecast what percentage of the work force will choose to participate in these programs.

Human Resources Management Systems (HRMSs)

Many aspects of Human Resources Management are purely administrative and encompass a lot of simple and repetitive tasks. HRM is therefore an ideal candidate for automation. Historically, *Human Resources Management Systems (HRMS)* were amongst the first Information Systems to be introduced in our organizations: as early as the mainframe era these systems were developed and deployed.

Smaller organizations with standard needs and without the proper resources to develop and deploy an HRMS will typically outsource the administrative part of their HRM; in fact, this is historically one first case for targeted outsourcing.

Larger organizations or organizations with special needs will buy or develop and deploy their own HRMS. Special needs typically occur in Public Administrations or other Government Agencies where recruitment, salaries and benefits, promotions and other aspects of an employee's career are subject to a set of rules and regulations (a Statute) which are not found in a private organization. In these cases the only option could be to develop an HRMS either from scratch or using an important customization project based on an off-the-shelf commercial package.

Buying (or developing) a HRMS is not like buying a word processing package. The cost of the project does not start and end with the purchase of the "shrink wrap" that the CDROM and user manual comes in. As the overall impact on the organization can be substantial, the time and care taken to buy the right application for your organization is much more critical. As the acquisition of a new HRMS is a major project it is important to structure it for success. A formal process should be developed to identify your organization's needs. This should include the identification of your current processes, resources, and costs. You should calculate the *Return on Investment (ROI)* that you can expect from your new system. Buying a new HRMS is not all cost, it should provide a pay back and pay for itself over time.

Typically, HRMSs are constructed around a database. The information stored within this database can serve a variety of purposes:

- *Payroll calculation* - the system that is used to calculate salaries and benefits of the employees is usually fed from the administrative database. This system can act directly on these data and in fact be a part of the HRMS or it can be a separate system - maybe even outsourced – that is loosely coupled to this database;
- Production of *pay checks* and other official documents;
- *Budget forecasting* – some HRMSs allow the input of simulated data thus enabling budget forecasts;
- *Time and attendance management* (e.g, time entry features, work schedule and shift roster management, time allocation);
- *Capacity planning* - enabling the line managers to view their work force capacity and helping them in the decisions with respect to holidays or training of their employees;
- *Turnover forecasting* - The HR department has to be able to identify where the organization is likely to lose key talent through turnover and retirements. This forecast, partially based on historical information, is designed to predict short-term vacancies in the next six months to prepare the appropriate recruitment or internal promotion strategies;
- *Vacancies and overhead* can easily be detected and even predicted when this tool is properly used;
- *Employment and position management* (e.g., job and position records, organization chart features, career planning, and succession management);

- *Appraisal management, recruitment management* (e.g., recruitment campaign features, job matching facilities, simulations);
- An organization chart can also be the basis for other systems that control the access to various resources (network access, roles in workflow applications, access to computer rooms etc.);
- *Activity Based Budgeting* - activities that incur costs in each function of an organization are established, relationships are defined between activities, and this information is used to decide how much resources should be allocated to each activity;
- Finally, an *organization chart* can also be used as the basis of an on-line consultation tool (yellow pages, who's who).

Best Practices

Apply an open privacy policy

Privacy has always been an issue that has created tension between employees and their employers and it is becoming more important and more complex as employers become more and more dependent on technologies such as email, telephone, and the use of the Internet.

What are the potential losses that could be caused by illegitimate employee behavior? The most important loss is probably *production time*; while an employee is hanging on the phone with his girlfriend or surfing on the Internet looking at undressed ladies he is not productive for the organization. Another cost can be the connection or communication cost; although most Internet connections are permanent the occupied bandwidth comes in debit of the productive use of the connection. Unlawful use of employer's resources can also cause unnecessary investments in network bandwidth, storage capacity, and computing power. Viruses or other insecure programs can be introduced in the corporate network. Copyrights and licensing agreements with third parties can be violated. Employees can cause heavy damage to the carefully built corporate image by communicating in an uncontrolled way. Finally, malevolent employees can abuse their employer's installations to disseminate corporate knowledge or even commercial secrets.

Therefore, to protect business assets and monitor employees without violating the law, employers should have a clear understanding of these matters, write down a policy and let this be known to their employees.

Avoid Strategic Outsourcing

Given the lack of effective project management, senior management awareness of the complex issues in managing major projects and professional cost tracking, the best case for most organizations with Strategic Outsourcing is neutral or slightly increased costs. This is coupled with loss of some of their best intellectual capital, as people prefer to resign rather than join the outsourcing organization. The worst case is total loss of control of the intellectual capital and capability to create strategic decisions. Clearly, few organizations have the project management capability to manage a relationship with big international outsource organizations, so avoid these situations.

Tactical and Limited Outsourcing, provided they are managed effectively, are workable options for most organizations.

Be fair and treat everyone equally and on merit.

There are no objective reasons to make a distinction in the working conditions, salaries and benefits and other ways we treat our people based on sex, race or religion. People have to feel that they are accepted as they are.

Do not forget your external staff: body shoppers, consultants or other collaborators. They should also be implicated in team-building activities, staff parties or even training programs. In that way they will better integrate and be more productive in the long run.

Diversity is a basic characteristic of human beings, so it has to be considered in a good HR policy. This can be done using work-life balance programs (flexitime, part-time work, sabbaticals...), cafeteria plans and by considering particular demands (e.g., religious events, kosher food etc...).

Behave as a leader, not as a boss

"People ask the difference between a leader and a boss.... The leader works in the open, and the boss in covert. The leader leads and the boss drives."

(Theodore Roosevelt)

Leadership is mostly about behavior, especially towards others. Some practical tips in this respect can be summarized as follows:

- Above all: integrity. Without integrity everything else will fail;
- Ask for people's views, but remain neutral and objective;
- Be decisive, but make balanced decisions;

- Be firm and clear in dealing with bad behavior;
- Help your people when they need it;
- Involve your people in your thinking and especially in managing change;
- Keep your promises;
- Give the good example: act as you like your people to act;
- Listen and understand, but make it clear that understanding is different to agreeing;
- Never get emotional with people, even if you feel very upset or angry;
- Relax, and give your people and yourself time to get to know and respect each other;
- Smile and encourage others to be happy and enjoy themselves.

Build a "win-win" relationship when you outsource

The conflict between the agendas of the client and outsourcing organizations makes it imperative that there is consideration within the relationship for long-term "win-win" scenarios.

The best option for ensuring that both partners in an outsource relationship have a shared agenda is for the client organization to buy part of or take an equity in the outsourcing organization. It must be emphasized that this type of relationship does not guarantee the client organization lower costs or any of the other justifications behind outsourcing. This option is really only available to large organizations that are considering strategic outsourcing.

The second option is more difficult to implement. By structuring the contract to include delayed payments based on proven savings as a result of the outsource partnership, the client organization can create a relationship where the outsourcing partner is focused on producing the expected savings, improved service and so on.

Concentrate on the Core Employees

Once it has been decided what work should not be outsourced, give some serious thought to how you will attract and retain your best talent. Charles Handy [56] identifies three groups of people in organizations. The first is the *professional core*, essential to your company's success. The second group, the *flexible labor force*, performs essential activities on a part-time or temporary basis. The third group is the *contractual fringe*, which does all the nonessential work. Each of these groups has different expectations and should be managed differently.

Members of the professional core are motivated by working in flat, collaborative organizations where they are compensated based on the group's results and given some kind of career promise. These are the people you want to retain. This is where you should invest your leadership energies.

According to Handy, managers should spend less time on the other two groups. The flexible labor force is motivated by fair pay and the flexibility to balance work with other interests. Members of this group may have transitioned from the professional core and may move back to the core if their priorities change. You can use skills training to keep this group up to speed. The contractual fringe is paid for results. It is important to compensate members of this group fairly and specify up front the mutual expectations for the relationship. Don't bother trying to get them to affiliate strongly with your organization; they work for somebody else.

Get legal advice when you outsource

The outsourcing of work has always been a part of industry sectors such as construction and manufacturing. The form and content of tenders and legal contracts within these sectors is well established. However, in the area of IT, the legal and contractual issues are more complex. For example, the issue of intellectual property and copyright remains a major challenge. The development of an outsourcing contract requires the client organization to ensure that they seek expert legal and accounting advice in the areas of performance measurement, intellectual property, valuation of intellectual property, fee structures and so on. Often, the size of the major outsourcing organizations and the fact that many are associated with important accounting and legal organizations means that the outsourcer often has better legal and contract advice than the client organization. Organizations considering outsourcing must also develop a plan to exit the contract before signing a contract with an outsourcer. By designing the exit strategy up front, organizations can ensure that the outsourcer understands it has an option to leave.

Hire for Attitude, Train for Skill

It is undeniable: you cannot build a great organization without great people, but how do you know them when you see them? Over the last years, many organizations have arrived at the same conclusion: <u>what people know</u> is less important than <u>who they are</u>. Hiring is not about finding people with the right experience, it's about finding people with the right mind-set. These organizations hire for attitude and train for skill.

This is, of course, only true for own staff. It can – to a certain extent – be applied for body shoppers as well. When hiring real consultants, however, the real skills will be more important.

Human Resources

Know the real costs

The truth is that many organizations have extremely poor costing and productivity measurement systems, especially in the project areas. The existing costing and productivity measures created in most organization are highly compromised by incorrect cost and effort tracking. As a result, the expectations of savings when introducing a new system or during reorganization are often based on incomplete or erroneous financial data. Also, when it is decided to outsource, there will be no effective benchmark for evaluating whether productivity has been improved.

Praise loudly, blame softly

This wisdom from Catherine the Great (1729-1796) still holds today. The single most important behavior to earn respect and trust is: always give your people the credit for your achievements and successes and never take the credit yourself. You must however take the blame and accept responsibility for any failings or mistakes that your people make. Never publicly blame another person for a failing; their failing is your responsibility.

Train your people

User training is one of the most powerful drivers to reduce costs. Research shows that the under-trained user consumes two to six times the amount of technical support (including peer support) than an adequately trained user. User training should be performed on systems and applications, being careful to match the training that is delivered in relation to the user's job. Training should include a mix of instructor-led classroom training, computer-based training, and just-in-time training to help increase user productivity and reduce support costs.

IT professional training is critical in preparing your staff to confidently plan and implement initiatives and solutions, and resolve user issues quickly and effectively. Professional training should significantly reduce the amount of casual learning and pay off in reduced time to implement and troubleshoot systems. Plan for losses

In times of high staff turnover, it is essential to have a strategy of identifying and developing individuals that can take over if an employee leaves. A *back fill plan* covers replacing key jobs within a single department; it is not company-wide. Individual managers are held responsible for developing at least one individual to fill every key job. Once again, this is particularly true for the IT department.

Use Job Enrichment

Job enrichment does not mean simply more work, but tasks your employees see as their own; so that when they succeed they can look back and think, "I did that." Job enrichment unleashes the motivators of achievement, recognition, interesting work, responsibility, advancement, and growth.

Give employees responsibility for a task they can make their own. Give them opportunities to make decisions, learn from the experience and put their personal stamp on their work.

Have faith in people to do great things - given space and air and time, everyone can achieve more than they hope for. Provide people with relevant interesting opportunities, with proper measures and rewards and they will more than repay your faith.

Online Resources

Benefits & Compensation - http://www.benefitslink.com/index.shtml
Benefits & Compensation - http://www.bls.gov/ncs/ebs/home.htm
Benefits & Compensation - http://www.datamasters.com
Benefits & Compensation - http://www.informationweek.com/731/salsurvey.htm
Benefits & Compensation - http://www.wageweb.com
Benefits & Compensation - http://www.worldatwork.org
Dictionary of occupational titles - http://www.oalj.dol.gov/libdot.htm
E-learning - http://www.onlinelearningmag.com
E-learning - http://www.tecweb.org
E-recruitment - www.rileyguide.com
Ethics - http://www.ethics.ubc.ca/resources/business/
Outsourcing - http://www.computerworld.com/managementtopics/outsourcing
Recruitment - http://www.erexchange.com
Recruitment - http://www.ipmaac.org/links.html
Recruitment - http://www.recruiting-links.com
Recruitment - http://www.recruitersnetwork.com
Recruitment - http://www.therecruitersbible.com
Teleworking- http://www.telecommute.org
Teleworking- http://www.gsa.gov

Further Reading

[52] Applegate, L., Cash, J. & Mills D.Q. *Information Technology and Tomorrow's Manager*, Boston, MA, Harvard Business School Press, 1988.

[53] Churchman, C.W. *The Design of Inquiring Systems*, Basic Books, New York, NY, 1971.

[54] Covey S. S., *Principle-centred Leadership*. Simon & Schuster, New York. 1992.

[55] Crosby, Philip B., *Running Things. The Art of Making Things Happen.* Mentor (Penguin), 1989.

[56] Handy, C., Bennis, W.G. *The Age of Unreason*. Harvard Business School Press ,1998.

[57] Herzberg, F., *Work and the Nature of Man.* Cleveland: World Publishing Co. 1966.

[58] Lawler, Edward E. III. *Pay and Organizational Effectiveness* New York: McGraw-Hill. 1971.

[59] Mabey, C., Salamn, G. and Storey, J. *Human Resource Management: A Strategic Introduction.* Blackwell, 1998.

[60] Maslow, A., *Motivation and Personality.* New York: Harper & Row. 1954.

[61] McGregor, D., *Proceedings of the Fifth Anniversary Convocation of the School of Industrial Management*, "The Human Side of Enterprise." Massachusetts Institute of Technology. 1957.

[62] Merriam, S. B., and Caffarella, R. S. *Learning in Adulthood: A Comprehensive Guide.* 2d ed. San Francisco: Jossey-Bass, 1999.

[63] Polanyi, Michael. *The Tacit Dimension.* London: Routledge & Kegan Paul.

[64] Vroom, V., *Work and Motivation.* New York: Jon Wiley & Sons. 1964.

5

Financial Resources

"Can anybody remember when the times were not hard and money not scarce?"
(Ralph Waldo Emerson)

Introduction

One of the least understood aspects of managing an IT department is *financial management*. Financial management is the sound stewardship of the monetary resources of the organization. It supports the organization in planning and executing its business strategy and requires a consistent application throughout the organization to achieve maximum efficiency and minimum conflict. Therefore, understanding the economics of the organization in general and Information Technology in particular is a major step toward developing sound financial strategies to accommodate technological advancement.

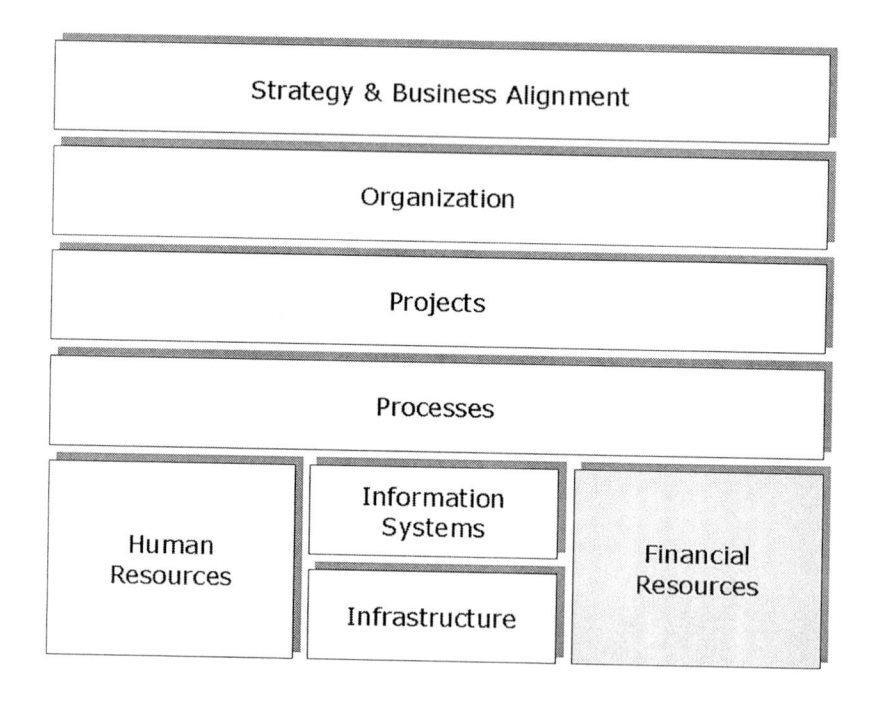

Fig. 5.1 – *Position of Financial Resources in the IT stack*

Within IT, financial management is visible in three main functions: budgeting, costing and charging.

Budgeting is the process of predicting and controlling the spending of money. It consists of a periodic negotiation cycle to set budgets (usually annual) and the day-to-day monitoring of the current budgets.

Costing is the set of processes that enable the IT organization to fully account for the way its money is spent.

Charging is the set of processes required to bill the customers for the services supplied to them.

Budgeting, costing and charging are interrelated and interdependent.

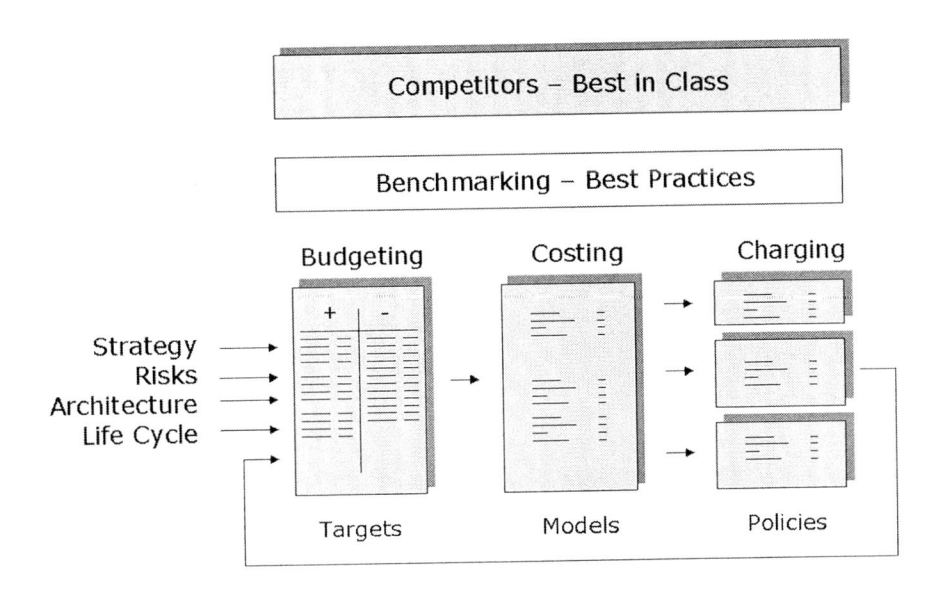

Fig. 5.2 – *Financial processes*

A *budget* is the overview of all the projected expenses and the way they will be paid for. An organization's budget is the financial expression of its strategy and so is the part of the budget that covers the IT expenses and incomes. The IT budget also takes into account other elements such as risks, the architecture of the IT environment and the life cycle of the IT systems.

Following a well-defined costing model a detailed follow-up of the actual spending is then made, particularly to identify costs by customer, by service, and by activity.

The charging policies ensure that customers are aware of the costs they impose on IT and try to influence the customer behavior. The actual recovery of the full costs is optional in many organizations, however the charging process allows for a formal evaluation of the IT services and to plan for future expenditures for operations and investments.

Ideally, budgeting, costing and charging follow the "Best Practices" of the industry and the results are compared with the competition and "Best-in-class" performers.

For the sake of clarity we will start with a more detailed discussion of the costing processes.

Costing

Managing an IT organization's financial resources starts with knowing the real costs. The costing processes provide management with information on the costs of providing IT services that support the organization's business needs. This information is needed to make well-informed decisions ensuring that there is a proper balance between the quality of service and expenditure. In this respect, costing helps the organization to:

- Provide top management with a justification of IT expenditures and investments;
- Demonstrate under- or over-consumption of service in financial terms;
- Make decisions about IT services in alignment with the business;
- Plan and budget with confidence;
- Understand the cost of not taking advantage of opportunities for change.

Cost elements

The major *Cost Types* to be taken into consideration are related to Hardware, Software, Human Resources, Accommodation and External Services. These cost types can be further divided in *Cost Elements*. Typical cost elements per cost type are:

Cost type	Cost elements
Hardware	CPUs, Storage, peripherals, WAN, LAN, Workstations, laptops, PDAs, Consumables…
Software	Operating Systems, Monitoring tools, Database Management Systems, Application Servers, Web Servers, Mail Servers, Packaged Applications, Homemade Applications, Personal Productivity Tools, Groupware, …
Human Resources	Payroll costs, Benefits, Re-location costs, Expenses, Training…
Accommodation	Offices, Furniture, Computer Rooms, Storage Areas, …
External Services	Security Services, Disaster Recovery Services, Outsourcing Services, Consultancy, Telecomm Charges…

Table 5.1 – *Cost Types and Cost Elements*

Cost elements can further be categorized in different ways:

- *Fixed Costs* – these are the costs that are not directly influenced by the business activities such as rent, salaries, license fees, maintenance contracts, etc...
- *Variable Costs* – these follow changes in business activity. Examples are consumables, telecomm charges, fees for contractors, ...

There is a trend towards converting fixed costs into variable costs in order to obtain a better alignment of IT and Business.

- *Direct Costs* – these costs can be allocated to a specific department or service like some application software, dedicated hardware, dedicated support teams, etc...
- *Indirect Costs* – these cannot be allocated to a specific department or service but are shared among more departments or services. Examples are management, system software, service desk, network, etc...

It is easy to demonstrate that a cut in direct costs will affect the quality of service delivered, but it is hard to prove how cuts to indirect costs will affect services. In general, only value-added services will be considered as direct costs, while indirect costs will be treated as business overhead.

- *Capital Costs* – these are typically those applying to substantial assets of the organization. It is not usually the actual cost of items purchased during the year that is included in the calculation of the cost but the annualized depreciation for the year.
- *Operational Costs* – these are the costs resulting from the day-to-day operations of the IT department such as staff costs, maintenance. These are repeating payments whose effects can be measured within a short timeframe, typically less than a year.

Total Cost of Ownership (TCO)

"TCO is the cost of owning, operating, and maintaining a computer system. TCO includes the up-front costs of hardware and software, plus the costs of installation, training, support, upgrades, and repairs."

(Bill Gates - Business @ the Speed of Thought)

Bill Kirwin (Gartner) introduced the concept of *Total Cost of Ownership (TCO)* in 1978 for desktops. The idea was to analyze direct and indirect costs of owning and using hardware and software. Over the years, Gartner and other consultants have developed models for various situations such as LAN, Client Server software, distributed computing, telecomm, mainframes, datacenters, etc.

Let's take as a simple example the annual costs associated with the ownership of a Personal Computer. A typical breakdown looks as follows:

- Hardware: 24%
- Administration: 24%
- Training: 17%
- End user downtime: 16.5%
- Software: 12%
- Co-worker time: 6.5%

Obviously, the larger part of these costs - the ones associated with administration, training, end user downtime and co-worker time - will not be taken into account at the moment when the purchase decision is made. These are "hidden costs". Furthermore, these costs will not necessarily appear on the IT budget as they are generated in other departments of the organization.

The purpose of a TCO analysis is to make the hidden costs visible and to make the other departments aware of the costs associated with typical IT investments.

A TCO analysis is performed in five steps:

- Step 1 – Identify all the cost factors, both direct and hidden
- Step 2 – Identify determining factors (quantities)
- Step 3 – Collect data, make assumptions where necessary
- Step 4 – Build and use the model, for different scenarios
- Step 5 – Follow-up and measure results, adjust as needed

It is important to note that a TCO model inevitably contains a number of assumptions and simplifications. A TCO analysis can be done on an existing asset to identify areas of potential savings; it can be done for the investment in a new asset, as a way of arriving at the lowest total cost, or the best value among several alternatives or as a benchmarking tool to compare your performance with others.

Activity Based Costing (ABC)

Activity Based Costing (ABC) is a costing model advocated by Cooper and Kaplan [67] that identifies the cost pools (or activity centers) in an organization and assigns costs to products and services (cost drivers) based on the volumes involved in the process of providing a product or service. ABC is a budgeting and analysis process that evaluates overhead and operating expenses by linking costs to customers, services, products and orders. It allows managers to see which products or services are profitable or losing money. Many companies are losing money on some of their products because they are unaware of the relationship of the price and real cost of their products. Traditional costing systems are unable to tell what to do with set-up, material handling and administrative costs on low-volume or difficult products.

The diagram below shows the normal relationship between real cost and volume. On the right hand side of the graph, a company using traditional costing methods will routinely set a price that is a little too high, losing bids for these "good" high-volume jobs to competitors who have better cost information. On the left hand side of the graph, the same company will set price too low on low-volume jobs, winning the contract but losing money on the sale.

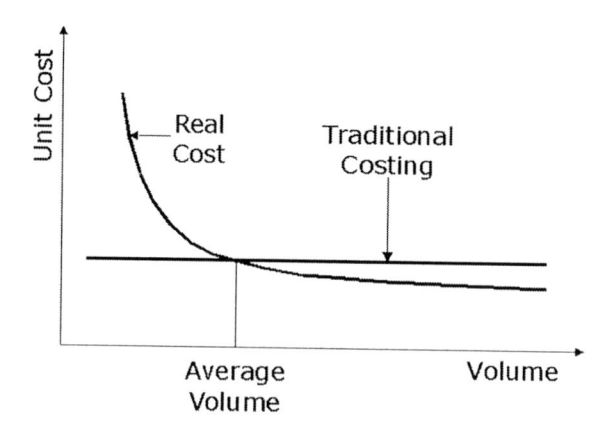

Fig. 5.3 – *Evolution of real costs*

The problem with traditional costing methods is that they arbitrarily allocate large portions of costs based on the volume, treating all costs as if they were variable. However, every product or service has both fixed and variable costs.

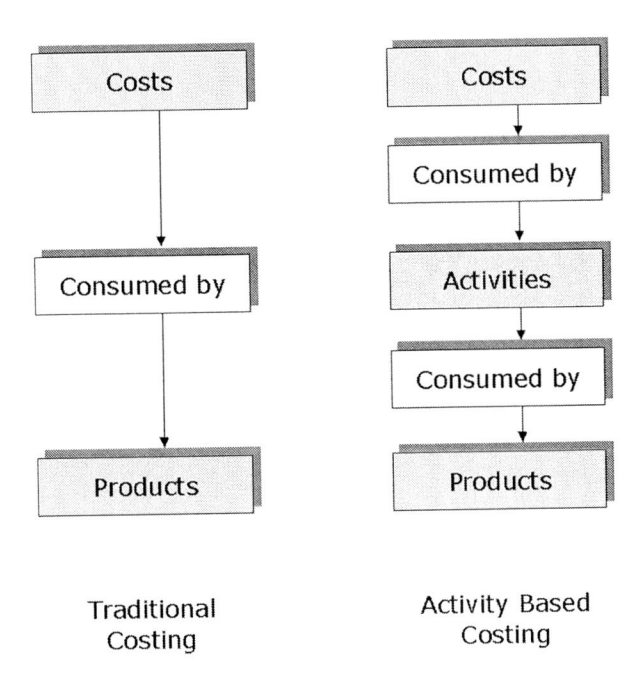

```
    Costs                    Costs
      │                        │
      ▼                        ▼
 Consumed by              Consumed by
      │                        │
      ▼                        ▼
                           Activities
                               │
                               ▼
                          Consumed by
                               │
      ▼                        ▼
   Products                 Products

  Traditional            Activity Based
   Costing                  Costing
```

Fig. 5.4 – *Traditional vs. Activity Based Costing*

ABC is a method that measures cost of a product or service, based on the activities to produce the product or service. The underlying assumption is that activities drive the costs, which are driven by the product or customer.

The reasons why an organization would implement ABC are multiple:

- Identify "money makers" and "money losers";
- Find a break even point;
- Compare different options;
- Discover opportunities for cost improvement;
- Prepare and actualize a business plan;
- Improve strategic decision-making.

The first step of ABC is to establish the activity centers and activities. For example, the IT help desk can be an activity centre. A help desk activity can be anything from installing software to routing a call to the appropriate technician who can assist the user with solving his problem.

Once the activities are established, you must determine the parts of each activity that cost money. These can be hidden such as the cost associated with each call to the help desk. The key is to determine what makes up fixed costs, such as the cost of a telephone, and variable costs, such as the cost of each phone call.

When the cost drivers and activities are established, the data is collected and input to a model. This can be a simple database, off-the-shelf ABC software or customized software.

It is important to note that the purpose of a proper ABC model is not to have the most accurate cost system but a good-enough model that balances the costs of errors made from inaccurate estimates with the cost of measurement. A properly constructed ABC model is a relatively simple system that contains 30-50 activities with accuracy in activity and process costs from 5 to 10%. Trying to build a more accurate model would lead to a far more expensive system where the cost of operating would be higher than the benefit of having better decisions.

Maintaining an ABC system can be a tedious job. Whenever there are changes in the processes, the ABC system has to be updated, employees have to be re-interviewed and resource-usage has to be re-estimated. Also, many managers feel uncomfortable with the degree of subjectivity involved in estimating employees' proportion of time spent on each activity. To cope with these problems, Robert Kaplan recently developed a new approach to ABC that simplifies the method and enables it to be updated very easily whenever changes occur in the structure of the model. In the new approach, time based cost rates are calculated and the costing is based on the time required to perform a transactional activity, hereby using cost equations. This approach is called *Time-Driven ABC*.

Charging

Charging customers is a method of balancing the quality and the quantity of IT services with the needs of the customers. Because customers are paying for IT services they have the right to influence decisions on their provision. Services are only provided if there is a business justification for it. On the other hand charging enables the IT management to make formal evaluations of the IT services and plan for investment based on cost recovery and to influence customer behavior.

The price of a service can be established according to different policies:

- Recover the costs;
- Recover the costs and also make some profit;
- Use the same price as other internal departments or similar external organizations;
- Use the current market prices;
- Use a fixed price agreed for a set period, based on anticipated usage.

Costs are important; they show the minimum level below which prices will not normally be set. Whatever pricing policy you decide to adopt, there will be a price below which it is simply not worth the effort. However, this is the only point at which costs should affect pricing decisions. Using a simple "cost-plus" formula for determining prices, takes no account of what your customers are willing to pay or how your products or services compare with the competition.

Remember that customers do not simply buy products - they buy benefits, i.e. the benefits that acquiring the product or service will bring. When fixing the price of a product or service you should ask yourself the following questions:

- What benefits do customers get by buying your product or service?
- What special benefits do they get by buying from you?
- What are these benefits likely to be worth to them?
- What might they be prepared to pay for these benefits?

Sometimes, you may be in a competition with other departments or external service providers. The main point to remember is that you don't necessarily have to undercut the others. A better service or a better understanding of your customer's needs can be as decisive.

Since costs, demand and competition can all change fairly frequently, it is important to keep your prices under review, to be sure that they stay in line with what you are trying to achieve.

Responsibility Centre

A department or organizational unit that is responsible for a group of activities, processes, functions or projects is also called a *responsibility centre*. Different types are distinguished:

- Standard cost centers;
- Revenue centres;
- Profit centres;
- Investment centres;
- Managed cost centres.

The most typical example of a *standard cost centre* is a production department. Input and output can be measured with high precision, both in units and in money and the relation between these two metrics is very clear. It is possible to set standards that show how much input units are needed to produce one or more output units.

An example of a *revenue centre* is a sales department. Both output and input can be measured in financial terms (sales figures, salaries, publicity costs…) It is however more difficult to show the relationship between input and output.

The management of a *profit centre* is responsible for both input and output in financial terms or in other words, for the profit as the result of the revenues minus the costs. Examples of profit centers can be found in organizations that commercialize different brands and in which every brand represents a profit centre.

An *investment centre* is a profit centre that has been given also the responsibility for the investments that are necessary to protect the long-term interests of the organization.

Managed (or discretionary) cost centers are responsibility centers where the input in financial terms can be measured precisely but for which the output cannot be measured clearly. Examples are Financial Administration, Human Resources, Infrastructure, and Public Relations. The first EDP departments certainly had to be considered as managed cost centers; the input was well defined but it was difficult to say how the output was distributed over the various other departments or activities. Over the years, this situation has changed: as more specialized Information Systems were introduced it became more apparent who the output was meant for: a CRM system for the sales department, a HRMS for the Human Resources department etc…

There are many organizations where IT is considered as a discretionary cost centre. There are, however, more and more organizations where the output of IT is considered in the financial balance of its internal customers. In this way, many IT departments have evolved into a *standard cost centre*. On top of that, more and more IT departments have created a better image of their relations with their customers using *Service Contracts* or internal *Service Level Agreements (SLAs)*.

The next step is the evolution into a *profit centre* in which profits are generated using internal transfer prices.

Finally, some IT departments have even evolved into an *investment centre*, for which the responsible manager can autonomously decide to invest for the future of his organization. Often, these IT departments become autonomous business units or even independent companies.

It should be clear that in an organization where the costs of IT are low with respect to the overall costs, or where the distribution of these costs are relatively stable over time it will probably not make sense to go through this evolution.

Budgeting

According to Webster's, a *budget* is:

1. An itemized summary of estimated or intended expenditures for a given period along with proposals for financing them: *submitted the annual budget to Congress.*
2. A systematic plan for the expenditure of a usually fixed resource, such as money or time, during a given period: *A new car will not be part of our budget this year.*
3. The total sum of money allocated for a particular purpose or period of time: *a project with an annual budget of five million dollars.*

Money is the lifeblood of an IT organization. Yet, most IT managers feel that the budgeting process is painful, takes too long, and yields little benefit for the effort invested. While IT professionals do not need to be budget experts, they must certainly know the basics. Progressive IT executives recognize that improvement of IT budgeting can help them do their job better because:

- Budgets are statements of IT plans quantified in financial terms;
- If the IT manager does not prove the need for money, no one else will;
- Senior management needs to know about IT in business terms, that is: "What is the benefit and how much will it cost?"

An interesting question with respect to the IT budget is of course how big it should be. Truth is that there is no single answer for this question. Each organization spends at a different level, largely depending on the activity of the business and what the importance of IT is within the organization. Figures of leading companies per industry are available and compare the level of spending with competitors or peers.

A typical figure is the *IT spending per employee*. This metric can be used as a single number for the entire organization, or it could be divided into subdivisions such as R&D, branches, field offices, geography, or division. There are industry averages available for IT spending per employee, with figures varying in a wide range. A good baseline is the *internal spend rate* of a selected base year. CIOs and IT Managers of growing organizations could find this to be a valuable metric, as budgets should be adjusted by the spend rate per employee without the increase being viewed as request for incremental funding.

Another measure is the ratio of *IT employees to total organization employees.* This number closely tracks the IT spending as a percent of revenue metric but is helpful in managing staffing requests. IT Managers can use this to justify increases in non-project based staffing as the organization grows. As with the other performance indicators managers could use this one when addressing Service Level Agreements or explaining the changes in service levels that would occur should IT staffing fail to keep up with the demands of growth.

One of the most used metrics is *IT spending as a percent of revenues.* IT budgets as a percent of total company revenue ranges from 8% in smaller companies to 4% in very large companies. IT budget is higher in smaller companies (8% in companies with less than $100 million in revenue) and lower in large organizations (4% in companies with revenue of $5 billion or more). Within financial services, banking and telecommunication companies, it averages 10 to 18 percent of revenues.

Each industry invests at different levels and although there are shifts each year, the percentages are consistent enough to allow CIOs or IT Managers to measure their organization's investments against their competitors or peers. While this is not the most accurate of measurements, it does allow determining whether their organization is investing at a rate similar to the rest of the industry. Long-term under-investment could be costing an organization its competitive edge and CIOs or IT managers should bring this fact under the eyes of their Senior Management.

Budgeting Processes

The *budgeting processes* consist of activities that encompass the development, creation, and evaluation of a plan for the provision of services and capital assets [65][66]. A good budgeting process is far more than the preparation of a document that appropriates funds for a series of line items. Good budgeting is a broadly defined process that has political, managerial, planning, communication, and financial dimensions. Several essential features characterize a good budget process:

- It incorporates a long-term perspective;
- It establishes links to broad organizational goals;
- It focuses budget decisions on results and outcomes;

- It involves and promotes effective communication with stakeholders;
- It provides incentives to management and employees.

Budgeting is not simply an exercise in balancing revenues and expenditures one year at a time, but it is strategic in nature, encompassing a multi-year financial and operating plan that allocates resources for identified goals. A good budget process moves beyond the traditional concept of line item expenditure control, providing incentives and agility to managers that can lead to improved efficiency and effectiveness.

Budgets can also be submitted to constraints such as:

- Limits on capital and operational expenditure;
- Limits on variance between actual and predicted spend;
- Guidelines on how the budget must be used;
- An agreed set of services to be delivered;
- Limits on expenditure outside the organization or group of organizations.

Budget preparation involves every part of the organization. From the Chief Executive's office to the cleaning services: every functional area prepares and submits requests to fund routine and non-routine activities and projects for the next period.

It is important to understand that, in this process, IT is just one more department asking for money. At this stage, the numbers reflect the operating plans and proposals for the entire organization stated in terms of their estimated costs and revenues. Project planning and justification are of vital importance.

Executives who develop the most compelling proposals and justifications, and demonstrate alignment with strategic goals and business objectives, significantly improve their chances of receiving the necessary funding.

Senior management evaluates the revenue plans and proposals, weighs them against expenditure plans and proposals, and decides how much can be spent and where. The result is the budget.

In fact, there are several budgets:

- *Operating budget* - Money to fund normal operations;
- *Capital budget* - Money for non-routine work such as projects;
- *Revenue budget* - Where the money will come from.

An organization's capital budget and budgeting process are usually distinct from its operating budget and budgeting process. The two kinds of budgets represent different expenditures, are planned through different processes, use different criteria, and can involve different managers. In order for expenditure to be funded from a capital budget, its sponsors can have to justify it with a formal business case analysis. The approved budget represents 100% of the money that an organization plans to spend (and receive) during the next budget period (typically, one year). Money has been spread over functional areas and within each functional area money is allocated. Every Euro or Dollar that is available to be spent has been linked to an expense item; from the network administrator that you want to hire in three months to the software license you proposed to buy next month.

During the execution phase, management monitors and controls spending to assure that it conforms to the approved plans. In that respect a budget provides a kind of early warning system that, when compared to actual results, can inform when something is going wrong that needs immediate attention. When the expenditures exceed the budget, there are several things that can be done to get back on track:

- *Review the budget* - Before anything else, take a close look at the budget and make sure that the assumptions on which it is based are accurate and make sense in your changing environment. Sometimes, it's the budget and not the spending that is out of line.
- *Freeze spending* - One of the quickest and most effective ways to bring spending back in line with a budget is to freeze expenses such as pay raises, new staff, and bonuses.
- *Postpone new projects* - New projects, including new product development, acquisition of new equipment, and research and development, can eat up a lot of money. However, if you are too fanatical in cutting spending when you need to develop new products or services to compete, the result can be disastrous for the future growth and prosperity of the organization.
- *Lay off employees and close facilities* - This is the last resort when you're trying to cut expenses. Although these actions will result in an immediate and lasting decrease in expenses, you also face an immediate and lasting decrease in the potential of your organization. Productivity and morale of remaining employees may also suffer.

Budgeting is sometimes confused with costing; both are expressions of an organization's activities in financial terms. There are however some important differences.

	Costing	Budgeting
Purpose	External reporting	Internal management
Perspective	Retrospective	Prospective
Reporting	General	Specific
History	Long	Recent

Table 5.2 – *Costing vs. Budgeting*

Both costing and budgeting are important for an organization, but they do not provide the same information and do not serve the same purposes.

Information Technology is a significant cost to most organizations. Often, IT is cited as the number two expense following personnel. It is therefore important to understand that the IT budget is in competition with the other department's spending: the money has to come from the same limited resources and it is up to the IT manager to persuade Senior Management that his operations and projects have to be chosen before the others. One should also realize that this competition is playing inside the IT budget as well: money that is spent in hardware or software maintenance cannot be used for paying extra staff and a software development budget cannot be spent for the purchase of new servers.

Budgeting Methods

Over the years, several different *budgeting methods* have been worked out. In the next sections the most important ones will be discussed.

Baseline or Incremental Budgeting

Many organizations have very predictable operations that vary little over time. In these cases *Baseline Budgeting* can offer the advantage of building on the organization's existing base of knowledge regarding its operations. Budgeters are often able to analyze historical data and extrapolate cyclical or seasonal trends quickly. Instead of recreating information, focus can be set on areas of the operations that can be exceptionally difficult to budget or represent opportunities to plan at an even greater level of detail. Analysis of historical data can remind budgeters to factor into their budgets events or trends that they can have otherwise forgotten or overlooked.

Incremental Budgeting is easy to understand and simple to administer. However, it encourages an organization only in a limited way to justify existing programs or to eliminate programs that are not productive. Thus, self-satisfaction is encouraged and an atmosphere of "business as usual" from year to year prevails. One of the most serious disadvantages of Baseline Budgeting is that managers will sometimes rely on historical data without considering its relevance. If the budgeter does not make the effort to determine whether the historical data includes extraordinary or irrelevant items, then the results are jeopardized; extrapolating historical trends without verifying the assumptions that underlie the data, risks compromising the integrity of the budgeted data.

Zero Based Budgeting (ZBB)

Zero Based Budgeting (ZBB) is the process of preparing a budget that starts with no authorized funds. In a zero-based budget, each activity to be funded must be justified every time a new budget is prepared. The objective of Zero Based Budgeting is to "reset the clock" each year. While an incremental budgeting process allows managers to start with last year's expenditures and add a percent for inflation to come up with next year's budget, ZBB means that managers need to build a budget from the ground up, building a case for their spending to start at zero. Peter Pyhrr [70] was the first to describe ZBB in the early 1970s. The Governor of Georgia, Jimmy Carter, asked Pyhrr to help him create the system for Georgia's state government in 1971. ZBB spread from Georgia to Texas and New Jersey and developed a following in several cities across the United States. When Carter became President, he mandated that all federal agencies use ZBB as well. Today ZBB is also used in business environments. ZBB can improve the cost containment, increase the discipline in developing budgets and yield more meaningful discussion during budget review sessions.

Applying the ZBB principle to all the budget lines turns out to be almost impossible, this is why many organizations in reality use a mix of incremental budgeting and Zero Based Budgeting, depending on the nature of the expense to be covered.

Activity Based Budgeting (ABB)

Activity Based Budgeting (ABB) [69] is a method of budgeting in which activities that incur costs in each function of an organization are established, relationships are defined between activities, and this information is used to decide how much resources should be allocated to each activity. ABB is budgeting by activities rather than by cost elements; it is another way of representing a budget.

Activity Based Budgeting is based on *Activity Based Costing (ABC)*, which defines the "real" cost of providing a product or service by capturing and analyzing how workers spend their time. Activity Based Budgeting uses these same models, and provides projected costs. The advantages of ABB are a detailed understanding of an organization's costs, increased control over expenditures and an improved understanding of the links between processes, activities and costs. It also encourages a healthy discussion of issues and cost drivers during budget reviews.

Responsibility Centre Budgeting (RCB)

Responsibility Centre Budgeting (RCB) - also called *Responsibility Centre Management (RCM)* - is a financial management system that requires predefined activity centers to be almost totally responsible for their expenditures and revenues, and that they manage their activities such that spending does not exceed revenues. RCM requires that unit managers and other individuals in the organization understand the need to identify paying constituencies (i.e., who their customers are) and to serve them efficiently. It creates management, budgetary, and reward structures that tie resources to performance so that individuals will see how their own actions influence the well being of their units and themselves. That, in turn, is intended to result in better responsiveness to the clients.

The Operations Budget

The *operations budget* is a financial plan for the provision of direct services and support functions. For an IT department this is typically structured as follows:

- Direct costs
    - Personnel
        - Employees;
        - External staff.
    - Non-Personnel
        - Hardware;
        - Software;
        - Contractual services;
        - Other.
- Indirect costs
    - Administrative;
    - Infrastructure;
    - Communications;
    - Other.

The Capital Budget

Organizations continuously invest funds in assets and these assets produce cash flows that can then either be reinvested or paid to its owners [71][72][73][74]. *Capital* is the organization's total assets and is comprised of all tangible and intangible resources. These include material properties (such as land, buildings, equipment, and machinery), as well as assets that represent property rights (such as accounts receivable, notes, stocks, and bonds). *Capital Budgeting* is the process of deciding which long-term assets to invest in and which ones to forego.

The value of IT in an organization is not a foregone conclusion and its benefits are not self-evident. IT professionals who believe that the value of technology is patently obvious run the risk of not getting the resources they need to do their job. Relying on people who do not understand the technology to make consistent judgments about what is important and what is not creates the risk of having IT funding decisions reduced to only two questions: *"how much does it cost?"* and *"how much will we save?"* As we have seen in the previous section both are important, but considering these two questions alone is not enough to make the best IT investment decisions. Other elements such as the relevance for the organization, risk and IT architecture have to be considered as well.

Depreciation

Depreciation is the reduction in the value of fixed or capital assets, through use, damage, weathering, or obsolescence. It can be estimated according to several methods.

Linear depreciation diminishes the value of an asset by a fixed amount each period until the net value is zero. This is the simplest calculation, as you estimate a useful lifetime, and simply divide the cost equally across that lifetime. Say you have bought a computer for $1500 and wish to depreciate it over a period of five years; each year the amount of depreciation is $300.

In a *geometric depreciation* scheme the asset is depreciated each period by a fixed percentage of its value in the previous period. In this scheme the rest value of an asset decreases exponentially leaving a value at the end that is larger than zero (*i.e.,* the resale value).

A third method most often employed in Anglo-Saxon countries is the *sum of digits method*. First, the initial value is divided by the sum of the number of years. For example, for a computer worth $1500 that is used over a period of five years you get D = 1500/(1+2+3+4+5)=100. Depreciation and asset value are then calculated as follows:

Year	Depreciation	Remaining Value
1	D*5=500	1000
2	D*4=400	600
3	D*3=300	300
4	D*2=200	100
5	D*1=100	0

Table 5.3 – *Depreciation*

The technical name for the depreciation of nonmaterial assets is *amortization*.

Costs and Benefits

Often, it is possible to express both costs and benefits of an IT project in dollars. The purchase price of computers, network components and software can be predicted with reasonable accuracy, and so can the costs of programmers and system designers. Examples of *hard* benefits are:

- Saved HR costs when automating a manual process;
- An improvement of the cash flows due to a better invoicing process; accountants are able to quantify the benefits of this with high accuracy;
- Reduction of the number of errors in the contacts with customers or suppliers can bring about considerable and quantifiable savings;
- Reduction of production dropout can save money;
- Lower stock levels by just-in-time processing reduce costs of storage infrastructure and immobilized capital;
- Shorter production cycles and better response times can be translated in financial terms.

There are also *intangible* or *soft* costs and benefits, which at the moment of decision cannot be expressed in hard figures. Senior Management accepts many IT projects on a basis of arguments like:

- Improvement of the customer relationship, higher customer satisfaction;
- Morale of the employees, job satisfaction;
- Confidence of the shareholders, image on the financial market;
- Relevance for society (environment, social justice, employment);
- Better decisions by faster and more accurate information for the management.

There are also intangibles on the cost side such as:

- Resistance to change from employees, suppliers or customers;
- Social turmoil because jobs are lost.

These benefits and costs are often *underestimated* during the budgeting phase of a project. The most frequent error during the estimation of the costs of an IT project, however, is not the underestimation of certain costs but simply forgetting them:

- Production of technical and other documentation;
- Consumables, tools, facilities;
- Data conversion and transfer from old to new system;
- Staff turnover, training and learning curves;
- Communication costs: formal and informal meetings, telecom;
- Administrative overhead;

- Time spent by functional management and end-users;
- Travel expenses.

If there are any expected costs over the lifetime of the new asset that are substantial or differentiate this purchase from others (e.g., high-end web server that requires 7x24 monitoring) these costs should also be mentioned and justified.

It must be clear that no sensible investor will spend his money on a project that, in the end, does not return the initial investment with some reasonable profit. It is important to distinguish between the responsibility of the IT planner and general management. It is useless to try to translate everything to money. The realization of an objective such as "Having the happiest customers in the market segment" can be a good justification for an IT project as it is the responsibility of Senior Management that these objectives are consistent with the ultimate strategic goals.

Return On Investment (ROI)

Business managers use *Return On Investment (ROI)* as a tool to analyze the financial benefits that an investment can create for their organization over a period of time. An ROI analysis typically correlates returns (due to productivity enhancements) to the investment required.

The *payback period* of a project is the number of years needed to recover the initial investment. For example: a project (A) that requires an initial outlay of $1,000,000 and pays $333,333 per year for four consecutive years has a payback period of 1,000,000/333,333 = 3 years. Let us consider, however, another project (B) with a yearly payback of $250,000 spread over five years:

	Project A	**Project B**
Initial investment ($)	-1,000,000	-1,000,000
Year 1	333,333	250,000
Year 2	333,333	250,000
Year 3	333,333	250,000
Year 4	-	250,000
Year 5	-	250,000
Total payback	1,000,000	1,250,000
Payback period (years)	3	4

Table 5.4 – *Payback period*

If the senior management has set a cut-off of three years, this would mean that project A should be accepted and project B rejected. However, over its total life cycle project B yields a higher payback and here is the main disadvantage of this technique: it ignores cash flows beyond the payback period.

Furthermore, the other disadvantages are:

- Cut-off periods are arbitrary;
- This method does not consider the time value of money;
- It does not consider any required rate of return;

The *discounted payback period* is the time needed to pay back the original investment in terms of *discounted* future cash flows. Each cash flow is discounted back to the beginning of the investment at a rate that reflects both the time value of money and the uncertainty of the future cash flows. This rate is the cost of capital; the return required by the suppliers of capital (creditors and owners) to compensate them for time value of money and the risk associated with the investment. The more uncertain the future cash flows, the greater the cost of capital.

This method is better than the previous one, however:

- Cut-offs are still subjective;
- All cash flows are still not examined;
- It requires an estimate of the cost of capital to calculate the payback.

The *Net Present Value (NPV)* is the present value of the net cash flows less the initial investment (INV).

$$NPV = \sum_{t=1}^{N} CF_t/(1+k)^t - INV$$

CF_t represents the cash flow at the end of period t; k represents the cost of capital, and N the number of periods comprising the economic life of the investment. If NPV is positive, the project should be accepted, if it is negative it should be rejected.

		Project A		**Project B**	
	Discount (at 5%)				
		CF	NV	CF	NV
Initial investment	1.0000	-1,000,000	-1,000,000	-1,000,000	-1,000,000
Year 1	0.95238	333,333	317460	250,000	238095
Year 2	0.90703	333,333	302343	250,000	226757
Year 3	0.86384	333,333	287946	250,000	215959
Year 4	0.82270	-	-	250,000	205676
Year 5	0.78353	-	-	250,000	195882
NPV			-92252		82369

Table 5.5 – *Net Present Value*

In this case it is clear that project A should be rejected and project B accepted. However, this method requires an estimate of the cost of capital to calculate the NPV (5% in the example) and the NPV is expressed in terms of dollars, not as a percentage, making it impossible to compare projects with different amounts of investment.

Rearranging the NPV formula yields the *Profitability Index (PI)*:

$$PI = \left[\sum_{t=1}^{N} CF_t/(1+k)^t\right] : INV$$

Instead of the *difference*, PI is the *ratio* of two present values. Hence, PI is a variation of NPV. By construction, if the NPV is zero, PI is one. If PI is greater than or equal 1 then the project can be accepted, otherwise it should be rejected. Projects A and B of the example would give a PI of 0.91 and 1.08 respectively.

The PI is often called the *cost-benefit ratio*, since it is the ratio of the benefit from an investment (the present value of cash inflows) to its cost (the present value of cash outflows). However, the PI cannot give the correct decision when used to compare mutually exclusive projects.

An investment's *Internal Rate of Return (IRR)* is the discount rate that makes the present value of all expected future cash flows equal to zero. We can represent the IRR as the rate that solves:

$$0 = \sum_{t=0}^{N} CF_t/(1+IRR)^t$$

If IRR is greater than or equal the required rate of return then the project can be accepted, otherwise it has to be rejected. In the case of project B of the previous example the IRR would be 0.0793081.

The disadvantages of this method are:

- It requires an estimate of the cost of capital to make a decision;
- It cannot give the value-maximizing decision when used to choose projects when there is capital rationing.
- It is difficult to calculate: various scenarios have to be compared to obtain the result.

Managing uncertainty

So far we have implicitly assumed that the cash flows and other relevant variables such as the cost of capital can be determined accurately and with certainty. These estimates are leading to a single result of for example the NPV. In real life however there are many uncertainties: a lack of data or gaps in available historical data can lead to assumptions. Projection of the future is inherently uncertain and there are many intangibles. For managing these uncertainties two approaches are used: sensitivity analysis and risk analysis.

During a *sensitivity analysis*, the goal is to find those variables that can change the resulting NPV, PI or IRR in such a way that the decision to accept or reject is altered or the ranking of alternatives is modified. These critical variables are found either based on a judgment or by experimenting with high and low estimates.

An alternative approach is *risk analysis*. Each critical variable is given a probability distribution. A software tool then samples at random from this distribution for each variable at calculates the resulting NPV, IRR or PI for many samples.

Other value factors

"Not everything that counts can be counted, and not everything that can be counted counts."

(A. Einstein)

Measuring the value of an investment is an integral part of business planning; however, an ROI calculation is only a small part of the total value of an investment as it is a purely financial metric. An ROI calculation may, in fact, even be negative but the intangible benefits such as user satisfaction may justify the expense..

In practice, only few organizations make a real ROI study before deciding on a project, instead they translate the acronym as *Running On Instinct*. Much more use more subjective criteria such as improved user satisfaction or reduced costs. IDC made a survey in 687 medium and large Dutch organizations and found that only 17% made an ROI study, the rest used other criteria:

Decision Criteria	%
Improved user satisfaction	58.2%
Reduced costs	52.7%
Increased productivity	52.0%
Within budget	37.1%
Meet deadlines	33.2%
Increased sales	18.6%
ROI study	17.0%
Reduced time-to-market	6.6%
No measure	14.7%

Source: IDC 2003

Table 5.6 – *Decision criteria*

This proves that ROI is an important metric but it needs to be balanced with a more complete analysis of all the value factors.

Business Alignment

Increasing complexity and the dependency of the organization on IT have made that business and IT can no longer be seen as independent; they mutually influence each other and this is reflected at different levels. These levels are mutually reinforcing, complementary, and interdependent. This means that IT investment has to be aligned with the business. This will be discussed in more detail in another chapter.

Risk Analysis

Many organizations have become totally dependent on Information Technology; vital business processes are supported or depend on IT. The failure or temporary unavailability of IT or one of its components could cause financial damage or even mean the end of the organization.

A successful IT project is not just the installation of a technical system, but also the institutionalization of its use in the context of formal and informal structures and personal or group processes. Issues such as organizational behavior, culture, structure and politics and the risks associated with these areas have to be considered if the project is to be a success.

Willcocks and Margett [73] define risk as:

"Exposure to such consequences as failure to obtain some or all anticipated benefits due to implementation problems and/or failure to complete the project on schedule, within budget, with adequate performance or in accordance with some measure of project success."

The risk level in IT projects is routinely underestimated, often due to human and organizational issues that are difficult to identify.

Risks also arise at different levels: strategic, tactical and operational.

Strategic-level risks are the risks emerging from the environment in which the organization operates. At this level consideration has to be given to the consequences of failing to realize the opportunities for business benefit as a result of not building the system. This can threaten business continuity or great financial risk, which can even endanger the viability of the organization. At this level the risks are arising out of factors such as the economy, government policy, markets, customer demands, sub contractors, competition, and in the Public Sector government guidelines, procedures and funding arrangements.

Risks at the tactical level are related to two categories of sources: content and process:

- *Content* includes project scope, type of technology, newness of technology, complexity, size and extensiveness of the project, whether radical or incremental in impact and whether other organizations or third parties are involved.
- *Process* relates to the availability of project management skills and resources. More specifically it includes formulation and specification of goals, planning

and monitoring of the actual realization. Attention is also to be given to user training and commitment, project team experience and IT staff retention rates.

Operational-level risks are those risks that arise out of the client environment: infrastructure integrity, acceptability within business and by the stakeholders and achievement of benefits.

Several risk analysis and management methods have been proposed. These methods are available either as guidelines to be applied manually or as interactive software packages. One of these is CRAMM: the UK Government's Risk Analysis and Management Method, another one is *Software Risk Management (SRM)* developed by the *Software Engineering Institute (SEI)*.

Architecture

All IT investments should be made in line with the organization's technical architecture unless there is a clear and persuasive reason not to do so. The technical architecture lists the different types of hardware, software, and networking infrastructure and protocols that are used and supported. The software architecture includes the development tools used to build custom Information Systems, desktop and networking operating systems, and personal productivity and groupware suites. The intention to create a homogeneous environment is in line with an investment that is consistent with the technical architecture. The idea is that the less diversity in IT assets, the less diverse and expensive will be the related support costs and TCO.

Any IT asset investment proposal is also supposed to consider the organization's entire portfolio of assets. In other words, one should purchase IT systems to maximize the benefits that derive not only from the newly purchased systems but also from existing systems as well. In part this requirement refers to the two items above; an organization should create a more homogeneous portfolio of systems to reduce support costs. In addition, one can develop an overall IT asset replacement strategy that considers individual purchases as part of a long-term strategy to purchase the newest, most powerful computers for the *power users*, then rotate their machines to a second tier of users, and so on.

Life Cycle of IT systems

The *economic life cycle* is the useful financial life of an item. In other words, the life cycle is the number of years one plans to keep a piece of hardware or software. For example, a life cycle of three years for a PC implies that at the end of three years, the PC is either no longer suited for its intended purpose, or maintenance and support have grown to the extent that it is cheaper to replace the computer than keep it, or new requirements or performance standards have required it's replacement to meet customer needs. Keeping IT assets longer than their economic life cycle is a mistake. Not only does it waste current money, but also it deprives you the advantages of newer technology.

When compared to other capital assets, the replacement of IT systems is unique; because you do not just replace what you had, you upgrade it significantly. Replacing traditional assets, like cars and office furniture, results in something the same as what you started with, only newer. On the other hand, a five-year-old PC could be replaced with a new one, which not only does the old things better but it does important new things that the original did not.

There are several ways of determining the economic life cycle of IT systems. One is to take into account technology generations. In the 1980s Intel produced a major new generation of microprocessors about every three and a half years. Currently, the time between generations is shorter, perhaps two years or less. The implications for life cycles are obvious; they are getting shorter. As a result, it is more expensive for organizations to stay on the leading edge and be competitive right now because of shorter technology life cycles, and it is likely to be even more difficult in the next decades.

The principles of asset management that apply to buying a computer are fundamentally different from those of buying a truck. If an organization purchases a truck for $25,000, with an expected life of, say, five years, it will have a capital cost of $5,000 per year. At the end of five years, the truck could be replaced with another truck that would cost more but still be functionally identical. One way to help make this investment pay better would be to invest more in maintenance and amortize the cost over more years. The rule of thumb to optimize this type of investment is to depreciate it for as many years as possible.

Computers, on the other hand, are different. If an organization purchases a $25,000 computer and depreciates the investment over five years it will also cost $5,000 per year. The difference comes when considering what happens when the machine is replaced. Here, the organization will be able to spend significantly less on the replacement and still receive a new computer that is superior to the one it is replacing. Given the superior performance of the replacement machine, the lower price, and the growing demand, the whole idea of evaluating IT investments by the same methods used to evaluate the truck seems impractical. Yet most organizations do just that. Instead of buying the biggest computer necessary to do the job for five years, it would be much better to buy the smallest computer that can do the job, say, for three years and then replace it. The organization is better off buying a $15,000 computer for three years, and then replacing it sooner than buying a $25,000 computer for five years. The first approach has the same annual cost but the organization gets the benefit of replacing its computer with a superior machine for less money after only three years instead of five.

In this example, the organization has a strategic choice of how to manage the replacement of IT. At the end of three years the organization can choose to either:

- Keep its computing power at a constant level and lower its annual expenditure by buying something with the same power for less money;
- Grow its computing power by holding IT spending constant and taking advantage of new economies;
- Expand its real investment in IT by growing its level of spending.

Case one can be rejected as it is a strategy of stagnation; regardless of the life cycle length, it assumes no growth in power or capabilities, so the strategic choice is between holding the capital budget constant and growing it.

Best Practices

Budget for hardware every year

Computer hardware should be classified as a yearly budgeted expense. It is recommended to replace computers at least every three years, however not all of them need to be replaced at the same time. Therefore, if you allocate money for each workstation annually, you will be able to purchase new computers for about a third of the organization each year. You will also be able to maintain systems that are not being replaced. The replacement scheme depends on the differences between the customers in the organization.

In an organization with a limited group of *power users* and a larger group of less-demanding users it could be decided to replace the computers of the power users every year. The "old" computers of this group can then be redeployed amongst the other users.

	A	B	C
Year 1	0	1	2
Year 2	0	2	1
Year 3	0	1	2

The figures represent the age of the computers at the beginning of every year. So, in year 2, the one-year-old machines of group A go to the users of group C, and the computers of group C are transferred to group B. This scenario is then repeated every year. On average, the users from group A will always dispose of a computer that is between brand new and one year old, while the users from groups B and C will have a machine that is between one and three years old. If the population is more *homogeneous*, a simpler scheme could be applied.

	A	B	C
Year 1	0	1	2
Year 2	1	2	0
Year 3	2	0	1

This scenario is simpler to create because it involves less moving around with computers between different user groups; the machines stay with the same users until they reach the age of their replacement.

It is obvious that both schemes can be mixed. One could for example apply the first scheme in the IT department (group A being the developers and B and C the others) and the second scheme to the rest of the organization. The only thing that is required is a good inventory control; to make sure that can be determined what type of user uses which computer.

Buy your systems "just in time"

You can save a lot of money when you invest at the proper time. There is no better way to illustrate this than with a simple example.

Suppose you are about to invest in a new system with an initial capacity of 100 units (processing power, storage, bandwidth...). You expect an increase in capacity requirement of 10% over the lifetime of the system yielding a total capacity requirement of 146 in year five. With a unit cost of 1.00 at the moment of purchase, buying the whole system in one go will cost you 146.00.

Year	Capacity	Increase	Unit cost	Cost
1	100	100	1.00	100.00
2	110	10	0.75	7.50
3	121	11	0.56	6.19
4	133	12	0.42	5.10
5	146	13	0.32	4.21
Total				123.00

Moore's law still holds, so the unit cost will drop over time by, say 25% a year. So, when you buy the additional required capacity units at the moment you need them, you will pay less. In the above example the total cost would drop to 123.00, which represent a nice saving!

This picture gets even better if you take into account the fact that you don't need all the money in the first year (so you don't have to pay interest if you have to borrow or you get the interest if you have the money). On top of that, you will pay less maintenance costs because these are usually proportional to the invested amount.

As a conclusion, it is better to buy systems that are slightly oversized for your current needs and extend their performance as your needs grow over time. Not only will you pay less but also you will be able to take better advantage of the continuous technological progress.

Good enough can be best

When defining the scope of a new project you should ask yourself how far the automation should go. Often, 80% of the work is simple and straightforward and only 20% is complex because of exceptions (Fig. 5.5). Focus on the automation of the "normal" cases and keep the exceptions out of the system using a manual procedure. This will yield cheap and easily maintainable systems that still add a lot of value to the organization.

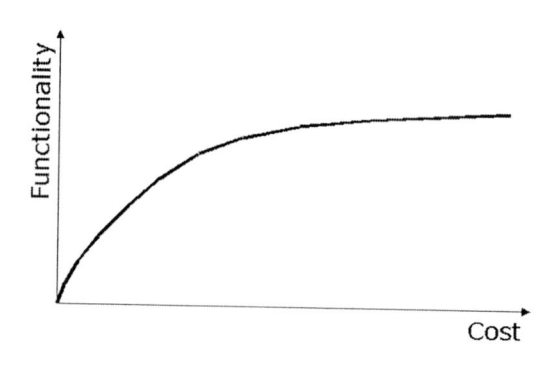

Fig. 5.5 – *Functionality vs. Costs*

Paradoxically, while the overall aim is to provide an excellent service, "good enough" IT Systems can best underpin this. The benefits gained from developing a perfect system for one activity can well be out-weighted by the costs of not developing an IT solution for another activity.

Invest to reduce TCO

Sometimes it can be cheaper in the long run to do an apparently unnecessary investment. Take for example the computing power of your machines. During the backup process the response time of a system are multiplied by 10, an operation that normally takes ten minutes now takes more than an hour. When there are 200 users this means a loss of 166 working hours! Investing in a more powerful machine could reduce this cost dramatically. Another example is downtime due to system trouble. Imagine the production time that can be lost because users cannot access their data anymore. This can be avoided by having some redundancy, an expense that at first sight could look superfluous but that could well turn out to be the lifesaver of your organization.

Note that – for the same performance – the price of technological resources is continuously dropping, while the costs related to Human resources keeps on increasing.

The annual cost of a programmer back in the 1960s was only a small fraction of the cost of the mainframe computer he was working on. That same programmer costs a multiple of the annual expenses for the much more powerful machines his programs are running on today.

The same holds for the end users of IT: in the 1960s human labour was relatively inexpensive compared with today's prices.

The conclusion of this is that it can be a good idea to spend more money on technology to reduce the costs in the HR area, thereby reducing the Total Cost of Ownership and at the bottom line the overall efficiency and effectiveness of the organization.

Link the project expenses to the objectives

When setting up a project you can agree on a cost-based charging and link the profit to the project objectives. All parties agree on the criteria to be met, such as improved user satisfaction or increased productivity and the way this will be linked to the profit. In that way, the contractor will be extra motivated to bring the project to a good end.

A pleasant side effect is that the users will be more involved and start thinking on how things can be improved.

Manage your software assets carefully

Software acquisition represents a significant portion of the IT budget, so it makes sense to control these costs effectively. On the other hand, the increased importance of software brings new risks: fraud, viruses, legal challenges and simple mistakes can have adverse effects on your profitability. It is therefore of prime importance to set up a *Software Asset Management (SAM)* policy that will help you to:

- Improve the software planning and cost control;
- Avoid legal issues;
- Manage technological change;
- Enhance information liquidity;
- Justify investments in technology.

When the volumes, diversity or physical dispersion of the software justifies this, this policy and associated procedures can be supported by automated tools but – once again – do not forget that the process is more important than the tool.

Financial Resources

Only go for win-win situations

Most of the time, financials will be the result of a negotiation between the IT department and its customers. Negotiation means that both parties are trying to agree on a good deal. A good deal is one that is fair for both parties at the time the agreement is made. It also provides for various unforeseen events before problems arise. In other words: a good deal is workable in the real world.

To be sure that there is a good deal, the answer to the following questions should be affirmative:

- Does the outcome of the negotiation fit into your short-term and long-term plans?
- Can both parties perform their side of the agreement?
- Do both parties have the intention to meet their commitment?

If you are hesitant about any one of these questions, take some more time to negotiate. See how the agreement could be changed in order to create a yes answer to each question.

Remember that the people you are dealing with are more important than the red tape. Know your counterpart very well before you enter into a long-term relationship. No lawyer can protect you from a crook; lawyers can just put you in a position to win a lawsuit.
Some people tend to be overly concerned about the other party's welfare in a negotiation, stifling their own goals in the process. The other party may not have that attitude so you risk ending up with a bad deal.

Push for equal treatment of the IT budget

The IT budget should be considered like any other part of the organization's budget, rather than as a separate category of expenses. IT investment decisions must be considered in the same manner that a manufacturer decides on investing in a new plant, for example. Also, the IT operating expenses are comparable to the other operating expenses such as energy, water and infrastructure maintenance.

Retire your old IT systems in time

How many organizations are still operating an old machine that is running some application critical to their business? You might think that just because the hardware was fully depreciated long ago, the system is "free." This is not true: there are real and hidden support costs to maintaining legacy hardware systems, provided you can even find replacement parts.

An even more critical and costly problem is supporting legacy software. If the application was written in-house, is the author still available to support it? If not, do you have enough documentation to support it now and in the future? Maybe you think you are safe because you purchased the software from a vendor. Is the company still in business? Even if it has not merged nor disappeared into oblivion, does the vendor still support your version of the software?

Here's a checklist of things to consider when reviewing legacy IT solutions:

- Is annual support less than replacement costs for both hardware and software?
- If the current support person would leave you, would you still be in business?
- Can you easily find people with the skills to maintain the system?
- Can you easily find replacement parts?
- Is the original vendor still in business and supporting your version of the system?

If you answered "no" to some of these questions, then you probably should be on the lookout for upgrading or replacing your legacy system before it causes serious harm to your business.

Set up pre- and post-implementation metrics

The business value of IT comes from the ability to conduct business processes more efficiently and effectively. However, once any new initiative is carried out, the value becomes embedded in the process. What remain apparent are the ongoing support costs. Unless pre- and post-implementation metrics are clearly defined, it becomes impossible to measure and report the value of the new initiative in the traditional language of business: cost, risk and time.

Start from the benefits, not the costs

When an organization develops Information Systems or sets up new IT projects it can only accurately determine the start costs, not the final costs. It is therefore better to start from the benefits you want to realize and calculate on that basis the costs you want to spend on the project. The questions to be asked should be: *"can we accept a failure?"* and *"what is the return if the project succeeds?"* Probably, the truth will be somewhere in the middle. This has to be accepted up front by all stakeholders.

Online Resources

ABC - http://www.pitt.edu/~roztocki/abc/abctutor/
ABC - http://www.offtech.com.au/abc/Home.asp
ABC benchmarking - http://www.abcbenchmarking.com/
IT metrics – http://www.informationweek.com
SRM - http://www.sei.cmu.edu/publications/documents/96.reports/96.tr.012.html
TCO - http://icdweb.cc.purdue.edu/~kimfong/TCO/models.html
TCO - http://www.zdnet.co.uk/pcmag/labs/1998/06/corp_pc/8.html
TCO - http://www-1.ibm.com/linux/RFG-LinuxTCO-vFINAL-Jul2002.pdf
Benchmarks and trends - http://www.info-edge.com/reports/CE-3601.asp

Further Reading

[65] Boynton, A., Victor, B. and Pine, B., *Aligning IT With New Competitive Strategies, Competing in the Information Age*, Luftman, New York, Oxford University Press. 1996.

[66] Bryson, John M., and Alston, Farnum K., *Creating and Realizing Your Strategic Planning*, San Francisco: Jossey-Bass Publishers, 1996.

[67] Cooper, R., Kaplan, R.S., *The design of Cost Management Systems*. Englewood Cliffs, NJ Prentice-Hall International, 1991.

[68] Gates, W., *Business at the Speed of Thought*. Time Warner. 1999.

[69] O'Guin, Michael C., *The Complete Guide to Activity Based Costing*, Englewood Cliffs, NJ, Prentice Hall, 1991.

[70] Pyhrr, P. A., *Zero-Base Budgeting: A Practical Management Tool for Evaluating Expenses*, New York, John Wiley & Sons, 1973.

[71] Remenyi, D., Money, A., Sherwood-Smith, M., *The Effective Measurement and Management of IT Costs and Benefits,* Butterworth Heinemann, 1990.

[72] Robson, W., *Strategic management and information systems*, Pitman Publishing, London, 1994.

[73] Willcocks, L. and Margetts, H. *Risk assessment and information systems*. European Journal of Information Technology, Vol. 3, N° 2. 1994.

[74] Willcocks, L., *Information management. The evaluation of information systems investments*, Chapman & Hall, London, 1994.

6

Processes

"Quality is a journey, not a destination."

(W.E. Deming)

Introduction

The term *Process* has already been used several times. Davenport [78] defines it as:

"A specific ordering of work activities across time and place, with a beginning, an end, clearly identified inputs and outputs: a structure for action."

A simple analogy would be to look at an organization as a wheel and the individual Business Processes as the spokes of that wheel. Having just one or two spokes loose can make a wheel roll out of balance. The longer a wheel runs out of balance the more damaging the effect to the wheel. When the wheel becomes so unstable that its primary function fails, you would simply replace the wheel. Obviously, an organization cannot replace itself... but your customers can and will do so if the organization does not perform to their needs and expectations.

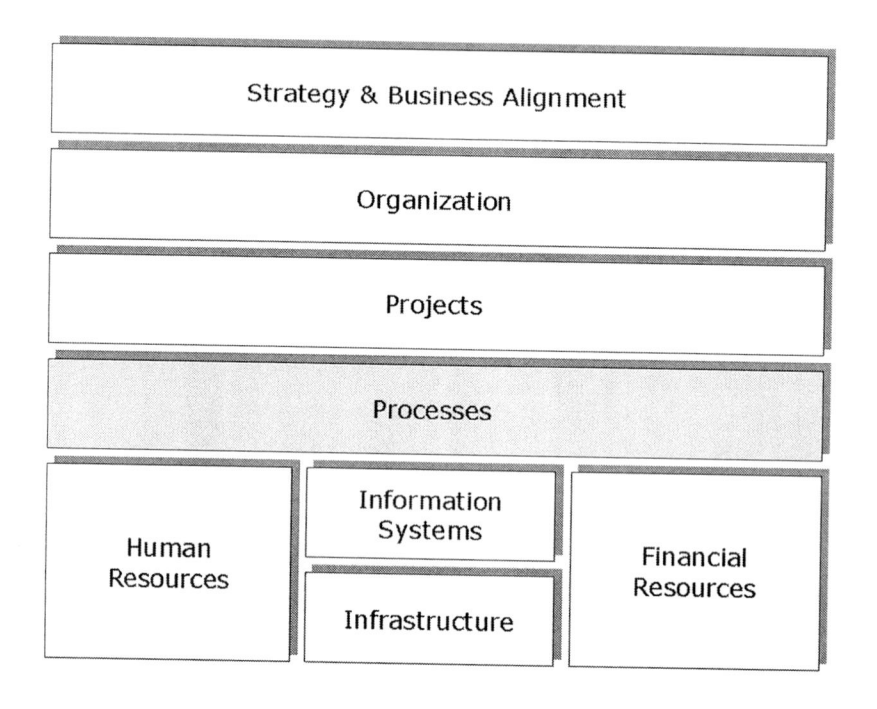

Fig. 6.1 – *Position of Processes in the IT stack*

Processes all have (internal or external) customers. They occur inside, across or between organizational subunits or between different organizations.

The purpose of a process is to *transform input* into *output*. This transformation is done through the support of *resources* (money, people, infrastructure, information) and according to predefined *specifications*.

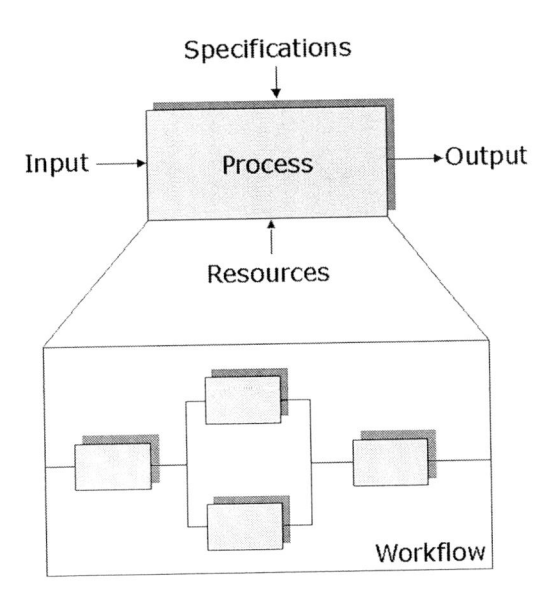

Fig. 6.2 – *Process Decomposition*

A process can be decomposed in several *steps*, organized in a workflow. Each step (or activity) is performed by an actor (a person or a group of persons) using a *role* in the workflow.

The output of a process can be material (a product) or non-material (a service). In fact, often it is a combination of both (e.g., a car is the material component, while maintenance the service component of the output of a car manufacturer's process).

The first part of this chapter will discuss the processes of the business itself, the second part will talk about the IT processes.

Business Processes

Typology

In general, an organization is situated between its suppliers and its customers. Inside the organization, a variety of processes are executed. The *operational processes* make the organization what it is; this is why these processes are sometimes called the *core business*. There are also several *support processes* such as financial management, accounting and Human Resources Management. The processes that occur between the organization and its suppliers or trading partners are called *Business-to-Business (B2B)* processes, while the processes between the organization and its customers are called *Business-to-Customer or Business-to-Consumer (B2C)*, internal processes are executed using *Enterprise Applications Integration*. The interaction with the customers and the suppliers or trading partners is also called *Front office*, while the other processes are categorized as *Back office*.

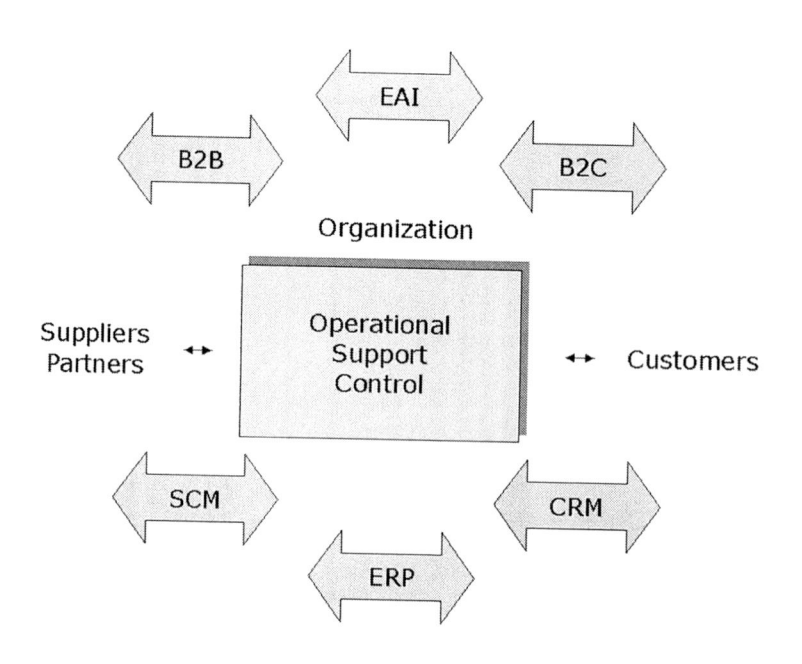

Fig. 6.3 – *Business Process Typology*

At the supplier side, the purpose of the processes is to reduce the processing cost by improving efficiency and speed. At the customer side, revenue enhancement is obtained by customer satisfaction. Inside the organization, an improved efficiency is achieved by reducing the internal cycle times. All this is underpinned by *integrating* the involved processes by means of *Supply Chain Management (SCM), Enterprise Resource Planning (ERP)* and *Customer Relationship Management (CRM)* systems.

Supply Chain Management

A *supply chain* is a set of facilities and distribution options that perform the functions of procurement of materials, transformation of these materials into intermediate and finished products, and the distribution of these products to customers [75]. Supply chains exist in both service and manufacturing organizations, although the complexity of the chain can vary much from industry to industry and organization to organization. Traditionally, marketing, distribution, planning, manufacturing, and the purchasing organizations along the supply chain operated independently. These organizational units had their own, often conflicting, objectives. For example marketing wanted to obtain a high customer service and maximum sales; this conflicted with manufacturing and distribution goals. Indeed, manufacturing operations are designed to maximize throughput and lower costs with little consideration for the impact on inventory levels and distribution capabilities. On the other hand, purchasing contracts were often negotiated with little information beyond historical buying patterns. The result was that there was not a single, integrated plan for the organization; there were as many plans as subunits. Clearly, there is a need for a mechanism through which these different functions can be integrated together. *Supply Chain Management (SCM)* is a strategy through which such integration can be achieved.

SCM is usually considered to be between fully vertically integrated organizations, where a single organization owns the entire material flow and each channel member operates independently. Therefore coordination between the various players in the chain is key in its effective management. SCM can be seen as a relay team. Such a team is more competitive when each player knows how to be positioned for the hand-over. The relationships are the strongest between players who directly pass the baton, but the entire team needs to make a coordinated effort to win the race.

There are four major decision areas in supply chain management:

- *Location* - geographic placement of production facilities, stocking points, and sourcing points;
- *Production* - what products to produce, and which plants to produce them in, allocation of suppliers to plants, plants to distribution centers, and distribution centers to customer markets;
- *Inventory* – which inventories exist and are managed (raw materials, semi-finished or finished goods);
- *Transportation and distribution* - shipment sizes (bulk versus lot-for-lot), routing and scheduling.

Customer Relationship Management

"And then you'll close the sale."

The Harvard Business Review states that the average US Company loses half its customers every five years. On the other hand, the Gartner Group found that a 5% increase in customer loyalty sometimes translates to a 75% increase in profitability. *Customer Relationship Management (CRM)* is a business strategy to select and manage customers to optimise long-term value. CRM requires a customer-centric business philosophy and culture to support effective marketing, sales, and service processes. CRM applications can enable effective Customer Relationship Management. CRM extends the concept of selling from an act performed by a salesperson to a continuous process involving every person in the company. It is the science of gathering and using information about your customers to build loyalty and increase customer value.

The key principles of CRM are:

- *Differentiation of customers* – not all customers are created equal. One should recognize and reward the best customers disproportionately;
- *Differentiation of offerings* – customers appreciate customized offerings;
- *Keeping existing customers* – it is five to ten times cheaper to retain your current customers than to acquire new ones. Furthermore, loyal customers are more profitable;
- *Maximizing lifetime value* – exploit up-selling and cross-selling potential.

There are four business process steps involved in creating a CRM system:

- Customer interaction;
- Customer data integration;
- Customer data analysis;
- Customer interaction personalization.

The last three steps all involve data warehousing.

Enterprise Resource Planning

Enterprise Resource Planning (ERP) is an industry term for the activities that help an organization to manage important parts of its business, including product planning, parts purchasing, maintaining inventories, interacting with suppliers, providing customer service, and tracking orders. ERP software can also include modules for the supporting activities such as Finance and Human Resources. Some important points to be kept in mind while evaluating ERP software include:

- Functional fit with the company's business processes;
- Degree of integration of the various components of the ERP system;
- Agility and scalability;
- Complexity and user friendliness;
- Amount of customization required;
- Implementation time;
- Ability to support multi-site planning and control;
- Technology: client/server capabilities, database independence, security;
- Availability of regular upgrades;
- Local support infrastructure;
- Total costs, including cost of license, training, implementation, maintenance, customization and hardware requirements.

The success of an ERP implementation depends on how quick the benefits can be acquired from it. The traditional approach to implementation has been to carry out a Business Process Re-engineering exercise before the ERP system implementation. This led to mismatches between the proposed model and the ERP functionality, the consequence of which was customizations, extended implementation durations, higher costs and loss of customer confidence. Another approach is to conduct a concurrent Business Process Re-engineering during the ERP implementation and aim to shorten the total implementation time.

Implementation of SCM, CRM and ERP processes

Packaged Solutions

In the last decade, several packaged, customizable and modular solutions that implement SCM, CRM and ERP have come on the market. The idea of using ready-made products, rather than homegrown applications is of course attractive, but there are also some risks attached to it. Indeed, you buy an empty shell that has to be adapted completely to your needs. To do this, customers typically rely on the intervention of external "experts."

The consequence of all this is that the costs associated with the implementation of an integration package are typically composed of two components: the licensing and maintenance costs for the products and the costs associated with the consulting assignment of analyzing your processes and modeling them in the tool.

The *licensing cost* is usually related to the number of (concurrent) users or the size of the machine and it has to be paid only once, the *maintenance cost* however is recurrent; it is a percentage of the license cost and usually only covers some support and minor software upgrades. For major upgrades a new license fee will have to be paid.

The *consulting costs* can be a multiple (three, ten or more times) of the licensing costs. As at the beginning of the project the consultant does not know anything about your business he will be reluctant to offer you a fixed price project and if he does, he will for sure take a royal margin to cover his risks. So you either pay too much (fixed price project) or have no idea at all what the project will cost at the end (and probably pay too much anyway). This is the main reason why many integration projects cost a multiple of what was initially planned for.

Besides the high costs there is another drawback with these packages. Because of the fact that the customization part is usually outsourced to an external consultant, the knowledge about the models of your business will usually leave your organization at the same time as the consultant does. That means that, whenever your processes change, you will be forced to ask for the intervention of that consultant. If he is still around it will just cost you, if he is not you will lose time and pay even more for the learning cycle of the newcomer.

Another approach is to adapt the business processes to the features that are offered by the package; in this way a lot of money can be saved on the invoice of the consultants. The question that can be asked in this context is of course what becomes of the differentiators between you and your competitors.

Therefore it is not advisable to use packaged solutions for your core business processes; they cost too much and make your business too vulnerable. When applied for the non-core processes it is recommended to adapt the processes to the package and to keep the knowledge in the heads of your own people.

Application Service Providers (ASPs)

Another interesting solution can be found in the *Application Service Provider (ASP)* model. IDC defines ASPs as providers of a contractual service offering to deploy, host, manage and rent access to an application from a centrally managed facility. ASPs are responsible for either directly or indirectly providing all the activities and expertise aimed at managing a software application or set of applications. The ASP model is sometimes called *Application Outsourcing*. The advantages of the ASP model are:

- The organization continuously disposes of the best IT infrastructure and the most recent software versions;
- The applications can be used anywhere, anytime; all that is needed is an Internet connection;
- Information can be shared with other users, provided they have the right to do so;
- There is no need for a heavy investment in either hardware of software. Moreover there is no need for staff for the maintenance of the infrastructure and the customer only pays for his real consumption.

Even though these are all real advantages, there are, as always, some drawbacks to this mode of operation as well:

- Who is responsible if, for some reason, the service is not good or not available?
- What about (intellectual) property of the information handled by the system?
- Do you keep the freedom to choose your supplier or is there a lock-in?

The above questions need some serious consideration before getting involved in an ASP scheme.

Quality and Quality Management

Definitions

ISO 8402 formally defines *Quality* as:

"The totality of features and characteristics of a product or service that bear on its ability to satisfy stated or implied needs."

In other words, quality is the extent to which a product or service meets or exceeds customer requirements and expectations. *Good* quality does not necessarily mean *high* performance; it means a predictable degree of uniformity and dependability at a reasonable cost, with a performance suited to the market.

Customer requirements can take many different forms; the spectrum of possibilities can be drawn as follows.

- Effectiveness
    - Internal
    - Availability
        - Timeliness;
        - Quantity;
        - Uniformity;
        - Agility.
    - External
        - Form;
        - User friendliness.
- Efficiency
    - Cost effectiveness;
    - Price.
- Reliability
    - Continuity;
    - Security;
    - Robustness.
- Customer Satisfaction
    - General satisfaction;
    - Functionalities.

Furthermore, these requirements can be descriptive or quantified. *Descriptive* requirements only contain a description while *quantified* requirements also contain a value that has to be met (norm). Obviously, it is preferable to have quantified requirements.

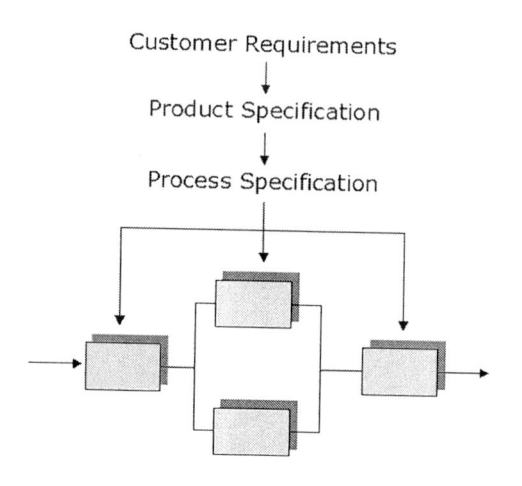

Fig. 6.4 – *Process Quality*

At the process level, these customer requirements are translated into product specifications, which in turn are decomposed into process specifications: these are the requirements to both input and output of the distinctive steps that form the process. For every step in the process both input and output then have to be measured and compared to the process specification. If this is not met corrective actions have to be taken.

Five notions have to be distinguished with respect to quality (ISO 8402):

- Quality Policy.
- Quality Management;
- Quality System;
- Quality Control;
- Quality Assurance.

Quality Policy is the overall intention and direction of an organization regarding quality, as formally expressed by top management.

Quality Management is that aspect of the overall management function that determines and implements the quality policy. The achievement of desired quality requires the commitment and participation of all members of the organization whereas the responsibility for quality management belongs with top management. Quality management includes strategic planning, allocation of resources and other systematic activities for quality, such as quality planning, operations and evaluations.

A *Quality System* is the organizational structure, responsibilities, procedures, processes and resources for realizing quality management.
Quality Control (QC) is the set of operational techniques and activities that are used to fulfill requirements for quality. Finally, *Quality Assurance (QA)* is the collection of all the planned and systematic actions necessary to provide adequate confidence that a product or service will satisfy given requirements for quality.

Total Quality Management (TQM)

Total Quality Management (TQM) [76][79][80] is the system that Japan has developed to create *Kaizen* or *continuing improvement;* it extends quality management to the resources and secondary (supporting) processes. TQM is an improvement on the teachings of Deming, Juran, Feigenbaum, and others. The term Total Quality Management contains three elements:

- *Total* - Quality involves everyone and all activities in the company;
- *Quality* - Conformance to Requirements (Meeting Customer Requirements);
- *Management* - Quality can and must be managed.

ISO 9000

ISO 9000 is a series of international quality standards. The guiding principle is the prevention of deficiencies through the planning and application of best practices at every stage of the lifecycle a product or a service. These standards focus on identifying the basic disciplines and specifying the general criteria by which an organization, regardless of whether it is manufacturing or service oriented, can ensure that the requirements of its customers are met. The ISO 9000 series comprises the following standards:

- ISO 9000 - Guidelines for selection and use;
- ISO 9001 - Design, development, production, installation and servicing;
- ISO 9002 - Production, installation and servicing;
- ISO 9003 – Final inspection and test;
- ISO 9004 - Quality management and quality system elements;
- ISO 10011 - Guidelines for auditing quality systems;
- ISO 10012 - Requirements for measuring equipment;
- ISO 10013 - Guidelines for quality manuals.

Fundamentally these standards can be grouped into two categories: requirements and guidelines. *Requirements* are mandatory standards that dictate what an organization must do. There are four requirements standards: ISO 9001, ISO 9002, ISO 9003 and ISO 10012. *Guidelines* help an organization to interpret the requirements standards, suggesting what a company should do. There are also four guidelines: ISO 9000, ISO 9004, ISO 10011 and ISO 10013.

Business Process Reengineering

"See everything. Overlook a great deal. Improve a little."

(Pope John XXIII)

Business Process Reengineering (BPR) is the analysis and redesign of the processes within and between organizations [67][77][81][82][83]. BPR became popular in the early 1990's when Michael Hammer and James Champy published their book, *Reengineering the Corporation*. The authors promoted the idea that sometimes, radical redesign and reorganization of an organization was necessary to lower costs and increase quality of service and that IT was the key enabler for that radical change. They suggested seven principles of reengineering to streamline the processes and thereby achieve significant levels of improvement in quality, time management, and cost:

- Organize around outcomes, not tasks;
- Identify and sort all the processes in the organization;
- Integrate information processing work into the real work;
- Treat geographically dispersed resources as though they were centralized;
- Link parallel activities instead of just integrating their results;
- Put the decision points where the work is performed;
- Capture information once and at the source.

By the mid-1990s, however, BPR had the bad reputation of being a kind way of saying "downsizing." Today, it is admitted that radical change should only be applied in specific situations, and that usually it is better to proceed in small steps (*Improvement*) rather than to go for a radical change (*Innovation*). Davenport [78] pointed out the fundamental differences between these two approaches.

Characteristic	Improvement	Innovation
Level of change	Incremental	Radical
Starting Point	Existing process	Clean Slate
Frequency of change	One-time/Continuous	One-time
Time required	Short	Long
Participation	Bottom-up	Top-down
Typical Scope	Narrow, within functions	Broad, cross-function
Risk	Moderate	High
Primary Enabler	Statistical Control	Information Technology
Type of Change	Cultural	Cultural/Structural

Table 6.1 – *Improvement vs. Innovation*

Davenport notes that continuous improvement (now known as *Total Quality Management*) refers to programs and initiatives that emphasize incremental improvement over an open-ended period of time. In contrast, BPR refers to separate initiatives that are intended to achieve radically improved work processes in a limited duration.

Many change projects fail for the following reasons:

- Unrealistic scope and expectations;
- Lack of sustained management commitment;
- Resistance to change.

There are no "silver bullets." No modification in the existing order of things, be it the introduction of a new technology or the application of a new management technique will have more than a marginal effect on the overall efficiency or effectiveness of an organization. Getting the attention and the commitment of management should not be so difficult. However, change always involves some kind of investment and often includes a transition period with lower rather than higher efficiency. The challenge is to keep the support of the management during these more difficult periods. Change and pain are two faces of one coin. Change will only occur when the pain of change is less than the pain of "status quo." One should also never forget that many individuals often benefit from the existing situation, because of:

- Individual power bases (trouble shooters);
- Prestige (heroes);
- Security (ad hoc processes);
- Lack of control (nobody knows what is really going on).

Furthermore, individuals act in their own best interests, NOT in the organization's best interest.

How to succeed a change project

Change must represent a benefit to individuals as well as the organization; therefore a change manager must first remove fear and uncertainty amongst the individuals [77]. All organizations are chaotic in a mathematical sense; they cannot be pushed into a new state, changes must be *seeded* throughout the organization before it will flip into a new state. A good way to do this is first convince the *opinion leaders*; once they are persuaded they will do the convincing of the others for you. It is important to realize that the implementation and execution of the redesigned processes depends on those who do the work. Hence, recognition, participation, and ownership at grass roots level are essential for a successful change process.

The relationship between Business Change and IT

In the early 1990s Hammer [81] designated IT as the key enabler of Business Change, which he considers as *radical change*. He prescribes the use of IT to confront the assumptions in the work processes that have existed since long before the introduction of modern computing and communications technology.

Davenport [78] argues that change requires taking a broader view of both IT and business activity, and of the relationships between them. IT should be viewed as more than an automating or mechanizing force: to reshape the way business is done. Furthermore, IT and Business Change have a recursive relationship. IT capabilities should support Business Processes, and Business Processes should be in terms of the capabilities IT can provide. Business Processes represent a new approach to coordination across the organization. The promise of IT is to be the most powerful tool for reducing the costs of coordination.

Although, BPR has its roots in IT management, it is primarily a Business Initiative that has broad consequences in terms of satisfying the needs of customers and the organization's other stakeholders. Nevertheless, the IT manager must play an active role in convincing Senior Management of the power of IT.

IT Processes

The IT department is an organizational unit like all the others. In that respect it participates in several the normal processes of the organization (financial procedures, purchasing processes, Human Resources processes, etc.) and there are no good reasons for the IT department not to do so. There are, however, several processes that are only encountered in the IT environment. The discussion of these processes is the subject of the following sections.

IT Service Management (ITSM)

IT Service Management (ITSM) is a set of cooperating processes that ensure the quality of IT services delivered to the rest of the organization. IT Service Management provides an overall framework within which to operate individual activities such as the Help Desk and the creation of Service Level Agreements (SLAs). The principal objectives of IT Service Management are:

- Providing customer focused IT Services;
- Aligning the IT services with the organization's objectives;
- Creation and managing of cost-effective SLAs.

ITSM is concerned with the planning, implementation and permanent control of operational IT services and the IT infrastructure on which these services run. Adopting ITSM introduces a service culture and provides the methodologies to deliver services that meet defined business requirements and priorities in a cost-effective way.

The adoption of ITSM empowers the IT department to change the perception that it is simply a significant cost centre. It helps put the IT organization on a proper business footing and to establish a profile as a professionally run unit that delivers cost effective services.

ITIL

An important set of documents managing ITSM is the *IT Infrastructure Library (ITIL)* developed by the *CCTA*, the UK Government's *Central Computer and Telecommunications Agency*.

ITIL consists of a series of books giving guidance on the provision of quality IT services, and on the accommodation and environmental facilities needed to support IT. ITIL has been developed in recognition of organizations growing dependency on IT and embodies best practices for IT Service Management.

The idea behind the development of ITIL is the recognition that organizations are becoming increasingly dependent on IT to satisfy their corporate aims and meet their business needs. This growing dependency leads to a growing requirement for high quality IT services.

From its beginnings in the UK and Europe, ITIL has rapidly become a world standard for measuring and improving standards of IT service delivery. ITIL is the only major non-proprietary set of IT service standards, crossing the boundaries of infrastructure type and industry, to provide objective measurement of service quality across the whole IT service spectrum.

ITIL was primarily targeted at people responsible for managing the delivery of quality IT services. The books describe what needs to be done, and therefore managed, rather than how the functions should be carried out. Nevertheless, all staff that delivers the IT services will have to have a general knowledge of ITIL. Many of the ITIL-processes are also of importance to business staff, both managers and day-to-day customers and end-users, involved in building good relationships with their IT service providers. The guidance is useful to any size of organization, in public or private sectors. ITIL intentionally describe functions and staff roles rather than work groups and job titles so that it can be applied to organizations of various sizes, whether they have a central, distributed or mixed IT infrastructure and service provision. ITIL divides the ITSM processes in ten disciplines, in turn grouped into two categories: Service Support and Service Delivery.

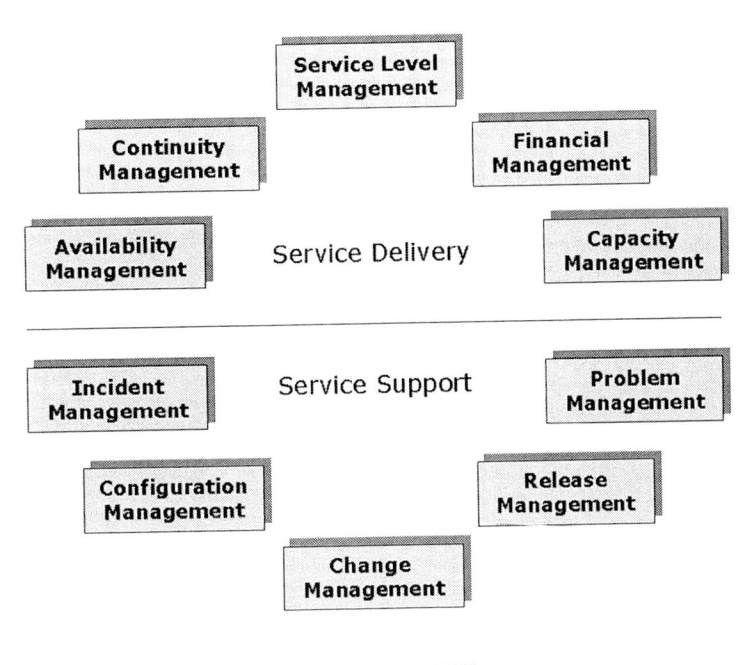

Fig. 6.5 - *ITIL*

Service Support is the practice of those disciplines that enable IT Services to be provided. Without these disciplines, it would be almost impossible to provide these services, and at best in an unmanaged and ad hoc way.

The five Service Support disciplines are:

- Configuration Management;
- Problem Management;
- Change Management;
- Incident Management;
- Release Management.

Service Delivery is the management of the IT services themselves, and involves several management practices to ensure that IT services are provided as agreed between the Service Provider and the Customer.

Service Delivery also consists of five disciplines. These are:

- Service Level Management;
- Capacity Management;
- Continuity Management;
- Availability Management;
- Financial Management.

Configuration Management

It is important for every organization to control it's production means, as they are the key to the creation of products or services that form the very reason of existence of the organization. Just like all other production means, the means of the IT department have to be managed. *Configuration Management* is the creation of a *Configuration Management Database* (*CMDB*) that contains the details of the *Configuration Items* (*CIs*) that are used in the provision and management of IT services. A Configuration Item is a component that is a part of, or is directly related to the IT infrastructure. A CI can be a physical or a logical component and can be composed of other CIs.

Some examples of CIs are:

- Personal Computer;
- Network card;
- Change Proposal;
- Manual;
- Service Level Agreement.

Configuration Management consists of five tasks:

- *Identification* – this is the specification, identification of all IT components and their inclusion in the CMDB;
- *Control* – this is the specification of who is authorized to change the CIs;
- *Status* – this task is the recording of the status of all Configuration Items in the CMDB, and the maintenance of this information;
- *Verification* – this task involves reviews and audits to ensure the information contained in the CMDB is accurate;
- *Information Providing* – mainly to the other processes of the IT Services.

Problem Management

Problem Management is the resolution and prevention of incidents that affect the normal running of the IT services. This includes ensuring that faults are corrected, preventing any recurrence of these faults, and the application of preventive maintenance to reduce the likelihood of these faults occurring.

Change Management

Change Management is the practice of ensuring all changes to Configuration Items are carried out in a planned and authorized manner. This includes ensuring that there is a business reason behind each change, identifying the Configuration Items and IT Services affected by the change, planning the change, testing it, and having a rollback plan should the change result in an unexpected state of the Configuration Item.

Incident Management

The *Help Desk* plays an important part in the provision of IT Services. It is often the first contact the customers have in their use of IT Services when something does not work as expected. The two main focuses of the Help Desk are Incident Control and Communication (Public Relations). There are different types of Help Desk, the selection of which is dependent on what the business requires. Some Help Desks provide a simple call logging function, and escalate calls to more experienced and trained staff. Others provide a high degree of business and technical knowledge with the ability to solve most incidents at the time that the business user reports them.

"Sorry, your problem doesn't make sense. Call back with a problem I understand."

Release Management

Software Control & Distribution (*SC&D*) is the management of all Software Configuration Items within the organization. It is responsible for the management of software development, installation and support of an organization's software products. There can be several versions of the same software within the organization, and there can also be unlicensed and illegal copies of externally provided software. The practice of effective Software Control & Distribution involves the creation of a *Definitive Software Library* (*DSL*), into which the master copies of all software is stored and from here its control and release is managed.

The DSL consists of a physical store and a logical store:

- The *physical store* is where the master copies of all software media are stored. This tends to be software that has been provided from an external source;
- The *logical store* is the index of all software and releases, versions, etc. telling where the physical media can be located. The logical store can also be used for the storage of software developed within the organization.

SC&D procedures include the management of the Software Configuration Items and their distribution and creation into the production environment. This will involve the definition of a release program suitable for the organization, the definition of how version control will be created, and the procedures surrounding how software will be built, released and audited.

Service Level Management

Service Level Management is the primary management of IT services, ensuring that agreed services are delivered when and where they are supposed to be delivered. The *Service Level Manager* is dependent on all the other areas of Service Delivery providing the necessary support that ensures the agreed services are provided in a secure, efficient and cost effective manner. The Service Level Manager is often the IT manager himself, although this function could be delegated to another collaborator of the IT department.

There are several Business Processes that form part of Service Level Management. These are:

- Reviewing existing services;
- Negotiating with the Customers;
- Reviewing the contacts of third party service providers;
- Producing and monitoring the Service Level Agreements (SLAs);
- Implementation of Service Improvement policy and processes;

- Establishing priorities;
- Planning for service growth;
- Involvement in the Accounting process to cost services and recover these costs.

Capacity Management

Capacity Management is the discipline that ensures IT infrastructure is provided at the right time in the right volume at the right price, and ensuring that IT is used in the most efficient manner. This involves input from many areas of the organization to identify what services are (or will be) required, what IT infrastructure is required to support these services, what level of Contingency will be needed, and what the cost of this infrastructure will be.

The Capacity Management processes are:

- Performance monitoring;
- Workload monitoring;
- Application sizing;
- Resource forecasting;
- Demand forecasting;
- Modelling.

From these processes come the results of Capacity Management, these being the capacity plan itself, forecasts, tuning data and Service Level Management guidelines.

Continuity Management

Contingency Planning is the process by which plans are put in place to ensure that IT Services can recover and continue should a serious incident occur. It is not just about *reactive measures*, but also about *proactive measures* - reducing the risk of a disaster in the first instance. Contingency planning is regarded as the recovery of the IT infrastructure used to deliver IT Services, but many businesses these days practice the much further reaching process of *Business Continuity Planning* (*BCP*); to ensure that the whole end-to-end Business Process can continue should a serious incident occur.

Availability Management

Availability Management is the practice of identifying levels of IT Service availability for use in Service Level Reviews with Customers. All areas of a service must be measurable and defined with a *Service Level Agreement* (*SLA*).

Availability is usually calculated based on a model involving the Availability Ratio and techniques such as Fault Tree Analysis.

Financial Management

Financial Management is the discipline of ensuring IT infrastructure is obtained at the most effective price (which does not necessarily mean the cheapest price), and calculating the cost of providing IT services so that an organization can understand the costs of its IT services. These costs can perhaps then be recovered from the Customer of the service.

Other frameworks

COBIT

The *Control Objectives for Information and related Technology (COBIT)* standard is published by the Information Systems Audit and Control Association (ISACA) and was originally released in 1996. The COBIT framework includes 34 high-level control objectives and 318 detailed control objectives that have been designed to help businesses maintain effective control over IT.

ISO 17799

The *ISO 17799* standard titled "Information Technology - Code of Practice for Information Security Management," was first released by the ISO in December 2000. It is based on the British Standard 7799. The intent of the standard is to focus on security and help organizations in the creation of an effective IT security plan. The standard has the following high-level groupings: security policy, organizational security, asset classification and control, personnel security, physical and environmental security, communications and operations management, access control, systems development and maintenance, business continuity management and compliance.

Which framework to select?

Interestingly, there is not much overlap between ITIL, COBIT and ISO 17799; they more or less complement each other:

- ITIL is strong in IT processes, but limited in security and system development;
- COBIT is strong in IT controls and IT metrics, but does not say how and not that strong in security;
- ISO 17799 is strong in security controls, but does not say how.

As a conclusion, rather than select one, organizations should get an overview of the three and plan an approach that blends the best practices of each along with the needs of the organization.

Best Practices

Apply the self-service concept where possible

Often, processes can be simplified and made more efficient by applying the *self-service concept*.

Take the example of a HR application that, amongst other functionalities, takes care of the management of the holidays of the staff. Typically, there is a paper form that is filled out by the employee, who asks his manager for his approval. The manager will then check with the planning of his department to verify if he can agree or not. The signed form is sent by internal mail to the HR department for encoding in the system. This is the ideal scenario; in reality managers tend to be hard to lay your hand on (they always seem to have a meeting somewhere) and the person of the HR department is not available. Furthermore, the paper circuit is slow and unreliable, so the real life process can take days, instead of the few minutes that are really needed. A better solution is of course a *self-service screen* on the organization's Intranet. The employee fills out the request form on-line. His manager is then informed about the request, which can approve or refuse the request. As everything is updated on-line, the HR department is not involved in the encoding of the information; all they have to do is provide for the management information, when requested.

This self-service concept can be applied to many real life situations: think of order entry and tracking, customized services, help desk, and so on.

Build generic solutions

Do not just automate a Business Process, as it exists today, as it is sure that at some point in the future it will change. Think in terms of *inheritance* and *polymorphism*: an employee is not just an employee but also a person and so are the contact persons of employees and business relations. They all share common attributes like names, birth dates, addresses and telephone numbers, so why making separate tables, methods and screens while most of the effort to create them can be shared.

Many Business Processes can be implemented with a workflow system, so do not build tailor made systems that hardcode these procedures, but try to catch them using parameters in an organization-wide workflow system that is also being used in other business areas. More generally speaking, hard coded logic should be avoided at all cost. Put as much as possible in parameter tables, initialization files or user definable options.

Create a unified view of the business objects

Can you imagine a company with different product lines and a set of customer data for every product line, or even worse, different identification systems for the components that are needed to make the products? Yet, in many real life organizations this is the case. Different Information Systems running on separate platforms show distinct views of the same business objects. This is of course not efficient and prohibits coherent management and strategic reporting. To avoid this, a unique identification system is the absolute minimum to exchange information between processes and supporting Information Systems. In this way you avoid multiple storage of the same data, ensure data integrity and allow for reporting. Ideally, a unique identification number has the following characteristics:

- *Unicity* – an entity has a single identification number that is attributed at the moment that the entity is created. An identification number is never attributed to more than one entity;
- *Exhaustivity* – all entities have an identification number;
- *Stability* – an identification number does not change during the lifetime of an entity. Therefore the identification number should not contain variable attributes or references to other entities nor does it change when the entity changes.

In this context, Microsoft introduced the concept of *Global Unique Identifier (GUID)*. A GUID is a number that creates a unique identity for an entity such as a Word document. GUIDs are widely used in Microsoft products to identify interfaces, replica sets, records, and other objects.

A *Digital Object Identifier (DOI)* is a permanent identifier given to a Web file or other Internet document. DOIs are submitted to a central directory and use the address of that directory plus the DOI instead of a regular Internet address. Initially, the only central directory was the one maintained by the DOI Foundation. It is possible, however, that other directories be created and maintained, for example by each major industry.

Make lightweight Information Systems

Most real life Business Processes are simple for most cases. What make them complex are the exceptions. These exceptions can be worked around by manual interventions (computation, manual data entry). Usually the special cases tend to vary in time and the normal cases remain stable. Hence, lightweight Information Systems will need much less maintenance than programs that handle eexception in the book. Ultimately this will mean that the Information Systems will be more available. Take care of the exceptions

Inexperienced system designers have a tendency to believe that they can take into account all the possible situations; they have a strong belief in the models of the real world they are using to build their system.

Experienced designers are aware of their own limitations. They know that it is impossible to take all the situations into consideration and acknowledge the fact that no single Information System is without bugs or that the underlying Computing Infrastructure can fail.

Building a system that allows no exceptions and that forces the customers into a limiting harness of screens and control flows will inevitably turn out into a disaster. The models are never perfect, users are human beings who need a certain freedom of action and, finally: no system is perfect and fails from time to time.

A way to overcome these problems is to provide for *exception handling tools*: special screens for manipulating data, shortcuts for procedures or direct access to internal variables. It is obvious that the access to these tools has to be limited to specialized users, helpdesk people or database administrators and their use should be rigorously limited.

Online Resources

ASP - http://www.allaboutasp.com
COBIT – http://www.isaca.org
CRM - http://www.crmguru.com
ebXML - http://www.ebxml.org/white_papers/whitepaper.htm
ERP - http://www.cio.com/research/erp/
Helpdesk - http://www.helpdesk.com
Helpdesk - http://www.helpdeskinst.com
ISO - http://www.isoeasy.org
ISO - http://praxiom.com/iso-index.htm
ITIL - http://www.itil.co.uk
IT Services - http://www.mspassociation.org
IT Services - http://www.computerworld.com/managementtopics/
OASIS - http://www.oasis-open.org/
Quality - http://www.quality.org
Quality - http://www.asq.org
SCM - http://www.cio.com/research/scm/
SCM - http://logistics.about.com/
SCM - http://www.stanford.edu/group/scforum/
SLA – http://www.service-level-agreement.net
SLA – http://www.sla-world.com/framework.htm
TQM - http://www.efqm.org

Further Reading

[75] Ballou, R. H., *Business Logistics Management*, Prentice Hall, Englewood Cliffs, NJ, Third Edition. 1992.

[76] Berk, J. and S. Berk *Total Quality Management: Realizing Continuous Improvement*, Sterling Publishing Co. Inc., New York NY. 1993.

[77] Carr, D. K. and H. J. Johansson, *Best Practices in Reengineering: What Works and What Doesn't in the Reengineering Process,* McGraw-Hill, Inc., New York NY. 1995.

[77] Crosby, P. B. *Quality is Free: The Art of Making Certain*, McGraw-Hill Book Company, New York NY. 1979.

[78] Davenport, T.H., *Process Innovation: reengineering work through information technology*, Harvard Business School Press, Boston, MA. 1993.

[79] Gevirtz, C. *Developing New Products With TQM*, McGraw-Hill, Inc., New York NY. 1994.

[80] Gitlow, H. S. and S. J. Gitlow. *The Deming Guide to Quality and Competitive Position*, Prentice-Hall Inc., Englewood Cliffs NJ. 1987.

[81] Hammer, M., *Reengineering Work: Don't Automate, Obliterate,* Harvard Business Review, (1990, July-August).

[82] Hammer, M. and Champy J., *Reengineering the Corporation: A Manifesto for Business Revolution,* HarperBusiness, New York NY. 1993.

[83] Peppard, J. and Rowland, P., *The essence of business process reengineering*, Prentice Hall, London, 1995.

7

Projects

"The only thing more expensive than writing software is writing bad software."

(Alan Cooper)

Introduction

Projects have always been a part of life - ever since the first groups of humans worked together to gather, plant and hunt. Over the years, the concept of *Project Management* - planning and directing the activities executed by a group of people with fixed objectives over a limited period of time - has been refined and formalized into a profession.

The *Project Management Institute (PMI)*, a leading organization in the development of project management principles and certification standards, defines a project as:

"Any undertaking with a defined starting point and defined objectives by which completion is identified. In practice most projects depend on finite or limited resources by which the objectives are to be accomplished."

In PMI's view, Project Management is:

"The art of directing and coordinating human and material resources throughout the life of a project by using modern management techniques to achieve predetermined objectives of scope, cost, time, quality and participant satisfaction."

The Project Management Institute published a set of guidelines known as the *Project Management Body of Knowledge (PMBOK)*. The PMBOK includes knowledge of proven, traditional practices, which are widely applied, as well as knowledge of innovative and advanced practices, which can have a more limited use. The *American National Standards Institute (ANSI)* approved the *PMBOK Guide* as a standard.

Also in the world of IT there are many projects, mostly situated in the area of software development. In fact, software development is often one of the most important posts on the budget of an IT department. Unfortunately, it is also a fact that many IT projects fail: they are delivered too late, are too expensive or do not come up to the expectations of the users. According to the Standish Group, in their CHAOS report of 2003, the following figures apply for software projects:

- 15% of software projects are terminated before they produce anything;
- 66% are considered to have failed;
- Of those that do complete the average cost overrun is 43%;

However, this is a significant improvement on the results reported in the previous years, because the way software projects are handled has matured.

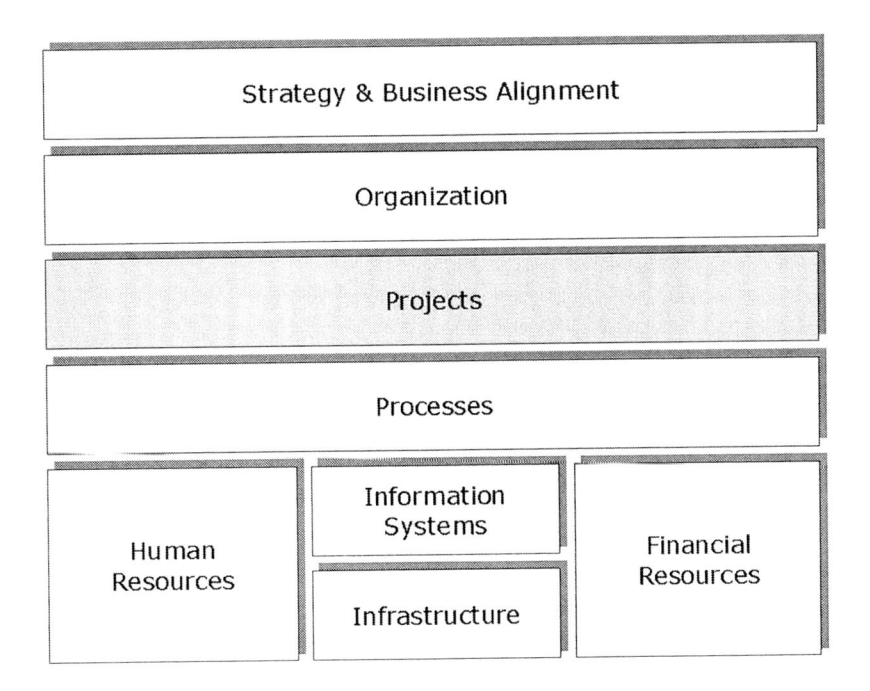

Fig. 7.1 – *Position of Projects in the IT stack*

The *Software Engineering Institute (SEI)* defines software development as:

"A set of activities, methods, practices and transformations that people use to develop and maintain software and the associated products."

An often-heard parallel is the one between the construction of a building and software development projects. At first sight there is indeed a lot of similarity between these two types of projects, there are however also some major differences.

It all starts with the *mismatch* between the functional and hierarchical organization model. It is almost impossible to run an IT project separate from the rest of the organization. Building a new plant can be done without affecting the rest of the company but with IT there is an influence on different parts of the organization and IT has to remain available all the time. Putting a sign "Closed for Work" is not an option. Another problem occurs because a lot of the work of an IT project has to be done by *non IT people*: management and staff of the end user community. Often, these people have to carry on with their normal work and have other priorities while the development team is constantly on their back with questions, tests etc.

Also, *measuring the progress* of an IT project is difficult: in a building project bricks are laid one by one and the progress can be seen right away, this is not so for a software development project; a lot of the work only becomes visible at the end, maybe when it is too late to correct mistakes.

Finally, in a building project, the allocation of some extra resources is easy but finding extra IT staff to speed up a project is less obvious. In a construction project everything is focused on the deadline. IT projects on the contrary are *resource-centric*; the resources are limited and the manager has to do with whatever is available. Furthermore, when new resources are added, they are not productive from the start.

The conclusion is that software development projects are different from projects in other areas; this is why a different approach in managing these projects has to be adopted. Understanding this is a first and necessary step for success.

Software Life Cycle

In the IEEE Standard Glossary of Software Engineering Terminology the *Software Life Cycle* is:

"The period of time that starts when a software product is conceived and ends when the product is no longer available for use. The software life cycle typically includes a requirements phase, design phase, implementation phase, test phase, installation and check-out phase, operation and maintenance phase, and sometimes, retirement phase."

A *Software Lifecycle Model* is a particular abstraction that represents a Software Life Cycle. A Software Life Cycle model is often called a *Software Development Life Cycle (SDLC)*.

The IEEE standard 1074 establishes a common framework for developing life cycle models. It describes the activities and processes needed for the development and maintenance of software. The standard divides the set of activities into *processes*, and processes into *process groups*:

Process Group	Processes
Life Cycle Modelling	Selection of a Life Cycle Model
Project Management	Project Initiation Project Monitoring and Control Software Quality Management
Pre-development	Concept Exploration System Allocation
Development	Requirements Design Implementation
Post-development	Installation Operation and Support Maintenance Retirement
Integral Processes	Verification and Validation Software Configuration Management Documentation Development Training

Table 7.1 – *Life cycle modeling*

Life Cycle Modelling

A variety of life cycle models have been proposed, most of which focus exclusively on the development processes. When formalized and combined with development techniques (modelling, prototyping…), they are called *methodologies*.

Code and Fix

Code and Fix is the simplest approach of product construction without specification or attempt of design. Coding, compilation, testing and fixing errors are repeated until the solution is good enough. This is a "trial and error" approach, which works fine for small software projects but is unacceptable for large or complex systems.

Waterfall Model

This is one of the first formalized development models.

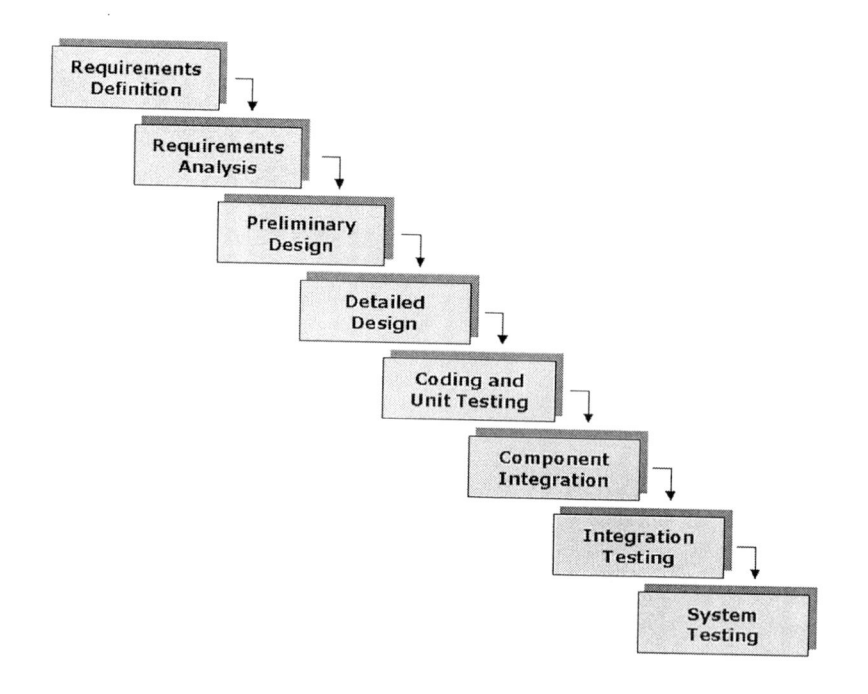

Fig. 7.2 – *Waterfall Model*

In this model, development proceeds in a stepwise manner from requirements, through design, implementation, testing, and finally operation.

The waterfall model has three underlying assumptions:

- The problem domain is well known by both client and development team;
- The problem domain is relatively stable over the development period;
- The client can wait for the entire solution to be delivered.

The Waterfall model is based on the approach used for the development of hardware systems, but there are differences between hardware and software that the waterfall model does not address. Unlike hardware, software requires no fabrication. One could use the analogies of house building and sculpting. Developing hardware can be compared to house building and developing software to sculpting. Sculpting is a less rigid exercise as moldable clay can be added, removed, or otherwise rearranged. Also, the criteria for judging successes in house building are largely objective, while the success of a sculpture is judged subjectively.

Some variants of the waterfall model allow revisiting the immediately preceding activity (*feedback loops*) if inconsistencies or new problems are encountered during the current activity.

Another variant of the waterfall model - the *V-model* - associates each development activity with a test or validation at the same level of abstraction. Each development activity builds a more detailed model of the system than the one before it, and each validation activity tests a higher abstraction than its predecessor.

The problems with the waterfall model are:

- It is difficult to define all requirements at the beginning of a project;
- This model has problems adapting to change;
- A working version of the system is not seen until late in the project's life;
- It does not scale up well to large projects;
- Real projects are rarely sequential.

Because these weaknesses, the application of the waterfall model should be limited to situations where the requirements and their implementation are well understood. For example, if an organization has experience in developing accounting systems then building a new accounting system based on the existing designs could be managed with the waterfall model.

The Incremental Model

The *Incremental Model* performs the waterfall in overlapping sections thereby attempting to produce usable functionality earlier in the project life cycle.

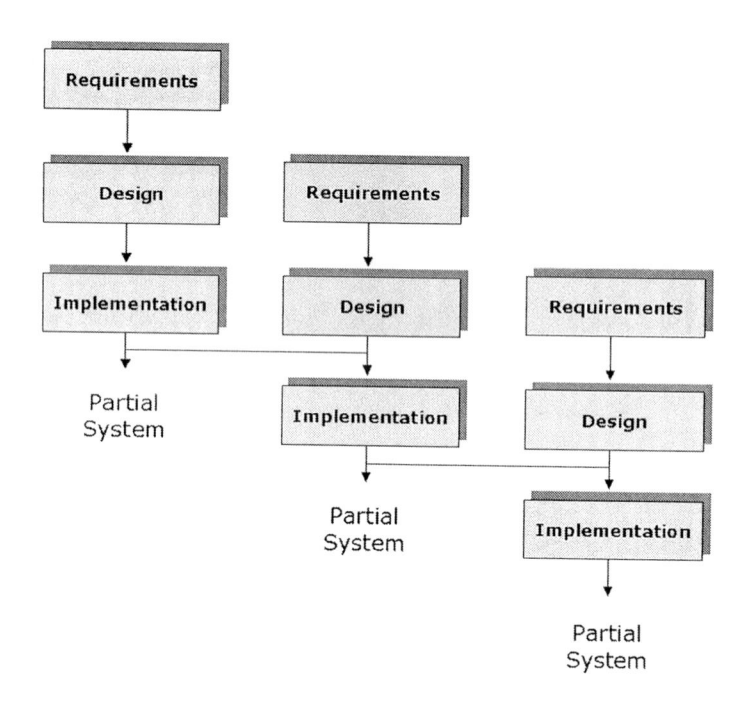

Fig. 7.3 – *Incremental Model*

As some modules are completed before others, well-defined interfaces are required. Also, there can be a tendency to push difficult problems to the future to demonstrate early success to management.

The Incremental Model can be used when it is too risky to develop the whole system at once.

The Spiral Model

The incremental model can also be represented as a spiral with every Requirements-Design-Implementation cycle as a coil. The spiral size corresponds with system size, and the distance between the coils of the spiral shows resources. This view illustrates the fact that resources can be kept constant while the available functionality grows.

In the *Spiral model* proposed by Barry Boehm [90] prototyping is used to control risk. The Spiral model describes development as an iterative four-phase process, for combining the various approaches:

- Expression of needs;
- Feasibility;
- Prototyping;
- Development of the final product.

The spiral model can be used when there is doubt about user requirements (for example in the development of a business intelligence system).

A popular variant of the spiral model is the *Component Assembly Model*. It tries to force reuse of components by:

- Attempting to identify candidate components for use in the system;
- Using the components if they exist;
- Develop new components when necessary and adding them to the component library;
- Constructing the application from library components.

Time boxing

In the models discussed above either the requirements are fixed (waterfall) or the resources are fixed (incremental/spiral) while the other elements can vary during development. Another approach is to *fix time* of the development and to fix the resources as far as possible. This means that the requirements that will be satisfied are allowed to change. Therefore, an important product of the business analysis is a *clear prioritization* of the high-level requirements. More detailed requirements are collected during the later stages of development and are also ranked.

This approach is used in a method known as *Dynamic Systems Development Method (DSDM)*. The flexibility of requirements to be satisfied has significantly affected the development processes and controls, and on acceptance of the system. Indeed, a fundamental assumption of DSDM is that nothing is built perfectly the first time, but that a usable and useful 80% of the proposed system can be produced in 20% of the time it would take to produce the total system. Another underlying principle of DSDM is that fitness for business purpose is the essential criterion for the acceptance of deliverables.

The mechanism for handling flexibility of requirements in DSDM is the *time box*. DSDM uses short time boxes of two to six weeks within the overall project duration. Each time box has a fixed end date and a ranked set of requirements assigned to it. Some of these are mandatory and some of a lesser priority. This mix is essential, since, if all the requirements that are to be satisfied in a time box were mandatory, there would be no room for maneuver when things do not go perfectly to plan or when new requirements surface. All necessary reviews and tests are contained within the time box.

DSDM can be summarized in nine principles that form a guideline throughout the whole theory:

- Necessity of active user involvement;
- Teams have to be allowed to take decisions autonomously;
- Frequent delivery of intermediate solutions;
- Fitness for purpose is the fundamental acceptance criterion;
- Iterative and incremental development;
- All changes can be undone;
- Requirements are set at a high level;
- Testing is integrated in the life cycle;
- Collaboration of all stakeholders is essential.

DSDM can be applied successfully in certain types of development projects. Especially when the functionality can be visualized easily using screens and reports as in these systems prototypes can be used for the visualization and validation of the design. It is also important that the user groups are well defined as in that case it is easy to select the right user representatives. These user representatives (the Ambassadors) are the link between the target organization and the developers. Finally, when the system to be developed is big and complex it has to be possible to cut down the system in smaller and manageable parts that can be developed and tested independently.

The time box approach is also used in other *Rapid Application Development (RAD)* methods. Developing applications rapidly is increasingly essential to business survival. There is, however, an inherent danger. Organizations are often tempted to use RAD techniques to build stand-alone systems to solve a particular business problem. Such systems, if they meet user needs, then become institutionalized. If an organization builds many isolated systems to solve particular problems, the result is a large, undisciplined mass of applications that do not work together (information islands). In practice, most business applications are closely related to each other, making a common infrastructure essential. In addition, as computing systems grow, they become more complex, and such systems are difficult to change unless they have been created within a well-designed architecture that allows one element to be changed without changing the whole system.

Agile Software Development

Agile means being both effective and maneuverable, agile development methods are both light and sufficient. In the introduction of his book *Agile Software Development* [97] Alistair Cockburn states:

"Knowing that perfect communications are impossible relieves you of trying to reach that perfection. Instead, you learn to manage the incompleteness of communication. Rather than try to make the requirements document or the design model comprehensive to everyone, you stop when the document is sufficient to the purpose of the intended audience. Managing the incompleteness of communications is core to mastering agile software development."

Agile software development methods are focusing on the people rather than on tools and processes, their goal is working code more than perfect documentation. They try to adapt to changes in the requirements rather than the execution of a predefined plan.

One increasingly popular Agile Development Method is known as *Extreme Programming (XP)*. It is a lightweight discipline of software development invented by Kent Beck based on principles of simplicity, communication, feedback, and courage [85]. XP is designed for use with small teams who need to develop software quickly in an environment of rapidly changing requirements. Extreme Programming was created in response to problem domains with *changing requirements*. In many software environments dynamically changing requirements is the only constant. XP was also set up to address the problems of *project risk*. If the system is needed by a certain date the risk is high. If that system is a new challenge for the software group the risk is even greater. If that system is a new challenge to the entire software industry the risk is greater even still. The XP practices are set up to diminish the risk and increase the likelihood of success.

There are 12 key practices in XP:

- *The Planning Process* - The XP planning process allows the XP "customer" to define the business value of desired features and uses cost estimates provided by the programmers, to choose what needs to be done and what needs to be deferred;
- *Small Releases* - XP teams put a simple system into production early and update it frequently on a short cycle;
- *Metaphor* - XP teams use a common "system of names" and a common system description that guides development and communication;
- *Simple Design* - A program built with XP should be the simplest program that meets the current requirements;
- *Testing* - XP teams focus on validation of the software at all times. Programmers develop software by writing tests first, then software that fulfills the requirements reflected in the tests. Customers provide acceptance tests that enable them to be certain that the features they need are provided;
- *Refactoring* - XP teams improve the design of the system throughout the entire development by keeping the software clean: without duplication, with high communication, simple, yet complete;
- *Pair Programming* - XP programmers write all production code in pairs, two programmers working together at one machine. Pair programming has been shown by many experiments to produce better software at similar or lower cost than programmers working alone;
- *Collective Ownership* - All the code belongs to all the programmers. This lets the team go at full speed, because when something needs changing, it can be changed without delay;
- *Continuous Integration* - XP teams integrate and build the software system multiple times per day. This keeps all the programmers on the same page and enables rapid progress;
- *40-hour Week* - Tired programmers make more mistakes. XP teams do not work excessive overtime, keeping fresh, healthy, and effective;
- *On-site Customer* - An XP project is steered by a dedicated individual who is empowered to determine requirements, set priorities, and answer questions as the programmers ask them. The effect is that communication improves, with less hard-copy documentation - often one of the most expensive parts of a software project;
- *Coding Standard* - For a team to work effectively in pairs, and to share ownership of all the code, all the programmers need to write the code in the same way, with rules that make sure the code communicates clearly.

Other models

There are many other models such as:

- *Sync-and-stabilize* – This is Microsoft's loosely structured, small-team style of product development [98]. Many small teams (three to eight developers) work in parallel. Changes are synchronized frequently so components will work together. Developers check in their code by a particular time. A new *build* (complete recompilation) is done at the end of the day or the next morning. The overall strategy is to quickly introduce products that are "good enough" to capture a mass market, and later improve the product, selling multiple product versions and upgrades;
- *Issue-Based Life Cycle Model* - The project is driven by a set of issues such as "How do we set up the initial teams?" and "What software architecture shall we use?" Issues are classified as open or closed, but closed issues can be reopened as changes occur in the application or solution domain. Issues are maintained in an issue base accessible to all project participants. Issues do not directly correspond to risks, as some issues are design problems, not risks. By organizing the project around issues, all life cycle activities can proceed concurrently, using dependencies between issues to determine which activities can be performed concurrently and what the impact of reopening an issue will be.

Concept Exploration

The activities of this process are:

- Identify ideas or needs;
- Formulate potential approaches;
- Conduct feasibility studies;
- Plan system transition;
- Refine and complete the idea or need.

Both management and the client identify an idea or need, and the manager establishes the initial system architecture. The need can be addressed through:

- *Green field engineering* for a new development effort;
- *Interface engineering* for a change to the interface of an existing system;
- *Reengineering* for a software replacement of an existing business process.

Note that, in real life, there are few green field projects.

A *Problem Statement* or *Statement of Need* (IEEE 1074) describes the *business* requirements to be addressed by the project.

Requirements

This process consists of an interaction with all the stakeholders to understand the place of the system in the wider context of the organization, to understand what the customer's business is/does, and how the system will fit in to the business [116].

A *Requirement* is a specification of what a system must do; the things about the system that users can observe, an external view.

Behavioral Requirements define *what* the system does. These describe the inputs and outputs of the system; these requirements are also called functional requirements.

"Is it too late to add the client's wish list of features to the project?"

Non behavioral Requirements define the attributes of the system as it performs its job. They include a complete description of the system.

The qualities of a good requirements document can be summarized as follows:

- *Correctness* – Every requirement is something required of the system;
- *Non ambiguity* – Every statement has only one interpretation;
- *Completeness* - Everything that matters is covered in the document;
- *Verifiability* - The built system can be checked to see if requirements are met;
- *Consistency* - There are no conflicts between requirements;
- *Understandability* - The form the document takes should allow the different audiences to gather the information they need;
- *Modifiable* - Changes to the requirements can be accommodated;
- *Traceability* - Each requirement exists because there was a need in the problem domain. Activity in the solution domain should relate back to the requirements.

For a long time developers have struggled with system requirements. They often assumed some requirements document, but were unsure of what such a document should look like. Here the impact of Ivar Jacobson's work on *Use Cases* has been important. So what is a Use Case? Jacobson [91] says they are when a user performs *"a behaviourally related sequence of transactions in a dialogue with the system."* The skill is to identify the users' goals, not the system functions. One way of doing this is to treat a user's business task as a use case, and to ask how the computer system can support it.

Use Case diagrams provide a way of describing the external view of the system and its interactions with the outside world. The outside world is represented as actors. Actors are roles played by various people, or other computer systems. The emphasis on roles is important: one person can play different roles, and a role can have many people playing it. Use cases are then typical interactions that the actor has with the system.

Project Initiation

Project Estimation

> "Crash programs fail because they are based on the theory that, with nine women pregnant, you can get a baby in a month."
>
> (Wernher von Braun)

The planning of a project is highly dependent on the estimation of the necessary effort, expressed in *Person-Days (PD)* or *Person-Months (PM)*, for every part of the project. It is important to realize that an estimate is NOT a single number, but a range of possibilities, a statistical entity. Everybody knows that if somebody wants to talk "for two minutes" it will probably take an average of 15 minutes and, if it is important it can even take 45 minutes, half an hour more than the average. On the other hand, there are no meetings with a negative duration, so the distribution of estimations is not symmetrical (Fig. 7.4).

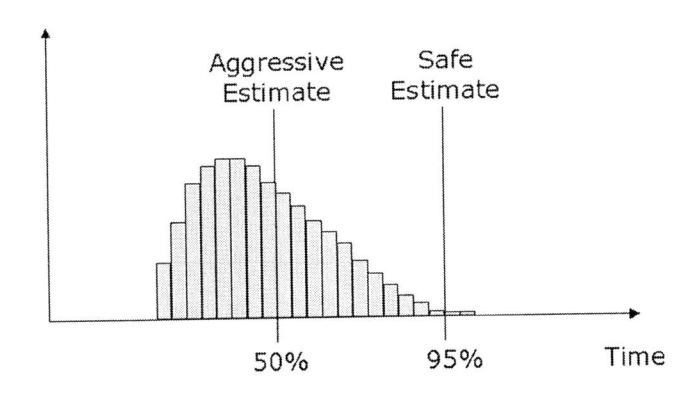

Fig. 7.4 – *Project estimation*

Project managers should also know that people have a tendency to give an estimate, which they think they can make in 95% of the cases (they make a *safe estimate*). A safe estimate can easily represent the double of the time of an *aggressive estimate*, one we think we can make in 50% of the cases.

Decomposition techniques

From statistics theory it is known that the relative error on the sum of many equally distributed and independent variables is smaller than the relative error of the individual variables. Underestimation of some variables will be statistically compensated by overestimation of others. This knowledge has led management consultants to develop the *bottom-up technique*; split a project into many small and comparable tasks that can be executed by one person. That person is then asked to make an estimate. The estimated effort for the whole project is the sum of the individual estimates.

Ideally, the people who will perform the tasks should make their own estimations. This is important, as productivity can vary a lot from one person to another (for programmers this can be as much as a factor ten!).

Below is a simple example. The functions are derived from the project definition. For each function, several tasks have to be performed. For every task, an estimate is made. As the qualifications of the persons performing the tasks are different, their rates are different as well. Total cost and effort result from this table.

Functions	Requirements	Design	Tasks Code	Test	Total
Database	2	8	8	8	26
Calculations	4	10	7	10	31
User Interface	10	15	10	15	50
Reports	7	8	7	7	29
Roll out	2	2	3	5	12
Total	25	43	35	45	148
Rate ($)	520	480	425	450	
Cost ($)	**13000**	**20640**	**14875**	**20250**	**68765**

This technique is simple and easy to understand by non-technical managers. It can however be abused to "blow up" the importance of a project (as it is difficult to argue about the estimates) and is vulnerable to "forgotten" activities and developers who systematically underestimate their own activities.

Empirical estimation methods

As opposed to the rather intuitive approach of the decomposition technique, the empirical estimation methods try to capture the estimation process in a mathematical framework, based on the size of the project expressed in *Lines of Code* or *Function Points*.

Lines of Code **(LOC)**

The idea of the *Lines of Code (LOC)* metric is that program length can be used as a predictor of program characteristics such as effort and ease of maintenance.

There are different versions of LOC:

- *Delivered Source Instructions (DSI)* – this metric is:

    o Only Source lines that are delivered as part of the product are included, test drivers and other support software are excluded;
    o Only source lines that are created by the project staff, code created by applications generators is excluded;
    o One instruction is one line of code;
    o Declarations arc counted as instructions;
    o Comments are not counted as instructions.

- *Source Lines Of Code (SLOC)* - a single SLOC can be several physical lines. For example, an "if-then-else" statement would be counted as one SLOC, but could be counted as several DSI.

The LOC metric has the advantage of being simple to measure. However, it is only defined on code; for example it cannot measure the size of a specification. LOC only characterizes one view of size: its length. It takes no account of functionality or complexity. Also, bad software design can cause excessive lines of code. Further, LOC is language dependent and has no significance for the customers. Finally, it is difficult to make an accurate estimate of LOC for code that still has to be written.

Function Points

In 1979 Allan Albrecht of IBM came up with the idea of *Function Points*. This technique quantifies the functions contained within software in terms that are important to the customer [100][105][106]. The measure relates directly to the business requirements, which the software is intended to address. It can therefore be readily applied across a wide range of development environments and throughout the life of a development project, from early requirements definition to full operational use.

All the functional components are analyzed and added together to derive an *Unadjusted Function Point (UFP)* count. Once the total unadjusted function point value has been calculated, the next step is to determine *General System Characteristics (GSCs)* and calculate the *Value Adjustment Factor (VAF)*. Fourteen GSCs are rated from zero to five, based on how they affect the application.

- Data communication;
- Distributed data processing;
- Performance;
- Heavily used configuration;
- Transaction rate;
- On-line data entry;
- End-user efficiency;
- On-line update;
- Complex processing;
- Reusability;
- Installation ease;
- Operational ease;
- Multiple sites;
- Help change.

The 14 GSGs are added, thus obtaining a number between zero and 70, the *Degree of Influence (DI)*. The Value Adjustment Factor is now computed as follows:

$$VAF = 0.65 + 0.01 * DI$$

The *Adjusted Function Point* count is then determined by multiplying the Value Adjustment Factor by the total Unadjusted Function Points.

Unlike LOC, FPA is not restricted to code and it is language independent. Furthermore, the necessary data is available early in a project; only a detailed specification is needed. These elements make FPA more accurate than estimated LOC.

Drawbacks of FPA are that it is based on a subjective counting and it is hard to automate.

The Function Point metric has been further improved to cope with specific situations (Feature Points, Mark II Function Points and 3D Function Points).

Organizations such as the *International Function Point Users Group (IFPUG)* have been active in identifying rules for function point counting to ensure that counts are comparable across different organizations. Readers should refer to the *IFPUG Counting Practices Manual* for more complete definitions and examples of characteristics to enable easy assignment of scores.

Constructive Cost Model (COCOMO)

The *Constructive Cost Model (COCOMO)* is based on a study of hundreds of software projects. Dr Barry Boehm published the original model in 1981 and continues to lead the research effort at the Center for Software Engineering at USC.

Typically, a project starts with only a rough description of the software system to be developed. As the knowledge of the problem is refined, COCOMO II can be used to produce more and more refined estimates.

COCOMO II is tuned to modern software life cycles. The original COCOMO model has been very successful, but it didn't apply to newer software development practices. COCOMO II targets the software projects of the 1990s and 2000s, and will continue to evolve over the next years.

COCOMO II distinguishes three different models:

- The *Application Composition Model* - Suitable for projects built with modern GUI-builder tools.
- The *Early Design Model* - To get rough estimates of a project's cost and duration before fixing the entire architecture.
- *The Post-Architecture Model* – Used for the actual development and maintenance of a software product.

Effort equation

The most fundamental calculation in the COCOMO II model is the *Effort Equation* to estimate the number of Person-Months required for developing a project.

$$PM = 2.94 \times EAF \times (Size)^B$$

In which PM is the effort in Person Months (exclusive of holidays, weekends accounted), EAF is the *Effort Adjustment Factor* derived from the *Cost Drivers* in order to capture the multiplicative effects on effort with projects of increasing size and B is the *Scale Factor* to account for the relative economies or diseconomies of scale encountered for projects of different size.

Most of the other COCOMO II results, including the estimates for Requirements and Maintenance, are derived from this quantity.

Project Size

The COCOMO II calculations are based on estimates of a project's size in Kilo Source Lines of Code (KSLOC). The SLOC approach is to measure the amount of intellectual work put into software development. The problem is of course that this is very difficult in the early stages of a project. Therefore, the Function Points cost estimation is based on the amount of functionality in a software project. Function Points measure a software project by quantifying the information processing functionality with major external data or control input, output or file types.

To determine the nominal person months the Unadjusted Function Points (UFP) have to be converted to source lines of code in the implementation language. COCOMO II does this by using conversion factors, for example:

Programming language	SLOC/UFP
Assembler	320
C	128
Pascal	91

Table 7.2 – *Function points to Lines of code conversion*

COCOMO II further adjusts for reuse by modifying the size of the module or project. It uses a non-linear estimation model:

$$AAF = 0.4(DM) + 0.3(CM) + 0.3(IM)$$

AAF is the amount of modification, based on the percentage of design modified (DM), percentage of code modified (CM) and percentage of modification to the original integration effort (IM).

The software understanding (SU), assessment and assimilation (AA) and relative unfamiliarity with the software (UNFM) further lead to the equivalent source lines of code (ESLOC):

$$ESLOC = (ASLOC[AA + AAF(1 + 0.02(SU)(UNMF)])/100$$

when AAF smaller or equal to 0.5, and

$$ESLOC = (ASLOC[AA + AAF + (SU)(UNMF)])/100$$

when AAF greater than 0.5

Scale Factor

The scale factor (B) is calculated as follows:

$$B = 0.91 + 0.01 \times \Sigma W_i$$

The five scale drivers determining the weights (W_i) are:

- Precedentedness (PREC)
- Development Flexibility (FLEX)
- Architecture / Risk Resolution (RESL)
- Team Cohesion (TEAM)
- Process Maturity (PMAT)

Scale weights have a value between 5 and 0, depending on their rating varying between "Very Low" and "Extra High". For example a 100 KSLOC project with "Very Low" (5) ratings for all the scale drivers will result in a B-value of 1,26 and a relative effort of 331 PM.

If B<1.0 then the project exhibits economies of scale: if the project size is doubled, the project effort is less than doubled. The project's productivity increases as the product size is increased.

If B>1.0 then the project exhibits diseconomies of scale. This is generally due to two main factors: interpersonal communications overhead and integration overhead.

If B=1.0 there is a balance between economies and diseconomies. This linear model is often used for small projects. It is also used in the Applications Composition model.

Effort Adjustment Factor

The Effort Adjustment Factor (EAF) in the Post Architecture Model is derived from 17 Cost Drivers. Project, development environment, and team are assessed to set each cost driver. The cost drivers are multiplicative factors that determine the effort required to complete the software project. For example, if the project will develop software that controls an airplane's flight, the Required Software Reliability (RELY) cost driver will be assessed to "Very High". That rating corresponds to an effort multiplier of 1.26, meaning that the project will require 26% more effort than a typical software project.

COCOMO II defines each of the cost drivers, and the Effort Multiplier associated with each rating:

Product factors:

- Required Software Reliability (RELY)
- Data Base Size (DATA)
- Product Complexity (CPLX)
- Required Reusability (RUSE)
- Documentation match to lifecycle needs (DOCU)
- Execution Time Constraints (TIME)
- Main Storage Constraints (STOR)
- Platform Volatility (PVOL)

Personnel factors:

- Analyst Capability (ACAP)
- Programmer Capability (PCAP)
- Applications Experience (AEXP)
- Platform Experience (PEXP)
- Language and Tool Experience (LTEX)
- Personnel Continuity (PCON)

Project factors:

- Use of Software Tools (TOOL)
- Multisite Development (SITE)
- Required Development Schedule (SCED)

The COCOMO II cost driver for Required Development Schedule (SCED) requires a special explanation. The SCED cost driver is used to account for the observation that a project developed on an accelerated schedule will require more effort than a project developed on its optimum schedule. A SCED rating of Very Low corresponds to an Effort Multiplier of 1.43 (in the COCOMO II.2000 model) and means that you intend to finish your project in 75% of the optimum schedule (as determined by a previous COCOMO estimate).

In the Early Design Model a reduced set of seven cost drivers is used. These are obtained by combining the Post-Architecture Model cost drivers.

Early Design Model	Post Architecture Model
Product Reliability and Complexity (RCPX)	RELY, DATA, CPLX, DOCU
Required Reuse (RUSE)	RUSE
Platform Difficulty (PDIF)	TIME, STOR, PVOL
Personnel Capability (PERS)	ACAP, PCAP, PCON
Personnel Experience (PREX)	AEXP, PEXP, LTEX
Facilities (FCIL)	TOOL, SITE
Schedule (SCED)	SCED

Table 7.3 – *Cost drivers*

An example will illustrate this approach. The Early Design cost driver PERS combines ACAP, PCAP, and PCON. Each of these has a rating from Very Low (1) to Very High (5). Adding up their ratings produces values from 3 to 15 and a corresponding rating of PERS.

	Extra Low	Very Low	Low	Nominal	High	Very High	Extra High
Sum	3,4	5,6	7,8	9	10,11	12,13	14,15

Table 7.4 – *The PERS Cost Driver*

Schedule Equation

The COCOMO II schedule equation predicts the number of months required to complete a software project. The duration of a project is based on the effort predicted by the effort equation:

$$TDEV = [\,3.67 \times PM^{(0.28 + 0.2 \times (B-1.01))}\,] \times (SCED\%/100)$$

Where TDEV is the calendar time in months from requirements baseline to completion of acceptance and PM is the effort but without the SCED effort multiplier.

Average Staffing

Average staffing is obtained by simply dividing the estimated effort by the project duration.

Design

System design is usually done using models that represent the business processes to be automated or supported. Modelling techniques share three common characteristics:

- They represent a *simplification* of the real world;
- They look at the real world from *different perspectives*;
- They use a *standardized notation*.

For Information Systems, three different approaches are commonly used: process, data and object-oriented.

Process oriented modelling

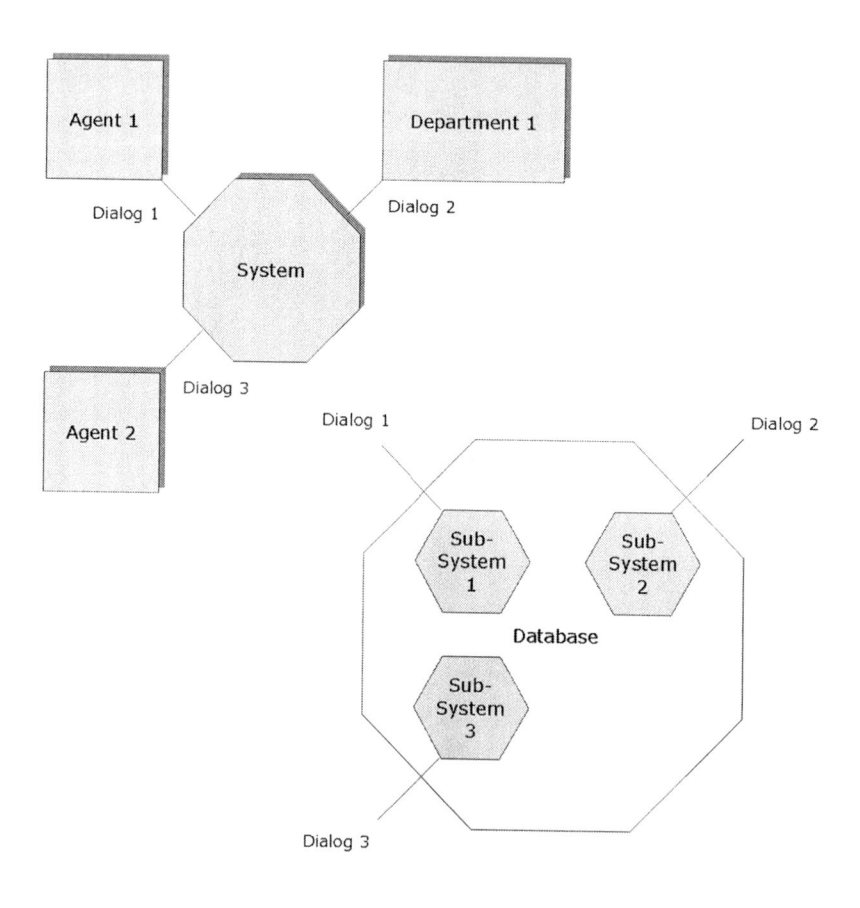

Fig. 7.5 – *SA/SD*

In this modelling approach, the process is the central element and all input and output data are grouped around the process; this is why it is also called the *IPO* (*Input–*

Process–Output) approach. A modelling technique used in this approach is called *Structured Analysis/Structured Design (SA/SD)*. It was invented by Yourdon and Constantine, and was later refined by DeMarco.

SA/SD looks at every process as a way to transform input data into output data. SA starts with the elaboration of *Data Flow Diagrams (DFDs)*. These diagrams contain the description of the data flows and the permanent data collections. Finally, the logic of the processes (system and subsystems) from the DFDs is described.

During the *System Design* (*SD*) phase, the subsystems are described as program modules, using *Structure Cards (SCs)*. The logic of the program is described in a pseudo-language.

Hatley & Pirbhai introduced the *Control Flow Diagrams (CFDs)*. Together with Ward & Mellor they adapted the technique for real-time systems. Gane & Sarson used this technique for the analysis of administrative processes; they also added physical flows besides the data flow.

The process oriented approach leads to the development of independent systems (information islands), which are difficult to link to one another. After some time there are many interfaces and a lot of data redundancy. This makes the maintenance as well as the exploitation difficult and expensive. Integration will only be possible if it has been taken in account from the beginning, but that implies a good idea of the total information needs of the organization.

Data oriented modelling

The introduction of database technology made the attention of the modellers shift to the data as the central and most stable part of an Information System. Data that were added to the database became immediately available for all existing or new applications. Business processes are variable and change with the developing insights and management methods. Data on the contrary are much more stable and do not change unless the business of the organization changes. In other terms, the data form a constant and stable kernel around which the business processes evolve.

Data modelling is intended to describe the things about which an organization wishes to collect data, along with the relationships among them.

Peter Chen invented entity-relationship modelling in the mid-1970s [95][139], and his approach remains widely used today. In Chen's notation, *entities* are shown as rectangles, *relationships* are shown with a diamond-shaped symbol on the relationship line between entities, and *attributes* are shown as separate circles. Relationships are in fact a special type of entity, so they also have a name (usually the combination of the two related entities) and they can have attributes as well. Over the years, several alternative notations have been devised, such as Richard Barker's notation, Information Engineering and IDEF1X.

The diagram in Fig. 7.6 is a model for a simple order entry system. An ORDER is always related to one CUSTOMER, a CUSTOMER however can have more than one ORDER. An ORDER only has a date and a number as attributes. The items that are ordered are contained in the relationship with the products entity: ORDERLINE. An ORDER can of course contain more than one PRODUCT and a PRODUCT can appear in several ORDERs.

From an *Entity Relationship Diagram (ERD)* as this one, it is easy to create a relational database schema with tables. An entity becomes a table with the attributes as columns. One-to-many relationships without attributes can be materialized as foreign keys (e.g., CustID in the ORDER table). Relationships with attributes or many-to-many relationships become separate tables.

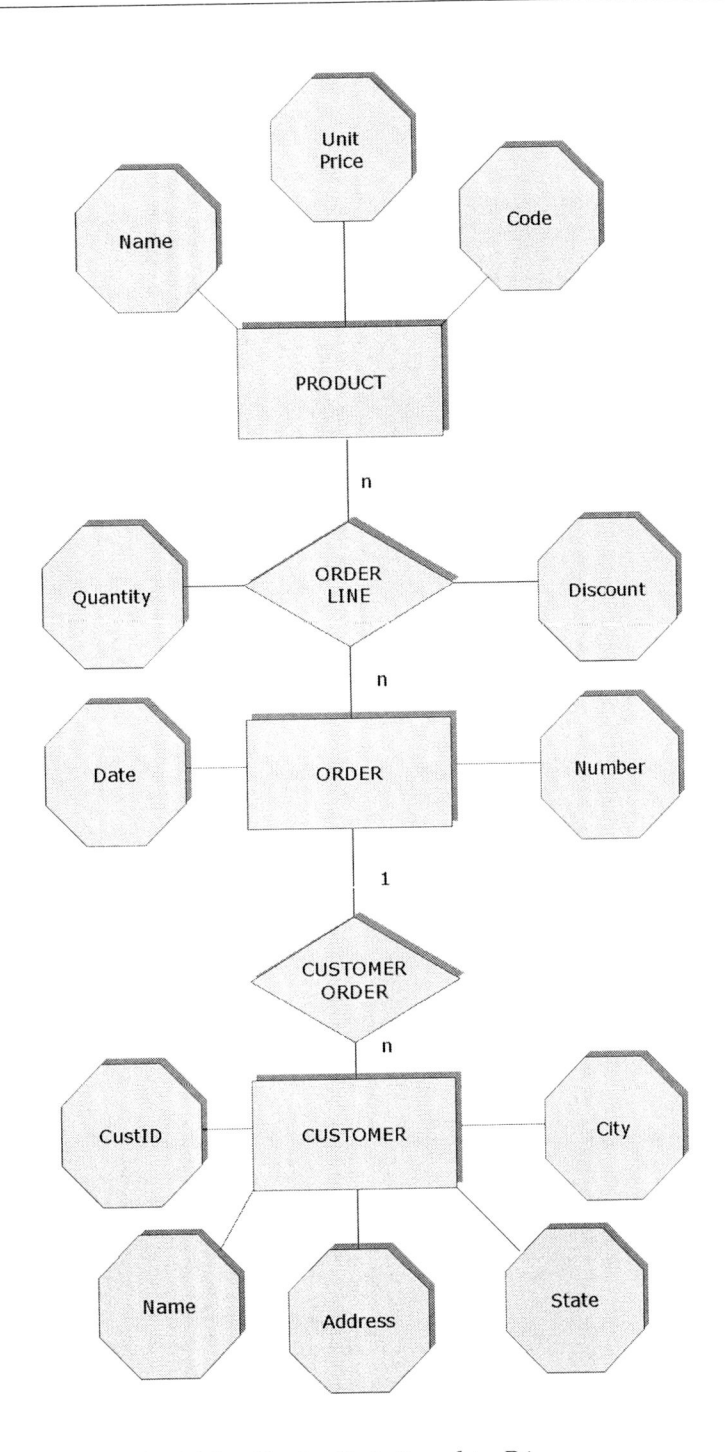

Fig. 7.6 – *Entity Relationship Diagram*

Object Oriented Modelling

In the object-oriented approach every system component is seen as an *object* [96][133][135]. An object not only has a *data structure* but also includes the *methods* that allow it to change its state. Objects can only communicate with the external world and with each other using messages. This leads to *information hiding* or *encapsulation*. Through a mechanism known as *inheritance* the reusability of components is promoted.

Several object oriented modeling techniques have been devised. Today, the *Unified Modeling Language (UML)* is recognized as the standard. Jim Rumbaugh and Grady Booch originally defined UML to contain all the constructs available in each of their own methods, but with a common graphical representation [91]. Later, Ivar Jacobson joined them. He added syntax for defining requirements with Use Cases.

Besides Uses Cases, UML has several other diagrams to model a system.

Class diagrams - The Class Diagram shows classes and their relationships. Classes define the types of objects that exist within the system. Classes can have *attributes*, which are primitive data members of objects, and operations, which define operations that can be performed on the object. Associations between classes show what links can exist between objects and define constraints on those links including the relative quantity of instances linked by an association (Fig. 7.7).

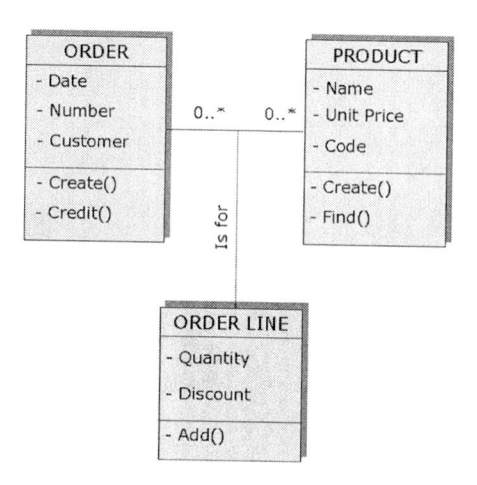

Fig. 7.7 – *Class diagram*

A static model will usually consist of many class diagrams which taken together, define the static structure of the system.

Sequence Diagrams - A sequence diagram shows the interactions that take place, both between objects inside the system, and across the system boundary, to fulfil the requirements defined through a use case.

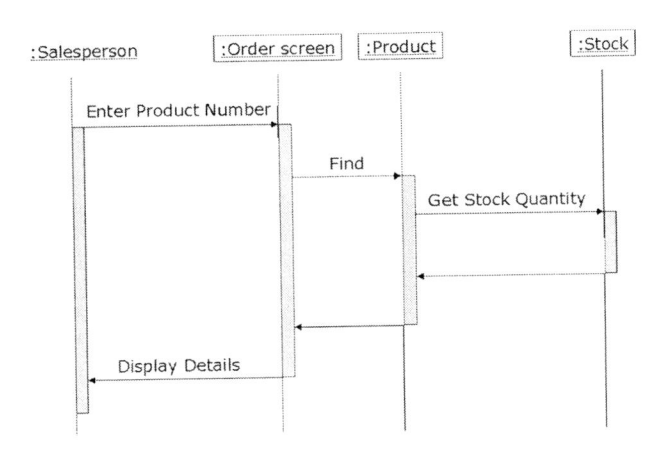

Fig. 7.8 – *Sequence diagram*

The vertical dotted lines in Fig. 7.8 represent the lifetime of the object and horizontal arrows the interactions or messages between objects. Messages can include sequence numbers, operation names and parameters. The boxes on the object lifelines represent the activation of the object when interactions are sequential and represent calls to operations. The operation remains open until all the sequential operations that it calls have completed.

Collaboration Diagrams – These are functionally equivalent to sequence diagrams and are useful for showing how groups of objects work together to perform a given functionality.

Activity Diagrams - Activity Diagrams can be used anywhere in the model to show a flow of activity. However, the Activity Diagram is usually reserved for defining the flow of business level events outside the scope of the system.

Component diagrams - Component Diagrams show the structure of actual software components that will be used to create the system. These can include source files, re-locatable code and executables. It shows the types of components that are in the system and the dependence between them including dependence on any specified component interfaces.

State Diagrams – These show how the functionality of an object depends on its state and how its state changes as a result of events that it receives (Fig. 7.9). Solid circles represent initial states, rounded rectangles intermediate states, and bull's eyes designate final states. Transitions between states are represented as arrowed lines that are labelled with an event name (the trigger).

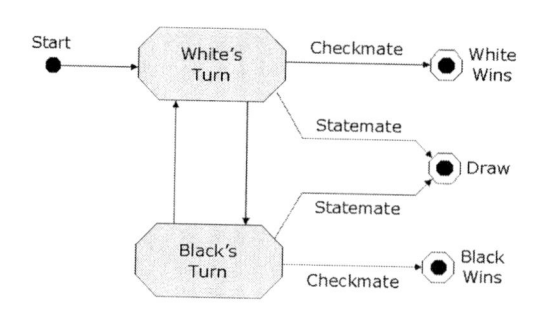

Fig. 7.9 – *State diagram*

Deployment diagram - A Deployment Diagram shows instances of processor nodes, their interconnection, and instances of the components that will run on them along with the dependence between the instances.

The syntax of UML has been designed to be independent of any particular target language, methodology or tool, but accommodates almost all language, tool or methodology requirements. Even though today UML is generally recognized as the universal modeling standard there are some negative remarks to be made as well:

- One of the biggest misunderstandings is to think that UML is a silver bullet. UML is only syntax; it will not solve the design problems. Neither does it present a standard way of doing things or best practices;
- UML is not simple. It takes a lot of time to master the syntax and there are many open questions about its use;
- It is impossible to use UML as a unique tool to specify a complete system. Tool suppliers tend to fill these gaps with proprietary add-ons, making the exchange of models between tools difficult;
- There is problem of scalability. For big systems the diagrams become too complex and unreadable;
- Finally, UML is not a methodology. How to apply it in to a particular project requires the definition of a set of semantics that are appropriate for a particular architecture and methodology.

The Object Management Group has defined a new version of UML (2.0). This version is supposed to solve the above-mentioned problems. It also fits in what is known as the *Model Driven Architecture (MDA)*. MDA propagates the approach of separating the specification of the functionalities of a system completely of any technological platform that can be used for the implementation. To create an MDA-based application one first has to make a *Platform Independent Model (PIM)*. This model is then translated to a Platform Specific Model (PSM) for a target platform such as J2EE, .Net or CORBA. UML 2.0 will also encompass the *Object Constraint Language (OCL)*. It specifies all kinds of constraints, pre- and post-conditions guards etc. over the objects in the different models.

Implementation

Programming languages

Software systems are built using *programming languages*. A programming language is a vocabulary and a set of grammatical rules for instructing a computer to perform specific tasks.

Programming languages, while simple compared to human languages, are more complex than the limited set of instructions the computer understands. Furthermore, as we already saw before, each different type of CPU has its own instruction set. This is why every program ultimately has to be converted into CPU instructions so that the computer can understand it. There are two ways to run programs written in a high-level language; the most common is to compile the program, the other method is to pass the program through an interpreter.

A *compiler* is a special program that processes statements written in a particular programming language and turns them into machine instructions. Typically, a programmer writes his programs one line at a time using an editor or a word processing program. The file that is created contains what are called the *source statements*. The programmer then runs the appropriate language compiler, specifying the name of the file that contains the source statements. While executing, the compiler first analyzes (or *parses*) all the language statements syntactically one after the other and then, in one or more successive passes, builds the output code, making sure that statements that refer to other statements are correct in the final code. The output of the compilation is called *object code*; this is machine code that the processor can execute one instruction at a time.

An *interpreter* analyzes and executes each line of source code at runtime, without looking at the entire program. The advantage of interpreters is that they can execute a program immediately. Therefore, interpreters are sometimes used during the development phase, when the programmer wants to add small sections at a time and test them quickly. Compilers require some time before an executable program is available, but the *executables* produced by compilers are much faster than the same programs executed by an interpreter.

With the Java programming language the possibility of compiling to an intermediate output called *byte code* was introduced. Byte code can run on any computer system for which a *Java Virtual Machine* or *JVM* (in fact a byte code interpreter) is provided. More recently, Microsoft introduced its *Common Language Runtime (CLR)*, a kind of virtual machine that executes intermediate code *(Microsoft Intermediate Language or MSIL)*. Byte code and MSIL are translated into machine code by a *Just In Time (JIT) compiler*. The application compiled as intermediate code is presented as *Portable Executables (PE)*. To be compilable the programming language used must comply with the *Common Language Specification (CLS)*. Versions of the CLR have been designed to run on non-Microsoft platforms, so one could imagine a Visual Basic program running on a mainframe or a COBOL system running on a Windows platform!

Programming language generations

Programming languages are often classified into *generations*. This does not necessarily mean that a language that belongs to an "older" generation was created later in time; for example Java is a third-generation language and Visual Basic belongs to the fifth generation, yet Java came later than Visual Basic.

1GL or *first-generation languages* are machine language or the level of instructions and data that the processor is given to work on. Below is a complete program for an Intel processor; it displays "Hello World!" on the screen.

Address	Instructions
000	4D 5A 27 00 02 00 01 00 20 00 11 00 FF FF 03 00
010	00 01 16 2F 00 00 00 00 1E 00 00 00 01 00 02 00
020	00 00 00 00 00 00 00 00 00 00 00 00 00 00 00 00
030	00 00 00 00 00 00 00 00 00 00 00 00 00 00 00 00
040	00 00 00 00 00 00 00 00 00 00 00 00 00 00 00 00
050	00 00 00 00 00 00 00 00 00 00 00 00 00 00 00 00
060	00 00 00 00 00 00 00 00 00 00 00 00 00 00 00 00
070	00 00 00 00 00 00 00 00 00 00 00 00 00 00 00 00
080	00 00 00 00 00 00 00 00 00 00 00 00 00 00 00 00
090	00 00 00 00 00 00 00 00 00 00 00 00 00 00 00 00
0A0	00 00 00 00 00 00 00 00 00 00 00 00 00 00 00 00
0B0	00 00 00 00 00 00 00 00 00 00 00 00 00 00 00 00
0C0	00 00 00 00 00 00 00 00 00 00 00 00 00 00 00 00
0D0	00 00 00 00 00 00 00 00 00 00 00 00 00 00 00 00
0E0	00 00 00 00 00 00 00 00 00 00 00 00 00 00 00 00
0F0	00 00 00 00 00 00 00 00 00 00 00 00 00 00 00 00
100	00 00 00 00 00 00 00 00 00 00 00 00 00 00 00 00
110	00 00 00 00 00 00 00 00 00 00 00 00 00 00 00 00
120	00 00 00 00 00 00 00 00 00 00 00 00 00 00 00 00
130	00 00 00 00 00 00 00 00 00 00 00 00 00 00 00 00
140	00 00 00 00 00 00 00 00 00 00 00 00 00 00 00 00
150	00 00 00 00 00 00 00 00 00 00 00 00 00 00 00 00
160	00 00 00 00 00 00 00 00 00 00 00 00 00 00 00 00
170	00 00 00 00 00 00 00 00 00 00 00 00 00 00 00 00
180	00 00 00 00 00 00 00 00 00 00 00 00 00 00 00 00
190	00 00 00 00 00 00 00 00 00 00 00 00 00 00 00 00
1A0	00 00 00 00 00 00 00 00 00 00 00 00 00 00 00 00
1B0	00 00 00 00 00 00 00 00 00 00 00 00 00 00 00 00
1C0	00 00 00 00 00 00 00 00 00 00 00 00 00 00 00 00
1D0	00 00 00 00 00 00 00 00 00 00 00 00 00 00 00 00
1E0	00 00 00 00 00 00 00 00 00 00 00 00 00 00 00 00
1F0	00 00 00 00 00 00 00 00 00 00 00 00 00 00 00 00
200	CC B8 01 00 CC 8E D8 CC BA 08 00 CC B4 09 CC CD
210	21 CC B8 00 4C CC CD 21 48 65 6C 6C 6F 20 57 6F
220	72 6C 64 21 0D 0A 24

The first row represents the address (the location in memory) in hexadecimal format of the first instruction of that line. The other rows contain the actual instructions (also in hexadecimal format). Note that, in conformance with the Von Neumann architecture, both instructions and data are stored in Main Memory and that no distinction is made between the two (the attentive reader will indeed notice that the "Hello World!" string, which is data in ASCII format, is stored from address 218H to 223H). The fact that so many memory locations contain only zeroes has to do with how the file format (.exe) is organized.

2GL or *second-generation languages* are also called *assembler* or *assembly language*. An assembly language contains the same instructions as a machine language, but the instructions and variables have names instead of being just numbers. The program that converts the textual instructions to machine instructions is called an *Assembler*. The program below is in fact the source code for the machine language of the previous example. It is obvious that this is already a much more manageable format.

```
        assume      cs:cseg,ds:dseg,ss:sseg

        cseg        segment
        start:
            mov     ax, dseg
            mov     ds, ax
            mov     dx, offset msg
            mov     ah, 09h
            int     21h
            mov     ax, 4C00h
            int     21h
        cseg        ends

        dseg        segment byte
            msg     db      'Hello World!',0Dh,0Ah,'$'
        dseg        ends

        sseg        segment stack
            db      100h dup(?)
        sseg        ends

            end     start
```

3GL or *third-generation languages* are "high-level" programming languages, such as C and Pascal. A compiler converts the statements of a high-level programming language into machine language. In the second half of the 1990s came C++. In this language, the "Hello World!" looks like:

```
#include <stdio.h>

int main(int argc, char *argv[]){
    printf("Hello World!\n");
    return 0;
}
```

Soon, it turned out that C++ was too complex for the average programmer so the market lost its heart to Java:

```
public class HelloWorld {
    public static void main(String[] args) {
        System.out.println("Hello World!");
    }
}
```

The big advantage of Java is its *portability* (*Write Once, Run Anywhere (WORA)*). This comes with the compilation of the source code into an intermediate, processor-independent byte code.

4GL or *fourth-generation languages* are designed to be closer to natural language than 3GL languages. These languages are typically oriented towards the access of information in a database; that is why some form of SQL is embedded. Examples are Informix4GL and SQL*Forms (now Oracle Developer). They offer a higher productivity for the development teams but are not generic; they can only be used to create administrative systems. *4GL+ languages* use a visual or graphical development interface to create source language that is usually compiled with a 3GL or 4GL language compiler. PowerBuilder, SQL-Windows and Visual Basic are the best-known examples. The "Hello World!" program could be realized in Visual Basic as shown in Fig. 7.10.

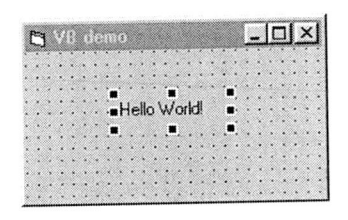

Fig. 7.10 – *4GL+ programming*

Productivity, performance and portability

Three important characteristics in selecting a programming language are *productivity, performance and portability*.

Even inside one generation important differences in productivity can be observed. According to the *International Software Benchmarking Standards Group (ISBSG)* the overall median productivity rate of Java is 20.3 hours per function point. As a comparison, C++ median productivity rate is 17.4 hours per function point. The overall median for 3GLs is 12.8 hours per function point and for 4GLs 10.4 hours per function point.

Java shows the lowest (worst) productivity of any of the main programming languages. There could be a number of reasons for this:

- Java is still a relatively new programming language and environment. Experience is still being built up.
- Given the very nature of the language, many of the projects are likely to be distributed Internet applications with complex multi-tiered architectures, hence more complexity and poorer productivity.
- The development tools available for Java are not yet at the same level as the ones for older 3GLs (e.g. IDEs are not yet as sophisticated).
- Many of the small and simple projects, which can be carried out with a very good productivity rate, are developed using languages such as Visual Basic or a 4GL, not with Java.
- Finally, due to the relative "newness" of the language, the projects being done may be predominantly new development projects, which often have a poorer productivity than certain types of enhancement projects, which would be included in the productivity figures for the older 3GLs.

Even with the powerful hardware platforms of today the *performance* of a software system remains an issue. The more primitive, lower-generation languages are translated more efficiently into machine instructions because there are fewer layers of abstraction in between.

Portability is a characteristic attributed to software if it can be used in an environment other than the one in which it was created, without requiring major rework. Obviously, 4GL systems targeting very specific environments will show a worse score than the others.

Table 7.5 summarizes the scores of the different language generations relative to each other. From this table it is obvious that the best solution has not been found yet; every generation is a compromise!

	Productivity	Performance	Portability
1GL	low	high	low
2GL	low	high	low
3GL	medium	medium	high
4GL	High	low	low
4GL+	high	low	low

Table 7.5 – *Comparison of programming language generations*

Scripting languages

Scripting languages form a special group of programming languages. To describe what a scripting language is one should first describe what a "script" is. Here is an attempt:

"A script is a user-readable and user-modifiable program that performs simple operations or that controls the operation of other programs. A scripting language is a programming language designed for writing scripts."

In UNIX, a script is a text file beginning with the line:

```
"#!" <full-path-to-interpreter> <space> <optional-flags>.
```

The command line interpreter is a program that accepts `<optional-flags> <text-file>` as arguments, ignores the first line, and does something sensible with the contents, like executing it. Awk, PERL, python, tcl and all UNIX shells are examples of such interpreters.

In Windows, an *Active-X Scripting Language* is a COM object that is registered properly and supports the appropriate interfaces for receiving and executing scripts. Other examples of scripting languages are VBScript and javascript. These are executed by the browser that is used to display web pages.

Scripting languages have the following properties:

- Source code is present at run time;
- Explicit compilation or linking phases are not needed;
- Variables, functions, and methods do not require type declarations;
- The ability to combine types into heterogeneous structures;
- Powerful iteration semantics;
- The interpreter can be embedded within other applications.

Procedural and Declarative programming

Probably the best-known type of programming style is the *procedural* (or *imperative*) style: the programmer specifies an explicit sequence of steps to follow to produce a desired result. One or more related blocks of statements that perform a complete function are grouped together into a single module (or *procedure*) and given a name. If the same function is needed elsewhere in the program, a simple statement refers to the procedure. Thus, large programs can be constructed by grouping together procedures that perform different tasks. Procedural languages allow programs to be shorter and easier to read, but they require the programmer to design each procedure to be general enough to be used in different situations. Well-known procedural languages are Basic, Pascal and C.

As opposed to procedural languages, *declarative languages* describe relationships between variables in terms of functions or inference rules. *Logic languages* use logic as their mathematical base. A logic program consists of sets of facts and if-then rules, which specify how one set of facts can be deduced from others. Many *Artificial Intelligence* (*AI*) programs are written in such languages. The most commonly known example of a logic programming language is Prolog. *Functional languages* treat procedures like mathematical functions and allow them to be processed like any other data in a program. Examples of functional languages are Haskell, Hope, and SML. Many other languages such as Lisp have a subset that is purely functional but also contain non-functional constructs.

Object-Oriented Programming languages

Object-oriented programming (*OOP*) *languages* are outgrowths of functional languages. In this type of language, the programmer defines not only the data type of a data structure, but also the types of operations (*methods*) that can be applied to the data structure. In this way, the data structure becomes an *object* that includes both data and functions. Objects are grouped together in *classes* who are in turn grouped into *hierarchies*.

To be truly OO, a programming language must support three properties: encapsulation, inheritance, and polymorphism.

Hiding of code is called *encapsulation*. Every class can hide some of its parts. If there is a piece of code that is called only by methods of the class itself, it is made *private* - invisible from outside the class. Some languages, for example C++ and newer versions of Java can even have classes inside classes, and these classes are private to the class that contains them.

Inheritance is the way to extend or change already existing parent class, and make a child class that stays linked with its parent class. If anything changes in parent class, automatically all children (and grand-children and so on...) are changed. This is the key for code-reusability.

A concept closely related to inheritance is *polymorphism*. This means that objects of different classes can be used in the same manner, but - depending on their actual class - will behave differently.

The first OOP language was Smalltalk, developed by Alan Kay at the Palo Alto Research Center of the Xerox Corporation in the early 1970s. Smalltalk, however, has not found widespread use. One of the most popular OOP languages is C++, developed by Bjarne Stroustrup at Bell Laboratories in the early 1980s. In May 1995 Sun Microsystems, Inc. released Java, a new OOP language, which has drawn worldwide interest. In some ways Java represents a simplified version of C++, but it adds other features and capabilities as well, and is particularly well suited for writing interactive applications to be used on the World Wide Web. Of course, Microsoft could not sit on the side of this evolution, it therefore introduced C# (pronounce "see sharp") as its alternative OOP.

Software reuse

Software reuse is the use of existing software assets to meet new business requirements. Program code is only one example of reusable software assets. Other assets include knowledge of the business domain, related design and technology, developer competencies, specifications, requirements, designs, tests, architecture, documentation, methods, procedures and tools. Reuse has been presented as the Silver Bullets of the IT industry and it is true that it can offer several advantages such as:

- Improved Productivity;
- Shorter development cycles;
- Improved Quality;
- Greater Agility;
- Lower maintenance costs.

There are, however, some drawbacks as well:

- Staff retraining and reluctance;
- How to find reusable assets;
- Added costs to make assets reusable;
- Practical organization of the repository.

A *component* is a reusable program building block that can be combined with other components to form a complete system. Components can be deployed on different servers across a network and communicate with each other. A component runs within a context called a *container*. Examples of containers are Web pages, Web browsers, and word processors. Component software is sometimes called *Lego software*, like the well-known toys.

Enterprise JavaBeans (EJB) is Java's server-side component model and are an integral part of the *Java 2 Enterprise Edition* (*J2EE*) platform. EJB provides full definition for component building and management using Java. EJB uses Java's communication protocol called *Remote Method Invocation* (*RMI*). RMI is independent of the underlying protocol so it can run on top of any protocol such as CORBA IIOP or even directly over TCP/IP. The answer from Microsoft to EJB is *ActiveX* [10][11]. This is a set of Object-Oriented programming technologies and tools. The main technology is the *Component Object Model* (*COM*). When used in a network with a directory and some additional support, COM becomes the *Distributed Component Object Model* (*DCOM*). The components in Microsoft's approach are known as an *ActiveX controls*. *Object Linking and Embedding* (*OLE*) used to be Microsoft's technology for compound documents. The Component Object Model now takes in OLE as part of a larger concept and Microsoft now uses the term *ActiveX control* for the component object.

Computer Aided Software Engineering (CASE) tools

Computer Aided Software Engineering (CASE) tools provide automated support for many of the systems analysis and design methods available to the information systems developer. CASE tools provide an environment, which automates many time-consuming aspects of the systems development process, such as:

- Drawing and redrawing of modeling diagrams;
- Cross checking of elements across the system model;
- Generation of system documentation;
- Generation of code structures and database schemas.

CASE tools are categorized as follow:

- *Upper case*: oriented towards the front end of the development cycle (requirements analysis, and design);
- *Lower case*: oriented towards coding, testing and understanding of existing code (reverse engineering).

CASE tools that cover both categories are sometimes called *Integrated* or *iCASE* tools.

An interesting feature offered by some CASE tools is known as *Round Trip Engineering*. A modeling diagram is linked to a piece of code that is generated, as the diagram is adapted. Inversely, when the code is changed with an editor the diagram is automatically adapted. Other functionalities can include Quality Assurance tools such as the determination of relevant metrics (LOC, cyclomatic complexity) and the verification of naming conventions and other coding standards.

CASE tools offer the advantage to provide a common set of tools to be used by everyone working on the same development project. Less effort has to be spent on document administration, such as redrafting diagrams as things are entered into the system instead of written down on scrap paper. An increased quality from extensive cross checking is provided. There is also a potential for reduction in system development time. Furthermore, system documentation is generated automatically.

In the 90s CASE tools were a real hype. In the mean time, many software developers have lost their faith in these products for several reasons:

- These tools usually enforce a single development model;
- The high training effort, difficult to justify with high staff turnover;
- The unstable marketplace with mergers and acquisitions, which makes the future of these tools uncertain;
- The poor interoperability (although XMI, a data modeling data exchange mechanism based on XML, could be a solution for this problem);
- The high price per developer seat.

Integrated Development Environments (IDEs)

IDE stands for *Integrated Development Environment*. In fact, the term comes from the embedded systems world, where the tools are included with the (hardware and software) building blocks used to compose the system. In a more recent history, this term has been associated with development environments wherein the appropriate tools needed for source code editing, compiling, linking, testing, debugging, profiling and executing are seamlessly integrated.

IDE tools are composed of the following elements:

- *Project Management* - This is where all current projects are managed. Files within a project can be separated into folders to ease conceptual separation of files and browsing/selecting the files;
- *Configuration Management* - possibility to check - out/commit files "on the fly" as needed without leaving the programming environment and online comparison of different versions of source files;

- *Application Framework Generator* - Automatic generation of projects and template files for several types of applications;
- *Editor Components* - Editors are usually realized as plug-in modules. This will allow for easy addition of new editors such as icon editors, GUI editors, etc.
- *Online Help* - these allow context sensitive help as well as help browsing by subject;
- *Compiler/build tool Integration* - The ability to build programs directly from the IDE with various (plug-in) compilers/build tools;
- *Debugger Integration* - The ability to debug programs from within the IDE.
- *Component gallery* - possibility to set all include and library variables to link in external libraries or a gallery of libraries and their locations;
- *Documentation tool* - IDE tools include documentation-generation facilities, or at least something that cross-references files, classes, variables etc.

It is to be noted that IDE tools concentrate on the more technical aspects of software creation; modeling is usually only secondary.

Using an IDE tools can bring an important productivity enhancement. Be aware of the inherent dangers: using the components delivered with the tool makes the project totally dependent on them. One will also be forced to follow the consecutive releases of the tool, to be assured of maintenance and support.

Project Monitoring and Control

"In preparing for battle I have always found that plans are useless, but planning is indispensable."

(Dwight D. Eisenhower)

Gantt Charts

Henry Gantt developed one of the first program management tools, today known as *Gantt charts*. Gantt Charts plot the activities necessary to complete a project on a timeline using a bar or line which begins and ends at a defined time. The Gantt chart also provides milestones, or markers, for assuring that a program is on track.

Fig. 7.11 shows a Gantt diagram with the project plan as the project manager defined it. As the same resource (Paul) will be performing two activities consecutively, the termination of the "Calculations" function is considered as a milestone. On the other hand, the "User Interface" should also be finished in time, as it determines the start of the "Roll out," so this is a milestone as well. Of course, the end of the project is another milestone.

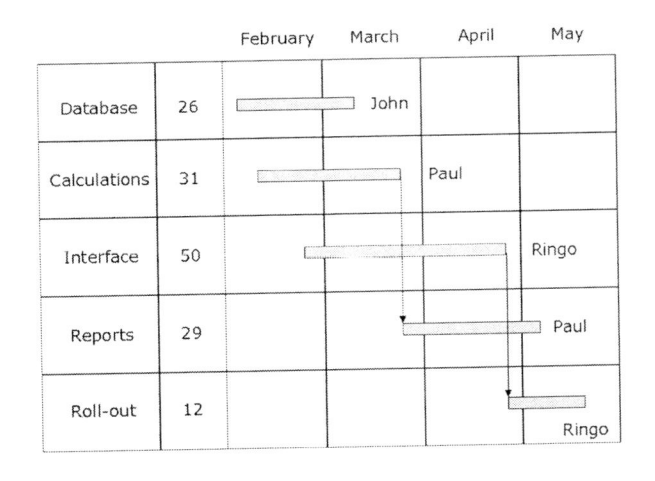

Fig. 7.11 – *Gantt chart*

While Gantt Charts have the advantage of simplicity, they can hide as much as they display. Indeed, the interrelationships among the various activities are not made explicit nor are the relationship between resources and the time to complete a task. Gantt Charts can tell a manager if a program is off track; however, they often cannot provide information about how to get it back on track.

Project Evaluation and Review Technique/Critical Path Method (PERT/CPM)

The most common method for documenting the relationships between tasks and determining their relative importance to the project is the *Project Evaluation and Review Technique/Critical Path Method (PERT/CPM)* [120]. PERT was developed in 1958 to help plan and schedule the U.S. Navy's Polaris submarine project. On the other hand, the DuPont Company and the Univac division of Remington Rand Corporation developed CPM to provide a method for controlling maintenance in the DuPont Chemical plants. Later, it was noticed that these two methods shared many similarities and their approaches were combined into one method.

PERT/CPM networks provide a general overview of a project. They consist of *activities* and *events*: activities are operations in the project that consume resources and take time; events occur at a point in time and represent the beginning, the end, (or both) of an activity.

The table below shows the interdependencies among the various tasks of the project example.

Function	Activity	Resource	Estimate	Dependencies
1. Database				
	a. Requirements	John	2	2a;3a;4a
	b. Design	John	8	1a
	c. Code	John	8	1b
	d. Test	John	8	1d
2. Calculations				
	a. Requirements	Paul	4	-
	b. Design	Paul	10	2a
	c. Code	Paul	7	2b
	d. Test	Paul	10	2c
3. User Interface				
	a. Requirements	Ringo	10	-
	b. Design	Ringo	15	3a
	c. Code	Ringo	10	3b
	d. Test	Ringo	15	3c
4. Reports				
	a. Requirements	Paul	7	-
	b. Design	Paul	8	4a
	c. Code	Paul	7	4b
	d. Test	Paul	7	4c
5. Roll out				
	a. Requirements	Ringo	2	1d;2d;3d;4d
	b. Design	Ringo	2	5a
	c. Code	Ringo	3	5b
	d. Test	Ringo	5	5c

The most time-consuming path in the network is called the *critical path*. The term critical is used for each activity within this longest path through the network, as any delays in realizing a critical-path activity will delay the entire project. The difference between the time it takes to create that path and the time it takes to create each other path is the *slack time* for each of the other paths. By definition, the critical path has zero slack time. Note that the shortest time possible to complete a project is the time it takes to complete the tasks on the critical path, also note that there can be more than one critical path and that the critical path can change during a project (as "slippage" extends the length of one path so that now it becomes the longest).

For the sample project, the PERT/CPM network looks like in Fig. 7.12.

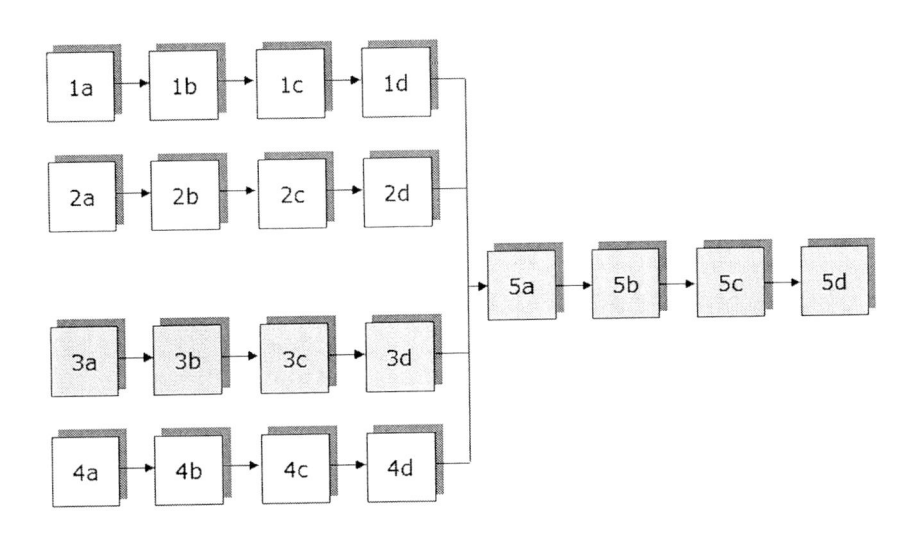

Fig. 7.12 – *PERT/CPM*

This diagram gives a much clearer view of the task dependencies. The critical path is formed by the activities related to the "User Interface" and the "Roll out." The critical path determines the minimal project duration; it is 62 days. Putting more resources (John) on these tasks could possibly reduce this duration. On the other hand, the slack times for the "Database," "Calculations" and "Reports" paths are respectively 36, 31 and 33 days.

There is a problem that cannot be shown in this diagram. Indeed, the whole picture would change if Paul, who is assigned to "Calculations" and "Reports," should exceed the allotted time. Although neither "Calculations" nor "Reports" are on the critical path, the fact that they are both performed (consecutively) by the same resource make them critical as well; this is known as *Resource Dependency*.

Critical Chain Scheduling and Buffer management

"Adding people to a late project makes it later."

(Brooks law, 1975)

As we saw before, estimates can have considerable safety margins: a safe estimate can easily be the double of an aggressive one. So, a manager could cut ten or 20 percent on the estimates of his collaborators and still have a lot of margin left. In practice, however, this margin will always be consumed and even be exceeded. There are three reasons for this: Murphy's Law, the Student Syndrome and Parkinson's Law:

- *Murphy's Law* - Edward A. Murphy, Jr. was an engineer on the experiments that were done by the US Air Force to test human tolerance to acceleration. One experiment involved a set of 16 accelerometers mounted to different parts of the subject's body. There were two ways each sensor could be glued to its mount, and somebody methodically installed all 16 the wrong way around. Murphy then made the original form of his law *"If there are two or more ways to do something and one of those ways can result in a catastrophe, then someone will do it."* After some years many variants had passed into the popular imagination. Most of these are variants on *"Anything that can go wrong will."* Murphy's Law applies to software development so nothing will go perfectly as it was intended and estimates will always be wrong.
- *The Student Syndrome* - Students are known to have a tendency to postpone their studying until the last minute. *"Why start right now, we still have all the time?"* There are so many other things to do or maybe Murphy already did his job so that we have something else to do first. Software developers often behave much like students and postpone their work until the last moment or even beyond.
- *Parkinson's Law* - Most software developers love their work, so even if they did it properly within the given duration they will add some extra features: make a screen look nicer, add a function somewhere etc. On the other hand, this is also a self-protection mechanism: if somebody has finished long before the allotted time he can go to tell his manager. The risk is then that the manager will reduce his next estimates so that he will be under a lot more pressure to finish his work. There are indeed better rewards. This phenomenon is known as Parkinson's Law: *"Work expands to fill the time available."*

In reality, things are even worse. This is because in most projects, tasks are executed in parallel. At the end of the project the result of the different tasks are then integrated, and this could cause some problems as well.

In the situation as shown in Fig. 7.14, tasks 1d, 2d and 4d are delivered on schedule; however, task 3d has a delay of ten days. As task 5a has to wait for all the others to be finished it will automatically be late as well; the more tasks that have to be integrated, the smaller the probability that the integration will be on time. For an aggressive estimate the probability for one task to be on time is 50%. For four tasks this becomes 0.5*0.5*0.5*0.5=0.0625 or just over 6%!

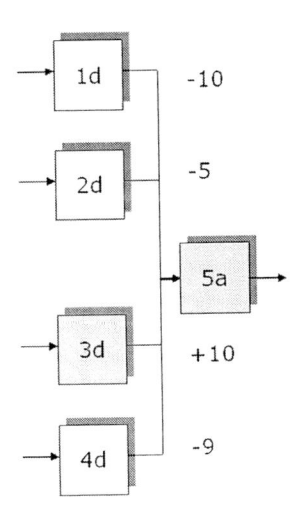

Fig. 7.13 – *Integration of tasks*

Clearly, traditional management techniques (managing the deadlines of the different tasks, putting our resources under pressure and switching them between tasks) are unable to cope with this situation. So, how can we protect the project due date without fixing intermediate deadlines? How can we make a systematic use of the time that is created by tasks that finish early and how can we effectively manage our project without intermediate deadlines?

An answer for these questions can be found in the *Critical Chain Scheduling and Buffer Management* method. This method is derived from the *Theory Of Constraints (TOC)*, invented by Eliyahu Goldratt [107][108][125]. The Critical Chain is the combination of task dependencies and resource dependencies. Resources that are performing tasks of the Critical Chain are asked to give an estimate of the time they still need to finish their task. In that way the resources that are occupied on less important tasks can prepare to "drop" these tasks to start the next task in the chain. The basic ideas are simple:

- Make use of the large amounts of spare time by isolating them from the tasks and aggregating them in one big project buffer, at the end of the project. This project buffer is used to "fight" against Murphy and can be smaller than the sum of the margins thanks to statistical effects;

- The project buffer is possible because we rely on aggressive estimates (50% probability) for the tasks, thus liberating half of the time allotted to each task. In this way the Student syndrome and Parkinson are eliminated for the tasks;
- The management of the project is no longer done on the task due dates, but on the size of the project buffer and how it is consumed by delayed tasks. The manager no longer has to concentrate on the different tasks, but can think of more global strategies to protect the project deadline.

Verification and Validation

"A common mistake that people make when trying to design something completely foolproof is to underestimate the ingenuity of complete fools."

(Douglas Adams)

Verification confirms that the software product works correctly; *"Are we building the product right?"* *Validation* confirms that the software product works according to the specifications, and therefore, the client's requirements; *"Are we building the right product?"*

Execution-Based Testing relies on running the program. *Non-Execution-Based Testing* relies on reviews, or sometimes on formal analysis [86][110][124].

White Box testing

The purpose *of White box testing* is to verify the control flow and is usually performed at the unit level. The goal is to obtain that all paths within a module have been exercised at least once, all logical decisions have been exercised with all possible conditions, loops have been exercised on upper and lower boundaries, and all internal data structures have been exercised. White box testing is also called *code-based testing* or *structural testing*. A metric that is used in the context of white box testing is the *Cyclomatic Complexity*. Thomas McCabe [123] introduced this metric in 1976; it measures the number of linearly independent paths through a program module. It is based on the idea that a program flow can be represented as a graph.

Consider for example the following C-function, which implements Euclid's algorithm for finding the greatest common divisors of two integers n and m.

```
0           Euclid(int m, int n)
            {
            int t;
1           if (n>m)
                {
2               r = m;
3               m = n;
4               n = r;
                }
5
6           r=m%n;              /* m modulo n */
7           while (r != 0)
                {
8               m = n;
9               n = r;
10              r = m%n         /* m modulo n */
11              }
12          return n;
13          }
```

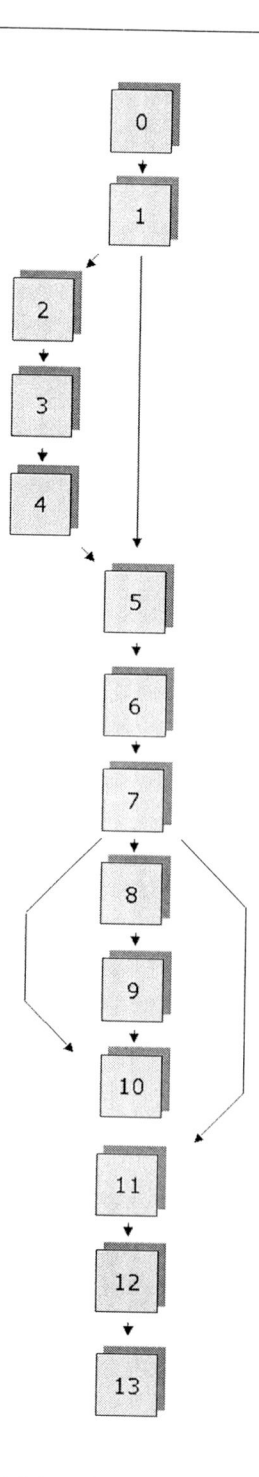

Fig. 7.14 – *Cyclomatic complexity*

n the control flow graph of Fig. 7.14 node 1 represents the decision of the "if" statement with the true outcome at node 2 and the false outcome at node 5. The decision of the "while" loop is represented by node 7 and the line shows the upward flow of control from node 10 to 7. When the test at node 7 is false, execution transfers out of the loop directly to node 11, then proceeds to node 12, returning the result of 2. The actual return is modeled by execution proceeding to node 13, the module exit node.

The cyclomatic complexity V(G) is defined to be (E − N + 2) where E and N are the number of edges and nodes. Thus, for the Euclid's algorithm the complexity is 3.

Studies show a correlation between a module's cyclomatic complexity and its error frequency and associated risk, and its testability. It gives the exact number of tests needed to test every decision point in a program for each outcome. An excessively complex module will require a prohibitive number of test steps; that number can be reduced to a practicable size by breaking the module into smaller, less complex sub-modules.

Cyclomatic Complexity	Evaluation
1-10	Simple program, low risk
11-20	More complex, moderate risk
21-50	Complex, high risk
> 50	Not testable, high risk

Table 7.6 – *Cyclomatic Complexity and Risk*

Unit Testing

Here, the focus is on the verification of modules. Testers define the input domain for the units in question and ignore the rest of the system. This testing is white box oriented. Unit testing can use drivers, which are control programs to coordinate test case inputs and outputs, and dummy subprograms (stubs), which replace low-level modules.

Black Box testing

This type of testing tests the functional capabilities (requirements) and is usually performed at the system level. This type of testing is used to find incorrect or missing functions, interface errors, errors in data structures, performance errors and initialization and termination errors. Black box testing is also called *functional testing*, *specification-based testing* and *behavioral testing*.

Integration Testing

Integration testing is used to verify the combination of the software units. Black box test case design techniques are the most prevalent during integration, although a limited amount of white box testing can be used to ensure coverage of major control paths. Integration testing provides a systematic approach for assembling the software in an incremental fashion. There are two approaches: top down and bottom up.

In a *top down integration* the top module is used as test driver. For all modules subordinate to top module stubs are developed and gradually replaced by the real modules. Additional stubs as required in the downward expansion are added and replaced. Tests are conducted as each stub is replaced with a real module. This approach has the advantage that major control flow is tested first, and it provides rapid demonstration for functionality.

In a *bottom up integration* a cluster of modules that perform a sub-function is combined. Then a driver is developed to test the cluster. Combine clusters and move upward, finally, interface with top control module. This approach has the advantage that "worker" modules are tested early, and there is no need for stubs or dummy simulation of data.

System Testing

System testing is a series of different tests whose primary purpose is to test a deliverable product. Although each test has a different purpose, all work should verify that all system elements (software, hardware, interfaces, etc.) have been properly integrated and perform allocated functions. There are four types of system level testing that can be performed: recovery testing, security testing, stress testing, and performance testing.

Regression testing

Usually, after correction of several faults, a new release of the software system is created. The problem is that correcting one fault can produce new faults (break something that was previously working). This means that several things have to be retested. This is called *regression testing*. It seems prudent to rerun every test from release n-1 on release n, but such a practice would be costly. Moreover, new software releases often contain new functionality, besides bug fixes, so the regression tests would take resources away from testing new code. So, to save resources, testers work closely together with developers to sort and minimize regression tests or use some form of automated testing.

Alpha and Beta Testing

If there are many customers, it is impractical to perform formal acceptance tests with each one. Most software manufacturers use a process called alpha and beta testing to uncover errors. Customers at the developer's site conduct *alpha testing* with the developer present. *Beta testing* is conducted at one or more customer's sites with the developer not present.

Automated testing

Automated Testing is automating the (manual) testing process [102]. This requires that a formalized testing process exists.

Minimally, such a process includes:

- *Detailed test cases*, including predictable expected results;
- A *test environment*, including a test database that is restorable to a known state, such that the test cases can be repeated each time there are modifications made to the application.

The real use and purpose of automated test tools is to *automate regression testing*. This means that a database of repeatable test cases has to be developed. This suite of tests is run every time there is a change to the application to ensure that the change does not produce unintended consequences. An *automated test script* is a program; therefore, automated script development must be subject to the same rules and standards that are applied to normal software development.

The conclusion is that test scripts have to be written by a technical person who knows what he is doing; they <u>cannot</u> be generated automatically.

Test Plan

A test plan is a formal, written document addressing the following issues [126]:

- The goal of the test: What do we want to achieve?
- Where and when will the test(s) take place?
- How long is each test session expected to take?
- What computer support will be needed for the test?
- What software needs to be ready for the test?
- What should be the state of the system at the start of the test?
- What should the system/network load and response times be?

- Who will serve as experimenters for the test?
- Who are the test users, and how are we going to get hold of them?
- How many test users are needed?
- What test tasks will the users be asked to perform?
- What criteria will be used to determine when the users have finished each of the test tasks correctly?
- What aids (manuals, online help, etc.) will be available to the test users?
- To what extent will the experimenter be allowed to help the users during the test?
- What data is going to be collected, and how will it be analyzed once it has been collected?
- What will the criterion be for pronouncing the interface a success?

Test Results

The test results are equally part of the project documentation and should therefore be kept in the Definitive Software Library (DSL). They give an idea of the known problem areas and, above all, allow the customer to judge if the product can be accepted or put into production.

Software Quality Management

"It is the mark of an instructed mind to rest satisfied with the degree of precision which the nature of the subject admits and not to seek exactness when only an approximation of the truth is possible."

(Aristotle)

The definition of the term *software quality* is an issue. A surprising number of people still think that software quality is simply the absence of errors. Many software engineering references define software quality as "correct implementation of the specification." It is true that such a definition can be used during product development but it is inadequate for comparing products. This is the reason why software quality is often defined in terms of the fitness of the product for its purpose.

It is also to be noted that different people have different purposes. A casual user could be more concerned about ease of use than about efficiency, a system integrator will be more concerned about failure detection and recovery and a third party maintenance organization is concerned about technical documentation. These examples show that software quality is not absolute, but it is a perception that depends on the person who is evaluating it and even evolves over time for the same person.

Over the years, a great amount of *Software Process Improvement (SPI)* models have been developed. They all have one common goal: transform software engineering from an ad-hoc, labor-intensive heroic activity into a managed, technology-supported engineering discipline, focused on technical and management practices that yield high-quality systems delivered on time and within expected cost, every time.

Capability Maturity Model (CMM)

The *Capability Maturity Model* (*CMM*) [129] was developed at the *Software Engineering Institute* (*SEI*) and is based on the premises that maturity shows capability and to obtain continuous process improvement it is much better to take small evolutionary steps rather than revolutionary innovations. It aims at guiding software organizations in selecting process improvement strategies by first determining their current process maturity before identifying the organization's critical quality and process improvement issues. The CMM provides a framework for organizing these evolutionary steps into five *maturity levels*. CMM is in fact an application of the *Total Quality Management* (*TQM*) concepts to software; both the CMM and TQM have the goal of customer satisfaction.

CMM distinguishes five levels of maturity:

- *Initial* - Characterised by an ad hoc process. Success depends on individual effort;
- *Repeatable* - Basic project management processes track cost, schedule and functionality. This process discipline enables the repetition of earlier successes on similar projects;
- *Defined* - Management and engineering activities in the software process are documented, standardized and integrated into an organization-wide software process;
- *Managed* - Detailed measures are collected, both for the software and for product quality;
- *Optimising* - Continuous process improvement results from quantitative feedback from the process and from testing new ideas and technologies.

The benefits that can be expected from the implementation of the CMM principles are substantial and can be situated in the domains of increased productivity and improved quality.

	1 to 2	2 to 3	3 to 4	4 to 5
Productivity	40-50%	20-30%	10-15%	5-10%
Quality	50-55%	30-35%	5-10%	1-5%

Table 7.7 *Benefits of CMM*

CMM has had a major influence on software process and quality improvement around the world. A lot of companies started using CMM and more standards, partially based on CMM, were developed.

ISO-9001

The *International Standards Organization* (*ISO*) developed the ISO 9000 series of standards. The ISO 9001 standard is intended to be used when conformance to specified requirements is to be assured by the supplier during several stages, which can include design, development, production, installation and servicing. There is a guideline, or a subset of guidelines, ISO 9000-3, for applying ISO 9001 to the development, supply and maintenance of software.

Like CMM, ISO is concerned with continuous Quality and Process Improvement. Both emphasize documented procedures and policies as well as reports and records of events and procedure implementations and both stress the need for prevention (Quality Assurance) rather than just detection (Quality Control). In all practicality, an ISO 9001 certification equals a CMM level 2 and some noticeable level 3 requirements satisfied.

TickIT

TickIT is a certification scheme developed to apply ISO 9001, but with the advantage of having been "tuned" for the special requirements of software development.

However, since the scope of TickIT is identical to ISO 9001, there is virtually no content relating to process improvement, except in the context of changes resulting from corrective and preventive actions.

Software Process Improvement and Capability dEtermination (SPICE)

SPICE is a major international initiative to support the development of an International Standard for Software Process Assessment [101]. SPICE stands for *Software Process Improvement and Capability dEtermination*. The objective is to assist the software industry to make significant gains in productivity and quality, while at the same time helping purchasers to get better value for money and reduce the risk associated with large software projects and purchases.

SPICE was intended to be a framework suitable for use in the primary contexts of process assessment, process improvement and capability determination. *Process Improvement* has the objective of changing or optimizing processes for greater effectiveness to achieve gains in product quality and productivity while *Capability Determination* is concerned with assessing an organization or project to determine risks to the successful outcome of a contract, development or service delivery. The assessment framework depends on an architecture that defines the practices and processes that should be realized. The process categories covered in the SPICE architecture address five *general areas of activity*:

- *Customer-supplier processes* - processes that directly impact the customer, support development and transition of the software to the customer, and provide for its correct operation and use of the software product or service;

- *Engineering processes* - processes that directly specify, create or maintain the software products, its relation to the system and its customer documentation;
- *Support processes* - processes that can be employed by any of the other processes (including other supporting processes) at various points in the software life cycle;
- *Management processes* - processes that contain practices of a generic nature that can be used by anyone who manages any type of project or process within a software life cycle;
- *Organization processes* - processes that establish the business goals of the organization and develop process, product and resource assets which, when used by the projects in the organization, help the organization achieve its business goals.

Software Configuration Management

Anybody who has been involved in software development has experienced one or more of the following problems:

- Developers overwriting each other's code;
- Wrong versions being put in production;
- Bugs reappear, although they were previously fixed;
- Customizations have to be refused;
- It is unclear which customer uses which release;
- It is unclear what has been fixed or realized.

At another level there are problems such as:

- Low level of reuse;
- Definition of responsibilities within a team;
- Inability to give the exact status of a project;
- Inability to give an accurate planning;
- Inabilities to determine which deliverables (source, documentation, executables) are affected by a change.

Clearly, these problems can have a negative effect for both the development team and its customers:

- Loss of productivity;
- Missed deadlines;
- Budget overruns;
- Stress and overtime;
- Too many status report meetings;
- Angry customers.

Professional teams avoid these problems using a good organization of their work and apply techniques of *Software Configuration Management (SCM)*.

Ovum defines SCM as follows:

"Software Configuration Management is a disciplined approach to managing and controlling the evolution of software development and maintenance practices and their software products as they change over time."

There are several factors that drive the need for SCM.

Application Size and Complexity - The size and complexity of applications continues to increase rapidly. The demands on functionality are relentless, and the result is typically larger and more complex applications. Directly related to the rise in object-oriented technologies is the fast-growing use of component-based development practices, often using objects developed in multiple languages and tools.

Size and composition of Development Teams - The larger the team, the greater the need for SCM; as teams grow, the problems of communication, coordination, integration, conflicts, and parallel development can quickly become overwhelming. Moreover, they are increasingly spread across multiple locations. SCM must support centralized, remote and distributed development teams. Another factor that has influenced team composition, as well as application size and complexity, is the rapidly increasing use of outsourcing, subcontracting and third party, vendor supplied code.

Parallel Development - Not long ago, the norm was for a software team to work on a single release of software, ship this release, and then move into a maintenance phase where the team would issue ongoing updates. Now, the typical case is that there are multiple teams working on the same code base, working simultaneously on patches, maintenance releases, and new generation releases, and delivering multiple variants of the code for different platforms, operating systems, databases, or native languages.

SCM provides full control of software products as they are developed. It also offers a mechanism for recording changes, during both development and production. It enables developers to:

- Track who, what, when, and why of any changes to the project deliverables (source code, documentation, executables);
- Identify the modules changed in response to a particular bug fix/requirement.
- Recreate any version of the product;
- Control access to the repository in which the deliverables are stored.

Even though a well-defined process is the most important, a good tool is needed to implement SCM in a cost-effective way. This tool can automate the process and help manage software projects more efficiently, from the beginning of development through testing, release, and maintenance.

Documentation Development

Software documentation [84][111] is another key activity in the construction of a software system. Documentation must serve a varied number of purposes:

- Analysts and designers use it to communicate the system requirements and design to users, management, and developers during the software development process;
- It provides customers with examples and explanations on how to use the software, thus improving their efficiency (and productivity);
- It also describes the algorithms, methods and techniques that the developers have used to create the software.

Brockmann [92] defines documentation as:

"Communication designed to ease interactions between computer software and the individuals who manage, audit, operate or maintain it."

Internal software documentation serves the purpose of communication among the different actors of the development team. It is composed of project plans, requirements specifications, design documents and progress reports but also testing strategies, test results and bug reports. *External documentation* is oriented towards the customers; it contains tutorials, user manuals, reference manuals, context-sensitive help, presentations, etc. It is important to understand that there are *different audiences* of external software documentation:

- *Novices* – These users understand isolated concepts but do not perceive the context so concrete examples should be used;
- *Intermediate* – These users perceive the context and begin to link concepts. Documentation should be task-oriented;
- *Advanced* – These users are competent and understand structure and relationships. They will use all the features of the system, so the documentation should be goal-oriented.

Brockman suggests two more groups:

- *Parrots* – These users have no experience whatsoever, they can only cope with small chunks and do not think, question or synthesize;
- *Intermittent* – These users can be novice, intermediate or expert but work infrequently with this system. They forget what they have learned previously and consequently rely heavily on the user interface.

Training

A *training program* can be conceived in different ways: it can be based on self study or be guided by a teacher, it can be done in a face-to-face, classroom approach or there can be a distance, both in space and in time, between the teacher and the student. A training program can be a guided exploration of the study domain or it can be composed of exercises.

Usually, a good training program is a balanced mix of all the above.

Some other reflections about training are:

- *Train the trainer* – The users who participated in the development (requirements, design, testing) can be good candidates to do the job of training the other users. They know the new system well and have a better credibility than some stranger from the IT department or an external company;
- *Different types of users have different training needs* – Refer to the reflections on this matter in the documentation development section;
- *Training should be immediately preceding system rollout* – People forget rapidly when they have no practice of the newly acquired skills;
- *A training schedule has to be prepared and communicated carefully* – euser should be reached and the availability of the new system to the users has to be synchronized with the training.

Installation

New software or changes to existing software come as *releases*. There are three types of releases:

- *Full Release* - All components of the release are built, tested, distributed and realized together. This type of release is used for the roll out of new software systems or totally new versions of existing systems;
- *Delta Release* - This only includes Configuration Items (CIs) that are new or that have changed since the last release and consequently it usually requires less testing and building effort. This is typically used in a maintenance situation;
- *Package Release* - This represents a large amount of change being grouped together. The particular advantages of this method are that it provides longer periods of stability, it reduces chance of older incompatible software still kept in use and it allows for testing of communications, links, dependencies across suites and systems.

The following elements have to be considered before a release:

- *Size* - The larger the release the greater the testing and required resources;
- *Interfaces* between the proposed unit and the other Information Systems.
- *Frequency of releases* is another key issue. Too many, too often will lead to instability, not often enough will lead to unnecessary complexity.

Urgent Releases are used to solve severe or high priority problems. These releases should be kept to a minimum, as they disrupt normal planned release cycles and are also error prone. Despite the urgency the following safeguards must still be maintained:

- Change Management;
- All actions must be reflected in the CMDB;
- The DSL version must be used as the basis for the change;
- The amended copy has to be stored in the DSL;
- The version number must be changed to reflect the release;
- Whatever testing is possible within the time available should be carried out;
- Notify customers as far in advance as possible (via the Helpdesk);
- Any documentation changes should be carried out as soon as possible.

Release frequency is governed by business needs, user requirements and technical considerations. Releases should be frequent enough to accommodate all necessary changes, but too frequent releases can result in high costs and a lack of stability.

A history, held in the *Definitive Software Library (DSL)* should be built up as a central point for release activity. The DSL will include only authorized versions of software and project documentation. It has to be totally separate from development, test or live environments.

For of a new system replacing an existing application, there are often overlaps: periods of time during which both systems are operated in parallel. During this period two approaches are possible: either the data in both systems are updated simultaneously or there can be an automatic process that transfers the updates in the old system to the new system (which is used in read-only mode). The first approach of course means a doubling of the workload of the users, while the second approach could be used to verify and improve the data.

Running a new system in parallel with the old one should only be considered as a way for the users to get used to the new system. It should never be seen as a supplementary test phase or being presented as a fallback scenario for if the new system should not work out well. Verification and validation of the new system are processes that have to take place before a system is put into operation, so relying on a period of parallel operation is risky and therefore a bad idea.

This being said, that does not mean that there could not be any "childhood diseases" that are only discovered during the first days or weeks of operation of a new system. After all it is the first time that the system is exposed to the real world with real data and real customers. The project planning should therefore provide for a "run-in" period during which these small problems are being corrected as they appear. Do not forget, however, to do this under configuration control.

Another aspect related to the release of a new system is the transfer of the data from old to new. Often, this is a non-trivial operation because of differences in the data structures (referential constraints), different formatting, different codes etc. Often, the data transfer operation has to be considered as a project in itself and there will be a high involvement of the end users for the verification.

Maintenance

Typology

Software Maintenance is a group of software engineering activities that occur after software has been delivered to the customer and put into operation.

Maintenance can be divided into four types:

- *Perfective* - Adding new capabilities, modifying existing functions and making general enhancements. This accounts for some 50% of all effort expended on maintenance;
- *Adaptive* – modification of software to interface properly with a changing environment (hardware and software). Some 25% of all maintenance effort;
- *Corrective* - diagnosis and correction of errors. Represents some 21% of the maintenance effort;
- *Preventive* - changing software to improve future maintainability or reliability or to provide a better basis for future enhancements. Only represents some 4% of the maintenance effort.

(figures: Van Vliet [140])

Problems associated with maintenance

The problems that are associated with maintenance are:

- Most software is not designed for change;
- Changes are not adequately documented;
- Badly structured code;
- It is difficult to understand someone else's program;
- Insufficient knowledge of system or problem domain;
- Maintenance tends to introduce new errors;
- Maintenance is not considered as interesting work;
- Staff turnover.

Lehman and Belady [119] have studied the history of successive releases in a large operating system. They found that the total number of modules increases linearly with release number, but that the number of modules affected increases exponentially with release number. All repairs tend to destroy the structure of the system, so less and less effort is spent fixing original design flaws but more and more is spent on fixing problems introduced in earlier fixes.

Software development can be seen as an *entropy-decreasing* process; order is created out of chaos. Program maintenance, on the contrary, is an *entropy-increasing* process, and even its most skillful execution only delays the subsidence of the system into unfixable obsolescence. Software maintenance, it seems, is like fixing holes in a dike; eventually it fails, and must be rebuilt. The result of all this is that the evolution of the development effort and the associated costs of any software system have a typical "bath tub" shape (Fig. 7.15); during the development phase, the costs are high. Once in the maintenance phase, the costs are relatively low and constant. Towards the end of the life cycle they are rising again.

Fig. 7.15 – *Bathtub diagram*

Many software organizations spend between 40 and 80 percent of all funds conducting maintenance. This leads to several unpleasant side effects:

- Loss of opportunity for new development with increasing misalignment between IT and business;
- Unsatisfied customers, because of faulty systems;
- Unsatisfied developers, because of frustrating jobs;
- Bad reputation of IT department as a whole.

Metrics

Efforts to measure and track maintainability are intended to help reduce or reverse a system's tendency toward *code entropy* or degraded integrity, and to show when it becomes cheaper or less risky to rewrite the code than to change it.

Several indicators have been developed to express the maintainability of software.

It seems logical that, the larger the system the more difficult it will be to maintain. This can be expressed using the *Lines Of Code (LOC)* metric.

On the other hand, the *internal complexity* of the program as a result of nested control structures will have an influence too. The *Cyclomatic Complexity* expresses this internal complexity.

Furthermore, the *Computational Complexity* will have an influence. A metric for this was developed by Maurice Halstead as a quantitative measure of complexity directly from the operators and operands in the module [109]. With n1 being the number of distinct operators and n2 the number of distinct operands, the *Program Vocabulary (n)* is n1+n2. Furthermore, if N1 is the total number of operators and N2 the total number of operands, the *Program Length (N)* is N1+N2. The Halstead Volume is then found as:

$$V = N * \log_2 n$$

Finally, if a program is well documented, more specifically using comments in the code, it will be easier to maintain.

All these elements were brought together by Oman [128] in a metric called *Maintainability Index (MI)*. The MI is a polynomial of the following form:

$$171 - 5.2 * \ln(aveV) - 0.23 * aveV(g') - 16.2 * \ln(aveLOC) - 50 * \sin(\sqrt{2.4 * perCM})$$

The terms are:

- aveV = average Halstead Volume V per module.
- aveV(g') = average extended cyclomatic complexity per module.
- aveLOC = the average count of lines of code (LOC) per module.
- perCM = average percent of lines of comments per module.

The coefficients shown in the equation are the result of calibration using data from numerous software systems being maintained by Hewlett-Packard. The larger MI, the better the system is maintainable.

The MI can be used in different ways:

- The system can be checked periodically for maintainability, which is also a way of calibrating the equations.
- It can be integrated into a development effort to screen code quality as it is being built and modified;
- It drives maintenance activities by evaluating modules either selectively or globally to find high-risk code.
- MI compares or evaluates systems: Comparing the MIs of a known-quality system and a third-party system can provide key information in a make-or-buy decision.

Application Mining

Making sure that Information Systems can adapt quickly and without risk to changing requirements has become an absolute necessity. But the problems of staff turnover, software complexity and a lack of appropriate tools make it increasingly difficult to meet this need. Just like Data Mining helps business managers make better decisions, *Application Mining* helps IT professionals improve application programming and maintenance. It has been found that developers spend nearly 50% of their time diving into the code, in search of application knowledge. Application Mining tools behave like an army of additional developers that would join the development team to read the code of the applications and understand it, much faster than humans would do. These tools break down source code and automatically populate an *Application Warehouse* with all the elements (tables, triggers, stored procedures, packages, classes, interfaces, methods...) and all the interactions between these elements (relations, inheritance, exception handling...). As opposed to error-prone manual updates of traditional repositories, it is the tool that keeps the Application Warehouse up-to-date.

Retirement

When a system has reached the end of its useful life it has to be retired. Among the things that have to be considered under these circumstances are:

- What is going to happen to the historical data (transfer to a new system, archiving…)?
- Training of maintenance staff and end users;
- Software licenses/maintenance contracts to be stopped;
- Phase out of related hardware.

Legal considerations

Intellectual Property

Intellectual Property (IP) refers to creations of the mind: inventions, literary and artistic works, symbols, names, images, and designs used in commerce. IP is divided into *Industrial property* (for patents, trademarks and industrial designs) and *Copyright* (for literary and artistic works).

Industrial Property

In the context of this book we are mainly interested in *patents*, more particularly for software. The definition of a patent by the *World Intellectual Property Organization (WIPO)* is:

"A patent is an exclusive right granted for an invention, which is a product or a process that provides a new way of doing something, or offers a new technical solution to a problem."

Since the essence of a patent is the right to exclude others from commercial exploitation of the invention, the patent holder is the only one who can make, use, or sell the invention. Others can do so only with the authorization of the patent holder.

All patent applications and granted patents are published; they offer a limited term of protection.

There is no single "international patent;" a patent gives rights only in the country (or group of countries) that issues it, so if an invention has potential foreign uses or markets, separate patent applications must be made for each country or region of interest. Each has its own requirements for patentability and patent applications.

Under the *US Patent Act*, for an invention to be patentable it must be:

- Statutory;
- New;
- Useful;
- Nonobvious.

The *statutory* requirement says that only processes, machines, articles of manufacture, and compositions of matter are patentable. Certain "inventions" are not patentable:

- Data structures or programs as such;
- Compilations or arrangements of non-functional information or a storage medium with such information;
- Methods of doing business;
- Mere printed matter.

However, if the patent requires the software program to operate on data, the invention can be considered a patentable process. Also, if the patent claims the software program in connection with the physical structure of a computer, the invention can be considered a patentable machine.

Some examples of patents are:

- The famous Diffie/Hellman secret key exchange patent;
- Use of different colors to distinguish the nesting level of expressions in computer programs.

A *European patent* can be obtained by filing an application in one official language of the *European Patent Office (EPO)* and is valid in as many of the contracting states as the applicant cares to designate. A European patent affords the same rights in the designated contracting states as a national patent granted in any of theses states. European patents are also granted for international applications filed under the *Patent Cooperation Treaty (PCT)*, under which the US, European and Japanese patent offices collaborate.

Copyright

A *copyright* is a property right that an author possesses in the literary, artistic or software work which he or she has created; it protects the expression of an idea not the idea itself. Copyright law protects the author from having the work copied by someone else. The *author* is the person who initially created the work. Under some circumstances, especially works created by employees as part of their employment, their company or employer is legally the author. The author is initially the owner of the work, but an author can transfer ownership of the copyright to someone else. Violation of copyright can have serious consequences as is illustrated by the case of Lotus versus Paperback Software and Mosaic Software (1990), who had produced spreadsheets that had the same menu structure as 1-2-3. There was no issue of copying code, but Lotus claimed that copying the interface itself constituted copyright infringement. Lotus won, and both companies went out of business.

The scope of software copyright protection available in different countries over the world varies greatly. Also, copyright laws operate territorially. This means that protection of a work is provided only for a country's nationals or for works first published in the country.

Treaties and bilateral agreements are in place to recognize the copyright interests of foreign authors beyond their country of origin:

- The *Universal Copyright Convention (UCC)* grants to each member state the same protection to works in a country as that country grants to its nationals for works originating in its territory. This form of reciprocity is called *national treatment*. The only formal requirement is that the copyright owner places a notice on the work with the word copyright or ©, the year of first publication and the author's name.
- The *Buenos Aires Convention (BAC)* also provides for national treatment. To be protected, works must bear the marking "All Rights Reserved." The UCC supersedes the BAC for member countries of both treaties.
- The *Berne Convention* is open to all countries of the world provided they meet certain minimum requirements for protecting copyright interests such as national treatment, the granting of moral rights to authors, the granting of economic rights and the adoption of a minimum term of protection of the life of the author plus 50 years.

Under US law, copyright protects computer programs in both source and object form, including software embedded as micro code. The methods and algorithms in a program are not protected. US copyright protection for computer programs extends to non-literal elements including the structure, sequence and organization of a program, and to its graphical user interface. Together these elements are called *look and feel*.

In 1991, the European Union adopted the Directive on the Legal Protection of Computer Programs calling for implementation of conforming legislation by Member States. The Directive provides for uniformity among Member States in several areas, including:

- Requiring protection of computer software as a literary work under copyright law;
- Defining the level of originality required;
- Providing a common term of protection;
- Allowing reverse engineering and decompilation under limited circumstances.

Which is best: Patent or Copyright?

The answer to this question is not simple, as it depends on the circumstances. Sometimes, a patent should be filed while in many others copyright protection is sufficient.

- Patent protection applies to the method or process, copyright protection only the expression of the method;
- Copyright protection is available the instant a work is completed, patent protection applies only after the application is approved, which can take several months;
- Another difference is the term of protection; in the US copyright protection can exist for 50 or more years. Patent protection lasts for only 20 years from the date of filing.
- Cost. A copyright registration application is cheap while a patent application for software can be extremely costly in terms of both time and money.

Licensing

The patent holder or author of a copyrighted work will, of course, try to take advantage of this situation. For this he or she will allow others to use or copy the work in exchange for a financial compensation; a license. A license sets out exactly how you can use the work. There are many different forms of licenses. Sometimes you pay per number of users ("seats"), the maximum number of concurrent users, per site, per processor, per transaction etc. Besides this, also the duration of the license agreement can vary. Until recently this was simple: you paid once for use during an unlimited period of time and something between ten and 20% for the annual maintenance. Now, more and more license agreements are specifying a limited period: a month, a year or longer but not forever anymore.

A special kind of licensing is applied for *Free Software* or *Open Source Software (OSS)*, this is software for which the source code is available. A big variety in OSS licencing agreements exists. These can be subdivided into a limited number of categories:

- *Copylefted software* - Copylefted software is free software whose distribution terms do not let redistributors add any additional restrictions when they redistribute or modify the software. This means that every copy of the software, even if it has been modified, must be free software;
- *Non-Copylefted free software* - Non-Copylefted free software comes from the author with permission to redistribute and modify, and also to add additional restrictions to it;

- *Public domain software* - Public domain is a legal term and means "not copyrighted." It is a special case of non-Copylefted free software, which means that some copies or modified versions cannot be free at all;
- *General Public License (GPL) software* - This software is one specific set of distribution terms for copylefting a program used by the GNU Project.

Besides OSS, other vaguely related licensing schemes exist:

- *Semi-free software* - This is software that is not free, but comes with permission for individuals to use, copy, distribute, and modify (including distribution of modified versions) for non-profit purposes;
- *Freeware* - The term freeware has no clear accepted definition, but it is commonly used for packages, which permit redistribution but not modification (and their source code is not available);
- *Shareware* - This is software, which comes with permission for people to redistribute copies, but says that anyone who continues to use a copy is *required* to pay a license fee. Shareware is not free software, or even semi-free because for most shareware, source code is not available; thus, you cannot modify the program at all and shareware does not come with permission to make a copy and install it without paying a license fee, not even for individuals engaging in nonprofit activity.

Best Practices

Aim for Conceptual Integrity

Like with most medieval European cathedrals, IT environments evolve over time and as a result have many different styles. This lack of integrity impacts new developments as well as maintenance and support. Sometimes, it even prevents organizations from adopting new technologies and work processes. Brooks offers us a metaphor: the Cathedral of Reims, where eight generations of builders followed an overall design. The same idea should be adopted for IT developments. Although its roots run deep in software engineering, there is no standard, universally accepted definition of the term *Software Architecture*. While there is no standard definition, there is also no lack of them: many industry gurus and software engineers have given their own definition. A good definition is the one given by Booch, Rumbaugh, and Jacobson in their book *The UML Modeling Language User Guide* [91]:

"An architecture is the set of significant decisions about the organization of a software system, the selection of the structural elements and their interfaces by which the system is composed, together with their behavior as specified in the collaborations among those elements, the composition of these structural and behavioral elements into progressively larger subsystems, and the architectural style that guides this organization-these elements and their interfaces, their collaborations, and their composition."

Architecture serves the role of a building plan for a system or set of systems. It is a specification describing how the system is structured and how the parts of a system coordinate their activities. It is, in large part, a set of design decisions that address important system-wide issues. It is the set of decisions that the architect has made to guarantee that the system elaborated from the architecture will successfully satisfy those important issues regardless of how low level design decisions unfold, providing the architectural specification is complied with. In short, the IT Manager should make sure that the Information Systems he deploys fit in a general architecture. As this architecture will inevitably evolve as technology evolves, the management of this architecture has to be considered as (part of) the job of one of his senior system designers. This person plays an important role in the software life cycle and should therefore have a strong profile:

- Down-to-earth and hype-indifferent vision on technology;
- Strong sense for the real needs of an organization and its employees;
- high capacity for abstraction;
- Creative, both on business issues and user interaction;
- Ability to listen, to present and to sell.

Design Twice, Code Once

The approach to design should never be to write code before design and then reverse engineer the design from this code.

Design should not be represented in pseudo code either, as this affects the partitioning and complexity management. Instead, graphical design methods (such as UML), based on diagrams avoid this problem. Use a tool that enforces notation and semantic rules, not a simple drawing tool.

Design should be done to minimize complexity and maximize understandability.

Do not be afraid of risks

It is in the nature of the work of any manager to take risks. Usually, decisions have to be taken based on incomplete, or even erroneous, information. This is no different for the IT manager. It is good practice to be open about this and to inform superiors, peers, and subordinates so that they will understand why a decision has been taken and possibly accept it if it turns out to be the wrong one.

Do not re-invent the wheel

A *design pattern* is the description of a solution to a recurring problem. The idea is simple: do not re-invent the wheel every time a new design problem occurs, but use the experience, knowledge and insights of others. Patterns provide ready-made solutions that can be adapted to different problems as necessary. Design patterns also provide a common vocabulary that can express large solutions succinctly.

Design patterns were introduced by a famous Gang of Four: Eric Gamma, Richard Helm, Ralph Johnson and John Vlissides [104], they can be seen as "best practices" for all aspects of software design.

A similar concept is known as *Universal Data Models*. The idea is to reuse the effort and experience of others in the creation of data models. It is worth having a look at the books of Silverston [136][137]. They contain hundreds of pre-cooked data models, ready-to-use.

Expect the unexpected

It would be naive to assume that people spend 100 percent of their time on the tasks assigned to them. Every organization has overhead. Overhead includes meetings, training, trade shows, and holidays Account for this time in the schedule. In addition include some margin for unexpected events like sickness, adverse weather conditions and technical problems. It is impossible to predict all the problems ahead, but it *is* predictable that there will be some.

Fit the methodology to the project, not the other way around

It is important to understand that every methodology has its limitations. Therefore it is impossible to name the best or correct way to develop software. It is also important to realize that a methodology is just a way to make people work together to reach a common goal. Therefore, project leaders with a lot of experience do not care so much about methodology any more. They simply observe and sense that more discipline is needed here, more freedom wanted there and more communication has to be organized in some other place. Ultimately, any software development methodology needs to be customized to the team and their circumstances. No methodology is just a collection of rules to be performed blindly, and there are no exceptions.

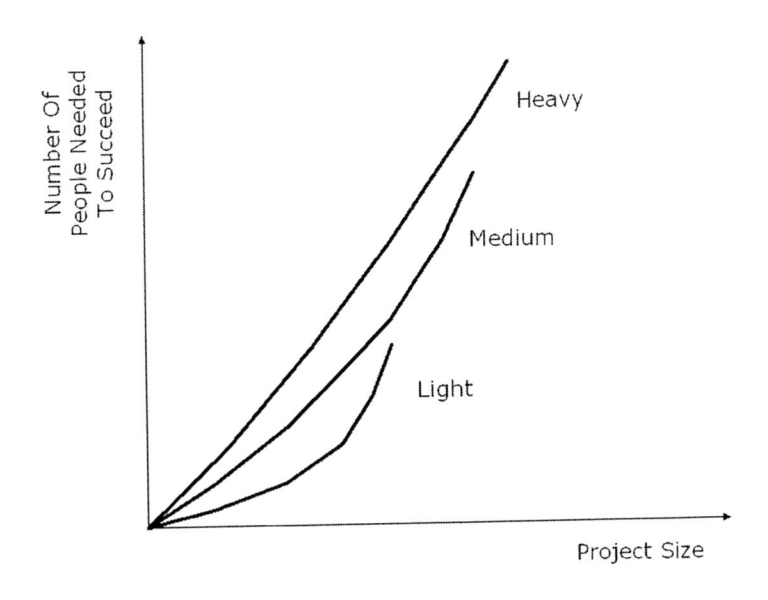

Fig. 7.16 – *Comparison of methodologies*

Although it is true that larger projects require heavier methodologies; it is possible to avoid using a heavy methodology on a small project. So the advice is to keep the selected methodology as light as possible for the particular project and team.

Have an Open Source strategy

"Open Source Software is like buying a car with a hood that you can open, as opposed to the traditional model in the software industry where the hood is locked shut."

(Bob Young, former chairman of Red Hat)

Free software or *Open Source Software (OSS)* is software that comes with permission for anyone to use, copy, and distribute, either word for word or with modifications, either for nothing or for a fee. This type of software can be considered as the ultimate form of software reuse: not only the work that has been done by other developers in the same organization can be reused but all the contributions of thousands and thousands of other developers around the world.

Total Cost of Ownership (TCO) for OSS is often less than proprietary software, especially when the number of platforms increases. It is important to understand that the TCO of a system based on OSS is composed differently; where in a more traditional approach these costs will be situated in the licensing part, for an OSS system these will be in the time and effort it will take for people to master the system and, of course, if you want services besides the software itself (such as guaranteed support, training, and so on), you will need to pay for those things just like you would for proprietary software.

Involve the users

Strangely enough, there are only two sectors where the *customers* are called *users*: IT and the drug scene. This is an indication of the bad reputation of what in fact are the most important stakeholders in any IT project. The Standish Group established the following list of success criteria for software development:

```
User Involvement                  19
Executive Management Support      16
Clear statement of Requirements   15
Proper Planning                   11
Realistic expectations            10
Smaller project milestones         9
Competent Staff                    8
Ownership                          6
Clear vision and objectives        3
Hard working staff                 3

Total                            100
```

The topics at the top of this list belong almost exclusively to the working domain of the IT management (including the project leaders). In practice, these criteria can be met with some simple project organization.

In *Steering Committees* the responsible managers of the user community can take decisions regarding what to do and with which priority. IT management can use this forum to obtain a clear statement of the requirements, explain the planning and adjust the expectations.

Through *user groups*, the users can exchange experiences and come up with useful ideas. Their work should of course be honoured and their ideas realized (after approval by the Steering Committee, of course).

Advanced Users (the brightest, quickest, oldest users that are well respected by their colleagues) can serve as Trojan Horses in the user community. Once these people are convinced, they will convince their peers. Programmers are lousy communicators; so do not let them make the user manuals but outsource this work to the advanced users.

It is also a good idea to give *names* to projects, not just numbers or acronyms but some fancy, if possible meaningful, name. Take a look at the Greek mythology, the animal world or lady's names to find some inspiration. What is the use? Well, this helps to create ownership, a common goal and team spirit, attitudes that will help to get things moving.

Another suggestion is to let the end-users; the analysts and programmers meet and know one another. Have some meetings, go to a bar together or even maybe organize a sport event. People who know each other will cooperate more easily than anonymous individuals that are separated from each other by walls of hierarchy.

Look for win-win situations. Where possible try to find solutions that will make life easier for everybody. People hate to do useless, boring or double work. Try to find these situations and eliminate them.

Limit the size of the project teams

Small teams have less communication problems. Brooks [93] uses the formula $n*(n-1)/2$ to quantify the number of communication interfaces, where n is the number of people on the team. The increased number of interfaces increases the potential for miscommunication and all its attendant problems. It has to be kept in mind that the more people work on a project the higher becomes the communication cost and the lower the effectiveness of the collaborators.

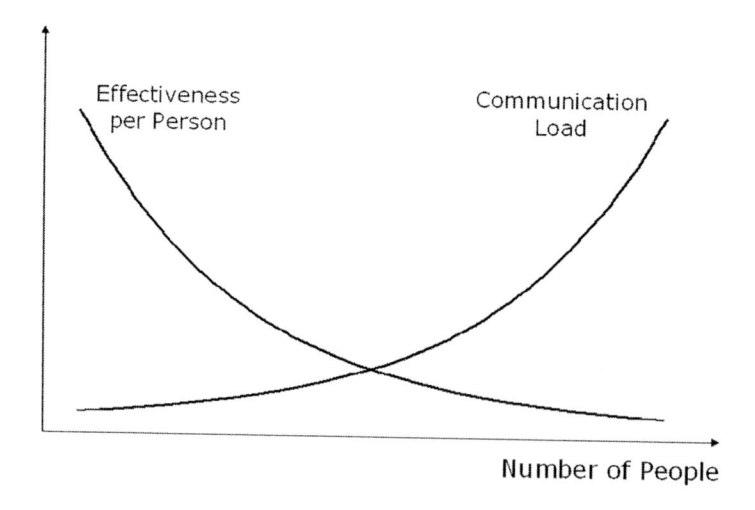

Fig. 7.17 – *Communication problems*

As a rule of thumb the size of a team should not exceed 12 people, if necessary the project should be broken down to smaller subprojects that can be handled by a smaller team.

Manage the requirements

Requirements will change; this is normal, frequent, and fine! The only systems for which requirements do not change are those that are not used. There are three measures to manage the inevitable changes to requirements:

- Maintain lists of requirements with estimated workload and priority;
- Develop iteratively; avoid "big bangs"
- Handle each change in a systematic manner.

Not all developers are created equal

One cannot assume that people are interchangeable and that tasks can be arbitrarily assigned. To start, some have more experience than others. Some people are productive, whereas others will have average or even poor productivity. Some developers are skilled with user interfaces; other like business logic and still others prefer to work on the database layer. The workload of the project has to be assigned as evenly as possible across the project team based on people's skills and capabilities. Do not assign too much of the workload to the best team members. Although they could be able to do more work than others, they also have their limits.

Organize the refactoring process

Refactoring is the process of changing a software system in such a way that it does not alter the external behavior of the code, but improves the internal structure [103]. It is a disciplined way to clean up existing code that minimizes the chances of introducing bugs. The purposes of refactoring are multiple:

- Improve the design of software;
- Make software easier to understand;
- Help to find bugs;
- Make programs faster.

Refactoring is not a major redesign; it is the application of simple steps the cumulative effects of which dramatically improve the understandability and maintainability. It can be as simple as renaming classes to follow a coding standard, moving attributes from one class to another or creating a new method that performs part of the work as another, more complex method.

Rank project elements up front

Every project is composed of three elements: the budget (resources), the timing and what the system will do, known as the functionality. In the beginning these three elements are defined but it is not unusual that during the life of the project problems occur. To know how to solve a problem, the project manager needs to know which of the three elements has the highest priority, which is secondary, and which is the least important. For example, assume that a problem occurs which could result in a delay and the project manager knows that it is of chief importance that the project is done by a certain date. The consequence is that he must either dedicate more resources to the project and therefore increase the budget or decrease the functionality to meet the schedule.

Remember Brook's Law

"Adding staff to a late software project makes it later." Anyone with some experience in IT projects will have witnessed this law in action. It seems to be a common mistake to confuse effort with progress. Instead of increasing the team size consider improving the performance of the team. Putting the right people on the right job, training and

better communication can do this. Also avoid people frequently switching tasks but give them well-defined goals they are capable to reach by themselves.

Separate concerns

Technical people should make technical choices and functional people should make functional choices. Once everyone agrees on that, a lot of frictions will disappear. First look at it from the users' point of view. They probably know best what their real need is, so if they come up with a request it will probably be justified. The technical person can then try to imagine a solution or make a counter proposition that is easier to create or fits better in the technical architecture. He should, however, never force his point of view to the user. On the other hand, the user should never impose technical choices to the IT department.

Separate stable and unstable elements

Unless an organization changes its business completely, which does not happen every month, the *data structures* remain pretty stable. A bank will keep working with clients who have different accounts, a wholesale company will need to manage its stocks and orders and a publishing company will always treat with authors and books. This means that the way these data are structured and stored (made persistent) should not be specific for one process (application) but should be kept at a generic (stable) level.

The *Business Processes* are of a more variable nature: they change and evolve over time, maybe because of a changing Business Strategy or because of changes in the legislation. Here we should try to build Information Systems that can be parameterized as much as possible. The *interfaces with the outside world* (users, other systems), finally, tend to be unstable: the underlying processes change, users want to have personalized settings and the market forces to follow the new versions and releases of their products. This is why one should go as much as possible for "generic" user interfaces such as browsers.

Therefore, it makes sense to build administrative applications in at least three layers where database logic, business logic and presentation logic are well separated. This separation should also be explicit, that is, not hidden in the code but realized with well distinguishable objects.

Separation into layers does have many advantages because it is one of the main enablers of agility. Layered applications are easier to integrate. It is possible to adopt new technology one layer at a time, without affecting the other layers. Layered applications have a longer lifetime and at the end, turn out to be cheaper solutions.

Separate Transaction Processing and Analytical Processing

There is a conceptual and technical difference between Transaction Processing and Analytical Processing. As Analytical Processing typically supports the change processes within an organization, the user requirements will be unstable. That is why it is not such a good idea to hard code too much reporting into an Information System: use (commercial) querying and reporting tools instead. In that way another problem is avoided: customers constantly asking for (urgent) reports and thereby disturbing the planning of the IT department. This separation can be physical (different hardware and software) or temporal (operational systems are on-line during the day time and informational systems run in batch during the night).

Take care of the installation process

Installing new software or changes to an existing software release is the most common reason for loss of Service; this has a major effect on the organization's performance and costs. The ability to quickly roll back to the previous situation consequently always has to be a part of the installation process. The *installation script* should always first be tested in a test environment that resembles as much as possible to the production environment (hardware, versions of other software and representative data). A *roll back script* must also be available and tested. Installation and roll back scripts are part of the project deliverables that are kept in the *Definitive Software Library (DSL)*.

Think Big, develop small

> *"You've got to think about big things while you're doing small things, so that all the small things go in the right direction."*
>
> *(Alvin Toffler)*

Organizations have a tendency to engage in big projects in an attempt to solve many business issues in one go. Such projects, however, create significant dangers. For instance, it takes a much larger amount of money to put such a project back on track if a problem occurs. Also, it tends to take longer to acknowledge fatal problems on a big project even if, sometimes, it is better to simply cancel a troubled project rather than try to fix it. Additionally, long project life cycles make it difficult to respond to new business needs or technological changes. On the other hand, smaller projects are easier to manage. For example, it is easier for IT staff to tell executives after three months of problem solving on a year long project to modify or abandon the project than it would be after investing three years. As a consequence, smaller projects reduce the risk of financial loss. Also, if the budget is the number one priority, the manager can delay the project or reduce its functionality.

As a rule of thumb, projects should be limited to a maximum duration of around nine months, much like a pregnancy. Longer projects tend to become unmanageable and get out of hand. It is also a good idea to build in a pause – or consolidation phase – allowing the organization to digest the changes incurred by the project.

Use the right tool for the job

The choice of development tools is a topic filled with opinion. Most programmers have their favorite tool and most programmers have tools they hate. Programming with a given development tool brings about similar responses to doing plumbing with a given toolbox. When every tool that is needed is in the box, then plumbing is a manageable task. When the box of tools has nothing but a hammer and a screwdriver it is going to be much more difficult, because these are just not made for the job. Similarly, development tools are all specialized for a particular type of problem: some are excellent for making hardware drivers others are good in string manipulations. Some languages are specialized for scientific and mathematical work others have been designed for business applications or for Artificial Intelligence. It should therefore not be considered as blasphemy to use a blend of different programming languages on the same project. A web system can well use a combination of HTML, JSP and javascript on the client side and Java technology (servlets and EJBs) combined with some shell scripting at the server side. Restricting the developers in the choice of their tools in an attempt to lower training costs may not be such a good idea. Training a good programmer to be able to program in any special language can in fact be the highest productivity method available if the special language fits the task.

An important thing to consider is the *target platform.* Compilers only generate executables for one target platform and also for interpreted languages there is no universal portability; think of the different versions Javascript and VBScript that do/do not run on different versions of popular web browsers. This can be a painful issue when developing applications for an unknown user community (e.g., Web applications). Java, XML and Web services are giant steps in the right direction in this respect. These technologies allow for portability and interoperability.

As a last remark it remains to be said that every technology will eventually loose the spotlight, even Java or .Net. It is, therefore, not a good idea to put all the eggs in the same basket, however promising it can look.

Online Resources

Agile development - http://www.agilealliance.org
Architecture – http://www.sei.cmu.edu/architecture/definitions.html
Critical Chain - http://www.aptconcepts.com/Articles/BuildingNetwork.html
CMM - http://www.sei.cmu.edu/
Cocomo - http://www.jsc.nasa.gov/bu2/COCOMO.html
Design Patterns – http://java.sun.com/blueprints/
Design Patterns – http://martinfowler.com/isa/
Design Patterns – http://www.theserverside.com
Extreme Programming - http://www.xprogramming.com
Extreme Programming - http://www.extremeprogramming.org
Function Point Analysis - http://www.ifpug.org
Java – http://www.jcp.org
Java – http://www.javasoft.com
J2EE - http://java.sun.com/jsee/
Methodology - http://www.geocities.com/itmweb/
Methodology - http://panoramix.univ-paris1.fr/CRINFO/dmrg/MEE/
Methodology - http://www.dsdm.org
Object Management Group - http://www.omg.org
Objects and Components - http://www.cetus-links.org
Open Group (X/Open and OSF) - http://www.opengroup.org
Open source IDE - http://www.eclipse.org
Open Source Software – http://www.apache.org
Open Source Software – http://www.free-soft.org
Open Source Software- http://www.gnu.org
Open Source Software – http://www.opensource.org
Patents – http://www.uspto.gov
Project management/PMBOK - http://www.pmi.org
Refactoring tools – http://cruisecontrol.sourceforge.net
Refactoring – http://www.refactoring.com
Requirements management - http://www.rmplace.org
Requirements management tools - http://www.incose.org/tools/
Software Benchmarking - http://www.isbsg.org
Software Development - http://swg.jpl.nasa.gov/resources/
Software development - http://www.standishgroup.com/
Software Engineering - http://www.sei.cmu.edu
Software Engineering - http://www.esi.es
Software Licensing – http://www.bsa.org
Software Patents – http://www.spi.org
UML - http://www.rational.com/uml/
UML - http://www.softdocwiz.com/UML.htm
Universal Data Models – http://www.universaldatamodels.com

Further Reading

[84] Barker, T.T. and Dragga, S. *Writing Software Documentation: A Task-Oriented Approach*, Allyn and Bacon, 1997.

[85] Beck, K., *Extreme Programming Explained: Embrace Change*, Addison Wesley, 1999.

[86] Beizer, B. *Software Testing Techniques*, Van Nostrand Reinhold, 1990.

[87] Birrell N.D. and Ould M.A. *A Practical Handbook for Software Development*, Cambridge University Press, 1985/88.

[88] Boehm, B. et al. *Software Cost Estimation with COCOMO II*, Prentice Hall, 2000.

[89] Boehm, B. *Software Engineering Economics*, Prentice-Hall, 1981.

[90] Boehm, B. *A Spiral Model of Software Development and Enhancement*, IEEE Computer, vol.21, #5, May 1988, pp 61-72.

[91] Booch, Rumbaugh and Jacobson *The UML Modeling Language User Guide*. Addison-Wesley, 1999.

[92] Brockmann, R. *Writing better computer documentation: From paper to hypertext*. John Wiley & Sons, New York. 1990.

[93] Brooks, Frederick P. *The Mythical Man-Month*, Addison Wesley, 1995.

[94] Brown, C. M. *Human-Computer Interface Design Guidelines*. Norwood, NJ: Ablex Publishing Corp., 1988.

[95] Chen, P., *The Entity-Relationship Model – Toward a unified View of Data*, ACM Transactions on Database Systems, Vol. 1, N°. 1, March 1976.

[96] Coad, P. and Yourdon, E. *Object-Oriented Analysis*, Yourdon Press, 1991.

[97] Cockburn, A. *Agile Software Development*. Cockburn-Highsmith Series. 2000.

[98] Cusumano, M.A. and Selby, R.W. *How Microsoft Builds Software*. Communications of the ACM, Vol. 40, No. 6, June 1997.

[99] Darwin, I.F., *Java Cookbook, Solutions and Examples for Java Developers*, O'Reilly, June 2001.

[100] Dreger, J. Brian. *Function point analysis*, Englewood Cliffs, N.J. Prentice Hall, 1989.

[101] El Eman, K., Drouin, J. and Melo, W. *SPICE The Theory and Practice of Software Process Improvement and Capability Determination,* IEEE Computer Society, 1997, *ISO/IEC Software Process Assessment - Part 1 - 9, DTR (ISO 15504).*

[102] Fewster, M. and Graham, D. *Software Test Automation*, Addison-Wesley: 1999.

[103] Fowler, M. *Refactoring: Improving the Design of Existing Code.* Addison-Wesley Co., Inc, Reading, MA, 1999.

[104] Gamma, E., Helm, R., Johnson, R. and Vlissides, J. *Design Patterns: Elements of Reusable Object-Oriented Programming.* Addison-Wesley,1995.

[105] Garmus, D. and Herron, D. *Measuring The Software Process: A Practical Guide To Functional Measurements*, Prentice-Hall, 1996.

[106] Garmus, D. and Herron, D. *Function Point Analysis: Measurement Practices for Successful Software Projects*, Addison-Wesley, 2000.

[107] Goldratt, Eliyahu M. *Critical Chain.* North River Press,1997.

[108] Goldratt, Eliyahu M. *Theory of Constraints.* North River Press,1999.

[109] Halstead, M. *Elements of Software Science, Operating, and Programming Systems Series* Volume 7. New York, Elsevier, 1977.

[110] Hetzeln, W.C. *The Complete Guide to Software Testing*, QED Information Services INC, 1988.

[111] Horton, W.K. *Designing and Writing Online Documentation: Hypermedia for Self- Supporting Products*, 2nd Edition, John Wiley & Sons, 1994.

[112] Howard, M., LeBlanc, D., *Writing Secure Code,* 2nd Microsoft Press, 2003.

[113] Jayazeri and Mandrioli. *Fundamentals of Software Engineering,* Prentice-Hall, 1991.

[114] Jones, C. *Applied Software Measurement - Assuring Productivity and Quality*, McGraw Hill, Inc. 1991.

[115] Keogh J. and Keogh J., *J2EE: The complete Reference*, McGraw-Hill Osborne Media, 2002.

[116] Kovitz, Benjamin L. *Practical Software Requirements - A Manual of Content and Style*, Manning Publications 1998.

[117] Lamb, D.A. *Software Engineering: Planning for Change,* Prentice-Hall, 1988.

[118] Laurel, B. *The Art of Human-Computer Interface Design.* Reading, MA: Addison-Wesley Publishing Co., 1990.

[119] Lehman, M., Belady, L. A. *Program Evolution: Processes of Software Change*, Ch. 5, APIC Studies in Data Processing No. 27. Academic Press, London, 1985.

[120] Levin, R.I., Kirkpatrick, C.A. *Planning and Control with PERT/CPM.* McGraw-Hill, 1966.

[121] Marciniak, John J., ed. *Encyclopedia of Software Engineering.* New York, John Wiley & Sons, 1994.

[122] Mayhew, Deborah J. *Principles and Guidelines in Software User Interface Design.* Englewood Cliffs, NJ: Prentice Hall, 1992.

[123] McCabe, T.J. *A Complexity Measure.* IEEE Transactions on Software Engineering, Vol. SE-2, 308-320. 1976.

[124] Myers, G.J. *The Art of Software Testing,* John Wiley & Sons, New York, 1976.

[125] Newbold, Robert C. *Project Management in the Fast Lane: Applying the Theory of Constraints*, St. Lucie Press, Boca Raton, FL. 1998

[126] Nielsen J. *Usability Engineering*, Academic Press, 1993.

[127] Nielsen, J. and Mack, Robert L. *Usability Inspection Methods.* New York: John Wiley & Sons, 1994.

[128] Oman, P. and Hagemeister, J. *Construction and Validation of Polynomials for Predicting Software Maintainability.* Moscow, ID: Software Engineering Test Lab, University of Idaho, 1992.

[129] Paulk, M.C., et al. *The Capability Maturity Model: Guidelines for Improving the Software Process*, Addison-Wesley Publishing Company, 1994.

[130] Pfleeger, S. *Software Engineering: The Production of Quality Software,* 2nd Edition, Macmillan, 1991.

[131] Pressman, R., *Software Engineering: A Practitioner's Approach,* 4th Edition, McGraw-Hill, 1996.

[132] Putman, *A general empirical solution to the macro software sizing and estimating problem.* IEEE Trans. on Softw. Eng., Volume 4, No 4, April 1978.

[133] Rumbaugh, J. et al. *Object-Oriented Modeling and Design,* Prentice-Hall, 1991.

[134] Schmidt, B. *Data Modeling for Information Professionals,* Prentice Hall, 1999.

[135] Shlaer, S. and Mellor, S.J. *Object-Oriented Systems Analysis,* Yourdon Press, 1988.

[136] Silverston, L.E.S. *The Data Model Resource Book. Revised Edition. Volume 1: A Library of Universal Data Models for All Enterprises.* Wiley, 2001.

[137] Silverston, L.E.S. *The Data Model Resource Book. Revised Edition. Volume 2: A Library of Universal Data Models for Industry Types.* Wiley, 2001.

[138] Sommerville, I. *Software Engineering,* Addison Wesley, 1996.

[139] Teorey, T.J. *Database Modeling and Design, the Entity-Relationship Approach,* Morgan Kaufman Publishers, 1990.

[140] van Vliet, H. *Software Engineering: Principles and Practice,* Chichester: John Wiley & Sons. 1993.

[141] Watts, S. Humphrey. *Managing the Software Process,* Addison-Wesley Publishing Co., Reading, Massachusetts, 1989.

[142] Watts, S. Humphrey. *A Discipline for Software Engineering,* Addison Wesley, SEI Series in Software Engineering, 1995.

[143] *ISO 9001: Quality Systems Model for Quality Assurance in Design/Development, Production, Installation and Servicing,* International Organization for Standardization, 1 July 1994.

[144] *ISO 9000-3: Guidelines for the Application of ISO 9001 to the Development, Supply and Maintenance of Software,* International Organization for Standardization, 1 June 1991.

[145] Microsoft Corporation. *The GUI Guide: International Terminology for the Windows Interface*. Redmond, WA: Microsoft Press, 1993

[146] Micorsoft Corporation. *The Windows Interface: An Application Design Guide*. Redmond, WA: Microsoft Press, 1992.

[147] NeXT Computer, Inc. NeXTSTEP User Interface Guidelines (Release 3). Reading, Mass.: Addison-Wesley Publishing, 1992.

[148] Open Software Foundation. *OSF/Motif Style Guide*. Englewood Cliffs, NJ: Prentice Hall, 1993.

Periodicals on Software Engineering

IEEE Software, IEEE Service Centre, 445 Hoes Lane, P.O. Box 1331, Piscataway, NJ 08855-1331, USA.

Software Engineering Notes, ACM, 11 West 42d St, New York, NY 10036, USA.

Software Maintenance News, ACM, 11 West 42d St, New York, NY 10036, USA.

Software Testing, Verification and Reliability, John Wiley & Sons Ltd, Baffins Lane, Chichester, West Sussex PO19 1UD, UK.

The Software Practitioner (TSP), Computing Trends, 1416 Sare Rd., Bloomington IN 47401 USA.

Journal of Software Maintenance: Research and Practice, John Wiley & Sons Ltd, Baffins Lane, Chichester, West Sussex PO19 1UD, UK.

Software: Practice and Experience, John Wiley & Sons Ltd, Baffins Lane, Chichester, West Sussex PO19 1UD, UK.

The Software Quality Journal, Chapman & Hall, Journals Promotion Department, North America. 29 West 35th Street, New York, NY 10001-2291, USA. Europe: 2-6 Boundary Row, London SE1 8HN, UK.

8

Organization

"No institution can possibly survive if it needs geniuses or supermen to manage it. It must be organized in such a way as to be able to get along under a leadership composed of average human beings."

(Peter Drucker)

Introduction

Organization

The term *Organization* has at least three different meanings:

(1) An organization is a collection of human, material, informational and financial resources; for example a company, a corporation or a public service.
(2) Organization is the activity of organizing.
(3) The organization is also how things in an Organization (1) are done. This is preferably the result of an organization (2) activity but can also be the result of a historical process. In this meaning the Organization is a set of (formal or informal) rules.

In the different chapters of this book, the three meanings are used in a mixed way and it is the context that determines which one is applicable. In this chapter the focus will be on the third meaning; the way things are done.

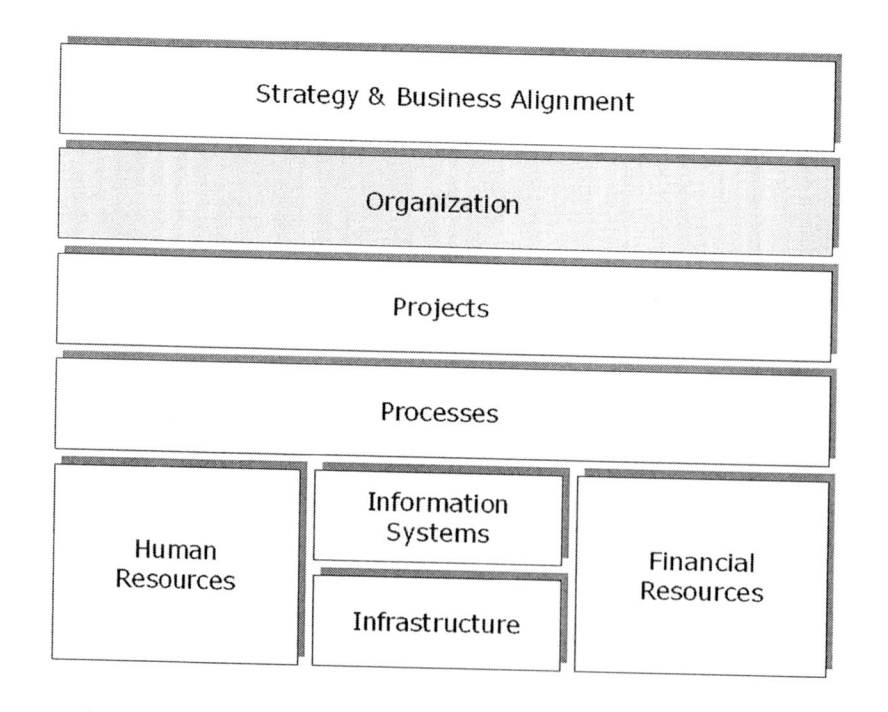

Fig. 8.1 – *Position of organization in the IT stack*

Objects in the organizational model

Activities

In an organization, work is performed using *activities*. One or more persons using tools to transform raw material or information into intermediate or finished products or services execute these activities.

Processes

Activities can be grouped into *processes*. Processes have known start and stop points and identifiable inputs and outputs.

The work that is executed inside a process has the following properties:

- It is repetitive;
- It spans a short time period (minutes, days);
- It is standardized and structured;
- It requires no creativity from its executers;
- It can be documented easily;
- It is easily quantifiable.

This work is found in factories, offices, restaurants, airlines, construction, hospitals, banks and so on, it is also called *process oriented*. Between 70 and 80% of all work in most organizations belongs with this category. Because of their characteristics, processes lend themselves easily to automation.

Procedures

Processes are concerned with <u>what</u> has to be done to operate an organization; *procedures* are concerned with <u>how</u> it is done. Procedures change as technology changes, processes do not. There are multiple types of procedures that accomplish given processes. Whereas procedures can be abandoned or changed, the processes still have to be carried out to run the organization.

Functions

A *function* is a group of processes that support one aspect of furthering the mission of the organization. Functions often have names that end with "ing," for example, purchasing, receiving, accounting. Functions can be grouped into *functional areas*. Functional areas refer to the major areas of activity: in a business organization for example they could be engineering, marketing, production, and distribution. Whereas processes have a definable start and stop, functions are ongoing.

Projects

Projects are another way of grouping processes. Unlike functions, projects are targeted on change; they act on the way things are done.

The work that is executed inside projects has the following characteristics:

- It is unique;
- It spans a long period of time (months, years);
- It is not standardized and difficult to structure;
- It requires much creativity of its executers;
- It is difficult to document;
- It is difficult to quantify.

This work is found in all organizations but, in most organizations, is clustered in groups such as Marketing, Information Technology, Research, Policy and other specialist groups. For most organizations, this work is around 20 to 30% of all effort. It is difficult to automate entire projects, although tools can support certain processes making part of them.

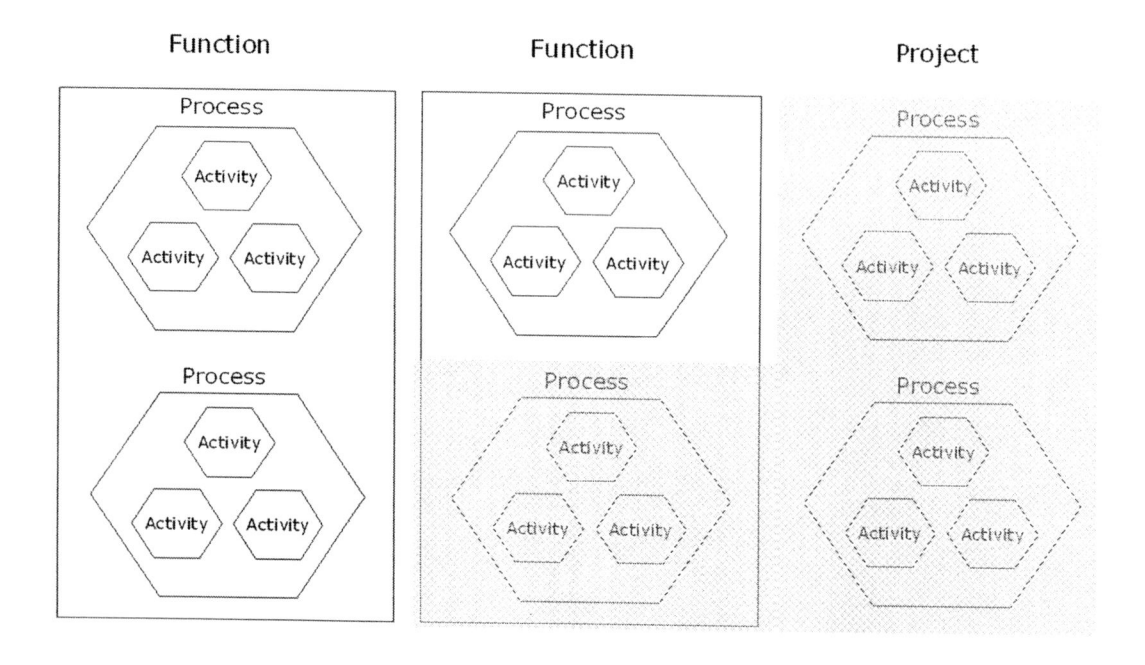

Fig. 8.2 – *Activities, Processes, Functions and Projects*

Organizational Units

To break down the complexity, organizations are usually split in smaller entities: *Organizational Units*. These units are responsible for certain aspects of the business and have well-defined boundaries and interfaces between them. An Organizational Unit can carry out several functions or projects, and more than one Organizational Unit can perform a given process or participate in it. We thus have a many-to-many association between functions, projects and organizational units. A matrix can be drawn and filled in to show which organizational units perform which functions or projects.

Management

"The primary job of the manager is not to empower but to remove obstacles."

(Scott Adams)

Management is the process of coordinating the available resources to achieve the goals of the Organizational Unit and, by extension of the whole organization.

Mapping Managers to Organizational Units

At the top of an Organizational Unit there is a Manager. On organization charts, managers are often shown as having a one-to-one association with Organizational Units. In practice, however, managers also carry out informal activities that are not identified on the organizational chart. A separate matrix is often created to document the real relationships between executives and business functions. The type of involvement an executive has with a business function can be one or more of the following possibilities:

- Direct management *responsibility;*
- Executive or policymaking *authority;*
- *Involved* in the function;
- Technical *expertise;*
- Actual execution of the *work.*

Managerial activities and roles

Professor Henry Mintzberg [163] groups managerial activities and roles as follows:

Activities	Roles
Interpersonal relationships	• figurehead • liaison • leader
Information processing	• monitor • disseminator • spokesman
Making significant decisions	• initiator/changer • disturbance handler • resource allocator • negotiator

Table 8.1 – *Managerial Activities and Roles*

Figurehead - Social, inspirational, legal and ceremonial duties must be carried out. The manager is a symbol and must be there for people and agencies that will only work with him because of status and authority.

Liaison - Networking to preserve internal and external contacts for information exchange are indispensable as these contacts give access to facts, needs and opportunities.

Leader - The manager defines the structures and environments within which subordinates work. The manager selects, encourages, promotes and disciplines and tries to balance subordinate and organizational needs for efficiency.

Monitor - The manager seeks and receives information from many sources to evaluate the organization's performance, condition and health. Monitoring of internal operations, external events, ideas, trends, analysis and pressures.

Disseminator - The manager brings external views into his organization and helps internal information flows among subordinates. The preferences of significant people are received and assimilated. The manager interprets and spreads information and values, for example policies, rules and regulations.

Spokesperson - The manager informs others, external to his own organizational unit. For outsiders, the manager is an expert in the field in which his unit works. A senior manager is responsible for his organization's strategy-making system, making and linking important decisions. He has the authority, information and capacity of control and integration over important decisions.

Initiator or changer – The manager designs and starts much of the controlled change in the organization. The manager starts a series of related decisions and activities to achieve improvement. The manager can delegate all design responsibility selecting subordinates or he can empower subordinates with responsibility for the design of the improvement program.

Disturbance handler – The manager takes charge when the organization hits a major problem unexpectedly where there is no programmed response. Disturbances can arise from staff, resources, threats or because others make mistakes or innovation has unexpected outcomes. The role involves stepping in to calm matters, evaluate, reallocate, support and buying time.

Resource allocator - The manager supervises allocation of all resources and implicitly sets organizational priorities. The managerial task is to ensure the basic work system is in place and to program staff work: what to do, by whom, what processing structures will be used. Managers develop models and plans in their heads. These models encompass rules, imperatives, criteria and preferences to evaluate proposals against. Loose, flexible and implicit plans are updated with new information.

Negotiator – The manager takes charge over important negotiating activities with other organizations. The spokesperson, figurehead and resource allocator roles demand this.

Organizational Forms

Organizational subunits

Henry Mintzberg [164][165] defines five basic *organizational subunits*:

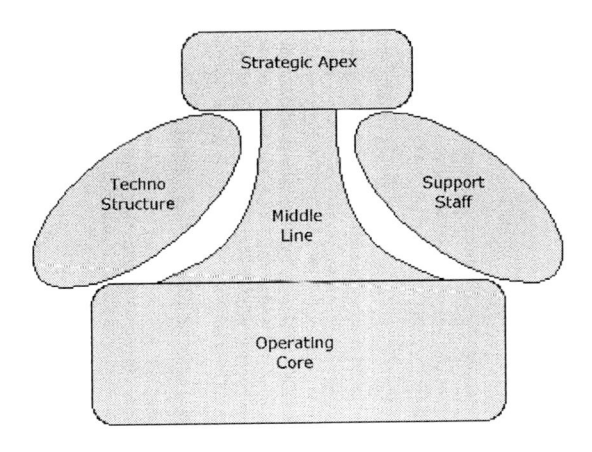

Fig. 8.3 – *Organizational subunits*

The task of the *Strategic Apex* is to guarantee the survival of the organization. To do this they set strategic goals, and develop a corporate policy. It contains the Board of Directors, the *Chief Executive Officer (CEO)* and the *Chief Operating Officer (COO)*. The CEO is the person responsible for setting the organizational strategy. The COO is next in line for the CEO. Other managers that belong to the strategic apex are the *Chief Financial Officer (CFO)*, the *Chief Technology Officer (CTO)* who is responsible for research and development and of course the *Chief Information Officer (CIO)*.

Seen from the top the *Middle Line* has an executing task and seen from the bottom a managerial task. In a manufacturing environment this could be VP Operations, VP Marketing, Plant Managers and Sales Managers. The line managers have a direct responsibility for the production of goods or services.

The *Operating Core* performs the real work. Here is where the products or services that are delivered to the customers are created. For example, in a manufacturing environment these are positions like Purchasing Agents, Machine Operators, Assemblers, and Sales Persons.

The *Techno structure* contains experts such as Strategic Planning, Personnel Training, Operations Research, Systems Analysis and Design. The customers of the techno structure are the other units of the organization.

Finally, the *Support staff* is composed of Legal Counsel, Public Relations, Payroll, Mailroom Clerks, Cafeteria Workers and maintenance staff.

Coordination mechanisms

Between the organizational subunits different *coordination mechanism* can exist:

Mutual Adjustment

Direct Supervision

Standardization of Work Processes

Standardization of Outputs

Standardization of Skills

Standardization of Norms

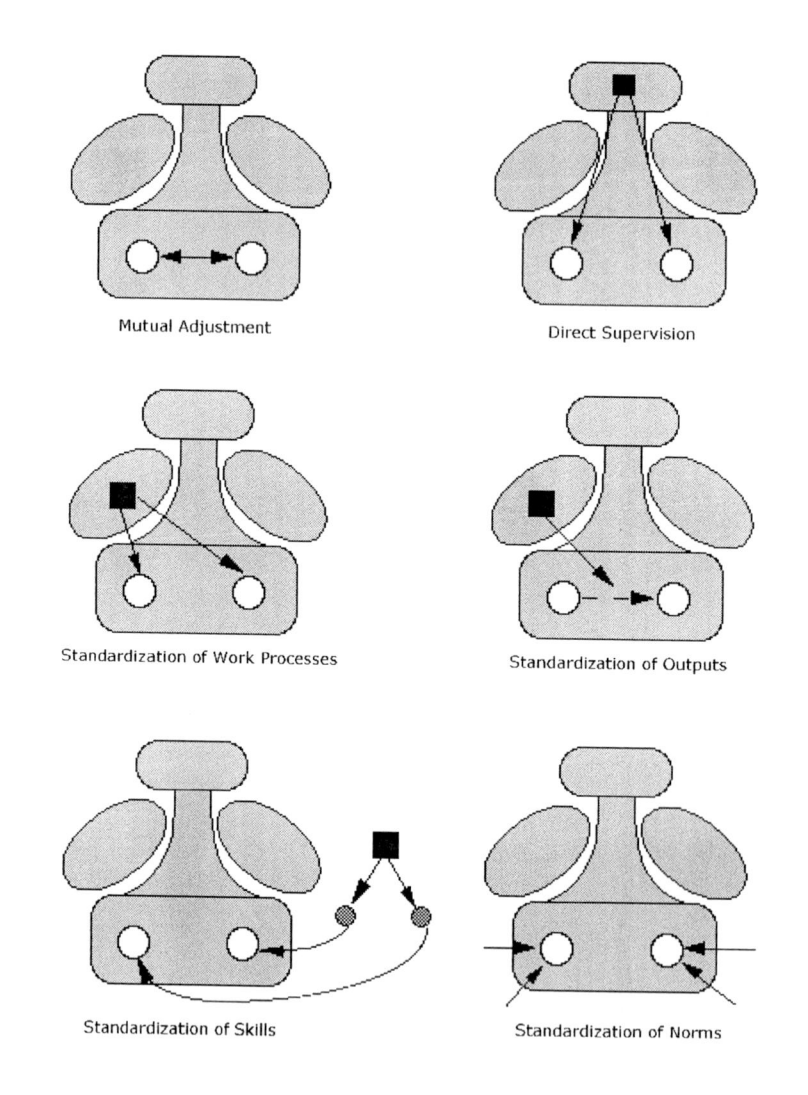

Fig. 8.4 – *Coordination mechanisms*

The first coordination mechanism is known as *mutual adjustment*. There is little formalization of behavior; specialists are grouped in small, market-based project teams to do their work with a reliance on liaison devices to encourage mutual adjustment, within and between these teams.

For *direct supervision*, power over all the important decisions tends to be centralized in the hands of the CEO.

In organizations that rely on the *standardization work processes* for coordination, the techno structure - which houses the analysts who do the standardizing - emerges as the key part of the structure.

With *standardization of outputs* there is a perpetual search for more efficient ways to produce given outputs. Thus, the entrepreneur function takes on a restricted form at the strategic apex.

Another coordination mechanism is the *standardization of skills*; duly trained and indoctrinated specialists (*professionals*) are hired for the operating core, and are given considerable control over their work. Control over his work means that the professional operates relatively independently of his colleagues, but closely with the clients he serves.

In the last mechanism, the change in the professional organization does not come from new administrators that announce major reforms. Rather, change comes as a slow process of changing the professionals by what they learn in professional schools; this is known as *standardization of norms*.

Organizational forms

Mintzberg distinguishes four organizational forms, depending of the characteristics of two environmental determinants, complexity and pace of change:

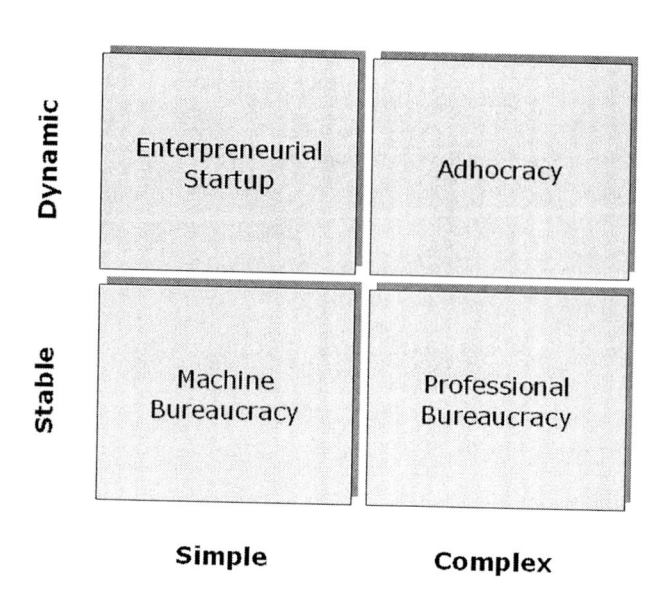

	Simple	Complex
Dynamic	Enterpreneurial Startup	Adhocracy
Stable	Machine Bureaucracy	Professional Bureaucracy

Fig. 8.5 – *Organizational forms*

The Entrepreneurial Start up

The environment of the *Entrepreneurial Startup* is typically <u>simple and dynamic</u>. A simple environment can be comprehended by a single individual, and so enables decision making to be controlled by that individual.

The Entrepreneurial Startup is characterized by what is <u>not</u> elaborated. Typically, it has little or no techno structure, a small support staff, a loose division of labor, minimal differentiation among its units, and a small hierarchy. Little of its behavior is formalized, and it makes minimal use of planning, training, and liaison devices. Typically, organizations pass through this form in their early years. Most of the dotcom companies started as entrepreneurial startups and did not manage to grow to a more mature form, with all the known consequences.

The Machine Bureaucracy

Machine bureaucratic work is found, in environments that are simple and stable. The machine bureaucracy is typically found in the mature organization, large enough to have the volume of operating work needed for repetition and standardization, and old enough to have been able to settle on the standards it wishes to use. Machine bureaucracies are typically found in manufacturing environments.

The *Machine Bureaucracy* is characterized by highly specialized, routine operating tasks; formalized procedures in the operating core; a proliferation of rules, regulations, and formalized communication throughout the organization; large-sized units at the operating level; reliance on the functional basis for grouping tasks; relatively centralized power for decision making; and an elaborate administrative structure with sharp distinctions between line and staff. The managers at the strategic apex of these organizations are concerned in large part with the fine-tuning of their bureaucratic machines. These are *performance organizations* not *problem solving* ones.

The Professional Bureaucracy

Whereas the machine bureaucracy generates its own standards the standards of the *Professional Bureaucracy* originate largely outside its own structure, in the self-governing association its operators join with their colleagues from other professional bureaucracies. The professional bureaucracy emphasizes authority of a professional nature - the power of expertise.

The strategies of the professional bureaucracy are largely ones of the professionals within the organization as well as of the professional associations on the outside. The technical system cannot be highly regulating, certainly not highly automated. The professional resists the rationalization of his skills - their division into simply executed steps - because that makes them programmable by the technostructure, destroys his basis of autonomy, and drives the structure to the machine bureaucratic form. Typical examples of professional bureaucracies are universities.

The Adhocracy

The *adhocracy* hires and gives power to experts, professionals whose knowledge and skills have been highly developed in training programs. However, unlike the professional bureaucracy, the adhocracy cannot rely on the standardized skills of these experts to achieve coordination. Rather, it must treat existing knowledge and skills merely as bases on which to build new ones. Moreover, the building of new knowledge and skills requires the combination of different bodies of existing knowledge. Whereas each professional in the professional bureaucracy can operate independently, in the adhocracy professionals must combine their efforts. In adhocracies the different specialists must join forces in multi-disciplinary teams, each formed around a project of innovation. Hospitals could be taken for example of this organizational form.

The role of IT

The role of IT depends heavily on the organizational form:

- In *Entrepreneurial Start-ups* IT will be an important driver for innovation.
- In a *Machine Bureaucracy* the Information Systems will mainly be used to support the routine operating tasks, execution of the formalized procedures and as a vehicle for the internal communications.
- The technical system of a *Professional Bureaucracy* cannot be highly regulating or highly automated, it can however provide for a specialized support of the professionals.
- Finally, in an *Adhocracy* the focus of IT will probably be on the collaboration mechanisms for the different specialists.

Organizational Culture

Organizational Culture is an arrangement of shared significance held by the members of an organization. It is largely based on what has been done before and the degree of success with it. It is kept alive by exposing the employees to a set of similar experiences. It is reinforced through the selection process, performance evaluation criteria, reward practices, training, career development activities and promotion procedures. Employees learn the organizational culture by stories, rituals, material symbols and language:

- *Stories* anchor the presence in the past and provide explanation and legitimation for current practices.
- *Rituals* are activities that express and reinforce the key values of the organization, what goals are most important.

- *Material symbols* tell to employees who is important and the behavior that is appropriate (e.g., size of offices, type of furnishing, reserved parking spaces, transportation means…)
- New employees are also familiarized with acronyms and jargon, a *language* that act as a common denominator that unites members of a given culture or subculture.

An organizational culture has many different functions:

- It defines the boundaries between the organization and others;
- It conveys a sense of identity;
- It helps the generation of commitment;
- It enhances social system stability;
- It guides and shapes attitudes and behavior.

The influence of the organizational culture is beneficial for both the employer and the employee; for the first it brings consistency and commitment and for the second it reduces ambiguity.

Work Teams

Work Teams are an essential part of the way organizations operate; they typically outperform individuals when the work requires multiple skills, judgment and experience. Teams allow for a better utilization of employee's talents. The possibility to assemble quickly, deploy, refocus and disband a team also gives a great agility and responsiveness. Furthermore, teams are an effective way to increase employee motivation.

Team versus Group

A Work Group is a group of people that interact primarily to share information and to make decisions to help one another perform within each member's area of responsibility. The collective performance of a Work Team results in positive synergy. Accountability is both individual and mutual. Skills are complementary and there is a potential to generate a greater output with no increase in inputs.

Types of teams

Problem-solving teams – members share ideas or offer suggestions on how work processes and methods can be improved. These teams rarely have the authority to implement unilaterally any of their suggested actions. Examples of problem-solving teams are quality circles.

Self-managed teams (SMTs) – ten to 15 people who take on responsibilities of their former supervisors: collective control over place of work, work assignments, organization of breaks, procedures, etc. If the team is fully self-managed it also selects and evaluates its own members [152].

Cross-functional teams – these are teams of employees of about the same hierarchical level but from different work areas with a goal to accomplish a task. Cross-functional teams are also called task forces or committees. This type of teamwork helps to exchange information, develop new ideas, solve problems and coordinate complex projects, but at the early stages it is time-consuming as it takes time for the members to learn to work with diversity and complexity and it takes time to build trust.

Virtual teams – these teams use computer technology to overcome time and space constraints of the members to achieve a common goal.

Turning individuals into team players

The barrier to work in a team is *individual resistance*; individuals must be able to communicate openly and honestly, to confront differences, to resolve conflicts and to sublimate their personal goals for the good of the team. The options available to turn individuals into team players are:

- *Selection* – ensure that candidates can fulfill team rules and have the required technical skills;
- *Training* – train people to improve their problem solving, communication, negotiation, conflict management and group development skills;
- *Rewards* – the reward system needs to be reworked to encourage cooperative efforts, however, the individual contribution should not be ignored. Teams also provide intrinsic rewards in forms of camaraderie.

Organizational Structures

Mechanistic and Organic Structures

There are two opposing concepts to address the way in which an organization works: the mechanistic and the organic concept.

Mechanistic structures are designed to induce people to behave in a predictable, accountable way. Situations leading to a mechanistic structure are:

- Individual specialization;
- Hierarchy is used as an integrating mechanism;
- Centralization: most communication is vertical;
- High standardization.

These structures are best suited for stable environments.

Organic structures, on the contrary, promote agility so that people can start change and adapt quickly. Situations leading to an organic structure are:

- Joint specialization;
- Loosely defined roles;
- Complex integration mechanisms;
- Mutual adjustment.

These structures are best suited for changing environments.

Organic and mechanistic organizations are the opposite ends of the spectrum; ideally, an organization achieves a good balance between the two.

Functional organization

In the *functional (traditional) structure* the departments are organized around the different functions of the organization such as Purchasing, Accounting, and Marketing. This structure is often found in commercial organizations.

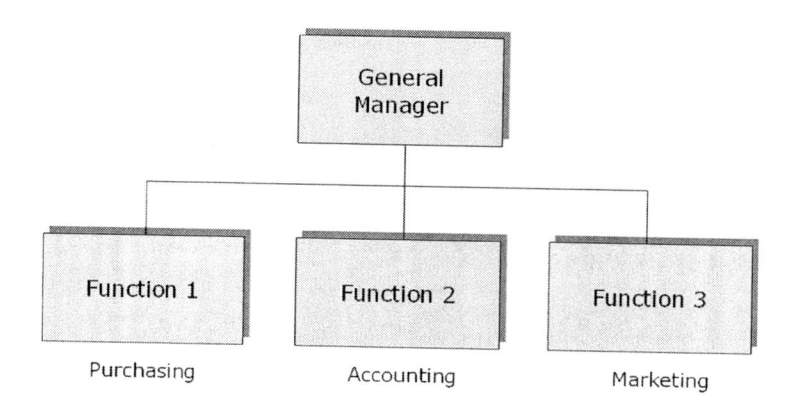

Fig. 8.6 – *Functional Organization*

Process-oriented organization

A variant of the functional organization is the *process-oriented structure*, in which every department is managing one particular (production) process. In an industrial environment this could for example be Founding & Castings, Screw Machining, Finishing & Heat Treating etc...

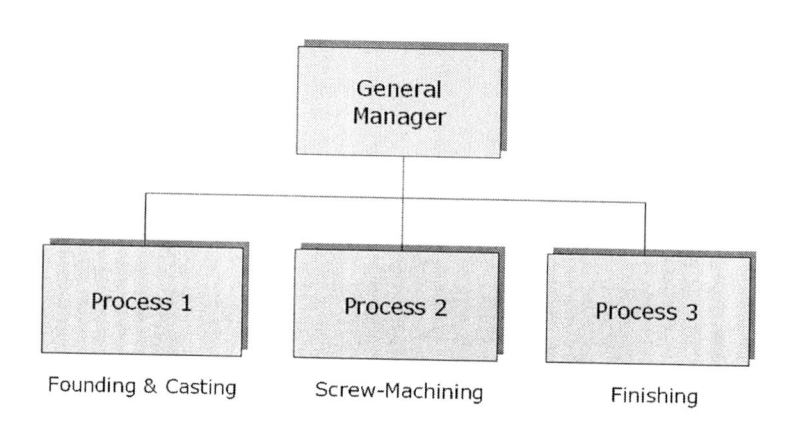

Fig. 8.7 – *Process-Oriented Organization*

Product-oriented organization

In a *product-oriented structure* every department handles all the processes related to one product or product line (e.g., Printed Media, Audio-visual, Internet...).

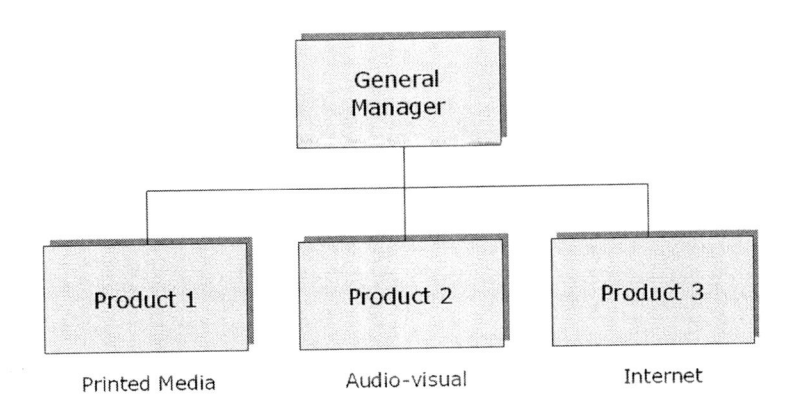

[Organization chart: General Manager → Product 1 (Printed Media), Product 2 (Audio-visual), Product 3 (Internet)]

Fig. 8.8 – *Product-oriented Organization*

A variation on this theme is the *market-oriented structure*. A consulting company could have different divisions focusing on Industry, Finance & Insurance and Government.

Geographical organization

Big and geographically dispersed organizations will often choose for a *geographical organization structure* (e.g., North America, Europe, Asia…)

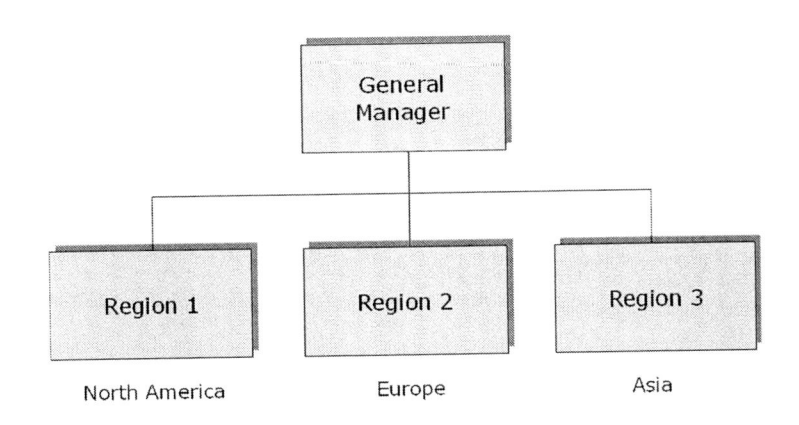

[Organization chart: General Manager → Region 1 (North America), Region 2 (Europe), Region 3 (Asia)]

Fig. 8.9 – *Geographical Organization*

Mixed structures

It must be clear that there is no such thing as an ideal organization structure; each design has advantages and disadvantages. A functional organization could lead to a poor communication across the organization and a process-oriented structure could lead to a mismatch between the production capacity and the sales. The marketing function could have difficulties in a product-oriented structure and in a regional structure may not be the best approach to enforce a global strategy. In reality, most organizations start with a basic structure that is modified to fit needs and complemented with coordinating mechanisms and communication arrangements. The result is a *mix* of different approaches.

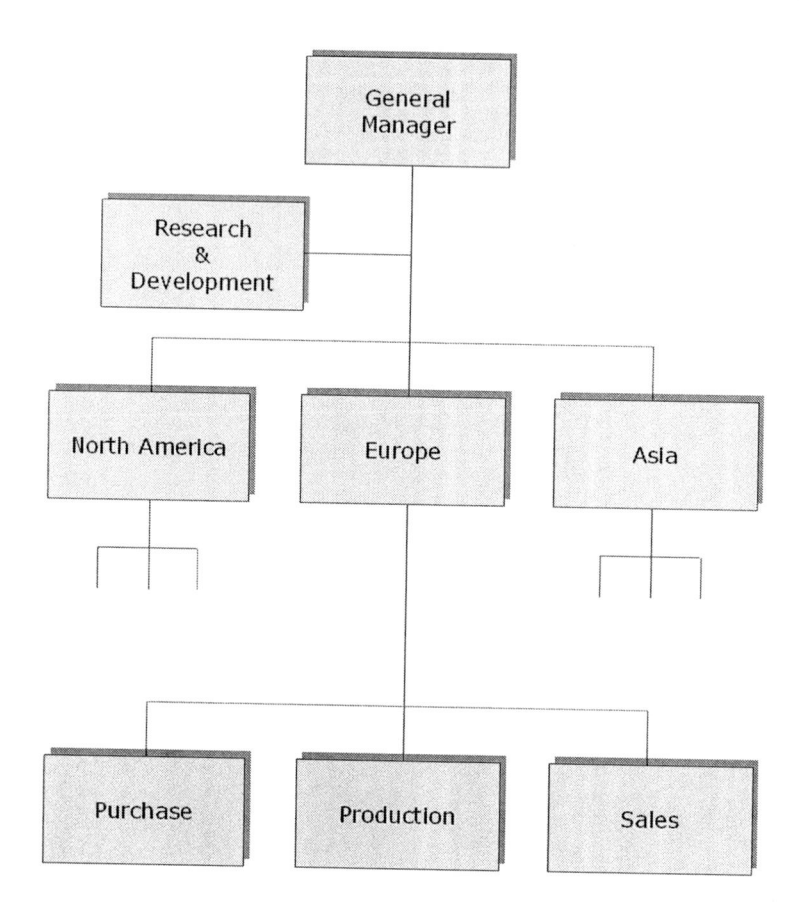

Fig. 8.10 – *Mixed Organization*

Organization of projects

The organizational structures discussed so far are only managing the functions, but how are projects organized? The most obvious solution is to keep the existing structure and to have project coordination done by a group of functional managers who all have a part of their staff participating in the actual execution of the project.

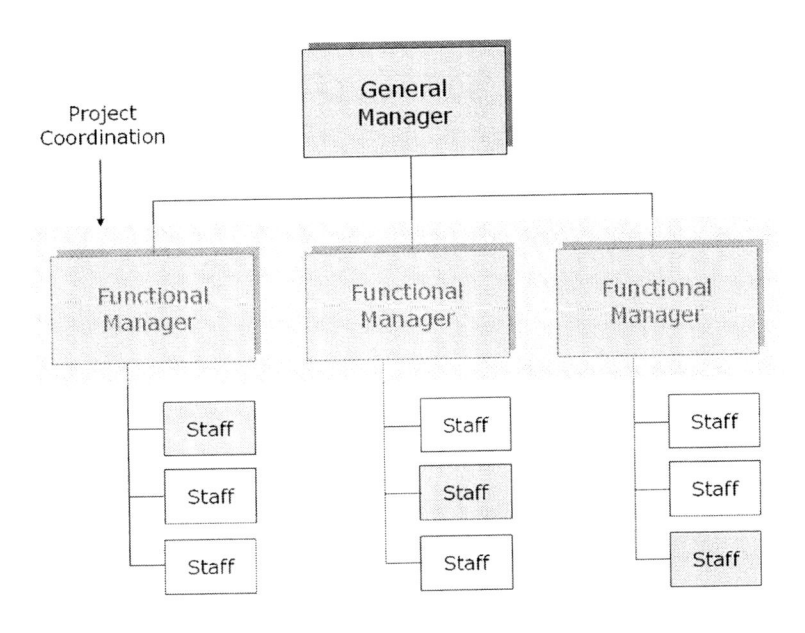

Fig. 8.11 – *Coordination of Project by the Functional Managers*

Organization

Another approach could be the following:

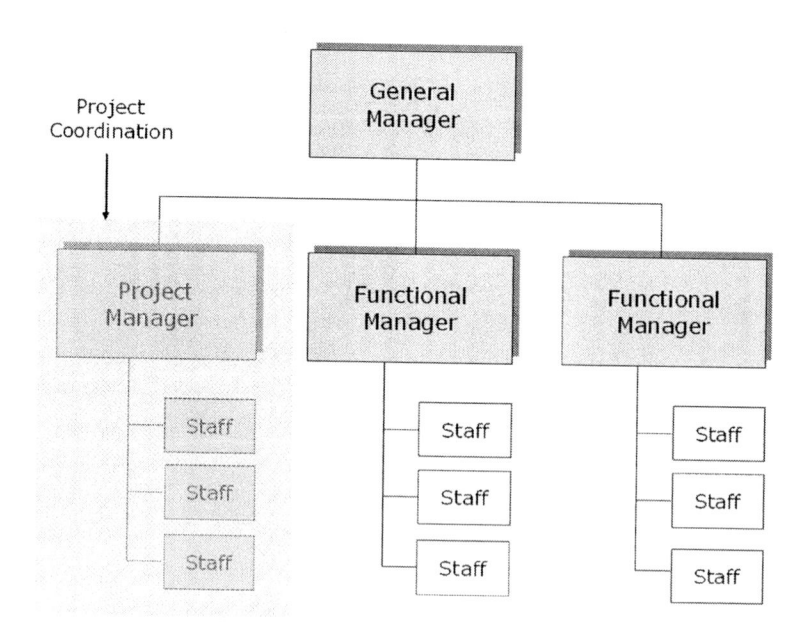

Fig. 8.12 – *Coordination of Project by a Project Manager*

Sometimes, staff members from different functional departments run projects without a hierarchical project leader. This is known as a *weak matrix organization*:

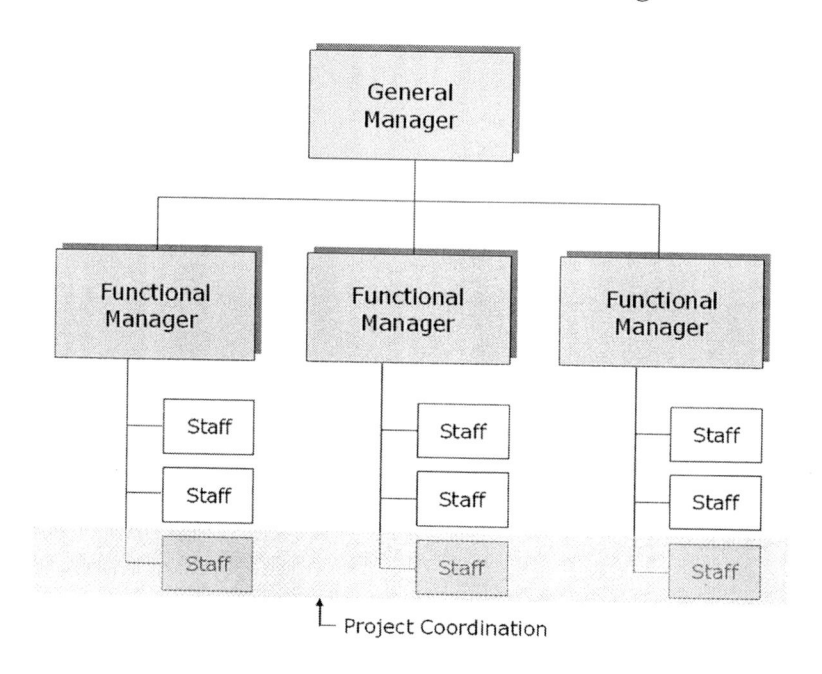

Fig. 8.13 – *Weak Matrix Organization*

This can be improved by having one of the staff members of a functional department responsible of the project. This is not necessary a full-time job. Then the organization is said to be a *balanced matrix organization*:

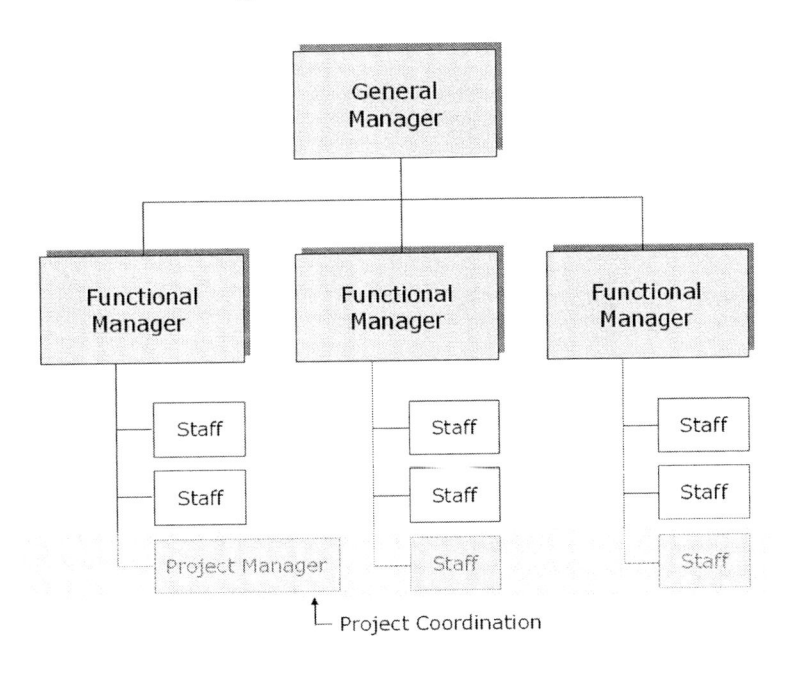

Fig. 8.14 – *Balanced Matrix Organization*

Having a specialized functional manager known as the Manager of the Project Managers could solve these problems; this situation is a *strong matrix organization*:

Organization

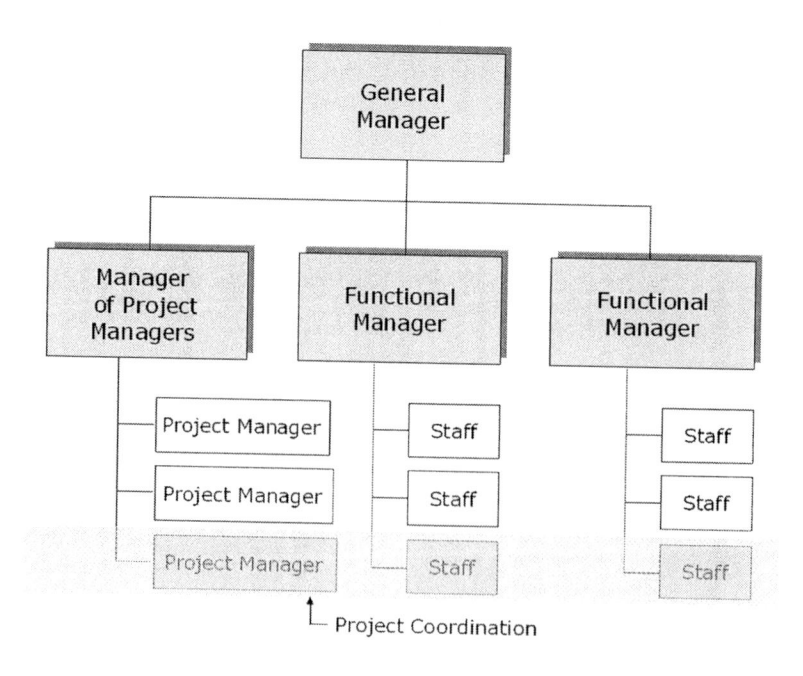

Fig. 8.15 – *Strong Matrix Organization*

It is important that his peers recognize the Manager of the Project Managers and that there is a good mutual understanding between them, otherwise the projects are bound to fail.

This last situation is often encountered in IT projects. The project manager is a staff member of the IT department and therefore reports to the IT manager (the Manager of Project Managers), however, the project team is mixed: people from the IT department (typically developers, database administrators, system administrators) but also future users from the functional departments.

Organization of IT

Strangely enough, while imposing processes and working methods on the rest of the organization, many IT departments seem to be unable to eat their own dog food. Often, the internal organization of IT is not transparent to the outside world and, worse, even its own staff does not know how things are structured or what other projects are ongoing. Of course, the fast pace at which both technology and the markets are moving, combined with outsourcing of work and a high staff turnover can partially explain this situation but these are no excuse for not getting things straight and allowing for clear communication.

Types of activities of an IT organization

Much like in the rest of the organization there are process-oriented activities and project-oriented activities that are deployed in an IT department.

Typical process-oriented activities are telecommunications, networking, systems- and database management and running of a helpdesk. Projects are typically found in application development but also major migration activities and the deployment of computing infrastructure can be considered as project work. It is important to realize that these two types of activities have to be managed in a different way and this should be reflected in the organization of the IT department. The most common way of doing this is the creation of two different "branches" in the organizational tree. A difficulty that can arise in this construct is of course the coordination of the activities that are common (e.g., user support, maintenance and configuration control).

Both process-oriented and project-oriented work will be discussed in the next chapters of this work.

Structure of the IT department

The actual structure of the IT department will depend on several factors, such as:

- The importance of IT within the organization;
- Structure of the organization (geographical, functional, product-oriented…);
- The size of the IT department;
- Available IT budget;
- Maturity of the IT organization;
- Deployed technology (both legacy and new);
- Skills and knowledge of IT staff.

This means that there are no standard solutions. It is, however, possible to make some general statements that are usually valid.

For small IT departments (in entrepreneurial start ups, small and medium organizations and organizations where the importance of IT is low) IT is a group of a few people, informally organized with one responsible manager who takes care of all the IT related domains. It must be clear that this situation is only possible where the deployed technology is limited and simple: a few PCs possibly interconnected with a LAN, running standard, shrink-wrapped software packages. Human resources management is a matter of some friends that collaborate in a tight team and financial resources are not formally managed, but more in an ad hoc, case-by-case manner. Processes and projects are not formally documented and there is no clear strategy or a need for strong business alignment.

As soon as the deployed Information Systems become a bit more elaborate or when the number of users increases, the need for more specialization arises and this almost automatically leads to an increase of IT staff. This can be coped with through outsourcing but – as explained before - this asks for additional management and should be limited to non-core activities. Responsibilities will probably be split over several persons and subunits will be created: one for the management of the infrastructure one for the Information Systems and an IT manager that takes care of human and financial resources in a more formalized way. There is still no need for a heavy process or project control, however, strategy and business alignment are gaining in importance.

When the organization becomes more and more dependent on the use of IT (usually, this coincides with the introduction of dedicated Information Systems for operations and control – layers 3 and 4) the need for more formalization of internal processes and projects will arise. A service manager will be appointed, who will be responsible for the interaction with the business users and the organization and follow-up of internal IT processes. The IT manager will take care of the general strategy and proactively assure the business alignment.

As the importance of IT grows, tactical or strategic decision support tools are being introduced (layers 5 and 6). Business analysts and other power users require the permanent attention of the IT department. This department is now composed of specialized subunits, each with their own manager.

Centralization and decentralization of IT

Centralization means allocating all IT resources to a single organizational unit that then provides IT services to the entire organization; *decentralization* gives units the responsibility for control over local IT resources with little or no consideration of other units.

Does IT have to be more centralized or more decentralized? The industry has been wrestling with this issue for decades. In the mainframe era, everything was strongly centralized but in the 1970s minicomputers gave rise to departmental computing. The next debate came with the proliferation of PCs in the 1980s. During both debates, managers argued over whom should control the computing anarchy that the new machines were causing inside their organizations. In the 1990s, the Internet has been reviving the argument, but what are the pros and cons of both scenarios?

Arguments for centralization focus on coordination, standardization and consolidation of equipment, processes, technology, customer, and vendor management. Centralization enables the creation and execution of a shared vision of how IT should support and drive market opportunities and growth. Centralization also provides significant economies of scale, reduction of redundancies and improved management practices. However, too much dominance of IT can have negative implications as well:

- Senior Management not involved in IT decision making;
- IT specializes in technology, not customer needs;
- Standardization dominates;
- All new systems must fit the data structure of existing systems;
- IT designs/constructs everything;
- Too much emphasis on database and systems maintenance;
- All requests for service require systems study and justification;
- Customers do not have much control over development;
- Build more often than buy;
- Unhappy customers.

At the same time, arguments for decentralization focus on allowing business units to make autonomous decisions about information and customer-related requirements. Of course excess of customer dominance has its drawbacks too:

- Lack of standardization and control;
- Duplication of technical staff and effort;
- Benefits/objectives of systems not systematically considered;
- Technically infeasible projects embarked on;
- Many suppliers, so hard to coordinate;
- No transfer of knowledge shared among user communities;
- High costs because of redundancies.

IT Staffing

"We've decided we need another 700 highly skilled IT professionals. How soon can you hire them?"

The contemporary IT organization relies on a wide variety of knowledgeable and skilled professionals. Knowledgeable and trained teams and individuals are behind hardware and software resources and systems, from conceptual development, through installation and integration, to training and adaptation for organization or user needs. IT systems and solutions are usually multi-faceted, requiring the involvement and collaboration of a variety of functional areas and individuals for successful implementation.

Daan Rijsenbrij, Professor at the University of Amsterdam (The Netherlands), distinguishes seven different profiles: IT specialist, Developer, Architect, Manager, Business Consultant, Project Leader and Auditor.

The *IT specialist* is a technological expert for a given domain within IT. With this expertise he can advise others, like the developer on the implementation of a technology, the business consultant and the customer on the application of that technology in the business domain. Examples are experts in domains like multimedia, CAD/CAM, databases, networks, operating systems, development tools, methodologies, etc...

The field of the *Developer* is the development and maintenance of Infrastructure and Information Systems. There are roughly three different types of tasks performed by the developers: gathering of system requirements in close collaboration with the users, designing and building the systems and finally roll out and make the systems operational. The developer focuses on the implementation of working solutions.

The *Architect* is the link between the customers and the developers. He listens to the different users and creates a model of (a part of) the IT solution. He can explain to the users the concepts of the model and obtain their approval for it. The model is also sufficiently clear to the developers to perform their job. The Architect also develops and explains the general principles, norms and rules by which the systems have to be developed.

The primary task of the *Manager* is to keep the automated systems "in the air." The manager should have a service-oriented attitude; he has to make sure that other people can do their work properly. There are different forms of management: management of the technical infrastructure, change- and problem management, helpdesk for managing user calls and solving user problems, and service level management.

A *Business Consultant* is specialized in a particular business domain. This can be oriented towards a certain market or towards a certain aspect of the business. The Business Consultant gives advice on changes in the business processes (Business Process Redesign BPR) and innovation. For technical question he relies on the IT specialists.

A *Project Leader* is responsible for the management of the processes that form a given project. His task is to make sure that the outcome of the project is what has been agreed with the customer and to keep outcome and expectations in sync (expectation management). The project manager controls and motivates the project team and tries to solve issues that could endanger the success of the project (such as conflicts).

The *Auditor* evaluates (parts of) an IT environment. This can be at all levels from infrastructure, over Information Systems, organization, processes, projects and IT strategy. The result of his work must guide the IT department to improve itself. When an auditor lacks detailed knowledge he uses the help of an expert.

Every profile requires specific knowledge, skills and personality type.

Knowledge:

	IT		Business	
	Specialized	**General**	**Specialized**	**General**
IT specialist	High	Medium	Medium	Low
Developer	Medium	High	Medium	Low
Architect	Low	High	Medium	High
Manager	Low	High	Medium	Low
Business Consultant	Low	Medium	High	High
Project leader	Medium	Medium	Medium	Medium
Auditor	Low	Medium	Medium	Medium

Table 8.2 – *Knowledge of IT Staff per profile*

Skills/Personality:

	Execution	Management	Communication	Social
IT specialist	High	Low	Medium	Medium
Developer	High	Medium	Medium	Medium
Architect	Medium	High	High	Medium
Manager	Low	High	High	High
Business Consultant	Low	Medium	High	High
Project leader	Low	High	High	High
Auditor	High	High	High	Medium

Table 8.3 – *Skills and personality of IT staff per profile*

The CIO/IT manager

The head of IT occupies a special position in the IT department. When IT is part of, or close to the core business of the organization, this is reflected by the presence of a representative in the highest decision organs of the organization (the Strategic Apex) by the *Chief Information Officer (CIO)*. The CIO is not a technology manager, but more a marketer who can detect opportunities and see through the technological implications of business issues. He is in charge of both technology managers and business managers and makes the link between these two. When IT is merely a support function in the organization, the *IT Manager* plays his role in the middle line as a manager of a technologically oriented department. Much like the CIO, the IT manager has to detect technological opportunities and give his advice on feasibility and implementation of business-oriented issues.

CIOs and IT Managers have to be multifunctional individuals.

Should he or she have a technical background? Not surprisingly, around 80% of the IT heads list IT as the area that they worked in before and that had an impact on their career path. Most frequently, CIOs and IT Managers previously were director of systems or applications, administrator, controller or planner (in that order). Although having a technical background is not really a must, it will certainly be helpful to be accepted by the technical people. Anyway, a sound interest in the subject is a must and so is some relevant experience in IT, for instance as a project leader for a reasonable amount of time. An additional MBA can certainly be a plus, just to give him/her that mandatory business feeling.

CIO/IT Managers spend a bulk of their time meeting, whether with the executive team, their IT staff or business partners. The ability to clearly *communicate* ideas, give direction and negotiate is of the highest importance. A manager's role can be defined as "getting work done through other people". In order to get this work done instructions must be given, clearly and precisely. Stimulation and training must be carried out. Staff should be able to air grievances, ask for help or pass on information they feel is relevant. In order to facilitate this exchange of information and ideas, managers must be good communicators. Their communication skills are vital in getting their message across to their staff. They are also essential in helping managers understand what their people are thinking and feeling. CIO/IT Managers communicate in every direction within the organization. When managers communicate to other groups in the organization, they cannot rely on their authority alone; they must exert influence. Good communication skills are vital in this respect.

The CIO or IT Manager must be an excellent *people manager* and a *motivator*; he is somebody who can transfer his enthusiasm both to his superiors and his collaborators. CIOs and IT Managers must be able to recognize, cultivate and retain IT talent. While a great number of candidates are applying for jobs, finding qualified personnel with the right balance of skills and experience in key technology areas is an ongoing challenge.

Understanding the company's *business strategy* and its competitive landscape add greatly to the CIO's ability to bring value to the organization. Additionally, strong business sense will help the CIO develop good relationships with the other managers. The CIO/IT Manager also has to be a *strategic thinker*. He should not only look for the low hanging fruit (quick wins) but for solid solutions that can survive the storms that lie ahead. This key person is often the driving force for innovations in the organization. Indeed, as he is aware of the developments of technology on the one hand, and he is in the middle of the action of his organization on the other hand. He is in a good position to see new opportunities.

Links between IT and the rest of the organization

Committees

To encourage and help understanding, and to obtain critical user support, many organizations have established a variety of standing *Committees* to provide a means by which strategic decisions and policies can be openly and collaboratively addressed. Typical examples of IT Advisory Committees include:

- Strategic Planning;
- Infrastructure Planning and Development;
- Facilities Planning and Development;
- Software Applications Acquisition;
- Resource Allocation and Planning;
- Programmatic Objectives;
- Policies and Standards.

These committees are composed of representatives of both the customer community and the IT department with a sufficient level of specialized business and technical knowledge.

Focus Groups

Focus groups are a valuable way to compile data and insight to help in planning new services or projects, or for testing or conducting an evaluation of services or projects in process.

Local Service Agents and Advanced Users

Some organizations make use of individuals to create a special link between IT and their user communities: Local Service Agents and Advanced Users.

Local Service Agents are employees that functionally depend on the IT department but that are physically located near the users; they are a kind of *liaison officers* between IT and its users. Being IT employees they have a good IT background, which they use to help and support their users.

Advanced Users are "normal" users but with a high affinity for IT. As they know the business domain well and are trusted by the other users they are excellent candidates for supporting development teams in the specification, testing and rollout of new systems.

Best Practices

Act normal

In many organizations the IT department is still considered as "something special." The human resources are not recruited in the same way as the others and they have special privileges, they apply different procedures for purchasing their systems, have a budget that nobody understands etc. All these things are of course not in favor of a good integration of IT in the rest of the organization and, in the long run, a good collaboration between the different players. Consequently, the IT department should avoid in as many domains as possible to differ from the other organizational units.

Create high-performance teams

As a team leader, your success depends largely on to what degree your staff is motivated and productive. One of your main tasks is to ensure your team's best efforts on a consistent basis. High-performance teams have a common vision that provides direction, momentum and commitment. The common purpose has to be translated into specific, measurable and realistic goals. Furthermore, successful teams hold themselves accountable both at individual and at team level for purpose, goals and approach.

To be effective, the size of work teams should be kept small (< 12); if larger they cannot develop cohesiveness, commitment and mutual accountability.

The following suggestions will help to create a sense of team commitment:

- Create a relaxed, informal and open work environment;
- Encourage and provide time for group discussion and interaction;
- Establish clear and concise individual and team goals;
- Be open to the discussion of differing points of view;
- Encourage criticism of ideas without allowing personal attacks;
- Avoid "B teams."
-

Eliminate redundant administration

Create a single point of inventory control, supported by a good distribution workflow and maybe an automated configuration control using the corporate network.

Every department its own responsibility

In an organization every unit has its own responsibility and this should also be the case for IT. The IT department should be considered as an internal service provider who builds and deploys Information Systems, but who does not operate them. IT has to make sure that Information Systems meet the user requirements, that they are available and have a good performance, but IT should not be involved in the operational processes. This means that Information Systems have to be built in such a way that once deployed, the users are fully self-supporting. They have to be able to run the Information System without the intervention of IT staff (except for the inevitable maintenance). They have to have access to all the relevant data and system parameters to influence the behavior of the application and the in-depth knowledge of the functionalities of the system has to be present in the user community. Organizing your Information Systems that way will effectively increase the availability as the users will no longer have to wait for the intervention of IT when a parameter has to be modified.

Flat or tall?

Organizational height refers to the number of levels or layers of management in an organization. In a *flat* organization there are few layers and managers perform more tasks, while in a *tall* organization there are many levels.

In the 1990s it was popular to plea for flatter organizations, as these were supposed to overcome the problems associated with tall ones:

- *Communication* – As the chain length increases communication takes longer and gets distorted, the decision-making gets slower and the information could be manipulated or selectively passed on, both resulting in a loss of control;
- *Motivation* – As the number of levels increases, the relative difference in authority of managers at each level decreases. Studies have shown that the more authority a person has the more motivated he is;
- *Bureaucratic costs* – The greater the number of levels, the greater the costs associated with running and operating the organization.

However, there are also problems related to flat organizations. These are mainly related to what is known as the *span of control* of the managers. The span of control of a manager is the number of subordinates he manages directly. Already in 1937 Graicunas [157] summed up the prevailing view of the reason for limiting the span of control:

"One of the surest sources of delay and confusion is to allow any superior to be directly responsible for the control of too many subordinates."

The most important factor limiting the span of control is the inability to supervise increasing numbers of subordinates adequately as an arithmetic increase in the number of subordinates is accompanied with an exponential increase in numbers of subordinate relationships.

The ability to supervise directly is limited by the complexity of the subordinate's tasks (the more complex, the smaller the span of control) and the interrelatedness of tasks (the more closely interrelated, the smaller the span of control). Also, qualified, experienced and well-motivated staff requires much less supervision. On the contrary, a manager can more easily supervise the work of many people doing the same, simple, job.

So, the fundamental question remains: "how many is too many?" The answer is probably to be sought in the work of General Sir Ian Hamilton, who, in 1922, wrote the following:

"The nearer we approach the supreme head of the whole organization, the more we ought to work towards groups of three; the closer we get to the foot of the whole organization, the more we work towards groups of six."

These figures, of course, have to be adapted to the reality of the organization but the rule of thumb is still valid in today's reality.

Harmonize, don't centralize

Neither centralization nor decentralization are sustainable in their pure form; this is why the trend is a shift towards structures that enable the best attributes of centralization and decentralization to be applied based on the requirements of a given function or business unit. In other words, IT is moving towards a scenario where centralized IT and decentralized IT coexist under the same structure (Fig. 8.16).

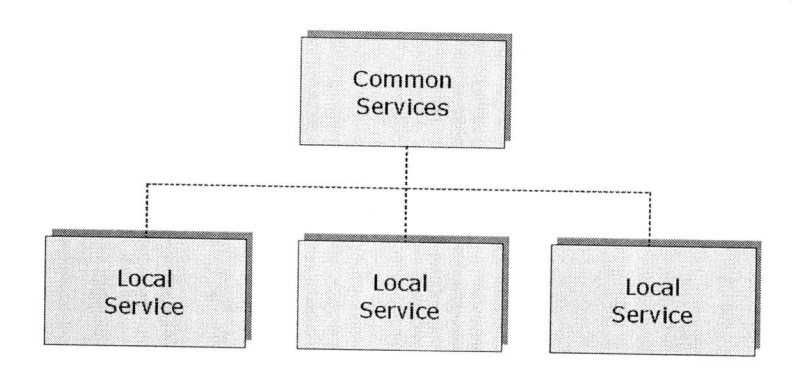

Fig. 8.16 – *Coexistence of centralized and decentralized IT*

Several common services are executed by a *horizontal* IT component. The activities of this component could be at all levels:

- Grouping of purchase contracts;
- Shared Helpdesk activities;
- Common component libraries and development frameworks;
- Pooling of IT staff;
- Training and education of users and IT staff;
- Elaboration of standards for hardware, software, tools and procedures;
- Coordination of projects;
- Exchange of knowledge and experience;
- Benchmarking;
- IT/Business Alignment;
- Internal and external relations.

On the other hand, the local services are performed by *vertical* IT components that are situated at the level of the organizational units they are part of (organized by region, function, product line, or any other dimension). These IT departments are specialized in the support of their own organizational unit and make use of the common services supplied by the central IT component. It is important to stress that there is *no hierarchical relationship* between the horizontal and the vertical IT units; the local IT departments report to their local management and benefit of the advantages offered by the centralized services.

Integrate in the Organizational Culture

Assessing an organizational culture is mostly intuitive; nevertheless, do not underestimate the importance of fitting in to the microcosms of the organization, also – and especially - beyond your own IT department. Observe your colleagues closely and consciously, study the tone of the internal memos and see how managers interact with their subordinates. An organizational culture is hard to describe and there are usually only small clues to follow: how do people dress, how do they communicate, is socializing important, do people call each other by their first name, are titles important? If you are new in an organization it is a good idea to inform about the past of the organization as a whole and of the IT department in particular. You will end with valuable insights on failures of the past, topics to avoid, sensitive zones and above all the "informal hierarchy." This knowledge will most certainly be helpful in setting out a path through the minefields of the organization.

Know and use the informal organization

The *informal organization* refers to the behaviours and interactions that result from personal relationships rather than organizational structure. The *grapevine* is the informal communications network within the organization.

Build a personal network. Try to find managers of your own level in the hierarchy that you can trust and discuss with on an informal basis. They will provide you with much information that is not available through the official channels and they will help you build the necessary credibility.

Also, having a personal assistant whom you trust can be helpful. He or she has access to information that will never reach you through the regular channels. Of course, this person must also trust you, so be as open and frank with him as you possibly can and keep the channel strictly confidential.

Participate in networks

A *Network* is a cluster of different organizations whose actions are coordinated by contracts and agreements rather than through a formal hierarchy of authority. The advantages of networks are:

- Lower production costs by avoiding the costs of a complex structure;
- Allows organizations to act in a flexible way;
- Partners can be replaced if necessary;
- Allows low-cost access to foreign sources of input and expertise.

Networks exist in many different environments: big multinationals, collaboration between federal and local authorities, armed forces, and even amongst competitors within a given industry. Networks are so successful because they are combining the "best of both worlds," it can only work however if the local management is prepared to spend effort, time and resources to keep the network alive.

Separate development and maintenance

Development and maintenance are two completely different types of activities: one is project-oriented while the other is process-oriented. In practice this means that, when executed by the same people, there will be interference; project planning will be constantly disturbed because of bug fixes, modifications or other urgent interventions such as ad hoc reporting. It is therefore a good idea to have the development and maintenance done by different people (if the size of your organization permits). Avoid, however, the emergence of "B-teams" by explaining to the maintenance people the importance of their work.

Online Resources

Management - http://www.aom.pace.edu
Management - http://www.insead.fr
Management - http://www.ccl.org
Management - http://www.nlma.org
Management - http://www.managementhelp.org
Management - http://www.solbaram.org/indexes/genmgt.html
Organization - http://www.brint.com
Organization – http://www.henrymintzberg.com
Methods - http://www.mapnp.org/library/org_perf/methods.htm
Teams - http://www.workteams.unt.edu/links.htm

Further Reading

[149] Ackoff, R. *Recreating the corporation*. Oxford University Press. 1999.

[150] Bartlett, C. and Ghoshal, S., *Managing Across Borders,* Harvard Business School Press, 1998.

[151] Chandler, A., *Strategy and Structure: Chapters in the History of the American Industrial Enterprise*. Cambridge, MA: MIT Press. 1962.

[152] Chang, R.Y., Curtin, M.J., *Succeeding as a Self-Managed Team: A Practical Guide to Operating as a Self-Managed Work Team*, Wiley, 1999.

[153] Cyert, R.M. & J.G. March, *A Behavioral Theory of the Firm*. 2nd ed. Blackwell Publishers: Cambridge, MA, 1992.

[154] Drucker, P.F. *The coming of a new organization*. Harvard Business Review. January-February 1988.

[155] Evan, William M. *Organization Theory and Design*. New York: MacMillan, 1993.

[156] Garvin, David A. *Building a Learning Organization*. Harvard Business Review (July-August). 1993.

[157] Graicunas, V.A., *Relationship in Organization* in *Papers on the Science of Administration*, edited by Luther Gulick and Lyndall F. Urwick, published by Columbia University's Institute of Public Administration. 1937.

[158] Hannan, M.T. and Carroll, G.R., *Dynamics of Organizational Populations*. New York: Oxford University Press, 1992.

[159] Jones, R.G. *Organizational theory: text and cases*. Reading Mass. Addison Wesley. 1999.

[160] March, J.G. and Olsen, J.P., *Rediscovering Institutions: The Organizational Basis of Institutions*. New York: The Free Press, 1990.

[161] Meyer, M.W. and Zucker, L.G., *Permanently Failing Organizations*. Newbury Park, CA: Sage Publications, 1989.

[162] Miller, Lawrence M., *Barbarians to Bureaucrats, Corporate Life Cycle Strategies*. C.N. Potter: New York

[163] Mintzberg, H., *The Nature of Managerial Work*. Harper Row. 1973.

[164] Mintzberg, H., *The Structuring of Organizations*, Prentice Hall. 1979.

[165] Mintzberg, H. *Structure in fives: designing effective organizations*. Englewood Cliffs. Prentice-Hall. 1983.

[166] Mintzberg, H. and Quinn J., *The Strategy Process: Concepts, Contexts, Cases*, Prentice Hall. 1996.

[167] Mintzberg, H., *Crafting Strategy*, Harvard Business Review, July-Aug, 1987.

[168] Nelson R.R. and Winter, S.G., *An Evolutionary Theory of Economic Change*. London: The Belknap Press of Harvard University Press, 1982.

[169] Perrow, C., *Normal Accidents: Living with high risk technologies*. New York, NY: Basic Books, Inc., 1984.

[170] Pfeffer, J., *New directions for organization theory: problems and prospects*. New York : Oxford University Press, 1997.

[171] Pfeffer, J., *Managing with Power. Politics and Influence in Organizations*. Boston, MA: Harvard Business School Press, 1992.

[172] Powell, Walter W. and Paul J. DiMaggio (eds.), *The new Institutionalism in Organizational Analysis*. Chicago: The University of Chicago Press, 1991.

[173] Porter, Michael E. *Competitive Strategy: techniques for analyzing industries and competitors*. New York. The Free Press. 1980.

[174] Porter, Michael E. *Competitive Advantage: creating and sustaining superior performance*. New York. The Free Press. 1985.

[175] Scott, W. Richard and Meyer, J.W., *Institutional Environments and Organizations*. Newbury Park, CA: Sage Publications, 1994.

[176] Senge, P.M., *The Fifth Discipline, the Art and Practice of the Learning Organization*. New York, Currency Doubleday, 1990.

[177] Shapiro, C. and Varian, H.R., *Information Rules: A Strategic Guide to the Network Economy*. Harvard Business School Publishing. 1998.

[178] Singh, Jitendra (ed.). *Organizational Evolution.* Newbury Park, CA: Sage Publications, 1990.

[179] Staw, B.M. & L.L. Cummings (eds.), *The Evolution and Adaptation of Organizations.* Greewich, CO, 1990.

# 9

Strategy and Business Alignment

"If you don't know where you're going, you'll end up somewhere else."

(Yogi Berra)

Introduction

In May 2003 the Harvard Business Review published a controversial article called *"IT doesn't matter"* [183]. In this, Nicholas Carr asks the question if all the IT investments over the last decades were really worthwhile. His conclusion was negative. Obviously, this article created a lot of debate, because it sharpened the discussion on cost and benefit of IT. Smith & Fingar [191] riposted in their book *"IT doesn't matter, business processes do."* They put forward that a new approach to business automation centered on business process management, instead of the data-centric world that Carr describes, show the greatest growth opportunity companies have ever seen.

Organizations have become totally dependent on Information Technology; vital Business Processes rely heavily on IT and the failure or temporary unavailability of IT or one of its components can cause important financial damage or even the end of the organization.

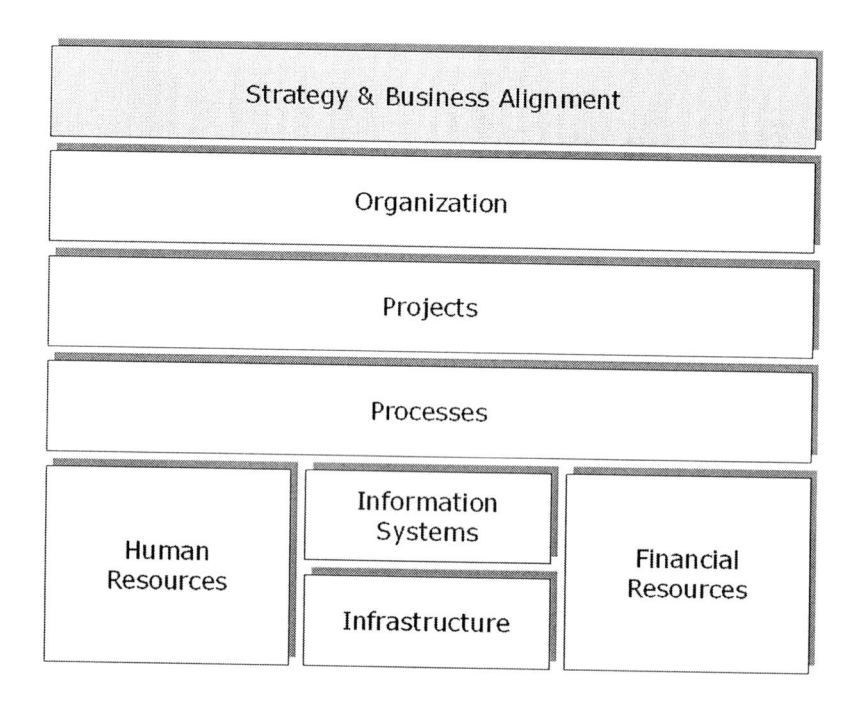

Fig. 9.1 – *Position of Strategy in the IT stack*

Increasing complexity of IT and the dependency of the organization on IT mean that business and IT can no longer be seen as independent; they influence each other and this has to be reflected on the strategic, the tactical, and the operational level.

Business Strategy

"No wind favors he who has no destined port."

(Montaigne)

The commonplace "If you don't know where you are going, any road will take you there" is equally valid in business. Organizations define this concept as having a mission or vision, and organizations lacking vision usually flounder.

A *Business Strategy* is the match an organization makes between its internal resources and skills and the opportunities and risks created by its external environment. The process of *Strategic Planning* determines *where* the organization is going to over the next couple of years, *how* it is going to get there and how it will *follow up* on the progress [151]. There are a variety of perspectives about strategic planning and a variety of approaches used in the strategic planning process. Usually, the strategic planners already know much of what will go into the strategic plan. However, the process of developing a strategic plan greatly helps to clarify the organization's plans and ensure that everybody is on the same track. So, in fact, the planning process itself is more important than the resulting planning document. The benefits of a Strategic Planning exercise are multiple:

"Our goal is to revolutionize the electronics industry, turn the old hierarchy upside-down, and put us in first place. Anyone have an idea how we can do that?"

- The purpose of the organization is clearly defined and realistic goals and objectives consistent with that mission in a defined duration within the organization's capacity of implementation are established;
- These goals and objectives are communicated;
- The most effective use is made of the organization's resources by focusing them on the key priorities;
- A base is provided from which progress can be measured;
- Clearer focus of organization is provided, thus producing more efficiency and higher effectiveness.

There are three major activities involved in the creation of a Strategic Plan:

- *Strategic Analysis (Where are we today?)* - This activity includes a review of the organization's environment. Planners look at the various *Strengths, Weaknesses, Opportunities and Threats* (*SWOT*) regarding the organization;
- *Setting Strategic Direction (Where do we want to go?)* - Planners determine what the organization must do. These conclusions include what strategic goals the organization should achieve and the strategies to achieve these goals. Goals should be S*pecific, Measurable, Acceptable, Realistic* and *Timely* (*SMART*);
- *Action Planning (How are we going to get there?)* - Action planning is laying out how the strategic goals will be accomplished by specifying objectives, or results, with each strategic goal. An objective is still a goal, but on a smaller scale. Action planning also includes specifying responsibilities and timelines with each objective, or who needs to do what and by when. It should also include methods to monitor and evaluate the plan, which includes knowing how the organization will know who has done what and by when.

It is common to develop an *annual plan* (sometimes called the *operational plan* or *management plan*), which includes the strategic goals, strategies, objectives, responsibilities and timelines that should be accomplished in the coming year. Often, organizations will develop plans for each major function, division department, etc., and call these *work plans*. Usually, *budgets* are included in the strategic, annual and work plans. In his book, *Competitive Strategy* [173], Michael Porter identifies three fundamental competitive strategies and lays out the required skills and resources, organizational elements and risks associated with each strategy: Cost Leadership, Differentiation and Focus.

Cost Leadership – To implement this strategy sustained capital investment and access to capital is needed. Furthermore, process-engineering skills, intensive supervision of labor, products that are designed for ease of manufacture and a low-cost distribution system are required. On the organizational side a tight cost control system with frequent, detailed reports is needed, so are a structured organization and a system of incentives based on meeting well-defined targets.

Differentiation – The skills and resources needed for this strategy are strong marketing abilities, good product engineering, creative flair, and strong capability in basic research, technological leadership and a long tradition in the industry or unique combination of skills drawn from other businesses. From the organizational point of view there has to be a strong coordination between R&D, product development, and marketing.

Focus – This strategy is the combination of the above policies directed at a particular target.

Integration of business and IT

"Imagination is more important than knowledge."

(Einstein)

Organizations use technology in general and IT in particular to become more efficient, more effective and to innovate.

Obviously, IT can be used to increase the *efficiency* of an organization. Efficiency stands for output versus consumed resources; higher efficiency means fewer resources for the same output or a higher output with the same resources. The contribution of IT can come in different flavors by:

- Unification of the business view of the different objects used by the organization;
- Enabling better collaboration through groupware;
- Avoiding double encoding and transcription errors;
- Rationalization and simplification of business processes;
- Automation of highly repetitive tasks;
- Automation of business workflows;
- Introduction of self-service concept for the customers;
- Or any combination of the above.

In times of economic recession, organizations tend to focus on efficiency and IT will be used to do the same with fewer resources. In times of economic prosperity, IT will be used to do a better job with the same resources. A better job could mean better or cheaper products or services, shorter delivery times, better customer support, etc.

Effectiveness is the degree to which a system's features and capabilities meet the customer's needs. In this way, the effectiveness of an organization is the degree to which it meets its strategic goals, which normally are derived from its customer's needs. Information systems can largely contribute to an organization's effectiveness, especially those systems that are situated in the higher layers of the IT stack. Much like a lever that is used to amplify physical force these Information Systems amplify the effectiveness of the organization. Typically, the spending on IT represents a few percent of the total turnover. Thus, an improvement of the efficiency of the IT support could proportionally improve the effectiveness of the organization as a whole (provided that the core processes are targeted).

Operational efficiency and effectiveness are important, but not enough to obtain a sustainable competitive advantage. Although lower prices and effectiveness are clearly differentiators, many organizations separate themselves from their competitors by operating differently, offering different services or making different products. Therefore, to sustain their advantage, organizations must also continue to *innovate*. Innovation concerns the search for and the discovery, experimentation, development and adoption of new products, processes and organizational set-ups.

The Strategic Alignment Model

"In the majority of failures – we estimate 70% - the real problem isn't bad strategy, it's bad execution."

(Why CEO's Fail – Fortune)

Henderson and Venkatraman [186] proposed a model for business – IT alignment: the *Strategic Alignment Model*. This model was intended to support the integration of IT into business strategy by promoting alignment between and within four domains.

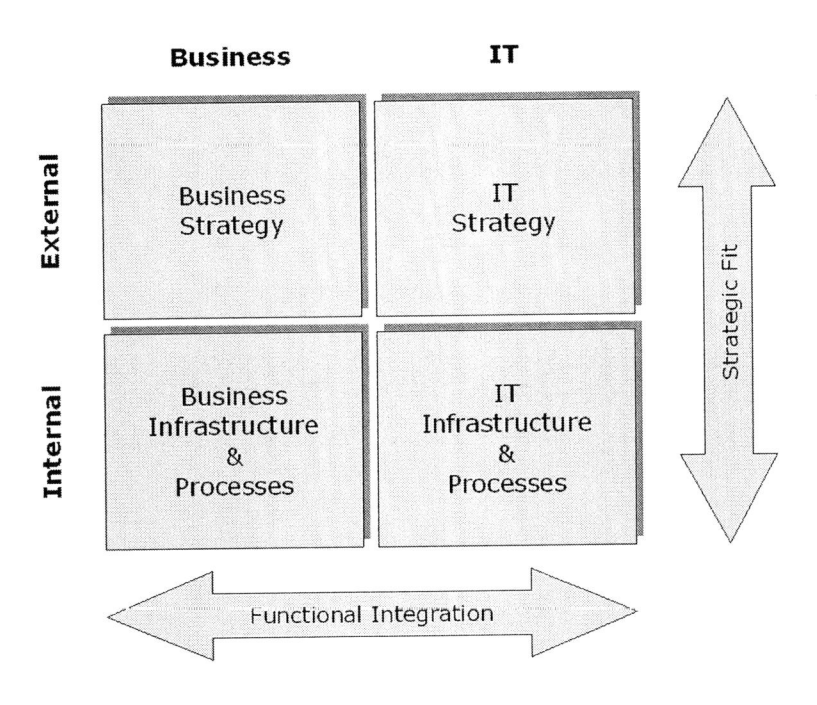

Fig. 9.2 – *Strategic Alignment Model*

Alignment is practiced along two dimensions: *Strategic Fit* (between the external and internal domain) and *Functional Integration* (between the business domain and the IT domain). The objective of this model was to provide a way to align information technology with business objectives to realize value from IT investments. Almost all later models start from this original model.

This model clearly shows that IT strategy and plans should be deduced from and aligned with Business strategy and plans, the main goal being to exploit IT for a competitive advantage for the organization as a whole.

Ultimately, the benefits of such an IT strategy are:

- *Better, timelier information* - satisfying business management expectations;
- *Increased efficiency* - reducing duplication of effort, increasing utilization of personnel resources for the whole organization;
- *More effective management* - keeping on top instead of playing catch-up;
- *Predictable budgets in future years* - eliminate major surprises;
- *Lower costs* - reduce the chance of stranded investments.

Functional Integration

"A goal is a dream with a deadline."

(Harvey Mackay)

External domain

The *Information Architecture* is a mapping of the overall information needs on the needs of the organization as determined by the organization's Business Strategy. The Information Architecture encompasses the application level aspects that map the information needs onto the organization's business needs. This mapping is also constrained by the various limitations present at the Business Strategy level. For instance, the viability of the proposal for systems or projects could be limited by the availability of the budget requirements.

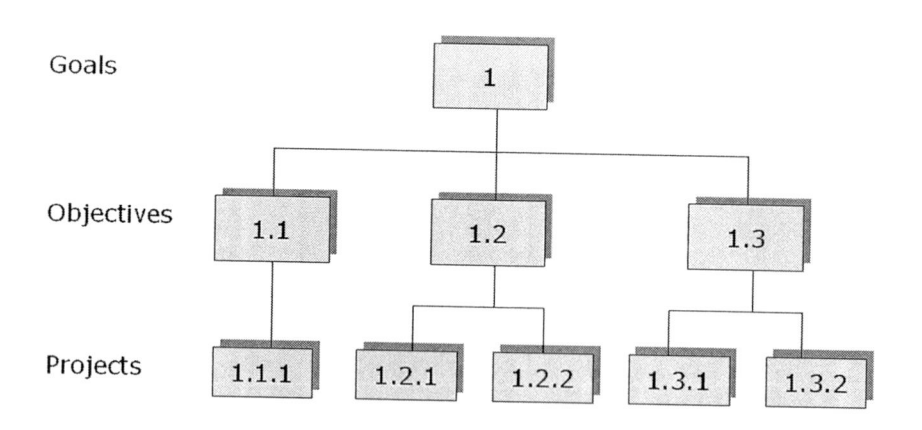

Fig. 9.3 – *Functional Integration*

The Information Architecture encompasses the Data Architecture, Systems Architecture and Computer Architecture.

Data Architecture - The organization will have to make decisions about how data will serve its business needs. It needs to define its current and future needs for accumulation, usage, renewal, maintenance and transfer of data within, and outside, the organization's boundaries.

Systems Architecture – These are the systems that the organization is going to deploy. The systems architecture includes issues such as the Client Server Architecture, Intranets, and the various Networking Protocols.

Computer Architecture – These are the hardware and software that constitute the technological base for the above architectures. The products available on the market and the budget allocations also determine hardware and software requirements. "Build, borrow or buy" decisions are made at this level; however the issues at other levels guide them. For instance the decision to outsource the telecommunication setup or data centre is guided by issues such as development of proprietary know-how, and focus on the core competencies. It must be observed that the above-discussed issues have cross-level implications. For instance, the decision related to Client-Server is not just a technological decision; it has implications for the organization's productivity, human resources, and competitive advantage. Similarly, decisions about Intranets entails financial, technological, and business aspects.

A "down to earth" approach for creating strategic IT plans for your organization is given below. This exercise should be performed at least on an annual basis:

- *Strategic Business Goals* - Meet with the key executives to make a list of the primary business goals for the next one to three years. These should include any new product introductions, geographic expansions, new facilities, customer service initiatives or revenue targets;
- *Current Infrastructure* - Establish the current state of the LAN, WAN, server, mainframe, PC, and software systems. Document the current strengths and weaknesses. Review any announced product upgrades;
- *Technology Goals* - Create a list of technology goals for the next one to three years which support the needs of the current business processes, and the new business initiatives. These goals could include LAN/WAN expansions or conversions, internet/intranet implementations, server deployments, major software upgrades, or application development;
- *Proposed Projects* - Based on the findings for the above, a list of projects with defined time requirements should be developed. Each project should be clearly linked to the business and technology goals;

- *Implementation Timeline* - The proposed projects should be put into a realistic time schedule (Gantt chart). This proposed schedule then becomes a key document for capital and expense budgeting during the upcoming time periods.

Internal domain

Processes

Functional integration between Business and IT in the internal domain can be obtained using *Service Level Agreements (SLAs)*. An SLA is a contract between a service provider (in this case, the IT department) and the end user, which stipulates and commits the service provider to a required level of service. An SLA should contain a specified level of service, support options, enforcement or penalty provisions for services not provided, a guaranteed level of system performance related to downtime or up time, a specified level of customer support and what software or hardware will be provided and – if applicable - for what fee.

Projects

Obviously, a good functional integration in the projects can only be obtained through the construction of systems that respond to the real needs of the users. On the methodological side this is a strong argument against the use of a classical waterfall approach because, as we know it is difficult to define all requirements at the beginning of a project, this model has problems adapting to change and working version of the system is not seen until late in the project's life. Far better approaches in this respect are the incremental and the spiral models or, when timing is important, the time box model. It is necessary to involve the customers – users at all levels in the organization – in the complete life cycle; from project definition over development up to post-development phases like operations and support, maintenance and finally retirement.

Strategic Fit

It is not sufficient to set goals and objectives in a strategic plan; there has to be a follow-up of the progress so that corrective actions can be undertaken if necessary. An interesting management technique in this respect is the *Balanced Scorecard (BSC)*. This methodology was introduced by Professor Robert Kaplan and Dr. David Norton in 1992 and has been used since by many organizations throughout the world.

Business domain

The BSC is a framework for describing, realizing and managing the operations of an organization by linking objectives, measures and initiatives. The BSC provides an overall view by integrating *financial measures* with other *Key Performance Indicators (KPIs)* concerning *customers, internal processes, learning and innovation*. The BSC is not just a static list of measures, but a framework for realizing and aligning complex programs of change.

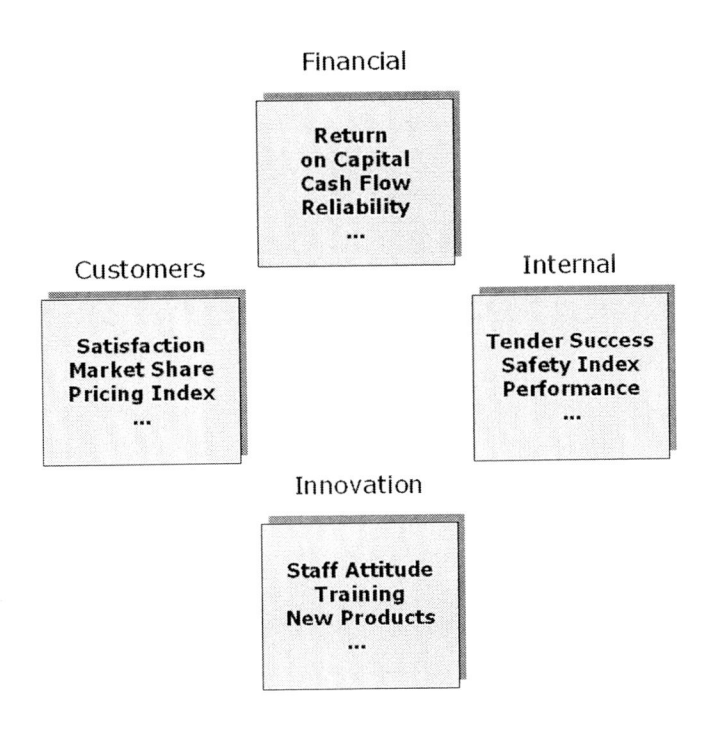

```
                        Financial
                    ┌──────────────┐
                    │   Return     │
                    │ on Capital   │
                    │  Cash Flow   │
                    │  Reliability │
                    │     ...      │
                    └──────────────┘
  Customers                                  Internal
┌──────────────┐                         ┌──────────────┐
│ Satisfaction │                         │Tender Success│
│ Market Share │                         │ Safety Index │
│ Pricing Index│                         │ Performance  │
│     ...      │                         │     ...      │
└──────────────┘                         └──────────────┘
                        Innovation
                    ┌──────────────┐
                    │Staff Attitude│
                    │   Training   │
                    │ New Products │
                    │     ...      │
                    └──────────────┘
```

Fig. 9.4 – *Balanced Scorecard*

The basic idea of the methodology is that focusing solely on the (short term) financial performance of an organization is not a good thing for its (long-term) survivability. Indeed, a business with unsatisfied customers is unlikely to survive, and so is an organization with badly organized internal processes or one that is not able to cope with technological and environmental changes. The BSC concept aims at finding a score against a set of representative performance indicators in these four domains (Finance, Customer, Internal and Innovation). Because optimization in every separate domain inevitably conflicts with one or more of the others a good balance has to be found, hence the adjective "balanced."

The BSC methodology has a tremendous potential for business benefit. Therefore, organizations should not consider a balanced scorecard as just a performance measurement. They should consider it as a method to align the organization and its processes with the strategic objectives.

The Balanced Scorecard has been quickly accepted by the business world. It is indeed easy to appreciate the value of a focused set of performance measurements. However, an effective Balanced Scorecard is more than a limited list of measures gathered into four categories. A good BSC should effectively reflect the organization's strategy in different ways:

- *Cause and Effect Relationships* – Every measure selected for a Balanced Scorecard should be part of a chain of cause and effect relationships that represent the strategy;
- *Performance Drivers* - Measures common to most organizations within a given sector of activity are known as "lag indicators." Examples include market share or customer retention. The drivers of performance or "lead indicators" tend to be unique because they reflect what is different about the strategy. A good Balanced Scorecard should have a mix of both;
- *Financial* - With the proliferation of change programs in most organizations today, it is easy to become preoccupied with a goal such as quality, customer satisfaction or innovation, however, although these goals are frequently strategic, they must translate also into measures that are ultimately linked to financial indicators.

IT domain

"You can't tell when you're winning if you don't keep score."

(Unknown)

The application of the BSC in an IT environment has also been intensively studied. The key difference between BSC within IT as opposed to the entire organization is that the customers are users within the organization, not external. The implementation of BSC has to be seen as part of a more profound cultural transformation in IT. Indeed, where the more traditional IT department is technology-driven it is the business that drives the modern IT department. Whereas the more traditional IT service was focused inward, the modern one is end-user focused. Individual performance has been replaced by team performance and finally, the measures – if any – that used to be centered on efficiency are now concerned with effectiveness.

This can formally be translated into Mission and Strategy according to the Balanced Scorecard methodology:

Customer	**Financial**
Mission To be the preferred supplier of IT solutions Strategy • Preferred supplier of applications • Preferred supplier of operations • Improve user satisfaction	Mission To obtain a good business contribution of IT investments Strategy • Control of IT expenses • Business value of IT projects • Provide new business capabilities
Internal	**Innovation**
Mission To deliver effective and efficient IT applications and services Strategy • Effective and efficient development • Effective and efficient operations	Mission Develop opportunities to answer future challenges Strategy • Training and education of IT staff • Expertise of IT staff • Research into emerging technologies • Reduce age of application portfolio

Table 9.1 – *Balanced IT scorecard*

This then has to be to be translated to *Key Performance Indicators (KPIs)* such as:

- Percentage of reusability for core application modules;
- Ratio of new IT investments and total IT spending;
- IT budget as percentage of total budget;
- Number of Service Level Agreements;
- Percentage of customers satisfied with IT product delivery;
- Percentage of customers satisfied with IT maintenance and support;
- Percentage of users covered by training for new IT solutions;
- Number of function points delivered per labor hour;
- Percentage of projects on time and on budget;
- Online system availability;
- Percentage of staff trained in relevant technology;
- Percentage of IT budget devoted to training;
- Number of training days followed by IT staff;
- Employee turnover.
- …

Zachman's Framework

Zachman's Framework for Enterprise Architecture[TM] is another interesting approach for developing and/or documenting an enterprise-wide IT architecture. It is owned and copyrighted by M. John Zachman. The purpose of the framework is to provide a basic structure which supports the organization, access, integration, interpretation, development, management, and changing of a set of architectural representations of the organizations information systems. The framework contains global plans as well as technical details, lists and charts as well as natural language statements. Any appropriate approach, standard, role, method, technique, or tool may be placed in it. In fact, the framework can be viewed as a tool to organize any form of meta-data for the enterprise.

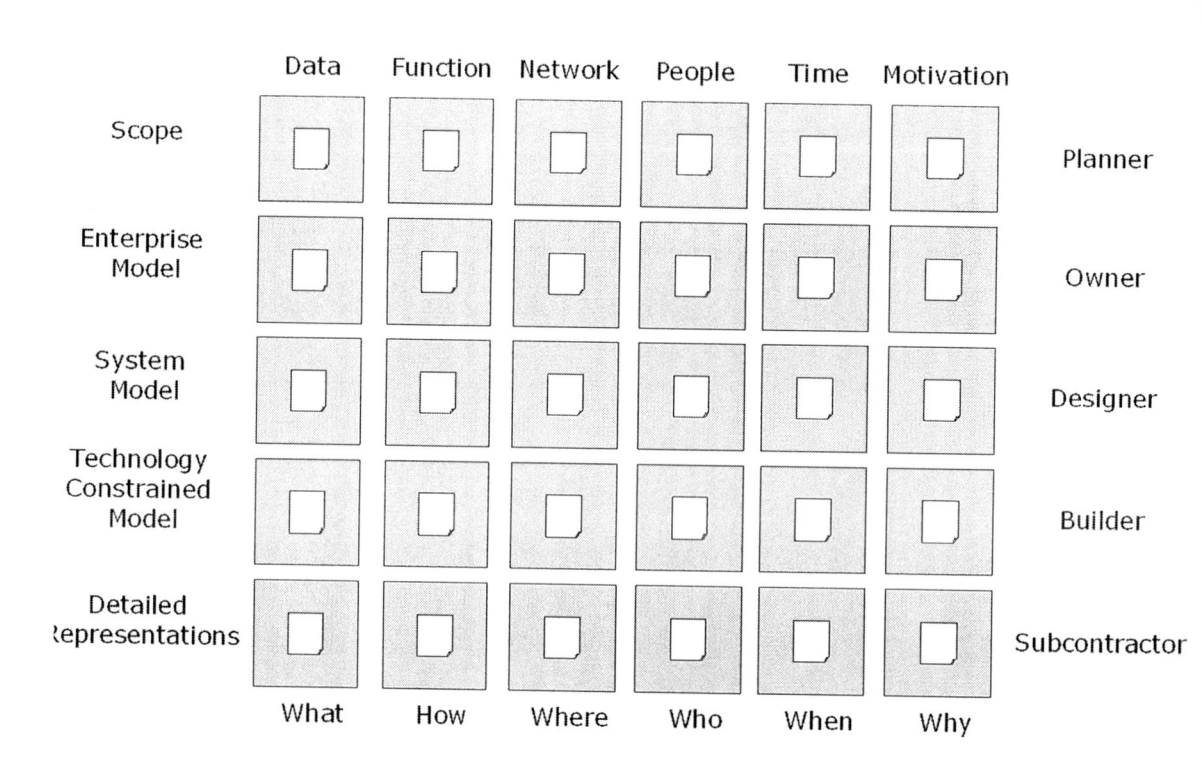

Fig. 9.5 – *Zachman's Framework*

The framework represents a grid showing in each row a particular stake holder's perspective. The two top rows are the business-oriented views (Planner and Owner), the IT views are Designer, Builder and Subcontractor while the bottom row shows the End-user's perspective.

The columns represent the answers to the questions "What?", "How?", "Where?", "Who?", "When?" and "Why?"

As an example let's consider an "employee". When a business user speaks about an employee he might do this in natural language and does not necessarily use the same conceptual model as the designer who might use a UML class diagram to define what an employee means. The developer probably still has another view, for example the table definition in the database schema of the database.

Modeling all aspects in this way allows the alignment of an element from a stake holder's perspective to another stake holder's perspective, serving as a communication and alignment tool for all stakeholders involved.

Business Continuity and Disaster Recovery

Disasters can take many forms. While calamities like terrorism, earthquakes and hurricanes may be infrequent events more common causes of disaster can strike at any time: from power outages over computer viruses to disruption by discontented employees. However, many organizations are not adequately prepared for these events.

According to the *Business Continuity Institute*, a Business Continuity Plan (BCP) is:

"A document containing the recovery timeline methodology, test-validated documentation, procedures, and action instructions developed specifically for use in restoring organization operations in the event of a declared disaster. To be effective, most Business Continuity Plans also require testing, skilled personnel, access to vital records, and alternate recovery resources including facilities."

In plain words, *Business Continuity* is the process of planning to ensure that an organization can survive an event that causes interruption to normal business processes. *Disaster Recovery* is the process that takes place during and after an organizational crisis to minimize business interruption and resume business as quickly as possible.

According to the (US) *National Institute of Standards and Technology (NIST)* the contingency planning for IT systems is a seven-step process:

- *Develop the contingency planning policy statement* - A formal policy provides the authority and guidance necessary to develop an effective contingency plan.
- *Conduct the business impact analysis (BIA)* - The BIA helps to identify and prioritize critical IT systems and components.
- *Identify preventive controls* - Measures taken to reduce the effects of system disruptions can increase system availability and reduce contingency life cycle costs.
- *Develop recovery strategies* - Thorough recovery strategies ensure that the system may be recovered quickly and effectively following a disruption.
- *Develop an IT contingency plan* - The contingency plan should contain detailed guidance and procedures for restoring a damaged system.
- *Plan testing, training, and exercises* - Testing the plan identifies planning gaps, whereas training prepares recovery personnel for plan activation; both activities improve plan effectiveness and overall agency preparedness.
- *Plan maintenance* - The plan should be a living document that is updated regularly to remain current with system enhancements.

Now, let us go quickly over the steps in this process.

Contingency Planning Policy Statement

To be effective, the contingency plan must be based on a clearly defined *policy*. The contingency planning policy statement should define the overall contingency objectives and establish the organizational framework and responsibilities for IT contingency planning. Key policy elements are as follows:

- Scope;
- Roles and responsibilities;
- Resource requirements;
- Training requirements;
- Exercise and testing schedules;
- Planned maintenance schedule;
- Backup policy.

Obviously, the backup policy is an important element of the overall contingency policy. *Backup* is the activity of copying files or databases so that they will be preserved in case of equipment failure or other catastrophe. Most new computer users neglect this essential precaution until the first time they experience a disk crash or accidentally delete the only copy of the file they have been working on for the last six months. Backup should be a routine part of the operation of large and small businesses. The retrieval of files you backed up is called *restoring* them.

"...and for remembering to make a system backup the night before the power failure..."

The first backup should always be a *full backup*. Subsequent backups (until the next full backup) can either be incremental or differential.

For an *incremental backup*, on the first day after the last full backup, only those files, which have changed since the last full backup, are backed up. With subsequent incremental backups, only those files, which have changed since the previous incremental backup, are backed up.

For a *differential backup*, every file that has changed since the last full backup is backed up during every backup. Thus incremental backups are, on average, much faster than differential backups; as fewer files need to be backed up. However, restoring data backed up using incremental backups is much slower, since data from the last full backup plus data from all the incremental backups must be restored. Restoring data backed up in differential mode only requires the last full backup plus the last differential backup.

Furthermore, a distinction can be made between online and offline backup.

An *online backup* takes place with the servers online and available to the users. A file can thus be open and not available for backup. There are applications that can protect open files, but if the file is changed while it is being backed up, the file on tape can be different with the file on disk. Specialized backup software is capable to handle this situation.

For an *offline backup*, the servers have to be taken offline first, making them unavailable to the users for the duration of the backup operation. Typically, these backups take place during the night or in the weekend.

Making a backup takes time; depending on the quantity of data to be backed up and the performance of the backup device the *backup window* can vary from less than an hour to 24 hours. This is of course no problem for an online backup, but for an offline backup this can mean that the system is not always available to the users when they need it. Creating several *backup domains* can solve this problem; these are manageable sub-segments of the production environment, each with a dedicated backup server with one or more tape drives or tape libraries.

Ideally the backup copies should be kept at a different site and in a fire safe. Another possibility is to use the services of specialized companies operating on the Internet; your records, files, and data are compressed and encrypted for a quick trip on the Internet to an *electronic vault*, far away from your own installation.

Business Impact Analysis (BIA)

The BIA is a key step in the contingency planning process. The BIA fully characterizes the system requirements, processes, and interdependencies and uses this information to determine contingency requirements and priorities. The BIA purpose is to correlate specific system components with the critical services that they provide, and based on that information, to characterize the consequences of a disruption to the system components.

First, BIA evaluates the IT system to determine the critical functions performed by the system and identifies the specific system resources required to perform them. Then, the impact(s) on IT operations if a given resource were disrupted or damaged is analyzed.

The Contingency Planning Coordinator should determine the optimum point to recover the IT system by balancing the cost of system inoperability against the cost of resources required for restoring the system.

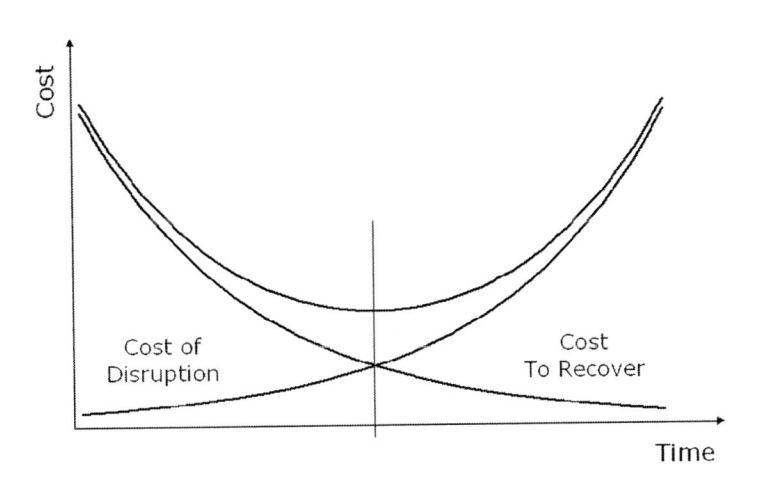

Fig. 9.6 - *Cost Optimization*

The point where the two lines meet will define how long the organization can afford to allow the system to be disrupted.

The impacts and allowable outage times are then used to develop and prioritize recovery strategies For example, if most system components could tolerate a 24-hour outage but some critical component can be unavailable for only 8 hours, the necessary resources for this critical component would be top priority. By prioritizing these recovery strategies, more informed, tailored decisions regarding contingency resource allocations and expenditures, saving time, effort, and costs can be made.

Identify Preventive Controls

In some cases, the outage impacts identified in the BIA may be mitigated or eliminated through preventive measures that deter, detect, and/or reduce impacts to the system. Where feasible and cost-effective, preventive methods are preferable to actions that may be necessary to recover the system after a disruption.

The following aspects need to be considered carefully.

Location and design – in a computer room there is no need for windows; usually, there is nobody inside who wishes to have a look outside and indiscrete eyes should not peek in. Furthermore, windows are weak points for burglars and disturbing elements in the thermal management of the room. Consequently, computer rooms are best situated at the inside of a building, if possible somewhere central, so that the cabling does not get too long. Putting a computer room in a basement is not a good idea either: water tends to flow to the lowest point and damage electronic installations. This water could come from a natural catastrophe or from the fire brigade trying to put out a fire.

Environmental control – temperature in the computer room has to be kept within certain boundaries and so is the case with humidity. The air has to be filtered to remove the dust. It is recommended to have a separate system monitor these conditions (e.g., the temperatures inside the computer cabinets), log the evolutions and give a warning when certain thresholds are exceeded.

Power Supply – a battery powered power supply called *Uninterruptible Power Supply (UPS)* guarantees the availability of power if interruptions in the incoming electrical power. Modern UPSs connect to the computer's network and provide information such as battery time remaining, allowing the systems to shut down gracefully before complete loss of power. For installations that are not allowed to go down, a generator can be installed; the role of the UPS is then to bridge the time gap needed for the generator to start. It is also important that the power supply is conditioned: the voltage has to be kept within certain boundaries and possible surges on the power network have to be effectively suppressed.

Fire Protection – Industry studies show that almost half of the businesses attained by a significant fire never reopen, and another 30% fail within three years; this is a strong argument for the value of good, effective, fire protection. Often, water is the primary tool to control fires. However, even a small fire controlled by a conventional sprinkler system can cause problems in a computer room; most sprinkler systems only activate when temperatures reach a certain level, often after a fire is established and equipment damage can have begun. Furthermore, water based agents are electrically conductive and can damage sensitive equipment. Even with the power off, water discharges often cause equipment problems. Other specialized extinguishing agents, such as foam and dry chemical powders, extinguish most fires but can have a destructive effect on equipment (as a consequence, these type of extinguishers should not even be available in the computer room, in order not to give any ideas to an uninformed volunteer).

Fortunately there are fire protection tools that do protect highly valuable and sensitive areas: the so-called *Clean Agent Fire Suppression Systems*. These systems not only protect an enclosure from fire, they protect the contents as well, including people, documents, and equipment. For many years, fire protection experts have called on Halon 1301 to protect essential property from fire. However, due to concern over potential ozone depletion, the use of Halon has been prohibited in most countries. There are several other excellent clean agents available: INERGEN (a mixture of nitrogen, argon, and carbon dioxide), FM-200 (heptafluoropropane), and FE-13 (trifluoromethane).

Security System – access control (code, smart card or biometry) combined with an intrusion detection system should avoid unauthorized personnel to enter the room. If for some reason a stranger has to be in the room, he has to be accompanied with somebody who does have the proper authorization.

Some other, organizational measures have to be taken:

- A computer room is a non-smoking area!
- Minimize the people traffic in your computer room; allow entrance only to authorized staff (the cleaning staff and the building maintenance people are not!)
- Always locate printers in a separate room to avoid dust contamination, and to reduce traffic in the computer room;
- Never store paper and cardboard boxes beyond what is needed for daily operations inside a computer room. This material is a source of dust, a potential fuel for fires and generates unnecessary people traffic;
- Make cleanliness part of your management program. Cleanliness is critical, and every body in your organization should understand why.

Develop Recovery Strategy

The Recovery Strategy provides a means to restore IT operations quickly and effectively following a service disruption. The strategy should address disruption impacts and allowable outage times identified in the BIA. Several alternatives should be considered when developing the strategy, including cost, allowable outage time, security, and integration with larger, organization-level contingency plans:

- *Do nothing* – This is – of course - the simplest and least expensive option.
- *Have the work done manually* – Some work that is usually performed by the IT system can be taken over by human beings. The problem is that there are probably insufficient staff/skills available;
- *Reciprocal arrangement* - Two organizations agree to provide the service if one fails or has an emergency. This should be supported by an agreement of service levels, stating what service is to be provided, when it can be used and for how long. To keep both sites compatible an agreed change management system should be created;
- *Cold start/fixed centre* – An empty computer room on a fixed site is available.
- *Cold start/portable centre* – A mobile facility with power, environment control, and telecom connections provided;

- *Hot start/external* - A computer room with hardware configured, fully compatible with the organization's needs is available;
- *Hot start/internal* – Using the inherent spare capacity of distributed systems;
- *Mobile Hot Start* – This is a computer room on the back of a truck.

If the IT system is damaged or destroyed or the primary site is unavailable, necessary hardware and software will need to be activated or procured quickly. Three basic strategies exist to prepare for equipment replacement.

- *Vendor Agreements* - SLAs with hardware, software, and support vendors may be made for emergency maintenance service.
- *Equipment Inventory* - Required equipment may be purchased in advance and stored at a warm or mobile site or at another location where they will be stored and then shipped to the alternate site.
- *Existing Compatible Equipment* - Equipment currently housed and used by the hot site or by another organization may be used.

Develop an IT Contingency Plan

The IT Contingency Plan contains detailed roles, responsibilities, teams, and procedures associated with restoring an IT system following a disruption. NIST proposes a plan with five sections:

- Supporting Information
    - Introduction
    - Concept of Operations
- Notification/Activation Phase
    - Notification procedures
    - Damage assessment
    - Plan activation
- Recovery Phase
    - Sequence of recovery activities
    - Recovery procedures
- Reconstitution Phase
    - Restore original site
    - Test systems
    - Terminate operations
- Appendices
    - POC lists
    - System requirements
    - SOPs
    - Vital records

Obviously, this plan should be tailored to the organization and its requirements.

Plan testing, training, and exercises

Testing is a critical element of a viable contingency capability because it enables deficiencies to be identified and addressed.

Training for personnel with contingency plan responsibilities should complement testing, it should be provided at least annually.

Plan maintenance.

Finally, to be effective, the plan must be maintained in a state that accurately reflects system requirements, procedures, organizational structure, and policies. IT systems undergo frequent changes because of shifting business needs, technology upgrades, or new internal or external policies. Therefore, it is essential that the contingency plan be reviewed and updated regularly.

Best Practices

Apply the right procurement process

Many organizations have a *standard procurement* process that is bureaucratic and slow. It was designed for the purchase of systems whose characteristics are well known from the start, which is different for most IT projects. Consequently, this process simply does not work properly for IT procurements. A key element of this process is the production of a large tendering document. Such documents typically have hundreds of requirements that are a mixture of cut-and-paste from previous purchases of completely different systems, new requirements invented by members of the selection committee to prove that they were awake during the dull meetings and requirements that were suggested by the already favored supplier whose sales team has been "helping" key team members "understand the issues." The creation of this document is often a rush job, so that questions frequently overlap or contradict each other (e.g., by wanting products both to be new and to have a large user base). Instead of having a carefully controlled short list, the document is often sent out to far too many suppliers. Eventually, all the responses have to be analyzed and scores assigned. Apart from being a tedious process, this sometimes has unexpected consequences, with an unexpected winner emerging. Corporate politics normally intervene at this point, and the scores or weightings are adjusted to ensure that the unwelcome intruder is ejected. There can also be two or more camps on the team, each preferring different products, and their political influence will be at least as important as the objective scores. In the end, after months of delay and significant cost to both the buyer and the participating vendors, the initially favored product is usually chosen, as could have been predicted on Day One. Obviously, this entire process is expensive; it is a waste of time and often leads to bad purchasing decisions.

A far better process is composed of the following steps:

- Understand the needs of the users;
- Make up a short list of possible vendors;
- See a demonstration and if possible visit references;
- Have the best two vendors make a proof of concept;
- Pick out the vendor with the best business terms, capable of meeting the needs. This is not necessarily the cheapest one.

In conclusion, the purchase process should concentrate on the business needs, not the supposed product features required to satisfy them.

Build a balanced portfolio of IT projects

Organizations and executives need to look more holistically at IT and treat it as a portfolio rather than an independent series of projects. Within the IT portfolio a balance must be found between the three areas where IT adds value to the organization: efficiency, effectiveness and innovation. Also, depending on the focus different metrics have to be used:

- When efficiency is at stake metrics like TCO, ROI, NPV, IRR, and Payback Period will be used;
- Project aiming at an improvement of the effectiveness of the organization will be measured using Economic Value Added, Activity Based Costing, cycle times and customer satisfaction;
- Finally, when innovating for strategic advantage elements such as market share and industry concentration will be measured.

By doing so, management can vary its approach to sponsorship and define its value expectations depending on the type of project.

The portfolio approach stresses balance and that includes balancing the sponsorship of initiatives controlled by the IT organization and those under the authority of the business units. For example, infrastructure projects fall in the "efficiency" category and lend themselves well to be managed centrally. Each business unit has similar needs in this area and the organization can enjoy the benefits of scale and standardization. On the other hand, applications such as CRM, which typically fall in the "effectiveness" or "innovation" categories may better be chosen and run by business units.

Create an "IT-friendly" environment

Here is where the marketing function of the IT manager comes in the game. The business benefits brought by IT have to be shown, as well to the top management as to the rest of the organization. Having a corner of the organization's intranet site reserved for IT related topics can be a good idea. Also, sending out on a regular basis an "IT newsletter" can promote your business. Openness and transparency are equally important in this context and the use of external consultants can be advisable because, after all, people have a tendency to pay more attention to the opinion of an external expert than the words of its own people, even if both say the same.

Concentrate on the core business

Every organization has what is commonly called a *core business*. This is what the organization is all about, its reason to be. For a commercial organization this will be selling things, a school or a university will concentrate on teaching and a hospital has to take care of its patients. In reality not all resources are devoted directly to this core business; an important part has a more supportive role. Take for example a hospital. The medical staff, doctors and nurses, executes the core business but a lot of people are occupied with patient administration, building maintenance, catering, laundry and all kinds of other activities that are needed to make the hospital run. This is a good case to show that often the resources spent on support activities exceed the operational resources, but also that there is ratio between operational and supporting resources: all other factors remaining unchanged doubling the medical staff will double the capacity of the hospital which will be reflected by a doubling of the needs for administration, maintenance, catering etc. This example can be somewhat oversimplified, however, it makes it obvious that one should concentrate on the efficiency of the core activities and that the rest will follow automatically.

Valuable resources should not be wasted on secondary things. The IT support therefore should be focused on the things that really count for the organization. Do not spend any time and effort on the development and deployment of a HR system, if you can use the services of an ASP. Do not host your own web site if it is not a vital part of your e-business strategy but let an ISP take care of that.

An IT strategy must define what really matters for the organization and spend the resources on those important things. Rather than spreading people and money thinly across too many activities one should concentrate on doing a few things well.

Do not confuse hypes with trends

Just because a technology, product or new version of an existing product is available does not mean it has to be deployed. The only reason for deploying an IT system is to meet a real need. There must be a demonstrable improvement over the pre-deployment situation; if possible the users themselves should even demonstrate this, not IT.

Because of the tremendous speed at which technology is evolving it is simply impossible to have all the different Information Systems over the different layers all at the same technological level. There will always be several technological generations living together in the same environment.

Gartner proposed a model to warn anyone not to fall into a common thought pattern: follow the latest technological development; they called it the *Hype Curve*.

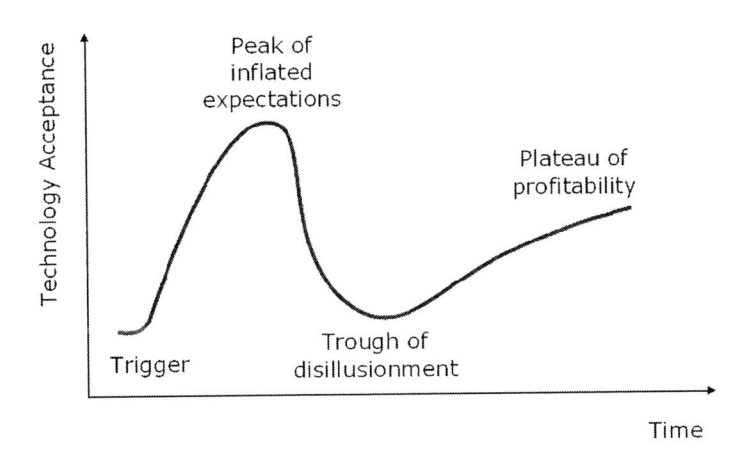

Fig. 9.7 – *Gartner Hype Curve*

Newly introduced technology usually follows this curve of being way over-hyped initially, driving it to the *Peak of Inflated Expectations*. Then, when it cannot possibly live up to that hype, critics jump on the immature technology with predictions of doom and gloom as it falls into the *Trough of Disillusionment*. Eventually, as the technology matures, more realistic expectations and clearer minds prevail as it climbs up the *Slope of Enlightenment*. As they figure out how to best use the new technology, it reaches the *Plateau of Productivity*. In general, it was not as good as was first said, and it is not as bad as the critics think.

An equally interesting model in this respect is the *Boston IT model*, derived from a model that was developed by the Boston Consulting Group.

In this model, a relation is made between the innovative status of a technology and its economical status. The typical lifecycle of a technology is shown by the curve; it starts high for innovative status and low for economical status, goes to a high economical status and a medium innovative status to end in a low position for both economical and innovative status.

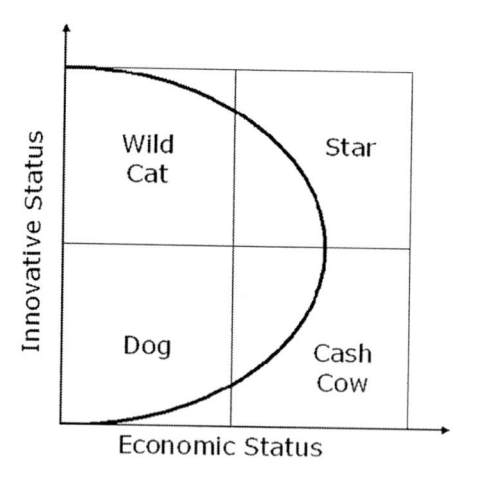

Fig. 9.8 – *Boston/IT model*

Four different zones in which a technology can be at a given moment are distinguished:

- *Wild Cat - Invest*. The technology is new and a possible introduction in the IT portfolio will have to be duly justified by a business-case. There is no guarantee for a return on investment;
- *Star – Implement*. The time has come to create new systems in this technology. The organization invests in new IT systems while the IT department invests in the construction of know-how and experience;
- *Cash Cow – Productivity*. The proven technology gives a maximal price/performance ratio. The IT department is optimally equipped for the implementation of new systems;
- *Dog – Phase out*. As the technology has become obsolete its economical status comes under pressure. High costs of IT are often situated in this phase so the best approach is to phase out these systems as fast as possible.

Have a written policy concerning the use of IT in your organization

Laws differ from state to state, from country to country and from region to region. Consequently, it is only possible to outline some general principles that will have to be adapted to the legal situation and that can have to be revised as technology changes. As a minimum, organizations should have in place a *written policy* that all employees who have access to internal or external email, Internet or similar communications systems have to acknowledge.

This policy should contain at least the following elements:

- A clear statement of what is considered to be *acceptable and unacceptable* use of your IT systems;
- Define who is *responsible* for administering and maintaining the systems.
- Protection of the *intellectual property* rights, both of external suppliers and of your own organization;
- Make clear that all the hardware, software and stored information is the *property of the employer* and is provided to the employees only for performing their job duties;
- Inform the employees about *monitoring activities* that are carried out in the context of system maintenance and security.

Know your Business

It can seem obvious, but the IT strategy of an organization, should take into account what kind of business the organization is managing. A bricks and mortar company will have to be handled differently than a high tech company. A competitive telecom operator which is commercialising new services every other month will have to be organized differently from a wholesale distributor of consumer goods, whose business is rather stable in time. Also, a small or medium sized company will have other IT needs than a multinational with tens of thousands of employees scattered all around the globe. The small company can only be interested in the basic services that can be offered by software applications (i.e., personal productivity tools), while a multinational will most certainly be interested in things like data warehousing, data mining and other sophisticated tools. The CIO or IT Manager should be aware of this and take it into account in his strategy.

What are the expectations? This will probably depend on the history of the organization. If there is a past of successful and high added value IT projects, these expectations can be high, even maybe too high. It is the role of the CIO/IT Manager to make the expectations realistic: it is better to aim a bit lower than to have to admit that you could not make the dreams come true. On the other hand, when there have been a lot of failed IT projects in the past, it can be a good idea to be modest, to create some credibility by making a couple of small projects work out well.

Protect Your Customers' Privacy.

Your customers are legitimately concerned about the protection and privacy of their information. That is why E-commerce sites must have privacy policies that are available on the site. From a legal point of view, regional differences occur, however, several commonly accepted principles could be observed:

- Personal information should only be stored or preserved for a *well-defined purpose*; irrelevant information should not be kept;
- Customers have to be *informed* about the fact that information is stored;
- Customer information should *not be communicated to third parties*;
- Customers have the *right to know* which information is stored and, if necessary to require corrections;
- In most countries it is prohibited to store information about *race, religion, political conviction or sexual preferences*;
- As a rule, *medical information* should only be accessible by users of a medical profession;
- *Historical and logging information* should only be kept for a limited period of time, statistical information should be made anonymous;
- The necessary measures have to be taken to guarantee the *quality* of the stored information;
- There has to be a *reliable backup* of the information;
- The access to the information has to be organized on a *need-to-know* basis.

Reduce complexity

The complexity of an IT environment is hard to determine in absolute terms. However, much like it is possible to measure the difference between two temperatures it is possible to compare complex and not so complex without having an absolute reference to measure up to. There are three factors that determine the complexity of an environment:

- The number of different elements that are interrelated;
- The number of different relations between the elements;
- The way in which the relations can change.

With these factors in mind it is possible to determine the contribution to complexity of any change to a system: adding a new element will result in new relations and possibly existing relations that are altered.

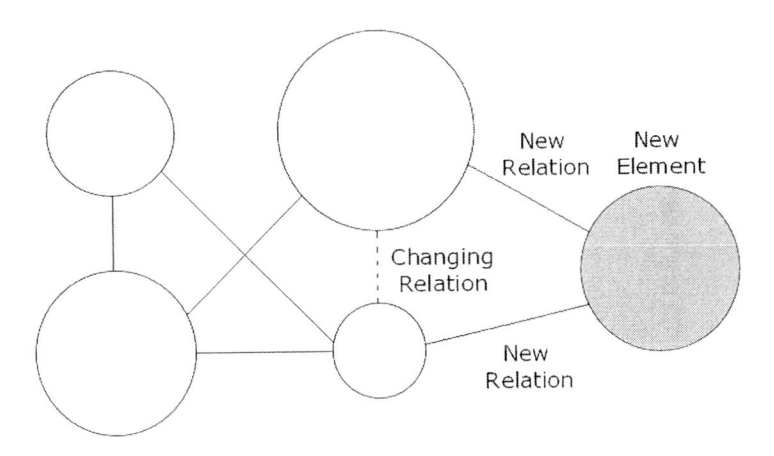

Fig. 9.9 - *Complexity*

One consequence of an increased complexity is a reduced agility. There are indeed more interfaces and functional dependencies to be considered and this costs a lot of extra design, build and testing effort. The conclusion is that, for an organization that depends heavily on IT, control and reduction of complexity of the IT environment is a critical success factor. Obviously, complexity can be reduced by limiting the number of elements, the number of relations and the changes in relations. In practice that means choosing for bigger elements with fewer interfaces, standardization, centralization and integration.

Select your suppliers carefully

The IT marketplace is a dynamic one. Companies are born and disappear, there are mergers and acquisitions and the marketing strategies change. All this has an important impact on the products these companies are trying to sell you: older versions are no longer supported, complete product lines disappear, the know-how of the support department gets lost etc. You, as a client of these companies, are dependent and vulnerable, so you cannot afford to select products without any kind of guarantee that they will be supported in the future or that the product or the vendor will survive.

An interesting model in this respect is Gartner's *Magic Quadrant*. This is a two-dimensional framework that places vendors from a technology industry sector into a strategic matrix.

Gartner Group analysts use multiple criteria to evaluate individual vendors, presented on two axes:

- *Completeness of vision (x-axis).* Measures the depth and breadth of a vendor's goals, its knowledge of the markets and customers it serves, and how it is positioned to address future industry scenarios;
- *Ability to execute (y-axis).* Measures the ability of the vendor to execute its vision. Focuses on the firm's management team and financial stability; sales channels; quality of research and development; its installed product base in the market; its service and support reputation; and its track record in delivering products on time.

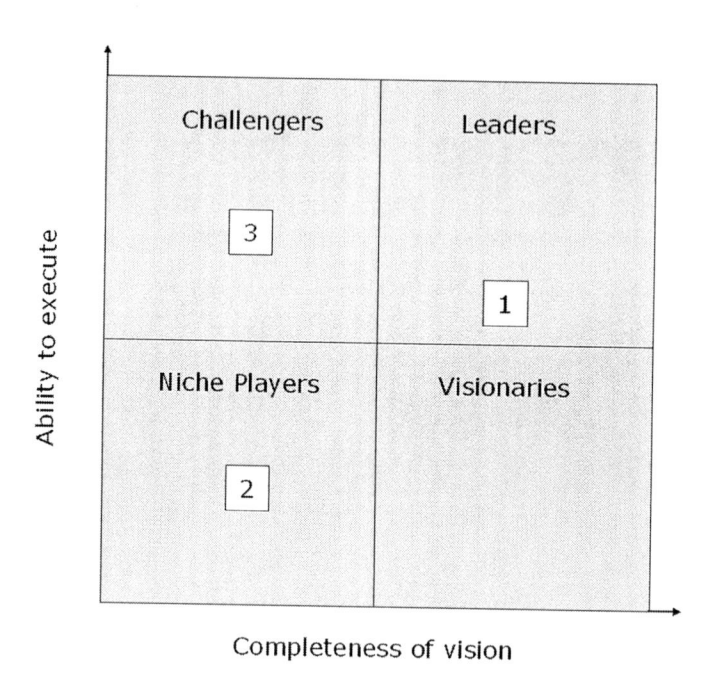

Fig. 9.10 – *Gartner's Magic Quadrant*

In viewing the graphic of the Magic Quadrant, Vendor 1 is positioned in the Leader quadrant, but not high in this quadrant. This can mean that Vendor 1's vision is not as strong as another Leader's vision or what Gartner views a true Leader's vision should be, and its ability to execute on this vision is not as complete as another Leader's or what Gartner views a true Leader's ability should be. Vendors 2 and 3 are in the centre of their respective quadrants, showing that the metrics that apply to each quadrant positions them squarely in the middle of the pack.

Set up a knowledge management strategy

"To conceive of knowledge as a collection of information seems to rob the concept of all of its life... Knowledge resides in the user and not in the collection. It is how the user reacts to a collection of information that matters."

(C.W. Churchman)

Many organizations are beginning to understand that *knowledge* is one of their most valuable assets, yet few have begun to actively manage this asset. *Corporate Knowledge* is the collective body of experience and understanding of an organization's processes for managing both planned and unplanned situations. There are many thoughtful and interesting reflections on knowledge; however, Michael Polanyi [63] was the first to make the distinction between explicit knowledge and tacit knowledge. *Explicit knowledge*, sometimes called *formal knowledge*, can be expressed in language and transmitted among individuals, while *tacit knowledge* (or *informal knowledge*) is personal knowledge embedded in individual experience and involving personal belief, perspective, and values. One could also distinguish a *hierarchy of knowledge*, based on how the rules are followed:

- *Skill* is the ability to act according to rules. The actor himself can judge whether the action has been successful or not. Skills could be the ability to chop wood or work with a text processor;
- *Know-how* includes skill and is the ability to act in social contexts. Other actors, like a professional institution or tradition establish the rules. Know-how also implies problem solving;
- *Expertise* is know-how complemented with the ability of reflection. Expertise implies the ability of know-how within a certain domain and the ability to influence the rules of the domain or the tradition. Expertise is thus not a property but a relation between actors and a social system of rules.

Knowledge Management (KM) is the collection of processes that govern the creation, dissemination, and utilization of knowledge [53]. These processes exist whether we acknowledge them or not and they have a profound effect on the decisions we make and the actions we take. It thus makes sense to recognize and understand these processes and, where possible, take steps to improve their quality and in turn improve the quality of those actions and decisions for which we are responsible.

State the alignment with strategies and objectives

Don't assume that every senior manager will relate IT proposals with the organizational strategies and objectives; you should make the explicit links when you present your plans. In some cases there will be no direct link, but still your proposal is important – tell them why.

State the benefits of your IT projects in clear, quantified business terms explaining what the outcome in efficiency, effectiveness and innovation will be.

Demonstrate that that the IT department is as professional in its management practices as the other departments.

Support the internal communication processes

"You can have brilliant ideas, but if you can't get them across, your ideas won't get you anywhere."

(Lee Iacocca)

Most organizations understand the importance of strategic communication with their customers and stakeholders; therefore they have marketing and communication specialists that make up and create communication plans for external use. Frequently, these communication methodologies for communicating with customers and the public are even included in strategic planning.

Few organizations, however, address *internal communication* in the same way. Determining <u>what</u> should be communicated to staff, <u>when</u> it should be communicated, and <u>how</u> it should be communicated is often treated on an ad hoc and reactive basis. Often, internal communication is organized around commotions like major organization changes, layoffs and downsizing. However, once the starting focus has been done away with, communication tends to go back to an unorganized and incoherent process.

It is known that some of the most successful organizations create a common culture yielding a work force that understands the mission, goals, values and procedures of the organization. The intent is not to dominate or control employees, but to direct them towards a set of common goals on which they can act eday. This brings coherence to the workplace, and allows better-coordinated action. By having staff that understands the basic values and purposes of the organization, people have the opportunity to make decisions that fall within those parameters. That means, for example, that more decisions can be made at the line level, which improves both efficiency and effectiveness.

Organizations that use their common culture as a strategic advantage create that culture through strategic, coordinated communication policies; they use multiple methods, consistently. Their training supports their cultural goals, as does their written communication. Their management communicates consistently with common messages in several forums and management behavior is consistent with the messages transmitted via other communication channels.

Obviously, the IT department has an important role to play in the processes of internal communication; as a provider of the transport mechanisms for the information but also as the faithful executor of the projects that fit in the strategic framework set by the top of the organization.

Online Resources

Balanced IT scorecard - http://www.esi.es/Projects/Metrics/Deliverables/bits.html
Balanced Scorecards - http://www.balancedscorecard.com
Balanced Scorecards – http://www.balancedscorecard.org
Business Continuity – http://www.thebci.org
Business Continuity – http://www.gcplc.com
Business Continuity – http://www.csrc.nist.gov/publications/nistpubs/800-34/sp800-34.pdf
Disaster Recovery – http://www.drj.com
E-commerce - http://www.commerce.gov
E-commerce - http://www.verisign.com
Enterprise Architecture - http://www.cs.vu.nl/~daan/arch/publ.htm
Enterprise Architecture - http://www.brint.com/papers/enterarch.htm
Fire Protection - http://www.fssa.net
Knowledge Management - http://www.bestpracticedatabase.com
Knowledge Management - http://www.brint.com/km/
Knowledge Management - http://www.kmworld.com
Knowledge Management - http://www.knowledgeassociates.com
Knowledge Management - http://www.knowledgeresearch.com
Strategic Alignment - http://www.strategic-alignment.com
Strategic Alignment - http://hsb.baylor.edu/ramsower/acis/papers/papp.htm
Zachman's Framework - http://www.istis.unomaha.edu/isqa/vanvliet/arch/isa/isa.htm

Further Reading

[180] Akdeniz, Y., Walker, C., and Wall, D.S., *The Internet, Law and Society*, 2001.

[181] Boar, B. *Strategic Thinking for Information Technology*, Wiley, New York, 1997.

[182] Boynton, A., Victor, B. and Pine, B., *Aligning IT With New Competitive Strategies, Competing in the Information Age*, Luftman, New York, Oxford University Press. 1996.

[183] Carr, N. *IT doesn't matter.* Harvard Business School Press; May 1, 2003.

[184] European Commission, *A European Initiative on Electronic Commerce*, (COM(97) 157).

[185] European Commission, *Globalisation and the Information Society, the Need for Strengthened International Co-ordination*, (COM(98) 50).

[186] Henderson, J., & Venkatraman, N. *Aligning Business and IT Strategies, Competing in the Information Age*, Luftman, New York, Oxford University Press. 1996.

[187] Keen, P., *Do You Need An IT Strategy? Competing in the Information Age*, Luftman, New York, Oxford University Press. 1996.

[188] Luftman, J. *Competing in the Information Age: Practical Applications of the Strategic Alignment Model*, New York: Oxford University Press. 1996.

[189] Papp R., *Strategic Information Technology: Opportunities for Competitive Advantage*, Idea Group Publishing

[190] Parker, M., *Strategic transformation and information technology*, Prentice Hall, Upper Saddle River (NJ), 1996.

[191] Smith, H., Fingar, P. IT doesn't matter, business processes do. Meghan Kiffer Pr. August 2003.

10

Beyond the Hype

"Advanced technology does not produce wisdom; it does not change human nature; it does not make our problems go away. But, it does and will speed us on our journey toward more human freedom"

(W.B. Wriston)

The future and IT

By considering the development of Information Technology within organizations in the past, it is possible to reflect about the importance of IT for the future. Although there can be differences in the speed with which various organizations, different industries and disparate regions of the world adopt a given new technology; IT has increasingly penetrated the heart of organizations and will continue to do so in the future.

In the 1970s, IT was only a means of mechanization. Organizations developed their "bread and butter" systems, and bookkeeping and payroll administration were the common applications for IT.

In the 1980s, organizations became aware of the need to integrate their applications. For example, the different definitions of "employee" as the term relates to data in separately developed applications for payroll and in human resources administration, where the term has a more widely defined use, caused problems, giving rise to the need for integration of payroll and human resources systems.

"Under our new plan we'll no longer sell products, have customers, or sit at desks. Money will simply appear in the mail while we go fishing."

In the 1990s, organizations realized that IT was a means for drastic improvement of their business processes. *Business Process Redesign* became the new buzzword, characterizing the strong impact of IT on organizational design. The theory of the *New Economy* held that computers and the Internet have so enhanced the prospects for higher profits that people could spend lavishly. The consumption boom inspired a boom in corporate investment, which was fed by flush profits, high stock prices and the promise of new technology [194][195][203][204].

At the end of the twentieth century, however, the New Economy got old. In the United States alone, hundreds of dotcom firms shut down, and the belief that Information Technology was going to lead to durable economic growth and low inflation was one of the first victims of the dotcom crash.

Nevertheless, it would be a mistake to neglect the lasting changes that have been introduced by the IT revolution. Indeed, the promise of new technology was not entirely false, and up to a point the theory of the New Economy works. Productivity is the term economists use for efficiency, and from 1980 to 1995, productivity (output per worker hour) in private business rose by an average of 1.5 percent annually. From 1995 to 2000, it rose by about three percent, which suggests that many productivity gains clearly flowed from technology, and there is no reason to believe that this will not continue.

According to the *United Nations Conference on Trade and Development (UNCTAD)* [204], the IT revolution will not be different from the previous technological revolutions that had such fundamental consequences for the economy. The steam engine, railroads and the industrial application of electricity resulted in the end of entire economic sectors, but they also enabled organizations to work differently and more efficiently. The consequences were higher productivity and an improvement in the quality of life. However, it took several decades before these changes affected the economy as a whole. UNCTAD believes that the recent acceleration of productivity in the United States is of a structural and lasting nature and that this increase is due to the changes that have been introduced by Information Technology and the Internet. This organization also believes that these technologies will continue to support the improvement of productivity. The cost of computer capacity will continue to drop dramatically for some time. In fact, most companies are still learning to organize themselves to take the greatest advantage of IT and the Internet. Even if the growth in the US were to slow down, there is a lot of ground to be caught up by the rest of the world. In short, productivity worldwide can still grow dramatically as the enterprises in the other developed countries and the countries in development become active in e-business.

When we have a look at the list of victims and survivors of the dotcom crisis, clearly, the importance of IT is not so much the growth of its share of the total economy but in the changes that are introduced into the organizations that use and assimilate IT. Technological revolutions have always had different effects on different segments of the economy. Railroads enabled the creation of national markets in both Europe and the United States, but one cannot say that they affected the financial sector. The application of electricity changed industrial production processes dramatically but had almost no effect on agriculture or retailing. In the same way, Information Technology will have an even bigger effect on the economy overall in as much as it can be applied to most aspects of production, distribution and consumption. Also, as opposed to the previous technological revolutions, IT can improve productivity in the creation of new services.

Today, IT increasingly affects systems, skills, structure and staff, and even the shared values of our organizations. Undoubtedly, in the coming decades, the use of Information Technology will prove to be a strategic dimension of business development and will drastically impact the style of management.

It is still too soon to make a reliable evaluation of the changes that our economies will go through. However, and a comparison with electricity can illustrate this fact: the penetration of IT in the most developed countries (expressed in number of PCs per hundred people) today is close to the share of electricity in the total energy consumption of American industry around 1920: some 50 percent. Imagine the effects of a higher penetration of IT in all sectors of the economy worldwide, a penetration comparable to the penetration of electricity at present, and you get an idea of the scope of the changes that IT will give rise to in the future.

Undoubtedly, the conclusion is that we are in the early stages of an historic transition from mass-production to agile production, from single-company operations to Web Enterprises and from the Industrial Age with capital, raw materials, land and labor as the primary economic resources to the Information Age with information and knowledge as the primary economic resources.

Online Resources

History of computing - http://www.computer.org/history/
History of computing - http://www.elsop.com/wrc/h_comput.htm
SETI Institute – http://www.seti.org
The Extropy Site – http://www.extropy.org
UNCTAD – http://www.unctad.org

Further Reading

[192] Dyson, E., *Release 2.0. A design for living in the digital age*, Broadway Books, 1997.

[193] Philip Evans, Ph., Wurster, S.T., *Blown to Bits: How the New Economics of Information Transforms Strategy* Harvard Business School Press.

[194] Gates, W. Hemingway C. *Business @ the Speed of Thought: Succeeding in the Digital Economy,* Warner Business Books.

[195] Gates, W., *The Road Ahead*, Viking Penguin, 1995.

[196] Hagel, J., Armstrong, A.G., *Net Gain: Expanding Markets Through Virtual Communities.* Harvard Business School Press.

[197] Kaplan, P.J., *F'd Companies: Spectacular Dot-Com Flameouts.* 2000.

[198] Kurtzweil, R., *The age of spiritual machines*, New York: Viking Penguin, 1999.

[199] Naughton, J., *A Brief History of the Future: The Origins of the Internet*, London: Weidenfeld & Nicolson, 1999.

[200] Negroponte, N.P., *Being Digital*, Vintage Books, 1995.

[201] Shapiro, P. And Varian, H. R. *Information Rules: a strategic guide to the network economy.* Boston: Harvard Business School Press. 1999.

[202] Toffler, A., *The Third Wave: The Classic Study of Tomorrow*, Bantam Books, 1980.

[203] Toffler, A., *Future Shock*, Bantam Books, New York, 1970.

[204] UNCTAD, *E-commerce ande Development Report 2001*

Glossary

ABB - Activity Based Budgeting. Preparation of cost budgets using *Activity Based Budgeting (ABC)* to help estimate workload and resource requirements.

ABC - Activity Based Costing. An accounting method used to identify and describe cost objects and the activities they consume, and the amount of resources the activities consume.

ADSL - Asymmetric Digital Subscriber Line. A digital phone-line technology that supports high-speed connections to the Internet using ordinary telephone lines.

AGP - Accelerated Graphics Port. A bus specification by Intel that gives low-cost graphics cards faster access to main memory on personal computers than the usual *Personal Computer Interface (PCI)* bus.

AI - Artificial Intelligence. The branch of computer science concerned with making computers behave like humans. Artificial intelligence includes games playing, expert systems, natural language, neural networks and robotics [Webopedia].

AIT - Advanced Intelligent Tape. A magnetic tape and drive specification developed by SONY for storing large amounts of data. AIT features high-speed file access, long head and media life.

ALU - Arithmetic and Logic Unit. The part of the CPU that executes the mathematical and logical operations.

ANSI - American National Standards Institute. This organization maintains commercial standards for a variety of industries.

ANSI X12 - A numbered set of commercial *Electronic Data Interchange (EDI)* transactions defined by the American National Standards Institute's Accredited Standards Committee X12. These uniform rules for the interchange of business documents are defined for cross industry EDI use and are based on the variable-length X12 standard.

Glossary

API - Application Programming Interface. The calling conventions by which an application program accesses common services.

Application - A functional system made up of software that performs some useful task.

ARP - Address Resolution Protocol. The protocol that translates *Internet Protocol (IP)* addresses into physical network addresses. ARP is a key player in the process that allows a packet of data addressed to a particular Internet host to find its destination.

ARPANET - A pioneering wide area network funded by DARPA. It became operational in 1968 and served as the basis for early networking research, as well as a central backbone during the development of the Internet.

ASCII - American Standard Code for Information Interchange. A coding convention that almost all computers understand. Each letter is assigned a numeric value that will fit in eight digits of binary notation. For example "a" is 97 in ASCII, and "A" is 65. All the numeric digits, and punctuation marks also have numeric values in ASCII.

ASP – (1) Application Service Provider. Provider of a contractual service offering to deploy, host, manage and rent access to an application from a centrally managed facility (definition by IDC). (2) Active Server Pages. A technique developed by Microsoft to embed active program code into HTML web pages.

Assembler - A computer program that translates programs expressed in assembly language into their machine language equivalents. [IEEE Std 610.12-1990].

Asynchronous - A communications mode where one character is sent at a time, which is surrounded by a start bit and a stop bit and sometimes a parity bit. There is a time interval between characters.

ATM - Asynchronous Transfer Mode. A high-bandwidth, controlled-delay fixed size packet switching and transmission system.

Authentication - A procedure, which verifies that the data sent to a receiver, is authentic, and has not been tampered with during its transmission.

Availability - Ability of a component or service to perform its required function at a stated instant or over a stated period of time. It is usually expressed as the availability ratio, i.e., the proportion of time that the service is actually available for use by the Customers within the agreed service hours [ITIL].

B2B – Business-to-Business. Electronic commerce between businesses, as opposed to between a business and its customers (B2C).

B2C – Business-to-Consumer or Business-to-Customer. Electronic commerce between a business and its customers or consumers.

Bandwidth - The measure of the capacity of a telecommunications channel to carry data.

Benchmarking - (1) Measuring the performance of computers using standard programs, which can be run on different computers. A benchmark attempts to show the overall power of a system by including a "typical" mixture of programs or it can attempt to measure more specific aspects of performance, like graphics, I/O or computation. (2) Comparing the performance of DBMSs. (3) Measured, "best-in-class" achievement, a reference or measurement standard for comparison, this performance level is recognized as the standard of excellence for a specific business process [APQC].

Best Practice - A policy, procedure, process, technique, tool or methodology that, through experience and research, has proven to reliably lead to a desired result.

Biometry - Automated methods of verifying or recognizing the identity of a living person based on a physiological or behavioral characteristic.

BITS – Balanced IT Scorecard. The ESI Balanced IT Scorecard is an instrument for quantitatively monitoring the technical and business performance of a *Software Producing Unit (SPU)*. This Generic model provides an understanding of the most important goals for excellent business performance of a SPU, how to measure it and what are the drivers helping to achieve these goals [ESI].

BLOB - Binary Large Object. A large block of data stored in a database, such as an image or sound file. A BLOB has no structure that can be interpreted by the database management system but is known only by its size and location.

Bluetooth – A Wireless LAN specification that describes how mobile phones, computers, and PDAs can interconnect with each other and with other devices.

Bootstrap - A short computer program that is permanently resident or easily loaded into a computer and whose execution brings a larger program, such as an Operating System or its loader, into memory. [IEEE Std 610.12-1990].

BMP - Graphical file format, used on the Windows platform only. The BMP format stores image data from bottom to top and pixels in blue/green/red order. Compression of BMP files is not supported, so they are usually large. File extension is ."bmp."

BPR - Business Process Redesign. Completely redesigning or reengineering a process to achieve a new, much higher standard of performance. Also known as Business Process Reengineering.

Browser - A program which allows a person to read hypertext. The browser gives a means of viewing the contents of *Hypertext Markup Language (HTML)* pages and of navigating from one page to another.

BSC - Balanced Scorecard. An aid to organizational performance management. It helps to focus, not only on the financial targets but also on the internal processes, customers and learning and growth issues [ITIL].

BTP – Business Transaction Protocol. An XML-based protocol being developed by the *Organization for the Advancement of Structured Information Standards (OASIS)* as a standardized Internet-based means of managing complex, *Business-to-Business (B2B)* transactions. The protocol is intended to be especially useful in a Web services environment. BTP can be run on top of any transport technology, such as the *Simple Object Access Protocol (SOAP)* or the *Electronic Business XML (ebXML)* project.

Business Process - A group of business activities within an organization that enables that organization to successfully deliver its products and services. A business process rarely operates in isolation, i.e., other business processes will depend on it and it will depend itself on other processes.

Business Strategy - **The match an organization makes between its internal resources and skills and the opportunities and risks created by its external environment.**

CA - Certification Authority. An organization that issues digital certificates to other organizations or individuals thus allowing them to prove their identity to others. Also known as "Trusted Third Party."

CAD/CAM - Computer Aided Design/Computer Aided Manufacturing.

CardBus - PC Card standard. The 32-bit version of the PCMCIA bus.

CASE - The use of computers to aid in the software engineering process. Can include the application of software tools to software design, requirements tracing, code production, testing, document generation, and other software engineering activities [IEEE Std 610.12-1990].

CCD - Charge-Coupled Device. A semiconductor technology used for light-sensitive electronic devices such as cameras and image scanners. Each CCD chip consists of an array of light-sensitive photocells that are sensitized by giving an electrical charge before exposure.

CCITT – Comité Consultatif International de Télégraphie et Téléphonie. (International consultative committee on telecommunications and telegraphy). CCITT changed its name to ITU-T in 1993.

CDDI - Copper Distributed Data Interface. CDDI is the implementation of the *Fiber Distributed Data Interface (FDDI)* protocols over twisted-pair copper wire.

CD-R - Recordable Compact Disk.

CD-ROM – Compact Disk Read Only Memory.

CD-RW - Rewritable Compact Disk.

CEO - Chief Executive Officer. The person responsible for setting the organizational strategy. He reports to the board and often also is a member of it, or even the chairperson.

CGI - Common Gateway Interface. A means for transferring information that users have typed into forms found on Web pages to scripts or programs run on a Web server, and vice versa. The most popular language for writing CGI programs is PERL.

CI – Configuration Item. Component of an infrastructure - or an item, such as a Request for Change, associated with an infrastructure - that is under the control of Configuration Management. CIs can vary widely in complexity, size and type, from an entire system (including all hardware, software and documentation) to a single module or a minor hardware component [ITIL].

CIO - Chief Information Officer. When IT is part of, or close to the core business of the organization, this is reflected by the presence of a representative in the highest decision organs of the organization. The CIO is in charge of both technology managers and business managers.

CISC - Complex Instruction Set Computer. A processor where each instruction can perform several low-level operations such as memory access, arithmetic operations or address calculations. Opposite of *Reduced Instruction Set Computer (RISC)*.

Class - An implementation of an abstract data type. A definition of the data structures, methods and interfaces of software objects. A template for the instantiation (creation) of software objects [ESI].

Client – (1) The economic buyer of the results of a business activity. (2) An element that requests a service from another element.

CLR - Common Language Runtime. The environment in which .NET applications that have been compiled to a common language, the *Microsoft Intermediate Language (MSIL),* are executed.

Cluster - The close connection of several systems to form a group using the appropriate software.

CMDB – Configuration Management Database. A database that contains all relevant details of each *Configuration Item (CI)* and details of the important relationships between CIs [ITIL].

CMM - Capability Maturity Model. This describes the principles and practices underlying software-process maturity and is intended to help organizations improve the maturity of their software processes through an evolutionary path from ad hoc, chaotic to mature, disciplined. It can also be used by an organization's customers to identify the strengths, weaknesses, and risks associated with their software suppliers. Authorized appraisers must go through both CMM and appraisal training [Mark Paulk].

COCOMO - Constructive Cost Model. A method for evaluating the cost of a software development proposed by Dr Barry Boehm. There are several different types that can be used under different distances.

Code - In software engineering, computer instructions and data definitions expressed in a programming language or in a form output by an assembler, compiler, or other translator [IEEE Std 610.12-1990].

COM – Component Object Model. A software architecture Microsoft, allowing interoperation between ObjectBroker and OLE. Evolved into *Distributed Component Object Model (DCOM)*.

Commercial Software - Software that is being developed by a business that aims to make money from the use of the software.

Complexity - (1) (Apparent) the degree to which a system or component has a design or implementation that is difficult to understand and verify [IEEE]. (2) (Inherent) the degree of complication of a system or system component, determined by such factors as the number and intricacy of interfaces, the number and intricacy of conditional branches, the degree of nesting, and the types of data structures [Evans].

Contingency Planning - Planning to address unwanted occurrences that can happen at a later time. Traditionally, the term has been used to refer to planning for the recovery of IT systems rather than entire business processes [ITIL].

Contracting or Targeted Outsourcing - This is the most common form of outsourcing. It involves the contracting out of parts of projects or sub-functions.

COO – Chief Operating Officer. The COO is next in line for the *Chief Executive Officer (CEO)*. Normally the CEO is responsible for managing the relationship with external stakeholders while the COO is primarily responsible for managing the internal operations.

Copylefted software - Copylefted software is free software whose distribution terms do not let redistributors add any additional restrictions when they redistribute or modify the software. This means that every copy of the software, even if it has been modified, must be free software [GNU].

CORBA - Common Object Request Broker Architecture. An *Object Management Group (OMG)* specification, which provides the standard interface definition between OMG-compliant objects.

CPU – (1) Central Processing Unit. The part of a computer, which controls all the other parts. (2) Occasionally used to refer to the system unit of a PC.

CRM - Customer Relationship Management. Enterprise-wide software applications that allow companies to manage every aspect of their relationship with their customers. The aim of these systems is to assist in building lasting customer relationships and to turn customer satisfaction into customer loyalty.

CSS - Cascading Style Sheet. Creates a common style reference for a set of web pages.

CSMA/CD - Carrier-Sense Multiple Access Collision-Detect. The low-level network arbitration protocol used by Ethernet.

CTI - Computer Telephone Integration. Enabling computers to know about and control telephony functions such as making and receiving voice, fax, and data calls, telephone directory services, and caller identification.

CTO - Chief Technology Officer. The person who is responsible for research and development and possibly for new product plans.

CU - Control Unit. The part of the *Central Processing Unit (CPU)* that coordinates all the activities going on within the computer, and manages the flow of data as it travels from place to place inside the machine.

Customer - Recipient of a service; usually the Customer management has responsibility for the cost of the service, either directly through charging or indirectly in terms of demonstrable business need [ITIL].

Cyberspace - A term used to refer to the electronic universe of information available through the Internet.

DAT - Digital Audio Tape. A format for storing music on magnetic tape, developed in the mid-1980s by SONY and Philips. DAT is also used for recording computer data.

Data mining - Analysis of data in a database using tools, which look for trends or patterns without knowledge of the meaning data.

DBMS - Data Base Management System. A suite of programs which typically manage large structured sets of persistent data, offering query facilities to many users.

DCOM - Distributed Component Object Model. Microsoft's extension of their *Component Object Model (COM)* to support objects distributed across a network.

Design Pattern - The description of a solution to a recurring problem.

DHCP - Dynamic Host Configuration Protocol. System that allows for dynamic allocation of IP addresses. Often used by Internet Access Providers for dynamically allocating addresses to dial-up clients.

DLT - Digital Linear Tape. A kind of magnetic tape drive originally developed by DEC.

DMA - (1) Document Management Alliance. (2) Direct Memory Access.

DMS - Document Management System. A system that can coordinate the changes, access, and availability of business critical information on an organization wide scale.

DMZ - Demilitarized Zone. Optional part of the organization's network that contains stations configured with an official IP-address, given by the Internet Service Provider.

Domain Name - Alphanumeric string used to identify an Internet host. Domain names are converted into IP addresses by a *Domain Name Server (DNS)*.

DNS - Domain Name System. A general-purpose distributed service mainly used on Internet for translating hostnames into Internet addresses.

DRAM - Dynamic RAM. A type of semiconductor memory in which the information is stored as an electrical charge in a storage cell consisting of a capacitor and a transistor.

DSDM - A high level framework with proven *Rapid Application Development (RAD)* techniques and management controls that work to improve on quality, cost and time involvement of system development projects, which can be used with object oriented or structured analysis and design approaches using iterative and incremental lifecycle style. [E.D. Wijendra].

DSI - Delivered Source Instructions. One line of source code (LOC) developed in a project. The term "delivered" is meant to exclude non-delivered support software, however, if these are developed with the same care as delivered software, with their own reviews, test plans, documentation, etc., then they should be counted.

DSL – (1) Digital Subscriber Line. A family of digital telecommunications protocols designed to allow high-speed data communication over the existing telephone lines. (2) Definitive Software Library. The library in which the definitive authorized versions of all software CIs are stored and protected. It is a physical library or storage repository where master copies of software versions are placed. This one logical storage area can in reality consist of one or more physical software libraries or file stores. They should be separate from development and test file store areas. The DSL can also include a physical store to hold master copies of bought-in software, e.g., a fireproof safe. Only authorized software should be accepted into the DSL, strictly controlled by Change and Release Management. The DSL exists not directly because of the needs of the Configuration Management process, but as a common base for the Release Management and Configuration Management processes [ITIL].

DSS – Decision Support System. A generic term for interactive Information Systems that support decision making.

DSSS - Direct Sequence Spread Spectrum. A transmission technology where a data signal at the sending station is combined with a higher data rate bit sequence that divides the user data according to a spreading ratio thus increasing the signal's resistance to interference.

DTD – Document Type Definition. A set of rules concerning the element types that are allowed within an XML document.

DTP - Desktop Publishing. Using a Personal Computer or workstation to produce high-quality printed documents.

DVD - Digital Versatile Disk (formerly Digital Video Disk).

DW – Data warehousing. Storing, managing and retrieving large amounts of data.

EBCDIC - Extended Binary-coded Decimal Interchange Code, developed by IBM. EBCDIC used a 5 bit encoding technique; if all the bits were set high (11111), then the encoding would switch to a different "page." Each "page" stored a set of 31 different characters, with the encoding (11111) reserved for the page switch. Many legacy systems still use EBCDIC.

ebXML - Electronic Business XML. A project to use the *Extensible Markup Language (XML)* to standardize the secure exchange of business data. The *United Nations body for Trade Facilitation and Electronic Business Information Standards (UN/CEFACT)* and the *Organization for the Advancement of Structured Information Standards (OASIS)* launched the project as a joint initiative.

EDI - Electronic Data Interchange. A set of standardized electronic business documents, which are exchanged in agreed on formats. The two largest EDI standards are ANSI X12 and EDIFACT.

EDIFACT - Electronic Data Interchange For Administration, Commerce and Transport. The international EDI standards developed within the framework of the United Nations. This EDI standard is ratified by the International Standards Organization (ISO). The Data Interchange Standards Association (DISA) administers these standards in the United States.

EDO - Extended Data Output. An improvement of the standard DRAM technology.

EDP - Electronic Data Processing.

EEPROM - Electrically Erasable Programmable Read Only Memory. The term used to describe all non-volatile memories whose contents can be changed or deleted electrically.

Effectiveness - the degree to which a system's features and capabilities meet the user's needs.

Efficiency - the degree to which a system or component performs its designated functions with minimum consumption of resources [IEEE].

EIA - Electronics Industry Association. A body that publishes *Recommended Standards (RS)* for electronic devices and their means of interfacing.

EIS – Executive Information System. A tool that provides direct on-line access to relevant information in a useful and navigable format.

EJB - Enterprise JavaBeans. A server-side component architecture for writing reusable and portable business logic. EJB is the basis of Sun's Java 2 Enterprise Edition (J2EE).

EMS – (1) Enterprise Management Suite. (2) A memory paging scheme-enabling access to memory other than conventional memory.

Encryption - Scrambling data with a mathematical algorithm to make it unreadable to outside users.

ERD - Entity Relationship Diagram. An approach to data modeling in which the database is divided in two logical parts; entities and relations.

ERP - Enterprise Resource Planning. A software system designed to support and automate the business processes of organizations such as manufacturing, distribution, HRM, project management and accounting.

Escrow - Software Escrow is the placing of a copy of the source code version of a computer program along with explanatory technical information and documentation according to the terms of an agreement with a trusted third party to be held until the occurrence of a specified event (e.g., bankrupcy of the supplier), whereupon the deposit is released.

Ethernet - See IEEE 802.3.

ETSI - European Telecommunications Standards Institute.

FAR - False Acceptance Rate. In biometric authentication, the chance that a non authorized person is granted access.

FC-AL - Fiber Channel-Arbitrated Loop. A fast serial bus interface standard intended to replace the *Small Computer System Interface (SCSI)*.

FDDI - Fiber Distributed Data Interface. A *Local Area Network (LAN)* protocol, primarily used in mission critical and high traffic networks.

FHSS - Frequency Hopping Spread Spectrum. A transmission technology where the data signal is modulated with a narrowband carrier signal that "hops" in a random but predictable sequence from frequency to frequency over a wide band of frequencies thus reducing interference.

Flexibility - The ease with which a system or component can be modified for use in applications or environments other than those for which it was specifically designed [IEEE].

Firewire - See IEEE 1394.

FPM - Fast Page Mode. An improvement of the standard DRAM technology.

Frame Relay - A form of packet switching with smaller packets and fewer error checking than traditional forms of packet switching (such a X.25). Frame relay is the international standard for efficiently handling high speed, bursty data over WANs.

Free software - Free software or Open Source software is software that comes with permission for anyone to use, copy, and distribute, either verbatim or with modifications, either gratis or for a fee. In particular, this means that source code must be available [GNU].

Freeware - The term freeware has no clear accepted definition, but it is commonly used for packages, which permit redistribution but not modification (and their source code is not available) [GNU].

FRR - False Rejection Rate. In biometric authentication, the probability that a person is not granted access to his account.

FTP - File Transfer Protocol. A client-server protocol which allows to transfer files to and from another computer over a TCP/IP network.

FP – Function points. A metric for the relative size and complexity of a software system, originally developed by Alan Albrecht in the late 1970s.

FPA – Function Points Analysis. Estimating a software project using the Function Point metric.

Global or Strategic Outsourcing - Type of outsourcing that involves the complete transfer of an entire function.

GPL - General Public License. A specific set of distribution terms for copylefting a program used by the GNU Project [GNU].

GPRS - General Packet Radio Services. A data transmission technique that transmits and receives data in packets, thus making efficient use of available radio spectrum.

GP-IB - See IEEE 488.

Groupware - Software tools to support groups of people working together, often at different locations.

GSM - (Digital) Global System for Mobile Communications.

GUI - Graphical User Interface. A pictorial way of representing the capabilities of a system and the work being done [ESI].

GUID - Global Unique Identifier.

HDSL - High Bit Rate Digital Subscriber Line. A form of DSL, providing connections over two or three twisted-pair copper lines.

HiperLAN2 - Wireless LAN protocol.

Glossary

HRM – Human Resources Management.

HP-IB - See IEEE 488.

HTML - Hypertext Markup Language. A text-based page description language that uses tags to describe formatting idioms and allows richly formatted documents to be created using everyday text editors. HTML is the language used to create Web pages.

HTTP - HyperText Transfer Protocol. The text-based protocol that serves as the official language of the World Wide Web. HTTP defines high-level commands, or methods - such as GET and PUT - that browsers use to communicate with Web servers. The GET command requests a page of HTML data, a .GIF file, or other resource from a Web server in preparation for displaying it in a browser window.

I20 - Intelligent I/0. A specification that provides an I/O architecture that is independent of both the specific device being controlled and the Operating System.

IDE – (1) Integrated Drive Electronics. A standard interface used between a computer motherboard's data paths and the disk storage devices. (2) Integrated Development Environment. A programming environment that has been packaged as an application program, typically consisting of a code editor, a compiler, a debugger, and a graphical user interface (GUI) builder [Whatis].

IEEE 1394 - Industry-standard implementation of Apple Computer, Inc.'s digital I/O system, known as Firewire. It is a serial, versatile, high-speed, low-cost method of interconnecting a variety of Personal Computer peripherals and consumer electronics devices. Developed by the industry's leading technology companies, the specification was accepted as a standard by the IEEE Standards Board in 1995, with succeeding revisions since then.

IEEE 488 - An 8-bit parallel bus common on test equipment. The IEEE 488 standard was proposed by HEWLETT-PACKARD in the late 1970s and has undergone a couple of revisions since then. HP documentation calls it HP-IB, or HEWLETT-PACKARD Interface Bus; the other manufacturers also refer it to as *General-Purpose Interface Bus (GP-IB)*.

IEEE 802.3 - Local Area Network Protocol, also known as Ethernet.

IEEE 802.5 - Local Area Network Protocol, also known as Token Ring.

IEEE 802.11 - Wireless LAN protocol.

IETF - Internet Engineering Taskforce. The body that defines standard Internet operating protocols such as TCP/IP. Standards are expressed as *Requests for Comments (RFCs)*.

IMAP – Internet Message Access Protocol. A protocol allowing a client to access and manipulate e-mail messages on a server.

Information - The meaning of the representation of a fact (or of a message) for the receiver.

Infrastructure - Permanent facilities that provides services to the higher layers.

Inheritance – In object-oriented systems this term denotes the way a developer can build customized objects without having to re-create all objects' functionality. A child object can be created which has (inherits) all the attributes of another (its parent) - except where specified [ESI].

Internet - A worldwide "network of networks" connected to one another using the TCP/IP and other similar protocols. Internet services include electronic mail, connections to remote computers, information diffusion and information retrieval. There is no single authority that controls the Internet.

IP – (1) Internet Protocol. The protocol responsible for transmitting packets of data over the Internet and routing them to their destinations. Tagging a packet with an IP address identifying an Internet host and transmitting it using IP is analogous to addressing an envelope and dropping it in the mail. IP plays the role of post office, allowing the networks and routers involved in the delivery process to talk to one another as the packet finds its way to the addressee. (2) Intellectual Property.

IP Address - Internetwork Protocol Address or Internet Address. A unique number assigned by an Internet authority that identifies a computer on the Internet. The IP address is four groups of numbers, separated by dots, each ranging from 0 to 255.

IPsec – A protocol that provides security over unprotected networks such as the Internet. IPSec acts at the network layer, protecting and authenticating IP packets between peers.

Ipv6 – A new version of IP that solves the problem of the shortage of IP addresses.

IR - Infrared. Electromagnetic waves in the frequency range just below visible light corresponding to radiated heat.

IrDA - Infrared Data Access. A non-profit trade association providing standards to ensure the quality and interoperability of IR hardware.

ISA - Industrial Standard Architecture. A type of internal computer bus.

ISDN - Integrated Services Digital Network. A set of communications standards allowing a normal telephone line or optical fiber to carry voice, digital network services and video.

ISO - International Standards Organization. Organization responsible for creating international standards in many areas, including computers and communications. Its members are the national standards organizations of the participating countries, including the ANSI.

ISP - Internet Service Provider. An organization which provides other organizations or individuals with access to, or presence on, the Internet.

IT - Information Technology. Technology that is used to store, communicate and manipulate information.

IT Infrastructure - The sum of an organization's IT related hardware, software, data telecommunication facilities, procedures and documentation [ITIL].

ITIL - IT Infrastructure Library. An important set of documents managing ITSM developed by the CCTA, the UK Government's Central Computer and Telecommunications Agency.

ITSM – IT Service Management.

ITU-T – International Telecommunications Union. Organization responsible for making technical recommendations about telephone and data communications systems. Before 1993 ITU-T was known as CCITT.

J2EE – Java 2 Enterprise Edition. A framework that simplifies application development and decreases the need for programming and programmer training by creating standardized, reusable modular components and by handling many aspects of development automatically.

JBOD – Just a Bunch of Disks.

JIT - Just In Time. (1) An approach to managing production that is designed to manufacture just the amount of products immediately required by customers. (2) In training, having trainees learn new practices just before they need to use them. (3) Technique of compiling intermediate program code (e.g., Java) to machine code at runtime.

JSP – Java Server Page. A freely available specification for extending the Java Servlet API to generate dynamic Web content.

KPI - Key Performance Indicator.

Laptop (computer) - Small, Personal Computer, small enough so it can sit on your lap.

LAN - Local Area Network. High-speed data network that covers a relatively small geographic area.

LCD - Liquid Crystal Display. An electro-optical device used to display information.

LDAP - Lightweight Directory Access Protocol. A protocol for accessing on-line directory services defined by the IETF. LDAP defines a relatively simple protocol for updating and searching directories running over TCP/IP.

Legacy System - When a new computer-based solution is developed, it can be necessary to retain hardware or software from the earlier system. In these cases, the software that has been retained is called a legacy system.

LLC - Logical Link Control. Sublayer of the OSI data link layer.

LOC - Lines Of Code. The total lines of code found in a program (source lines + blank lines + comment lines).

LSB - Least Significant Bit.

Manager - The person charged with the job of planning, organizing, staffing, directing and controlling the activities of others [ESI].

Mainframe (computer) - A large and expensive computer capable of supporting hundreds, or even thousands, of users simultaneously.

Metric - The quantitative measure of the degree to which a system, process or component posesses a given attribute [ESI].

Metadata - Information about what a set of data consists of and how it is organized.

Middleware - Set of business-unaware services that enable applications to interact with one another.

MIME - Multipurpose Internet Mail Extensions. A protocol for sending non-ASCII data - for example, sound, video, and graphics - over the Internet using text-based transport protocols such as the *Simple Mail Transfer Protocol (SMTP)*.

Minicomputer - A mid-sized computer system.

MIPS - Mega Instructions Per Second.

MIS - Management Information System. A general term for the Information Systems in an organization that provide information about its operations.

Model - An abstraction of a physical system, with a certain purpose. [OMG]

MOM - Message Oriented Middleware. A client/server infrastructure that increases the *interoperability*, *portability*, *flexibility* and the *complexity* of developing of an application by allowing the application to be distributed over multiple heterogeneous platforms.

MPP – Massive Parallel Processing. the coordinated processing of a program by multiple processors that work on different parts of the program.

MSIL - Microsoft Intermediate Language. Microsoft's .NET compilers create MSIL rather than native processor code. The MSIL is in turn compiled to native code by a JIT (just-in-time) compiler and then executed by the *Common Language Runtime (CLR)*.

Multiread - A specification for optical devices to be capable of reading discs created in CD formats. Any device adhering to the specification is capable for reading audio CD, CD-ROM, CD-R and CD-RW.

MSB - Most Signifcant Bit.

NAS - Network Attached Storage. Storage that is set up with its own network address rather than being attached to a computer that is serving applications.

NAT - Network Address Translation. The translation of an IP address used within one network to a different IP address known within another network.

NC - Network Computer, a Personal Computer with minimal memory, disk storage and processor power designed to connect to a network, especially the Internet.

Non-copylefted free software - Software that comes with permission to redistribute, modify and to add additional restrictions to it.

Notebook (computer) - An extremely lightweight Personal Computer, small enough to easily fit in a briefcase.

NVC - Noun Verb Count. A technique for estimating the size of a new project, or the amount of effort required to complete a project.

OASIS - Organization for Structured Information Standards. A nonprofit international consortium whose goal is to promote the adoption of product-independent standards for information formats such as *Standard Generalized Markup Language (SGML)*, *Extensible Markup Language (XML)* and *Hypertext Markup Language (HTML)*.

OCR - Optical Character Recognition. Recognition of printed or written characters by computer.

ODBC - Open Data Base Connectivity. A standard for accessing different database systems.

ODMA - Open Document Management API. An open standard allowing desktop applications to interface with document management systems.

OLAP - On Line Analytical Processing. The ability to organize data hierarchically in multiple dimensions to let users quickly create, calculate and analyze complex data relationships.

OLTP - On Line Transaction Processing. The processing of transactions by computers in real time.

OODBMS - Object Oriented Database Management System. A database management system that supports the modeling and creation of data as objects.

OOP - Object-oriented programming. Programming technique organized around "objects" rather than "actions," data rather than logic.

ORDBMS - Object Relational Database Management System. An RDBMS in which the management of objects is also supported.

Organization - (1) A collection of human, material, informational and financial resources; for example a company, a corporation or a public service. (2) The activity of organizing. (3) How things in an Organization (1) are done. This is preferably the result of an organization (2) activity but can also be the result of a historical process. In this meaning the Organization is a set of (formal or informal) rules.

Open Source software - Software that comes with permission for anyone to use, copy, and distribute, either verbatim or with modifications, either gratis or for a fee. In particular, this means that source code must be available. also known as Free software [GNU].

OS - Operating System. The low-level software which handles the interface to peripheral hardware, schedules tasks, allocates storage, and presents a default interface to the user when no application program is running.

OSI - Open Systems Interconnection. A model of network architecture and a suite of protocols to implement it, developed by ISO as a framework for international standards in heterogeneous computer networks.

Outsourcing - The process by which functions performed by the organization are contracted out for operation, on the organization's behalf, by third parties [ITIL].

Overhead - Also known as indirect costs, these are costs that cannot be assigned exclusively to any particular product, project, process, or activity. In traditional cost accounting, overhead includes most support services. ABC takes a much narrower view of overhead and strives to include only organizational activities in it.

PABX - Private Automatic Branch eXchange. A telephone exchange operated within an organization, used for switching calls between internal lines and between internal and external lines.

Partial or Tactical Outsourcing - Tactical Outsourcing involves major sub-functions or projects being outsourced.

Patent - An exclusive right granted for an invention, which is a product or a process that provides a new way of doing something, or offers a new technical solution to a problem [WIPO].

PC - Personal Computer. A small, relatively inexpensive computer designed for an individual user.

PC/104 - Computer bus for embedded products, using 104 pins.

PCI - Personal Computer Interface. An internal computer bus.

PCMCIA - Personal Computer Memory Card Interface Association. A type of internal computer bus.

PDA - Personal Digital Assistant. Handheld device that combines computing, telephone/fax, and networking.

PERL – Practical Extraction and Reporting Language. Powerful scripting language designed by Larry Wall.

PERT/CPM - Project Evalutation and Review Technique/Critical Path Method.

PKI - Public Key Infrastructure. A system of public key encryption using digital certificates from Certification Authorities that verify and authenticate the validity of each party involved in an electronic transaction.

PMBOK - Project Management Body of Knowledge.

PMI – Project Management Institute.

Polymorphism - A term used in object-oriented systems to denote the effect of sending the same message to different objects and each object responding differently [ESI].

POP - Post Office Protocol. A text-based protocol used to send and retrieve Internet e-mail messages. Unlike SMTP, which is used primarily to transfer mail messages between mail servers, POP provides a way for mail programs to interact with virtual mailboxes in which messages wait until they are sent or retrieved. POP comes in two flavors: POP2 and POP3. The two are related in name only and are not compatible.

Port Number – Identification of a particular service on an Internet host to the TCP and UDP Protocols. They are 16-bit numbers, usually written in decimal, and known by convention. For example, port 25 is used for SMTP mail transfers, and port 80 for HTTP Web transfers.

POTS - Plain Old Telephone System.

Project Management - The art of directing and coordinating human and material resources throughout the life of a project by using modern management techniques to achieve predetermined objectives of scope, cost, time, quality and participant satisfaction [PMI].

Public domain software - **A** legal term and means "not copyrighted". It is a special case of non-copylefted free software, which means that some copies or modified versions cannot be free at all [GNU].

PSTN - Public Switched Telephone Network.

PPCP - PowerPC Platform, a computer hardware specification that allows a computer to run multiple Operating Systems.

PPP - Point-to-Point Protocol. Protocol for transmitting IP packets over serial point-to-point links.

Proprietary software - Proprietary software is software that is not free or semi-free. Its use, redistribution or modification is prohibited, or requires you to ask for permission, or is restricted so much that you effectively cannot do it freely [GNU].

Process - A specific ordering of work activities across time and place, with a beginning, an end, clearly identified inputs and outputs: a structure for action [Davenport].

Protocol - The common "language" between two computers when "talking" to one another. A protocol is a set of rules that define how a communications (sub) function is carried out. A protocol is independent of the computer hardware and operating system on which it runs.

Quality - The totality of features and characteristics of a product or service that bear on its ability to satisfy stated or implied needs [ISO 8402].

Quality Assurance - The collection of all the planned and systematic actions necessary to provide adequate confidence that a product or service will satisfy given requirements for quality [ISO 8402].

Quality Control - The set of operational techniques and activities that are used to fulfill requirements for quality [ISO 8402].

Quality Management - That aspect of the overall management function that determines and implements the quality policy [ISO 8402].

Quality Policy - The overall intentions and direction of an organization regarding quality, as formally expressed by top management [ISO 8402].

Quality System - The organizational structure, responsibilities, procedures, processes and resources for realizing quality management [ISO 8402].

QoS – Quality of Service. The performance properties of a network service, such as throughput, transit delay and priority.

RA - Registration Authority. An authority in a network that verifies user requests for a digital certificate and tells the *Certificate Authority (CA)* to issue it.

RAD - A generic term for development methods that involve users and developers working jointly to consolidate the steps of requirement definition, design and programming. Examples are prototyping, incremental and evolutionary development. The term "rapid" refers to the immediate feedback of design results to users rather than to rapidity in project completion [The TickIT Guide].

RADSL - Rate Adaptive Digital Subscriber Line. A version of ADSL where modems test the line at start up and adapt their operating speed to the fastest the line can handle.

RAID - Redundant Array of Inexpensive Disks. A mechanism for providing data resilience for computer systems using mirrored arrays of magnetic disks. Different levels of RAID can be applied to provide for greater resilience [ITIL].

RAM - Random Access Memory. Memory where the Operating System, application programs, and data in current use are kept so that they can be quickly reached.

RDBMS - Relational Database Management System. A program that lets you create, update, and administer a relational database.

Refactoring - The process of changing a software system in such a way that it does not alter the external behavior of the code, but improves the internal structure.

Resources - Money, labor, material, supplies, information and other economic elements consumed by activities to produce outputs.

Requirement - A desired feature, property, or behavior of a system. [OMG]

RFC – (1) Request For Comment. A formal document from the Internet Engineering Task Force (IETF) that is the result of committee drafting and subsequent review by interested parties. (2) Request For Change. Form, or screen, used to record details of a request for a Change to any CI within an infrastructure or to procedures and items associated with the infrastructure [ITIL].

RISC - Reduced Instruction Set Computer. A processor whose design is based on the rapid execution of a sequence of simple instructions rather than on the provision of a large variety of complex instructions. Opposite of *Complex Instruction Set Computer (CISC)*.

ROM - Read-only Memory. An integrated circuit programmed with data when it is manufactured.

RS232 - An *Electronics Industry Association (EIA)* standard for serial communication.

RTF - Rich Text Format. Format designed by Microsoft as an open format for interchanging documents between Microsoft Word and other word processing packages. WordPerfect, FrameMaker, Interleaf and many other packages on UNIX, Apple, Macintosh, Next, and PC platforms support it. File extension: ".rtf"

RTP – Real Time Protocol. The Internet-standard protocol for the transport of real-time data, including audio and video. It can be used for media-on-demand as well as interactive services such as Internet telephony.

RPC - Remote Procedure Call. A protocol that one program can use to request a service from a program located in another computer without having to understand implementation details.

SAN - Storage Area Network. A high-speed special-purpose network (or subnetwork) that interconnects different kinds of data storage devices with associated data servers.

SC&D - Software Control & Distribution. The management of all Software Configuration Items within the organization.

SCM – (1) Supply Chain Management. The oversight of materials, information, and finances as they move in a process from supplier to manufacturer to wholesaler to retailer to consumer. (2) Software Configuration Management. A disciplined approach to managing and controlling the evolution of software development and maintenance practices and their software products as they change over time [Ovum].

Scripting language - A script is a user-readable and user-modifiable program that performs simple operations or that controls the operation of other programs. A scripting language is a programming language designed for writing scripts.

SCS - Structured Cabling System. Cabling and components installed in a logical, hierarchical way.

SCSI - Small Computer System Interface. A set of evolving ANSI standard interfaces that allow computers to communicate with peripheral hardware such as disk drives, tape drives, CD-ROM drives, printers, and scanners.

SDLC – Software Development Life Cycle.

SDRAM - Synchronous DRAM.

SDSL - Symmetric High Bit Rate Digital Subscriber Line.

Security - The ability of a system to manage, protect, and distribute sensitive information.

SEI - Software Engineering Institute.

Semi-free software - Software that comes with permission for individuals to use, copy, distribute, and modify (including distribution of modified versions) for non-profit purposes [GNU].

Service Name - Short string that identifies a particular service on an Internet host. They must be converted to port numbers before use, which is commonly done using a services table, /etc/services on UNIX machines. Examples of service names are TELNET, SMTP, and HTTP.

SGML – Standard Generalized Markup Language. An ISO standard (8879:1986) that describes a markup scheme for representing the logical structure of documents in a system- and platform independent manner.

Shareware - Shareware is software that comes with permission for people to redistribute copies, but says that anyone who continues to use a copy is *required* to pay a license fee. Shareware is not free software, or even semi-free because for most shareware, source code is not available; thus, you cannot modify the program at all and shareware does not come with permission to make a copy and install it without paying a license fee, not even for individuals engaging in nonprofit activity [GNU].

SLA - Service Level Agreement. A written agreement between a service provider and Customer (s) that documents agreed service levels for a service [ITIL].

SLIM - Software Life Cycle Management.

SLIP - Serial Line IP. A widely used but somewhat outdated protocol for establishing dial-up connections to the Internet. Technically speaking, SLIP is a packet-framing protocol that defines how IP datagrams (packets of data transmitted over the Internet using IP) are packaged for transmission over serial data lines-for example, over a serial link between your modem and an Internet service provider.

SLOC - Source Lines Of Code. A metric used to estimate the size and complexity of a software program.

SNMP - Simple Network Management Protocol. The protocol governing network management and the monitoring of network devices and their functions.

SMP – Symmetric Multiprocessor. The processing of programs by multiple processors that share a common operating system and memory.

SMTP - Simple Mail Transfer Protocol. A text-based TCP/IP protocol used to exchange mail messages on the Internet. SMTP defines the format and content of transactions between mail servers.

SOAP - Simple Object Access Protocol. A way for a program running in different operating systems to communicate by using HTTP and XML as the mechanisms for information exchange.

Software development - A set of activities, methods, practices and transformations that people use to develop and maintain software and the associated products [SEI].

Software life cycle - The period of time that starts when a software product is conceived and ends when the product is no longer available for use. The software life-cycle typically includes a requirements phase, design phase, implementation phase, test phase, installation and check-out phase, operation and maintenance phase, and sometimes, retirement phase [IEEE].

SPICE - Software Process Improvement and Capability determination.

SPMP - Software Project Management Plan.

SQL - Structured Query Language. A language used to access data in a relational database.

STP - Shielded Twisted Pair.

Supercomputer - Special type of computer that is employed for specialized applications that require immense amounts of mathematical calculations.

SVGA - Super VGA permits resolutions of up to 1024 x 768 pixels. To display 16 out of 256 colors, a graphics card memory of 512 KB is required. With a 1 MB memory expansion, a total of 256 colors can be displayed from a palette of 16.7 million colors.

Tag - Generic term for language element descriptor.

Teleworking - A work arrangement in which employees work at any time or place that allows them to accomplish their work in an effective and efficient manner [Jack Nilles].

Testability - The degree to which a system or component helps the establishment of test criteria and the performance of tests to determine whether those criteria have been met [IEEE].

TCP - Transmission Control Protocol. The protocol that provides reliable stream deliservice to Internet applications. Using TCP, an Internet client can open a virtual connection to another Internet client and transmit streams of data. Unlike its counterpart, UDP, the TCP protocol ensures reliable deliby retransmitting lost and corrupted data packets. It also guarantees that an application on the receiving end of a TCP connection will receive bits and bytes in the same order in which they were sent.

TCO - Total Cost of Ownership. A type of calculation designed to assess both direct and indirect costs and benefits related to the purchase of any IT component.

TCO92/95/99 - Requirements in terms of quality and ergonomics for computer equipment from the Swedish Union of Employees.

Technology - The combination of skills, knowledge, abilities, materials, machines, tools and other equipment that people use to convert or change raw materials into valuable goods and services.

Telnet - A user command and underlying protocol for accessing remote computers.

TOC - Theory Of Constraints. A relatively recent development in the practical aspect of making organizational decisions in situations in which constraints exist.

Token Ring - See IEEE 802.5.

TPC - Transaction Processing Performance Council.

TQM – Total Quality Management. The philosophy of management where quality is the primary concern and goal in system development [ESI].

UDDI - Universal Description Discovery and Integration. An XML-based registry for businesses worldwide to list themselves on the Internet.

UDF - Universal Disk Format. A CD-ROM and DVD file system standard.

UDP - User Datagram Protocol. The protocol that allows packets of data, or datagrams, to be sent from one Internet application to another. UDP is a "connectionless" protocol, because, unlike TCP, it does not require the sender and receiver to establish a connection before data is transmitted. It's considered "unreliable," because it does not guarantee that datagrams will arrive in the same order they were sent, or even that they will arrive at all. If reliability is desired, it's up to the application using UDP to provide it.

UML – Unified Modeling Language. A standard notation for the modeling of real-world objects.

UMTS - Universal Mobile Telecommunications System.

UNCTAD - United Nations Conference on Trade and Development.

UNICODE - Unicode represents characters by a full 16-bit number. Each encoding is unique to that character, though how the character is displayed depends on the font used. Unicode also includes additional specifications to help when realizing Unicode text. Again like UTF-8, Unicode retains compatibility with ASCII by simply mapping the ASCII encoding to the same Unicode values. With Unicode also non-Latin characters such as Japanese, Cyrillic or Greek can be represented without any problem. Most probably, Unicode will be the universal standard for the coming decades.

UPS - Uninteruptible Power Supply. A device that allows systems to keep running for at least a short time when the primary power source is lost. It also provides protection from power surges.

URL - Universal Resource Locator. A human-readable string that identifies the location of a resource on the Internet (for example, a page of HTML data or a .GIF file) and the protocol used to retrieve it.

USB - Universal Serial Bus. A peripheral bus standard developed by industry leaders, eliminating the need to install cards into dedicated computer slots and reconfigure the system.

UTF-8 - UCS (Universal Character Set) Transformation Format, 8-bit. Developed as a lightweight version of Unicode. Instead of using the whole 16-bits specified by Unicode, UTF-8 simply uses the lowest 8-bits. ASCII is mapped to the same bit positions within UTF8 to help compatibility, and other control characters are mapped into the space left.

UTP - Unshielded Twisted Pair.

Understandability - The degree to which the purpose of the system or component is clear to the evaluator [Boehm].

VDSL - High Bit Rate Digital Subscribe Line.

VGA - Video Graphics Array. A display standard in the PC environment in which 640 x 480 pixels and 16 out of 256 colors can be displayed at the same time. An additional mode allows 256 colors to be viewed, however, the resolution in this case is limited to 320 x 200 pixels.

VoIP – Voice Over IP. A set of facilities for managing the deliof voice information using the Internet Protocol.

W3C – World Wide Web Consortium. A group of vendor companies that acts as a sort of standards body for the Web.

WAN - Wide Area Network.

WAP - Wireless Access protocol.

Web – Common name for the World Wide Web (WWW). The Internet service that uses the HTTP protocol and the HTML format to deliver documents.

WebDAV - Web Distributed Authoring and Versioning. A set of extensions to the HTTP protocol that allows users to collaboratively edit and manage files on remote web servers.

Web Farming - The systematic discovery and acquisition of business-relevant Web content as input to a data warehouse.

WLAN - Wireless Local Area Network.

WML - Wireless Markup Language.

Workflow – A way of implementing business processes that involves step-by-step progression of a task involving several users [ESI].

Workstation – A type of computer used for engineering applications (CAD/CAM), desktop publishing, software development, and other types of applications that require a good amount of computing power and high quality graphics capabilities.

WSDL - Web Services Description Language. An XML-based language used to describe the services an organization offers and to provide a way to access those services via the Web.

WWW - World Wide Web. The WWW provides a graphical interface for browsing (surfing) resources on the Internet. Resources are identified by a unique identifier (URL - uniform resource locator). Resources can include texts, images, sound and video clips. Texts are usually prepared using a standard format (HTML - HyperText Mark-up Language or XML - eXtensible Mark-Up language), which describes their presentation and can define "links" to other resources. The program used to access the World Wide Web is called a browser.

WYSIWYG – What You See Is What You Get.

XDSL - Generic name for Digital Subscriber Line.

XML - eXtensible Markup Language.

XMI - XML Metadata Interchange. A proposed use of XML that is intended to provide a standard way for programmers and other users to exchange information about metadata. Ideally, XMI will allow different cooperating companies a way to use one another's data repositories. XMI is similar to, but competing with, Microsoft's Open Information Model.

XP - Extreme Programming. A lightweight discipline of software development, designed for use with small teams who need to develop software quickly in an environment of rapidly changing requirements.

XSL – Extensible Style Language.

XSDL – XML Schema Definition Language.

Online Glossaries

http://databases.about.com/library/glossary/
http://foldoc.doc.ic.ac.uk/foldoc/contents.html
http://www.cknow.com/ckinfo/acronyms/
http://www.esi.es/Help/Dictionary/welcome.html
http://www.itil.co.uk/online_ordering/itil_glossary.htm
http://www.matisse.net/files/glossary.html
http://www.osicom.com/notes/glossary.html
http://www-rohan.sdsu.edu/glossary.html
http://www.sei.cmu.edu/str/indexes/glossary/
http://www.squareonetech.com/glosaryf.html
http://www.robertgraham.com/pubs/hacking-dict.html
http://www.techweb.com/encyclopedia/
http://www.webopedia.com
http://www.whatis.com

Index

.NET 74, 75, 108
A2A 123
ABB 219, 449
ABC 137, 145, 208, 449
Accountability 32
Active Server Pages 107
ActiveX 108, 310
Activity Based Budgeting 191, 219
Activity Based Costing 137, 208
Activity Diagrams 299
adhocracy 376
ADSL 52, 53, 449
Agile Software Development 279
Agility 7
AGP 22, 449
AIT 449
alpha testing 323
ALU 449
ANSI 270, 449
API 31, 69, 70, 101, 450
Application 450
Application Mining 338
Application Outsourcing 248
Application Servers 75
Application Service Provider 151, 248
Application-to-Application integration ... 123
APQC 136
Architect 390
archiving 83
ARP 450
ARPANET 450
Artificial Intelligence 138, 308, 354
ASCII 18, 63, 69, 95, 103, 304, 450
ASP 75, 107, 108, 248, 430, 450
Assembler 304, 354, 450
Asynchronous 52, 450
ATM 55, 450
Auditor 390, 391
Authentication 32, 65, 450
Authorization 32
Automated Testing 323
Availability 7, 261, 451
B2B 123, 127, 244, 451
B2C 244, 451
B2E 244
Back office 244
Backup 421
Balanced Scorecard 144, 145, 414, 415, 416
Bandwidth 451
Baseline Budgeting 218
BCNF 37
BCP 261, 420
Benchmarking 136, 182, 398, 451
Berne Convention 342

Best Practice 451
Beta testing 323
BIA 420
binary 18, 63, 73, 103, 140
Binary Large Objects 41
Biometry 451
bitmap graphic 97
bitmapped index 139
BITS 451
Black box testing 321
Blade computers 16
BLOB 41, 451
Bluetooth 50, 51, 452
BMP 452
bodyshopping 167
Bootstrap 452
Boyce-Codd Normal Form 37
BPR 253, 254, 255, 391, 452
Browser 452
BSC 144, 145, 414, 415, 416, 452
BTP 130, 452
B-tree 139
budget 214
Budgeting 202
budgeting process 215, 219
Buenos Aires Convention 342
Business Consultant 390, 391
Business Continuity 420
Business Continuity Institute 420
Business Continuity Planning 261
Business Intelligence 3, 94, 135
Business Process Redesign 444
Business Process Reengineering 253
Business Processes 134, 135, 242, 255, 260
Business Strategy 407, 452
Business Transaction Protocol 130
Business-to-Business 123, 244
Business-to-Consumer 244
Business-to-Customer 244
Business-to-Employee 244
CA 66, 453
cache 22
CAD/CAM 98, 453
Capability Maturity Model 325
Capacity Management 258, 261
Capital budget 216
Capital Budgeting 220
Capital Costs 206
CardBus 23, 453
CASE 310, 311, 453
CCD 453
CCITT 453
CDDI 453
CD-R 27, 453

Index

CD-ROM 26, 453
CD-RW 27, 453
Central Processing Unit 20
Centralization 379, 388, 389
Centronics 23
CEO 371, 373, 453
Certification Authority 66
CFO 371
CGI 106, 107, 453
Change Management 259
Charging 203, 211
Chief Executive Officer 371
Chief Financial Officer 371
Chief Information Officer 4, 371, 392
Chief Operating Officer 371
Chief Technology Officer 371
CHRP 14
cHTML 56
CIO 4, 371, 392, 393, 433, 454
CISC 20, 454
Class 75, 140, 298, 454
Class diagrams 298
Client 454
CLR 74, 75, 302, 454
CLS 303
cluster 16, 322, 399, 454
CMDB 258, 259, 454
CMM 325, 326, 327, 454
Coax 47
COBIT 262
COCOMO 289, 455
Code 455
Collaboration 278
Collaboration Diagrams 299
COM 73, 108, 310, 455
Commercial Software 455
Common Gateway Interface 107
Common Hardware Reference Platform 14
Common Language Runtime 74, 302
Common Language Specification 303
Compact HTML 56
compiler 302, 303, 304, 305
Complexity 434, 455
component 310
Component Bus 72
Component diagrams 299
Component Object Model 73, 310
Computational Complexity 337
Computer Aided Design 98
Computer Aided Manufacturing 98
Computer Aided Software Engineering 310
Configuration Item 258, 259
Configuration Management 258, 259, 311
Configuration Management Database 258
Constructive Cost Model 289
Contingency Planning 258, 261, 455
COO 371, 455
cooperative multitasking 31
Copylefted software 343, 456
CORBA 73, 310, 456
Corporate Knowledge 437
Cost Elements 205
Cost Types 205

Costing 203
Costs 7
CPU 20, 22, 302, 456
Critical Chain Scheduling 317
critical path 315
CRM 126, 244, 246, 247, 456
cryptography 65
CSMA/CD 49, 456
CSS 456
CTI 456
CTO 371, 456
CU 456
custom tags 108
Customer 456
Cyberspace 457
Cyclomatic Complexity 319, 337
DAT 457
Data Control Language 37
Data Definition.Language 37
Data Manipulation Language 37
data mart 138
Data Mining 146, 338
Data modeling 295
Data Warehousing 138
DataBase Management System 35
Datamining 3, 457
Datawarehousing 3
DBMS 35, 70, 457
DCL 37
DCOM 73, 310, 457
DCOM/COM+ 73
DDL 37
decimal 18
Decision Support Systems 94
Delivered Source Instructions 287
Demilitarized Zone 59
Deployment diagram 300
Depreciation 221
design pattern 346, 457
Desktop Publishing 96
Developer 390
DHCP 59, 457
differential backup 421
Digital 18, 114
Digital Audio Tape 27
Digital Linear Tape 27
Digital Object Identifier 264
Digital Subscriber Lines 52
Digital Versatile Disk 27
Direct Costs 206
directory 34, 63, 64, 66, 71, 106, 310
Directory 64
Disaster Recovery 420
disk caching 26
Distributed Component Object Model 73, 310
DLT 457
DMA 101, 113, 457
DML 37
DMS 101, 457
DMZ 59, 457
DNS 59, 64, 71, 458
Document Management Systems 101, 113
DOI 264

Index

Domain Name 457
DOS 31, 104
DRAM 21, 458
DSDM 277, 278, 458
DSI 287, 458
DSL 52, 260, 324, 334, 353, 458
DSS 458
DSSS 48, 50, 458
DTD 111, 459
DTP 96, 459
DVD 27, 459
DW 138, 459
Dynamic Host Configuration Protocol 59
EAI 123, 244
EBCDIC 18, 69, 459
ebXML 128, 459
ECP 25
EDI 114, 127, 128, 459
EDIFACT 128, 459
EDO 21, 459
EDP 3, 459
EEPROM 22, 459
Effectiveness 459
Efficiency 460
Effort Equation 289
EIA 47, 460
EIP 113, 114
EIS 460
EJB 310, 460
Electronic Data Interchange 127, 128
Email 102
Employee Recognition Program 181
EMS 145, 460
encapsulation 298, 308
Encryption 460
Enhanced Parallel Port 25
Enterprise Information Portal 113
Enterprise JavaBeans 310
Enterprise Management Suite 145
Enterprize Application Integration 123, 244
Entity Relationship Diagram 296
Entrepreneurial Startup 374
EPP 25
EPROM 22
ERD 296, 460
ERP 126, 137, 244, 247, 460
Escrow 460
Ethernet 23, 49, 57, 81, 82, 460
ETL 138
ETSI 460
Executive Information Systems 141
Executive Search 164
Expectancy Theory 174, 177
Extended Capabilities Port 25
Extensible Style Language 111
Extraction, Transformation and Loading 138
extranet 62
Extreme Programming 279
fabric mode 29
FAR 461
FC 28
FC-AL 461
FDDI 57, 461

FHSS 48, 50, 461
Fiber optic 47
Fibre Channel 28
file 26, 35
file server 16, 82
File Systems 34
File Transfer Protocol 63
financial management 202
Firewall 59, 67
Firewire 461
FireWire 25
Fixed Costs 206
Flexibility 461
Floppy disk 26
FLWR 43
FLWR expressions 43
FPA 287, 288, 462
FPM 21, 461
Frame Relay 55, 461
Free software 348, 461
Freeware 344, 461
Front office 244
FRR 461
FTP 63, 67, 106, 128, 462
full backup 421
function 167, 191, 288, 365
Function Point Analysis 287
Function Points 288
Functional Integration 412
Gantt charts 313
Garbage In, Garbage Out 143
General Packet Radio Services 56
General Public Licence 344
GIGO 143
Global Unique Identifier 264
goal 63
GP-IB 462
GPL 344, 462
GPRS 56, 462
Grid Computing 17
Group Calendars 114
Groupware 100, 120, 462
GSM 56, 462
GUI 14, 312, 462
GUID 264, 462
Hayes-compatible command set 52
HDSL 52, 462
Help Desk 256, 259
hexadecimal 304
Hierarchy of Needs 173
HiperLAN2 .... 51, 462
HP-IB 463
HRM 162, 163, 168, 189, 463
HRMS 189, 190
HRMSs 190
HTML 104, 108, 112, 124, 463
HTTP 65, 106, 113, 128, 130, 463
Human Resources 160
Human Resources Management Systems 189
Hygiene factors 173
Hype Curve 430
Hypertext Markup Language 104
Hypertext Transfer Protocol 106

Index

I20 463
IDE 311, 312, 463
IEEE 1394 .... 25, 463
IEEE 488 463
IEEE 802.11 .... 50, 51, 464
IEEE 802.3 .... 49, 463
IEEE 802.5 .... 49, 464
IETF 66, 67, 464
IFPUG 288
ILD 47
IMAP 65, 102, 103, 464
Incremental 254, 276
incremental backup 421
Incremental Budgeting 218
Indirect Costs 206
Information 464
Information Liquidity 7
Information System 92
Information Technology 2, 3, 366, 406, 444, 445
Infrared 48
Infrastructure 12, 66, 220, 413, 464
Inheritance 308, 309, 464
Injection-Laser Diode 47
instruction 287, 302, 304
instruction set 20, 302
Integrated Development Environment 311
Integrated Services Digital Network 54
Integration 115, 152, 280, 295, 312
Integration testing 322
Intellectual property 340
internal communication 438, 439
Internal Rate of Return 226
International Function Point Users Group 288
International Standards Organization 45
International Telecommunications Union 57, 118
Internet 61, 464
Internet Message Access Protocol 102
Internet Protocol 57, 62
interpreter 31, 302
intranet 62, 118
Inverted List 139
investment centre 212
IP Address 464
IPng 59
IPsec 66, 67, 465
Ipv6 .... 59, 60, 66, 465
IrDA 51, 465
IRR 226
ISA 128, 465
iSCSI 29
ISDN 54, 465
ISO 45, 327, 465
ISO 17799 262
ISO 8859 18
ISO 9000 .... 252, 327
ISP 57, 59, 430, 465
Issue-Based Life Cycle Model 281
IT Infrastructure 465
IT Infrastructure Library 256
IT Manager 4, 433
IT Service Management 256
IT specialist 390
IT strategy 433

ITIL 256, 257, 465
ITSM 256, 257, 465
ITU 118, 466
J2EE 74, 75, 108, 310, 466
Java 2 Enterprise Edition 74, 310
Java applet 105
Java Database Connectivity 70
Java Remote Method Protocol 74
Java Server Pages 75, 107
Java Virtual Machine 74, 302
Java/Remote Method Invocation 73
Java/RMI 73, 74
JBOD 466
JDBC 70
JIT 74, 302, 466
Job descriptions 162
Job enrichment 197
JPEG 97
JRMP 74
JSP 107, 108, 466
just-in-time 74, 222
JVM 74, 75, 302
Key Performance Indicators 135, 144, 415, 417
Knowledge Management 437
KPI 135, 144, 415, 466
LAN 48, 50, 466
Laptop 466
LCD 466
LDAP 64, 466
LED 47
Light-Emitting Diode 47
Lightweight Directory Access Protocol 64
Lines Of Code 287, 337
LLC 467
LOC 287, 288, 311, 337, 467
Local Area Networks 3, 51
LSB 18, 467
MAC 61
Machine Bureaucracy 375, 376
Magic Quadrant 435, 436
Mainframe 3, 17, 467
Managed (or discretionary) cost centres 212
Management By Objectives 181
Management Information Systems 3
Manager ... 368, 385, 386, 390, 391, 392, 393, 467
Massive Parallel Processor 140
MBO 181
MDA 300
Mean Time Between Failure 26
Media Access Control 61
memory management 30
Metadata 467
Metric 467
metrics 115, 135, 189, 337
microprocessor 20
Middleware 69, 73, 100, 467
MIME 104, 467
Minicomputer 467
Minicomputers 16
MIPS 21, 81, 467
MIS 467
Model Driven Architecture 300
MOM 468

Index

Moore 21
Motivators 173
mouse 14
MPP 140, 141, 468
MSB 18, 468
MSIL 302, 454, 468
MTBF 26
multiprocessing 31
Multiread 27, 468
Multitasking 31
multithreading 31
multi-user 31
Murphy's Law 316
Narrowband 48
NAS 28, 468
NAT 59, 468
national treatment 342
NC 468
Net Present Value 224
Network Address Translation 59
Network Attached Storage 28
Network Computers 15
NIST 420
Non-copylefted free software ... 343, 468
NPV 224, 225
NVC 468
OASIS 130, 469
Object Constraint Language 301
Object Management Group 73
Object-oriented programming .. 308
OCL 301
OCR 469
ODBC 70, 469
ODMA 101, 469
offline backup 422
Offshore Development 167
OLAP 114, 141, 142, 145, 469
OLTP 469
OMG 73
Online Analytical Processing 141
online backup 422
OODBMS 43, 469
OOP 308, 309, 469
Open DataBase Connectivity 70
Open Source 76, 114, 348, 470
Open Source software 343, 461
Open Source Software 348
Open Systems Interconnection ... 45
Operating budget 216
Operating System 30
Operational Costs 206
operations budget 220
Orange Book 32
ORDBMS 469
Organization 188, 328, 364, 469
Organizational Units 367, 368
OS 30, 470
OSI 45, 46, 49, 60, 62, 470
OSS 348
Outsourcing 167, 168, 462, 470
Overhead 470
P2P 73
PABX 470

Parkinson's Law 316
Patent Cooperation Treaty 341
payback period 223, 224
PC 3, 14, 470
PCI 22, 23, 471
PCMCIA 23, 52, 471
PCT 341
PDA 471
Peer-to-Peer 73
Personal Computer 3, 14, 186
Personal Productivity Tools 95
PERT/CPM 314, 315, 471
PKI 66, 471
Players 98
PMBOK 270, 471
PMI 270, 471
PML 114
Point-to-Point 72
polymorphism 309
Polymorphism 308, 471
POP 65, 102, 471
Port Number 471
Portal 113, 125
Post Office Protocol 102
POTS 53, 471
PowerPC Platform 14
PPCP 14, 472
PPP 81, 472
preemptive multitasking 31
presentation software 98
primary key 36, 39
print server 16
procedures 365
Process 452, 472
Production 190, 245
Professional Bureaucracy 375, 376
profit centre 212
Profitability Index 225
Programmable Read-Only Memory ... 22
Project Management 270, 311, 472
Project Management Body of Knowledge 270
Project Management Institute 270
Project Manager 390, 391
Projects 12, 80, 134, 270, 366, 387, 413
PROM 22
proprietary 84
Proprietary software 472
Protocol 57, 115, 452, 472
PSTN 51, 59, 117, 472
Public domain software 344, 472
Public Switched Telephone Network 51, 59
Publish-and-Subscribe 72
QA 251, 252
QC 251
QoS 118, 473
Quality 249, 472
Quality Assurance 251, 327, 359, 472
Quality Control 251, 327, 472
Quality Management 182, 251, 473
Quality of Service 118
Quality Policy 251, 473
Quality System 251, 473
query optimizer 39

Index

RA	66, 473
RAD	278, 473
RADSL	52, 473
RAID	26, 78, 473
RAM	473
Rapid Application Development	278
RCB	219
RCM	219, 220
RDBMS	35, 36, 37, 42, 70, 71, 473
Real-Time Protocol	118
Recruitment	163
Redundant Array of Inexpensive Disks	26
Refactoring	280, 351, 473
Registration Authority	66
regression testing	322, 323
Relationship Management	244, 246
Removable Disk	26
Requirement	283, 474
Resource Planning	244, 247
Resource Reservation Protocol	118
Resources	317, 474
Responsibility Center Budgeting	219
Responsibility Center Management	219
responsibility centre	212
Return On Investment	223
Revenue budget	216
revenue centre	212
RFC	115, 474
RISC	14, 20, 474
ROI	190, 223
ROM	22, 474
root directory	35
Routing	60
RPC	474
RS 232	474
RS232	23
RSVP	118
RTF	96, 474
RTP	118, 474
SA/SD	295
SAM	235
SAN	474
SC&D	260, 475
Schema Language	110
SCM	126, 244, 245, 247, 329, 330, 475
scripting languages	307
SCS	82, 475
SCSI	23, 475
SDLC	273, 475
SDRAM	22, 475
SDSL	52, 475
security	32, 179
Security	475
SEI	229, 271, 325, 475
Semi-free software	344, 475
Sequence Diagrams	299
Service Level Agreements	256, 260, 414
Service Level Management	258, 260, 261, 391
Service Name	476
servlet	107
SGML	469, 476
Shareware	344, 476
Simple Mail Transfer Protocol	102
Simple Network Management Protocol	63
Simple Object Access Protocol	129, 130
Single Points of Failure	78
SLA	261, 414, 476
SLIM	476
SLIP	81, 476
SLOC	287, 476
Small Computer System Interface	23
SMART	181, 408
smartcard	66, 425
SMP	140, 141, 476
SMTP	65, 102, 103, 477
SNMP	63, 476
SOAP	114, 129, 130, 477
Software Architecture	345
Software Asset Management	235
Software Configuration Management	329
Software Control & Distribution	260
Software development	271, 336, 477
Software Development Life Cycle	273
Software Engineering Institute	271, 325
Software life cycle	477
Software Life Cycle Model	273
Software Process Improvement	325
software quality	325
SPI	325
SPICE	327, 477
Spiral model	277
SPMP	477
SPOF	78
spooling	31
Spread Spectrum	48, 50
spreadsheet	95, 97, 101, 139
SQL	36, 69, 70, 477
standard cost centre	212
State Diagrams	299
Storage Area Network	28, 81
Stored procedures	41
STP	477
Strategic Alignment Model	411
Strategic Planning	371, 393, 407
Strategy	144, 408
Structured Analysis/Structured Design	295
Structured Cabling System	82
Structured Query Language	36
subdirectory	35
Supercomputer	477
Supercomputers	18
Supply Chain Management	244, 245
SVGA	477
Switching	61
Symmetric Multiprocessor	140
Synch-and-stabilize	281
Tag	477
TCO	206, 234, 348, 478
TCO92	478
TCO92/95/99	478
TCO99	176
TCP	62, 67, 310, 478
TCP/IP	46, 62, 69
Technology	2, 478
Telecommuting	186
Telework	185, 478

Index

Telnet	63, 67, 478
Testability	478
Theory X	173, 180
Theory Y	173, 174, 180
Thin Client	15
TickIT	327
TOC	317, 478
Token Ring	49, 57, 478
Total Cost of Ownership	206, 235, 348, 478
Total Quality Management	251, 254, 326
TP monitor	72, 75
TPC	43, 44, 478
TQM	251, 326, 478
transaction	43, 71
Transaction Monitor	72
Transaction Processing Performance Council	43
Transmission Control Protocol	62
Triggers	41
UDDI	129, 479
UDF	27, 479
UDP	62, 67, 479
UML	298, 300, 345, 479
UMTS	57, 479
UNCTAD	445, 479
Understandability	283, 480
Unicode	19, 479
Unified Modeling Language	298
Uniform Resource Locator	106
Uninteruptible Power Supply	424
Universal Copyright Convention	342
Universal Disk Format	27
Universal Serial Bus	23
UNIX	14
Unshielded Twisted Pair	47
UPS	424, 479
URL	106, 479
USB	23, 480
Use Case diagrams	284
User Datagram Protocol	62
UTF8	480
UTP	47, 480
Validation	319
Variable Costs	206
VDSL	52, 480
Vector graphics	97
Verification	259, 319, 334
VGA	480
Viewers	98
virtual memory management	30
Virtual Private Networks	66
viruses	67, 68
VoIP	117, 480
von Neumann	19
W3C	43, 108, 480
WAN	51, 81, 480
WAP	56, 480
Waterfall model	275
Web Authoring Tools	96
Web Content Management	112
Web Distributed Authoring and Versioning	113
Web Farming	147, 481
Web Services	114, 129
Web Services Description Language	129
WebDAV	113, 480
well-formed	111
White box testing	319
Wide Area Network	51
Windows	73
Wireless Application Protocol	56
Wireless LANs	50
Wireless Markup Language	56
WLAN	50, 481
WML	56, 481
Word processors	96, 97
Workflow	115, 481
workstation	3, 15, 102, 187, 232
WSDL	129, 481
WWW	26, 481
WYSIWYG	96, 481
X.25	54, 55
X12	128, 449
XDSL	52, 481
XMI	311, 481
XML	41, 108, 481
XP	279, 280, 482
XSDL	482
XSL	111, 482
Zachman	418
Zachman's Framework	418
ZBB	219
Zero Based Budgeting	219